鋼の錬金術師

FULLMETAL ALCHEMIST

16

HIROMU ARAKAWA

荒川弘

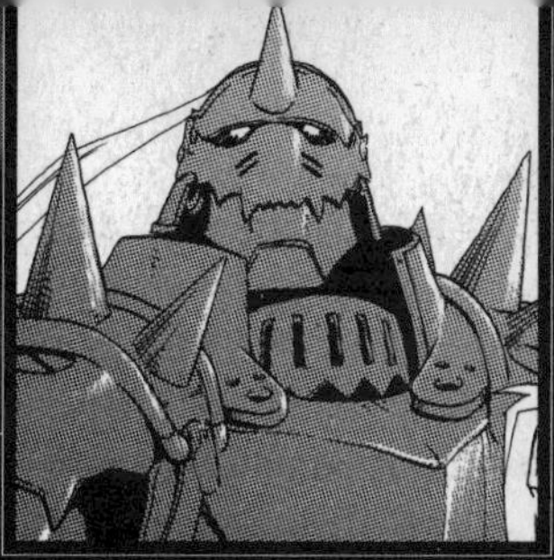

アルフォンス・エルリック

Alphonse Elric

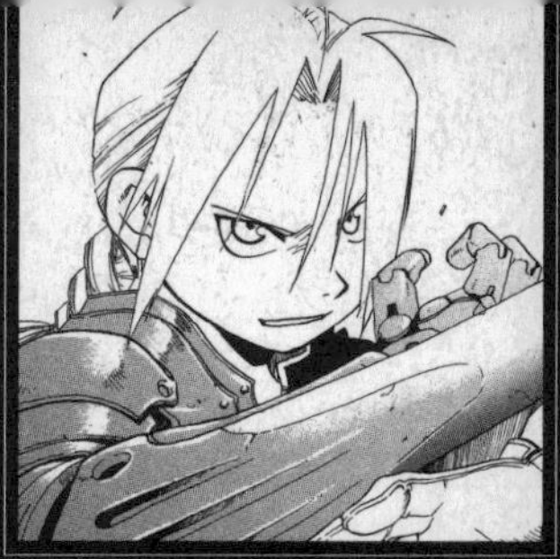

エドワード・エルリック

Edward Elric

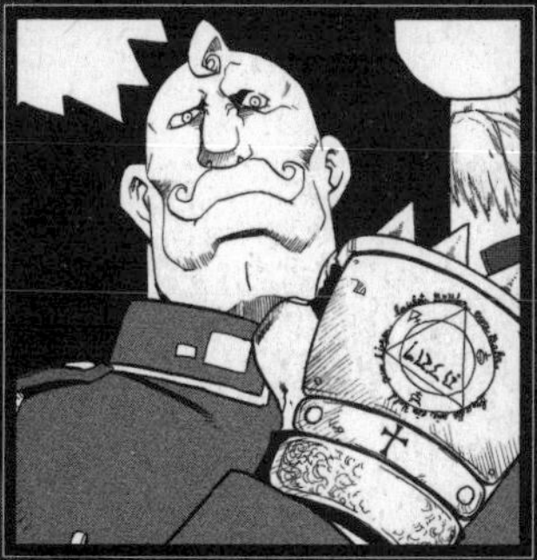

アレックス・ルイ・アームストロング

Alex Louis Armstrong

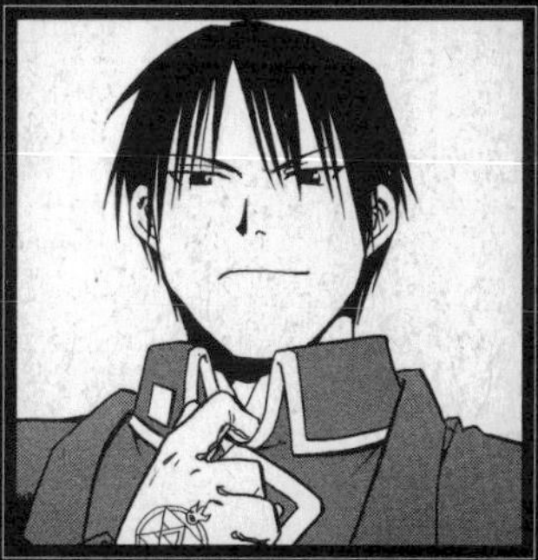

ロイ・マスタング

Roy Mustang

OUTLINE

FULLMETAL ALCHEMIST

ing a forbidden alchemical ritual, the Elric Brothers attempted to bring their dead other back to life. But the ritual went wrong, consuming Edward Elric's leg and phonse Elric's entire body. At the cost of his arm, Edward was able to graft his other's soul into a suit of armor. Equipped with mechanical "auto-mail" to replace s missing limbs, Edward became a state alchemist, serving the military, while aming the world with his brother in search of the Philosopher's Stone, the gendary substance with the power to restore what they have lost.

eir search hits a dead end when they learn the gruesome truth about the ilosopher's Stone and their government's complicity in its creation. Blackmailed by e enemy, Ed, Al and Colonel Roy Mustang are powerless to do anything with their wfound knowledge. As they adjust to their new reality, Ed gets a history lesson om Riza Hawkeye about the Ishbalan civil war and the atrocities that took place hen Amestrian soldiers followed [illegible] instead of their hearts.

鋼の錬金術師
FULLMETAL ALCHEMIST

CHARACTERS
FULLMETAL ALCHEMIST

■ ウィンリィ・ロックベル

Winry Rockbell

■ スカー

Scar

■ リザ・ホークアイ

Riza Hawkeye

■ キング・ブラッドレイ

King Bradley

■ ゾルフ・J・キンブリー

Solf J. Kimblee

■ メイ・チャン

May Chang

CONTENTS

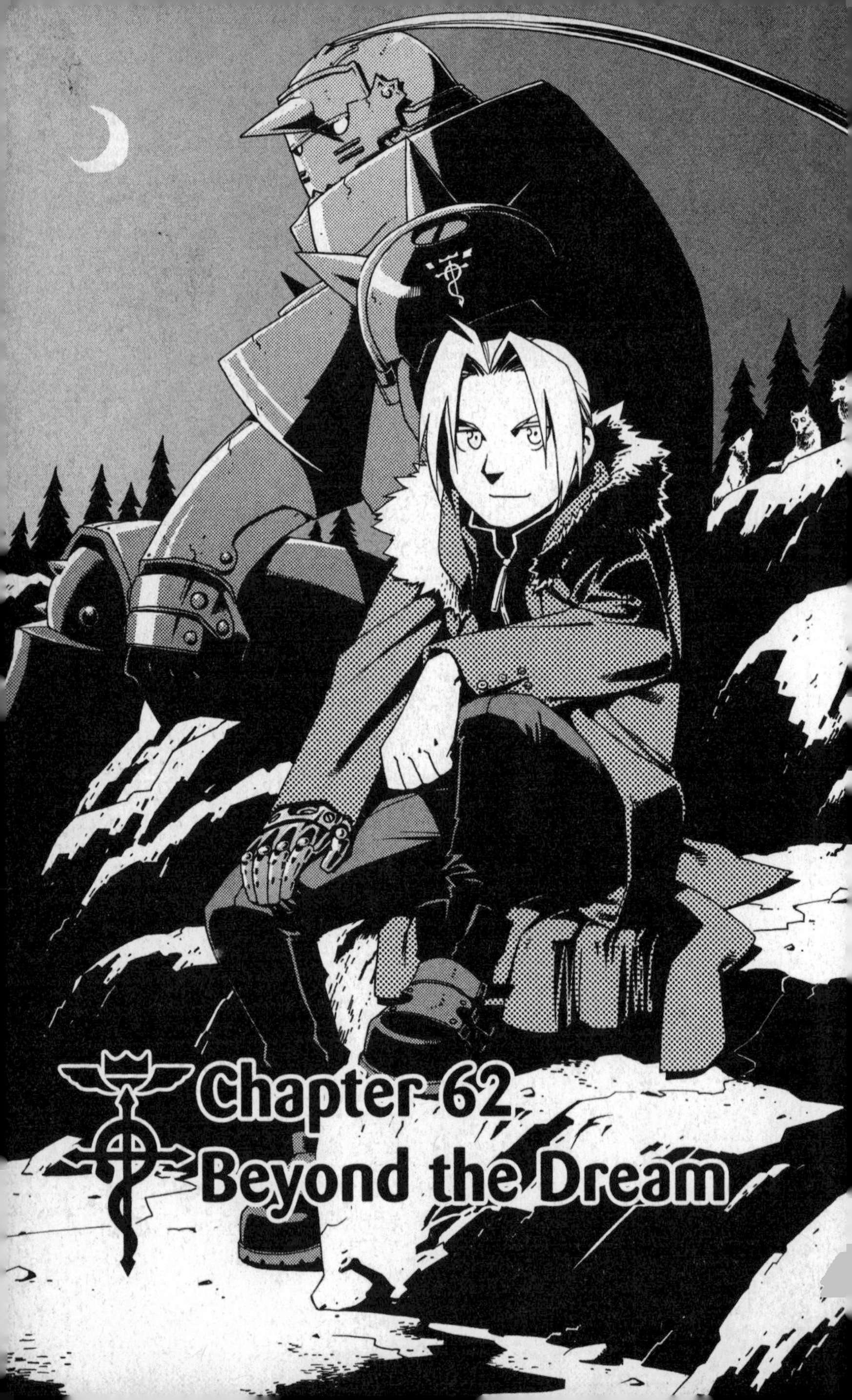

Chapter 62
Beyond the Dream

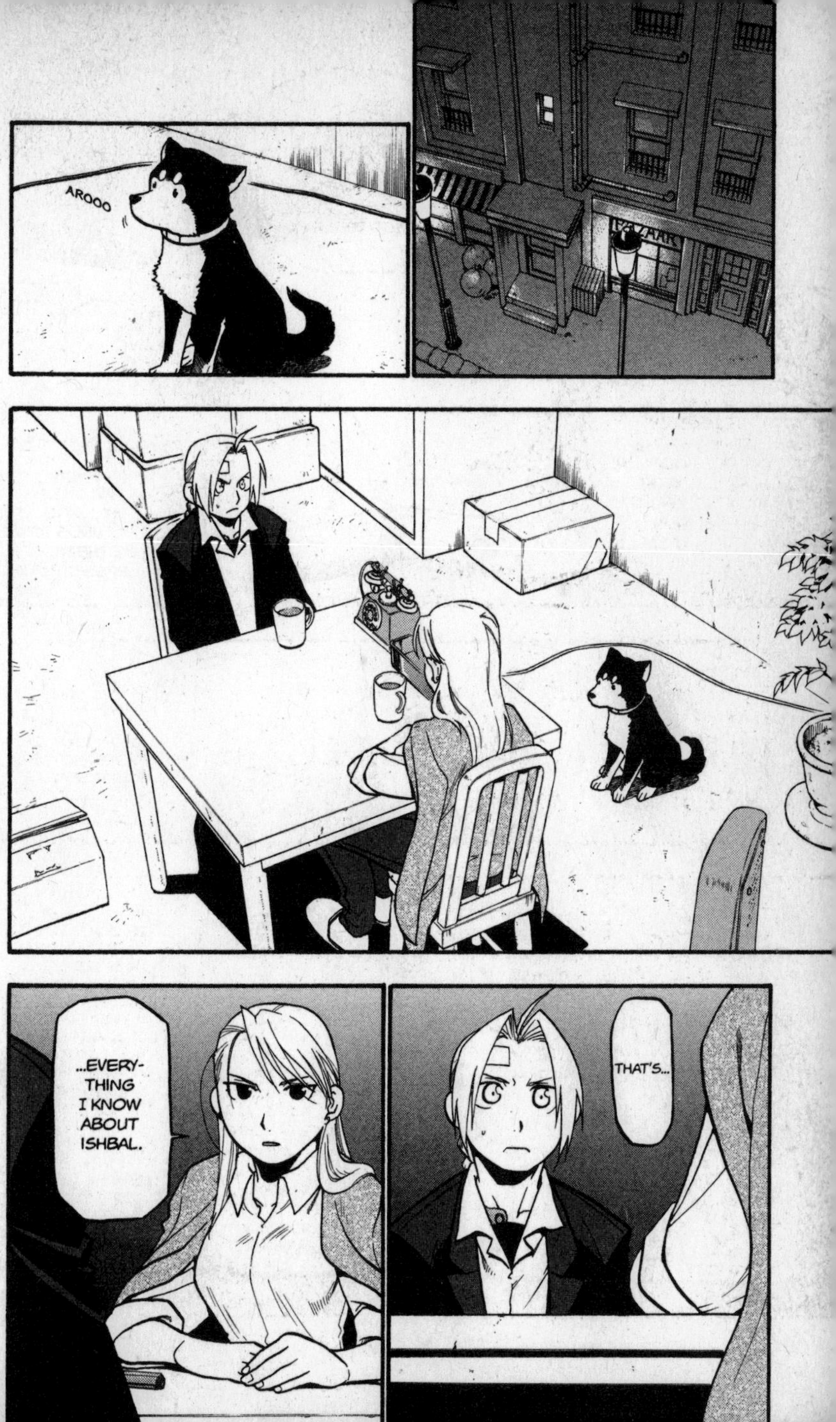
BAZAAR
AROOO
THAT'S...
...EVERY-THING I KNOW ABOUT ISHBAL.

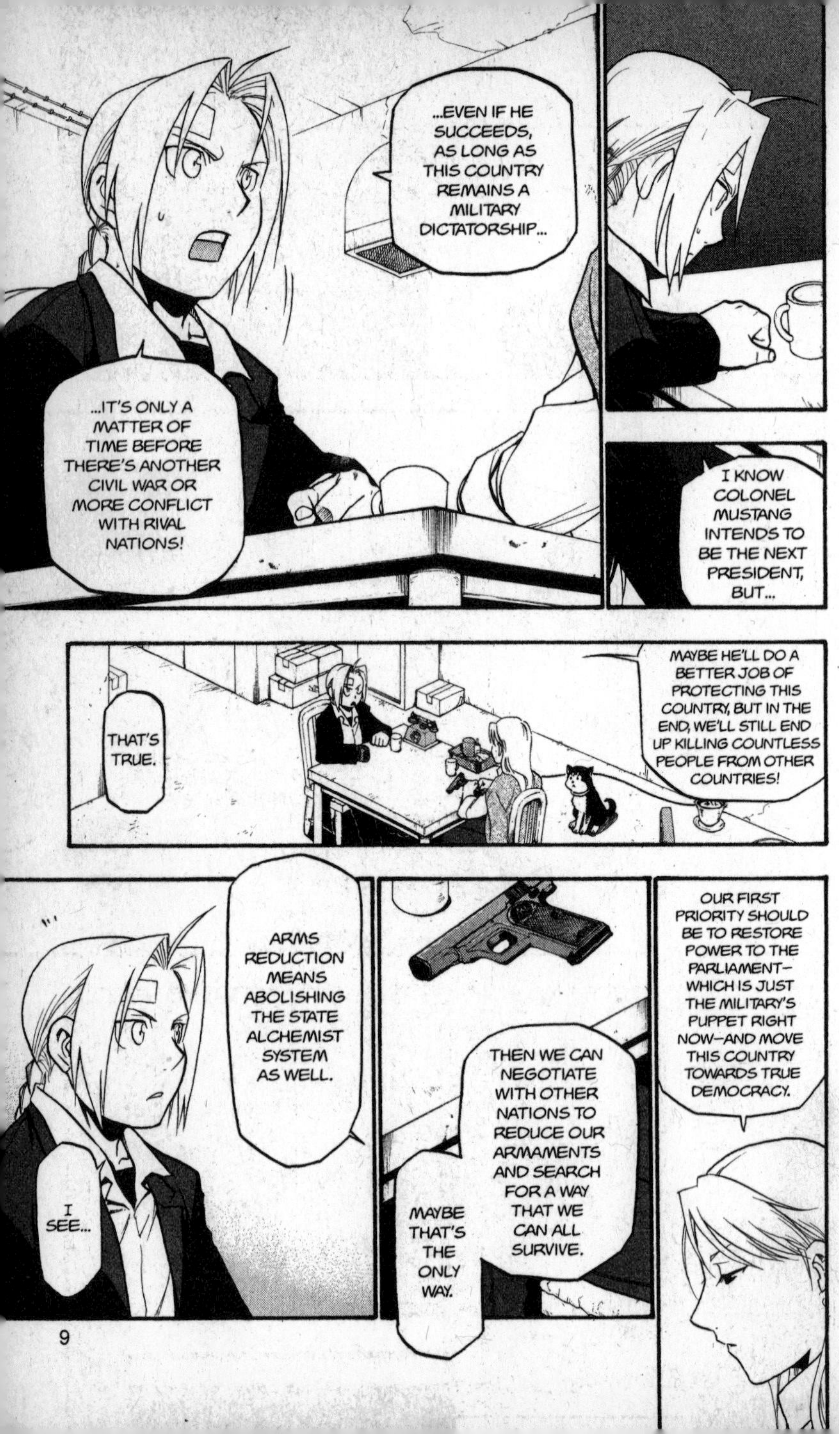
I KNOW COLONEL MUSTANG INTENDS TO BE THE NEXT PRESIDENT, BUT...
...EVEN IF HE SUCCEEDS, AS LONG AS THIS COUNTRY REMAINS A MILITARY DICTATORSHIP...
...IT'S ONLY A MATTER OF TIME BEFORE THERE'S ANOTHER CIVIL WAR OR MORE CONFLICT WITH RIVAL NATIONS!
MAYBE HE'LL DO A BETTER JOB OF PROTECTING THIS COUNTRY, BUT IN THE END, WE'LL STILL END UP KILLING COUNTLESS PEOPLE FROM OTHER COUNTRIES!
THAT'S TRUE.
OUR FIRST PRIORITY SHOULD BE TO RESTORE POWER TO THE PARLIAMENT—WHICH IS JUST THE MILITARY'S PUPPET RIGHT NOW—AND MOVE THIS COUNTRY TOWARDS TRUE DEMOCRACY.
THEN WE CAN NEGOTIATE WITH OTHER NATIONS TO REDUCE OUR ARMAMENTS AND SEARCH FOR A WAY THAT WE CAN ALL SURVIVE.
MAYBE THAT'S THE ONLY WAY.
ARMS REDUCTION MEANS ABOLISHING THE STATE ALCHEMIST SYSTEM AS WELL.
I SEE...

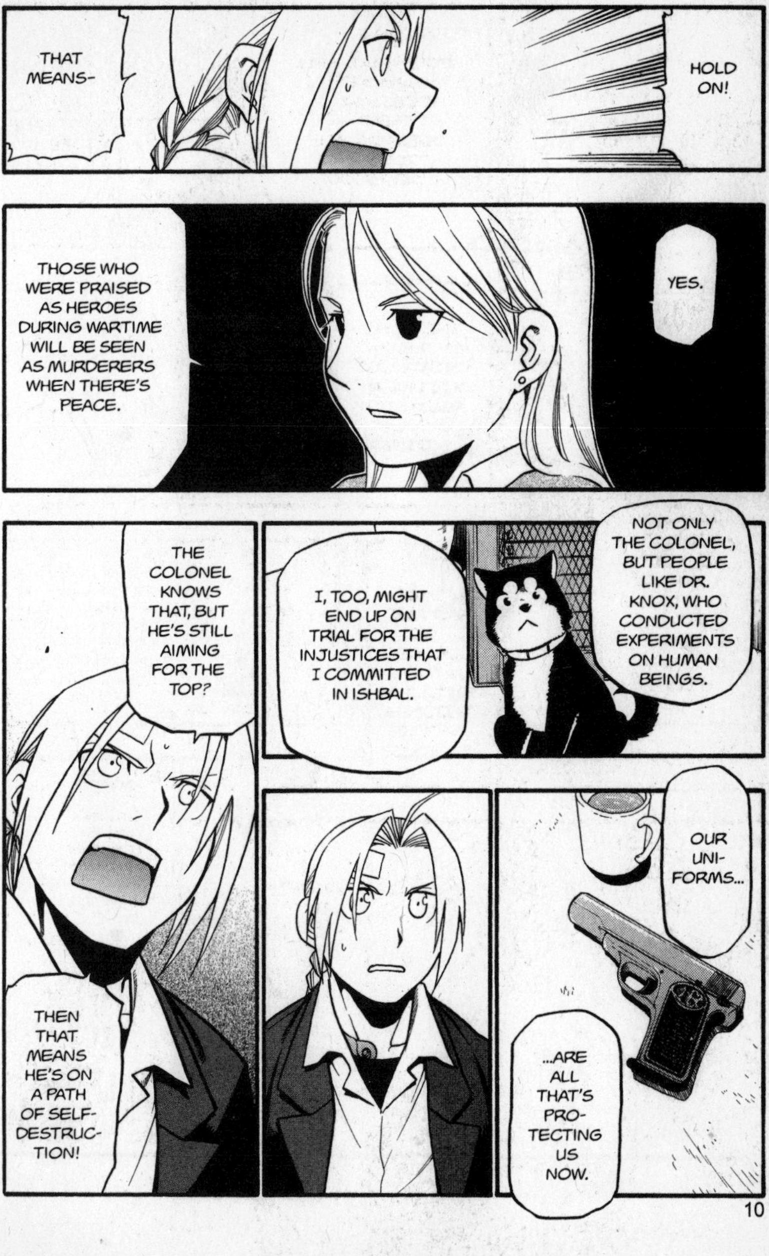
HOLD ON!
THAT MEANS-
YES.
THOSE WHO WERE PRAISED AS HEROES DURING WARTIME WILL BE SEEN AS MURDERERS WHEN THERE'S PEACE.
NOT ONLY THE COLONEL, BUT PEOPLE LIKE DR. KNOX, WHO CONDUCTED EXPERIMENTS ON HUMAN BEINGS.
I, TOO, MIGHT END UP ON TRIAL FOR THE INJUSTICES THAT I COMMITTED IN ISHBAL.
OUR UNI-FORMS...
...ARE ALL THAT'S PRO-TECTING US NOW.
THE COLONEL KNOWS THAT, BUT HE'S STILL AIMING FOR THE TOP?
THEN THAT MEANS HE'S ON A PATH OF SELF-DESTRUC-TION!

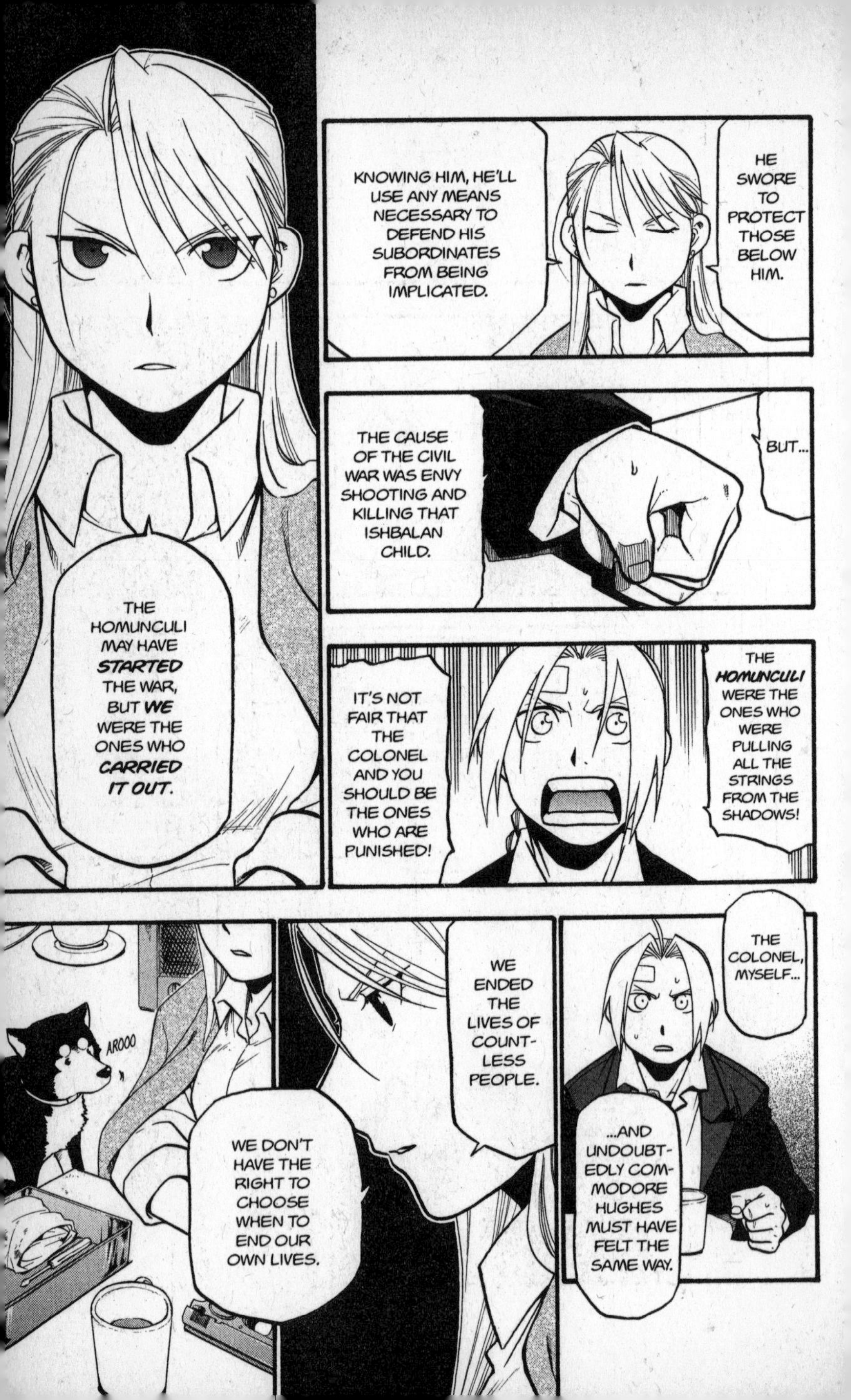
HE SWORE TO PROTECT THOSE BELOW HIM.
KNOWING HIM, HE'LL USE ANY MEANS NECESSARY TO DEFEND HIS SUBORDINATES FROM BEING IMPLICATED.
BUT...
THE CAUSE OF THE CIVIL WAR WAS ENVY SHOOTING AND KILLING THAT ISHBALAN CHILD.
THE **HOMUNCULI** WERE THE ONES WHO WERE PULLING ALL THE STRINGS FROM THE SHADOWS!
IT'S NOT FAIR THAT THE COLONEL AND YOU SHOULD BE THE ONES WHO ARE PUNISHED!
THE HOMUNCULI MAY HAVE **STARTED** THE WAR, BUT **WE** WERE THE ONES WHO **CARRIED IT OUT**.
THE COLONEL, MYSELF...
...AND UNDOUBTEDLY COMMODORE HUGHES MUST HAVE FELT THE SAME WAY.
WE ENDED THE LIVES OF COUNTLESS PEOPLE.
WE DON'T HAVE THE RIGHT TO CHOOSE WHEN TO END OUR OWN LIVES.
AROOO

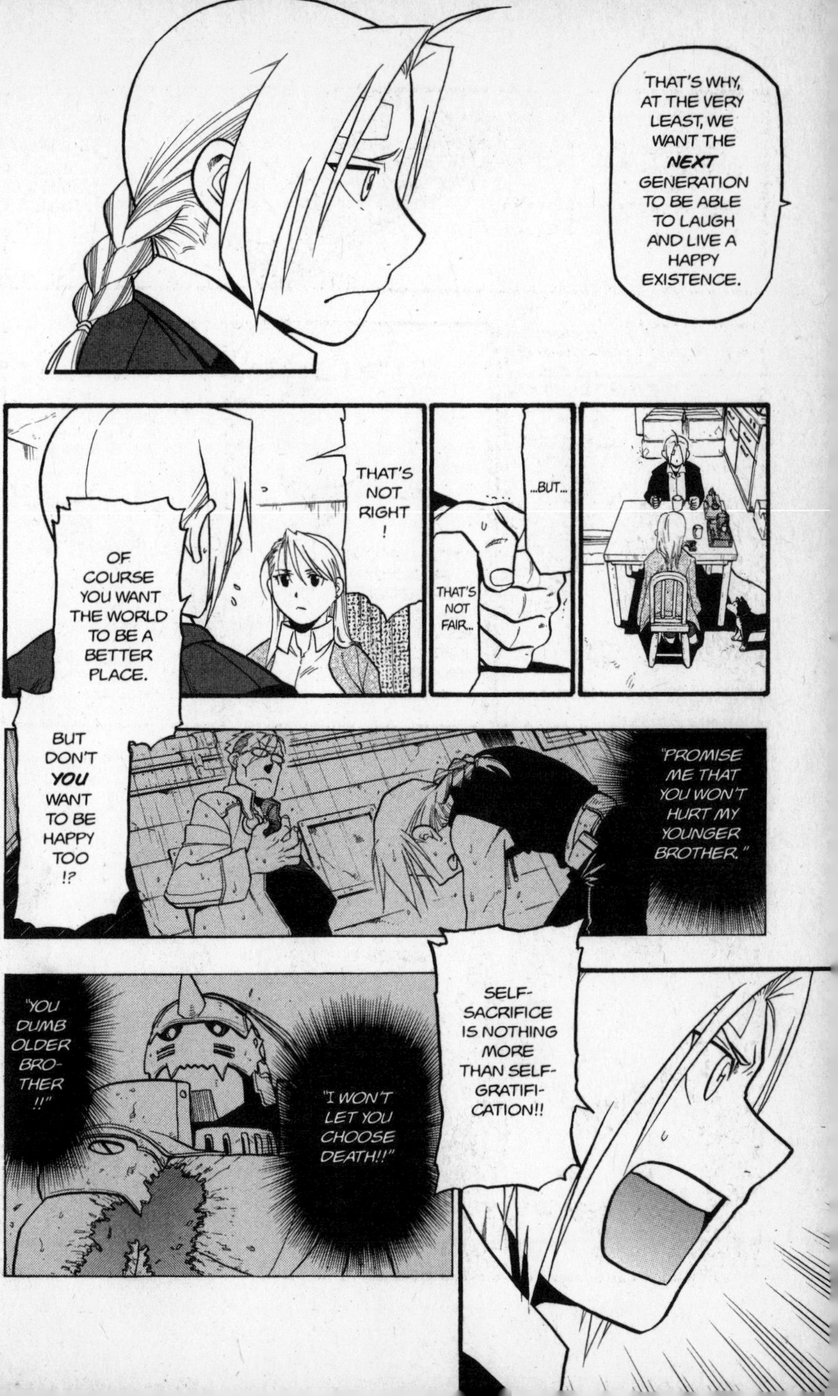
THAT'S WHY, AT THE VERY LEAST, WE WANT THE NEXT GENERATION TO BE ABLE TO LAUGH AND LIVE A HAPPY EXISTENCE.
...BUT...
THAT'S NOT FAIR...
THAT'S NOT RIGHT!
OF COURSE YOU WANT THE WORLD TO BE A BETTER PLACE.
"PROMISE ME THAT YOU WON'T HURT MY YOUNGER BROTHER."
BUT DON'T YOU WANT TO BE HAPPY TOO!?
SELF-SACRIFICE IS NOTHING MORE THAN SELF-GRATIFICATION!!
"I WON'T LET YOU CHOOSE DEATH!!"
"YOU DUMB OLDER BROTHER!!"

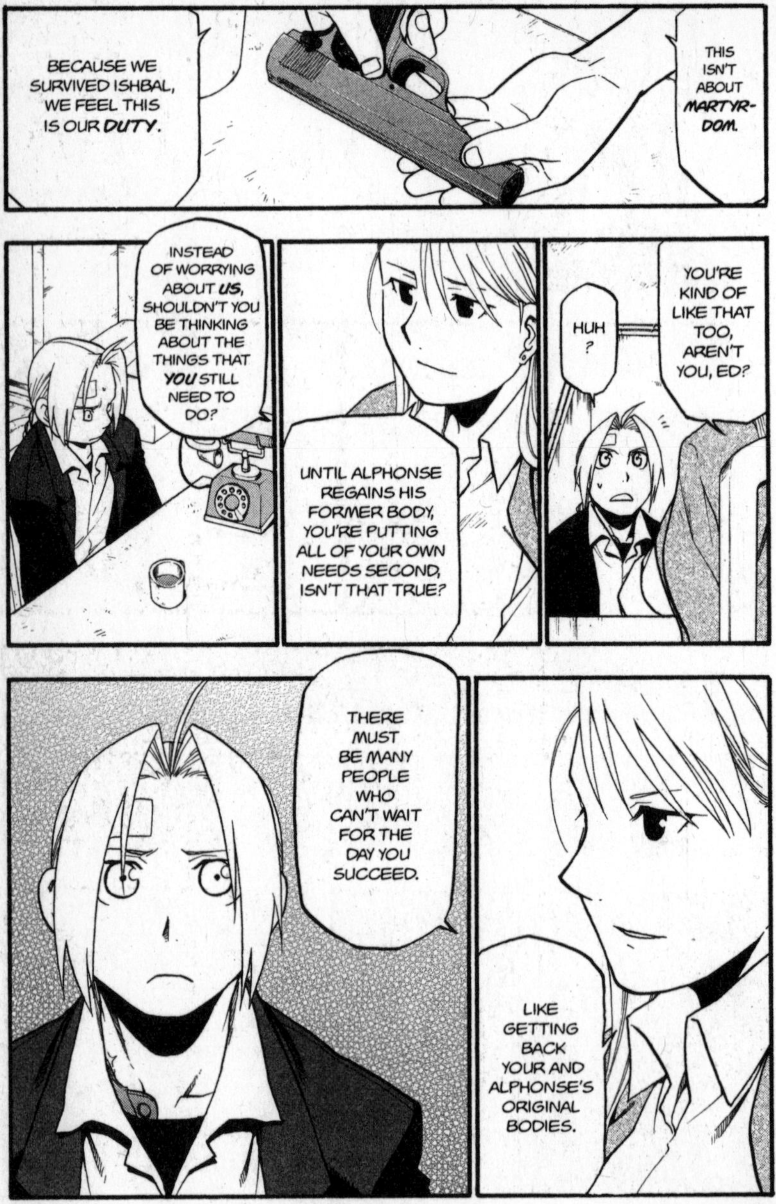
THIS ISN'T ABOUT MARTYRDOM.
BECAUSE WE SURVIVED ISHBAL, WE FEEL THIS IS OUR DUTY.
YOU'RE KIND OF LIKE THAT TOO, AREN'T YOU, ED?
HUH?
UNTIL ALPHONSE REGAINS HIS FORMER BODY, YOU'RE PUTTING ALL OF YOUR OWN NEEDS SECOND, ISN'T THAT TRUE?
INSTEAD OF WORRYING ABOUT US, SHOULDN'T YOU BE THINKING ABOUT THE THINGS THAT YOU STILL NEED TO DO?
LIKE GETTING BACK YOUR AND ALPHONSE'S ORIGINAL BODIES.
THERE MUST BE MANY PEOPLE WHO CAN'T WAIT FOR THE DAY YOU SUCCEED.

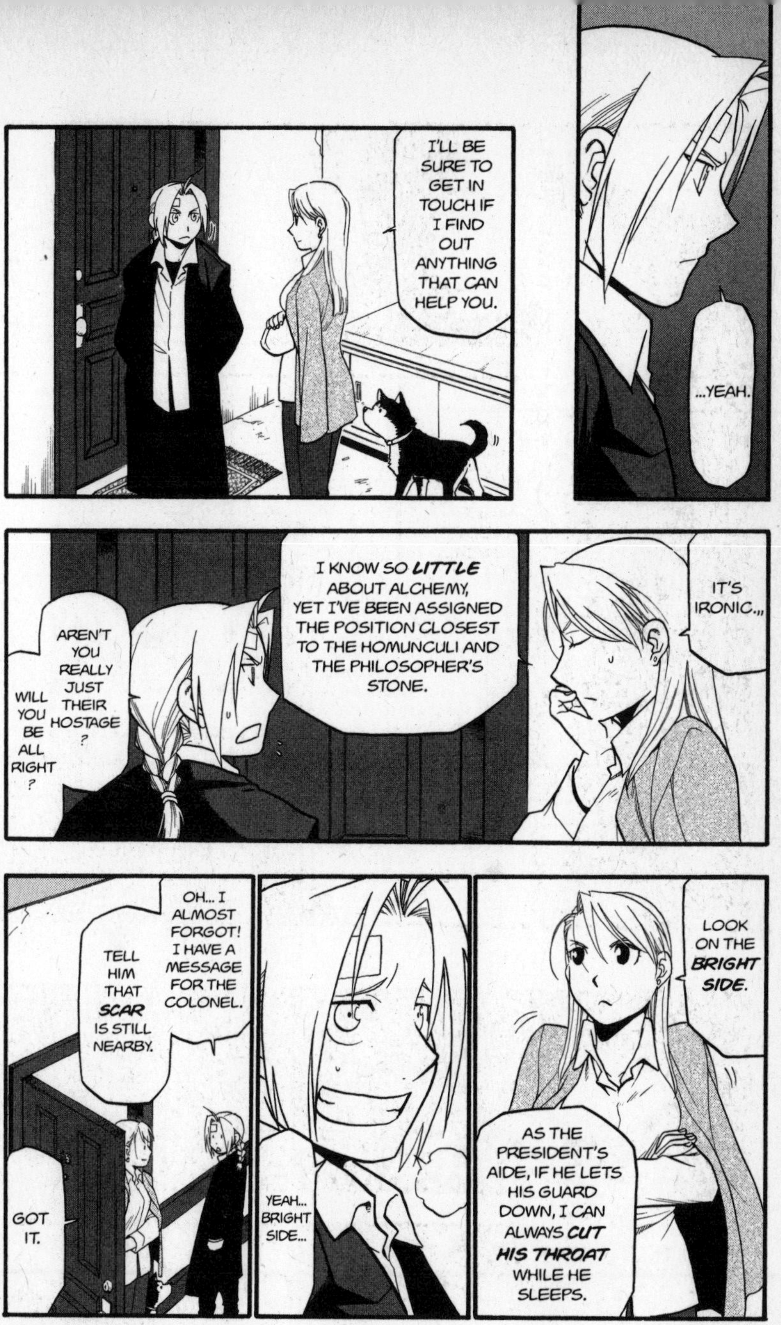
...YEAH.
I'LL BE SURE TO GET IN TOUCH IF I FIND OUT ANYTHING THAT CAN HELP YOU.
IT'S IRONIC...
I KNOW SO LITTLE ABOUT ALCHEMY, YET I'VE BEEN ASSIGNED THE POSITION CLOSEST TO THE HOMUNCULI AND THE PHILOSOPHER'S STONE.
AREN'T YOU REALLY JUST THEIR HOSTAGE?
WILL YOU BE ALL RIGHT?
LOOK ON THE BRIGHT SIDE.
AS THE PRESIDENT'S AIDE, IF HE LETS HIS GUARD DOWN, I CAN ALWAYS CUT HIS THROAT WHILE HE SLEEPS.
YEAH... BRIGHT SIDE...
OH... I ALMOST FORGOT! I HAVE A MESSAGE FOR THE COLONEL.
TELL HIM THAT SCAR IS STILL NEARBY.
GOT IT.

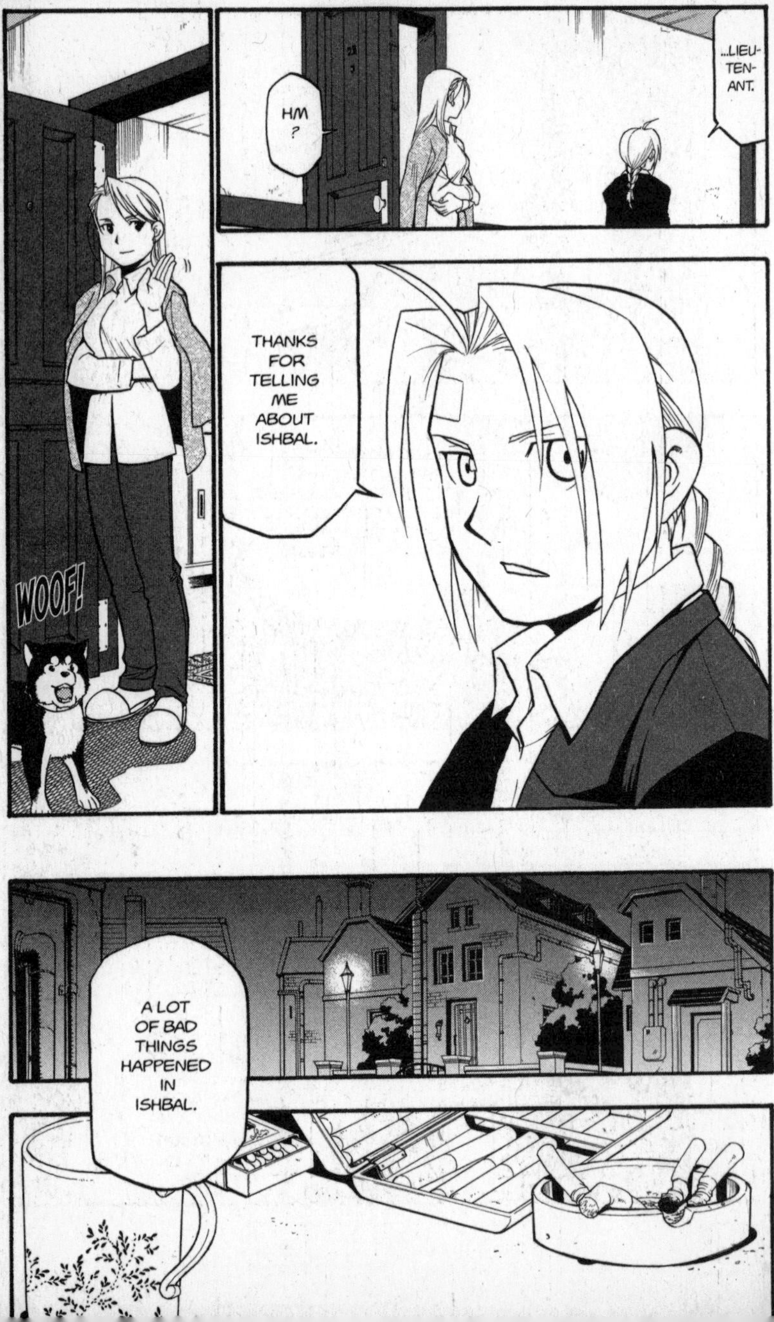
...LIEUTENANT.
HM?
THANKS FOR TELLING ME ABOUT ISHBAL.
WOOF!
A LOT OF BAD THINGS HAPPENED IN ISHBAL.

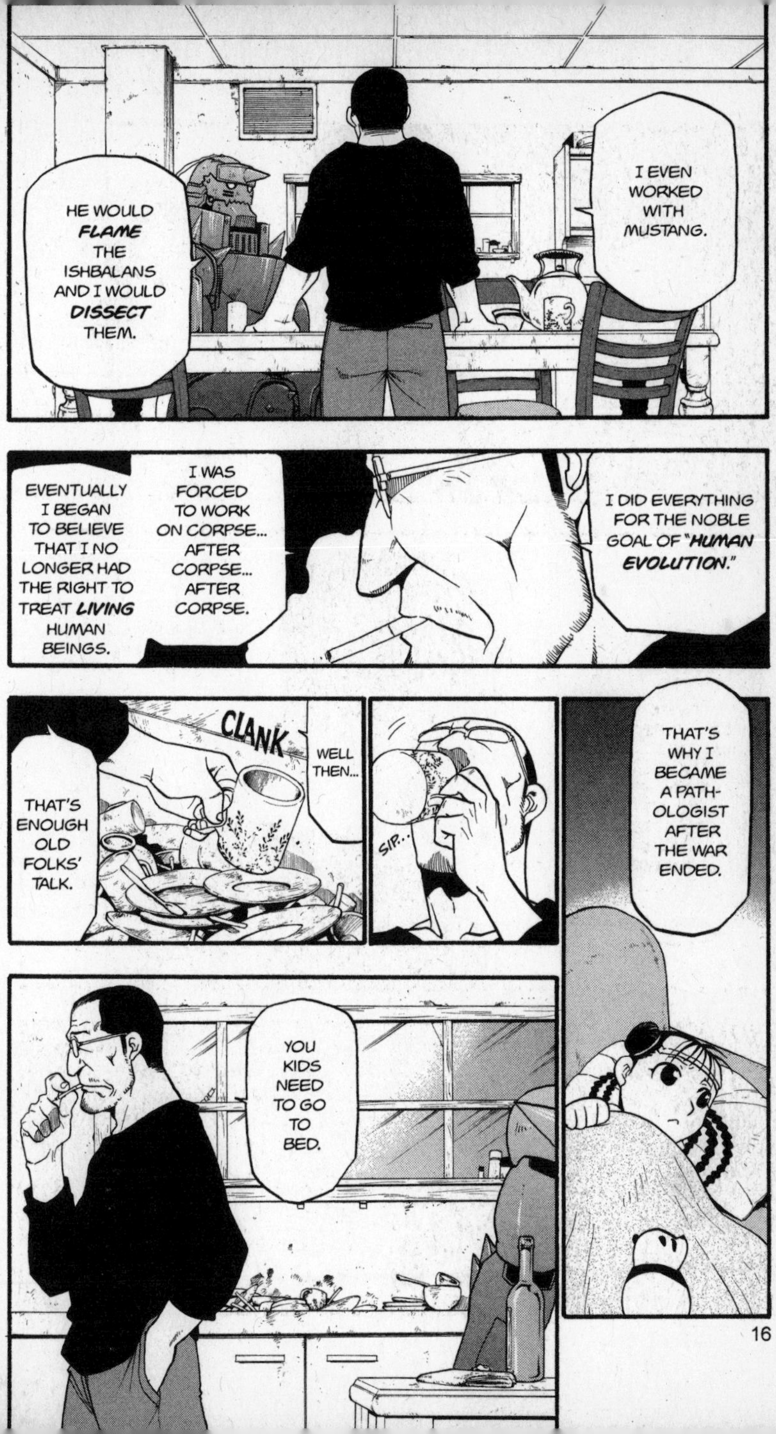
I EVEN WORKED WITH MUSTANG.
HE WOULD *FLAME* THE ISHBALANS AND I WOULD *DISSECT* THEM.
I DID EVERYTHING FOR THE NOBLE GOAL OF "*HUMAN EVOLUTION*."
I WAS FORCED TO WORK ON CORPSE... AFTER CORPSE... AFTER CORPSE.
EVENTUALLY I BEGAN TO BELIEVE THAT I NO LONGER HAD THE RIGHT TO TREAT *LIVING* HUMAN BEINGS.
THAT'S WHY I BECAME A PATHOLOGIST AFTER THE WAR ENDED.
SIP...
WELL THEN...
CLANK
THAT'S ENOUGH OLD FOLKS' TALK.
YOU KIDS NEED TO GO TO BED.

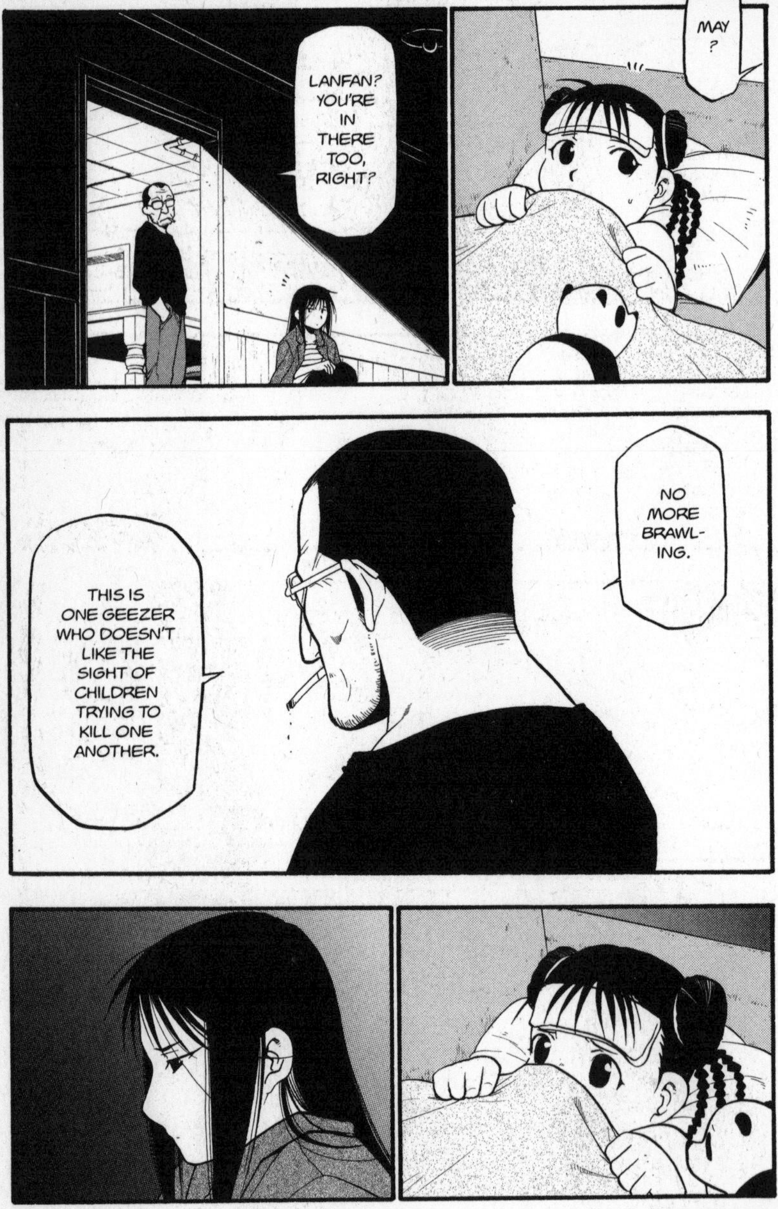
MAY?
LANFAN? YOU'RE IN THERE TOO, RIGHT?
NO MORE BRAWL-ING.
THIS IS ONE GEEZER WHO DOESN'T LIKE THE SIGHT OF CHILDREN TRYING TO KILL ONE ANOTHER.

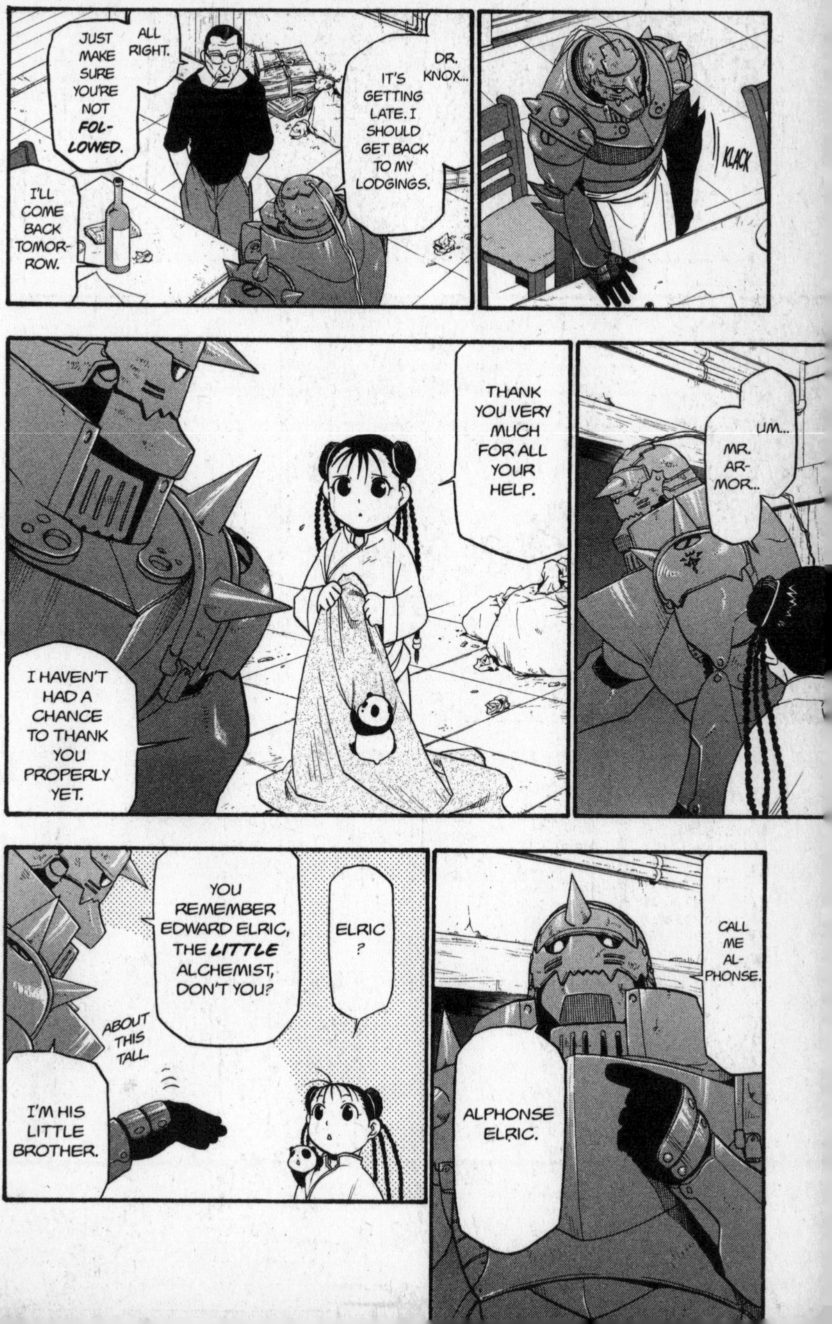
KLACK
DR. KNOX... IT'S GETTING LATE. I SHOULD GET BACK TO MY LODGINGS.
ALL RIGHT.
JUST MAKE SURE YOU'RE NOT FOL-LOWED.
I'LL COME BACK TOMOR-ROW.
UM... MR. AR-MOR...
THANK YOU VERY MUCH FOR ALL YOUR HELP.
I HAVEN'T HAD A CHANCE TO THANK YOU PROPERLY YET.
CALL ME AL-PHONSE.
ALPHONSE ELRIC.
ELRIC?
YOU REMEMBER EDWARD ELRIC, THE LITTLE ALCHEMIST, DON'T YOU?
ABOUT THIS TALL.
I'M HIS LITTLE BROTHER.

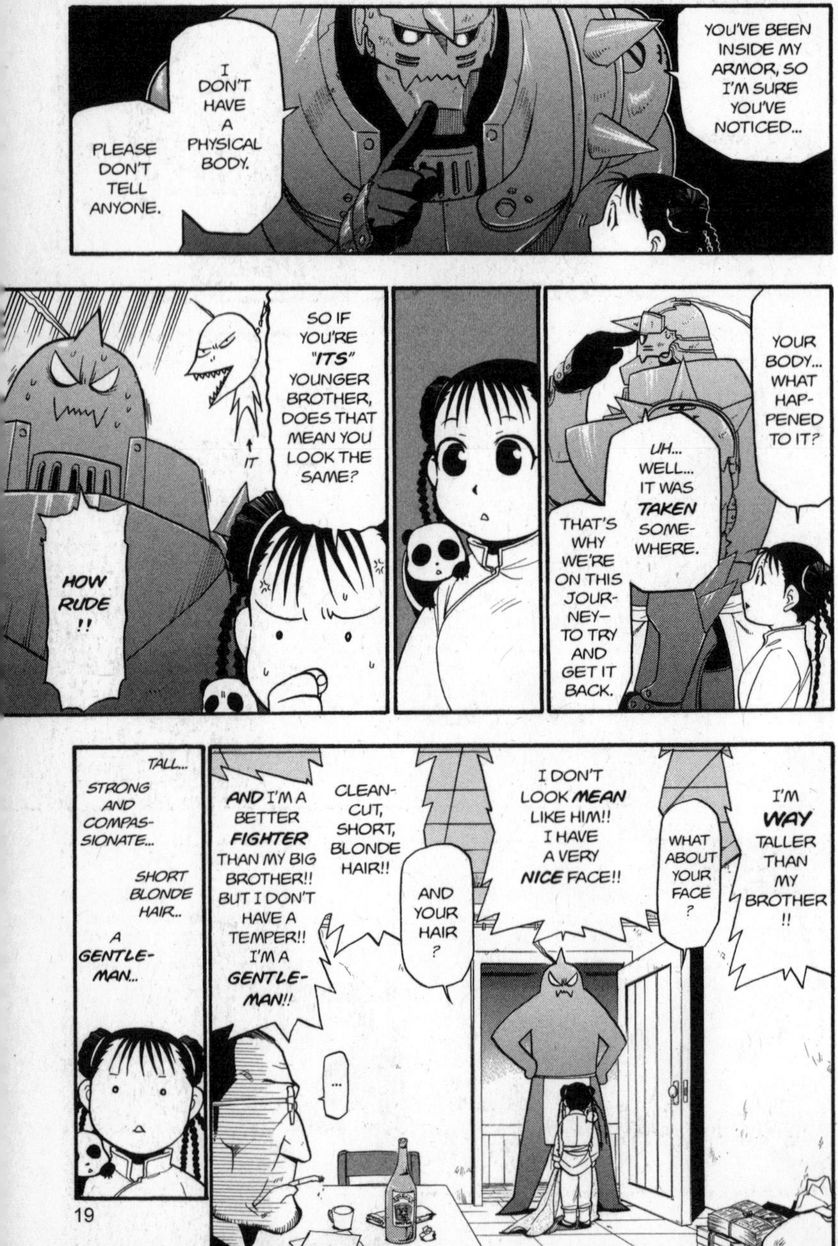
YOU'VE BEEN INSIDE MY ARMOR, SO I'M SURE YOU'VE NOTICED...
I DON'T HAVE A PHYSICAL BODY.
PLEASE DON'T TELL ANYONE.
YOUR BODY... WHAT HAPPENED TO IT?
UH... WELL... IT WAS TAKEN SOMEWHERE.
THAT'S WHY WE'RE ON THIS JOURNEY—TO TRY AND GET IT BACK.
SO IF YOU'RE "ITS" YOUNGER BROTHER, DOES THAT MEAN YOU LOOK THE SAME?
IT
HOW RUDE!!
I'M WAY TALLER THAN MY BROTHER!!
WHAT ABOUT YOUR FACE?
I DON'T LOOK MEAN LIKE HIM!! I HAVE A VERY NICE FACE!!
AND YOUR HAIR?
CLEAN-CUT, SHORT, BLONDE HAIR!!
AND I'M A BETTER FIGHTER THAN MY BIG BROTHER!! BUT I DON'T HAVE A TEMPER!! I'M A GENTLEMAN!!
...
TALL...
STRONG AND COMPASSIONATE...
SHORT BLONDE HAIR...
A GENTLEMAN...

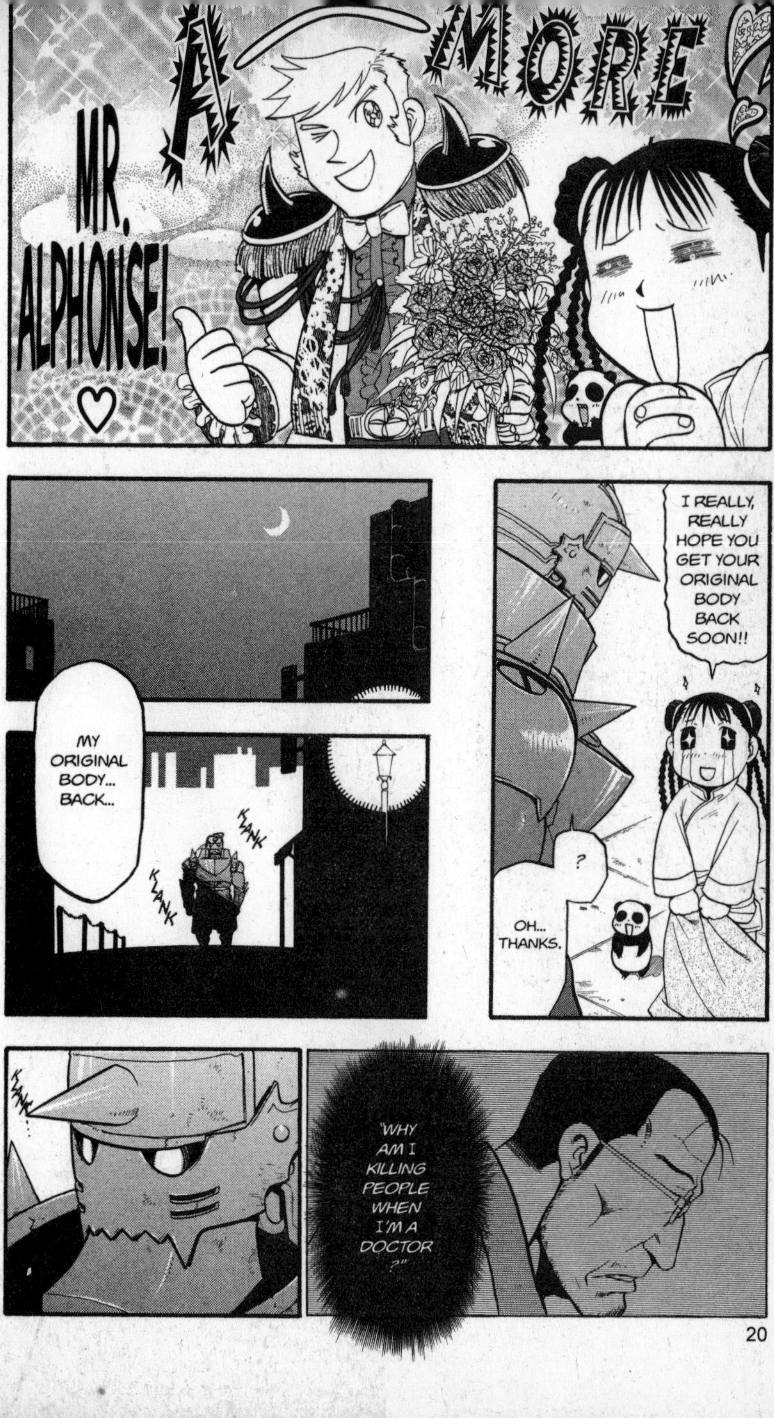
A MORE
MR. ALPHONSE!
♥
I REALLY, REALLY HOPE YOU GET YOUR ORIGINAL BODY BACK SOON!!
?
OH... THANKS.
MY ORIGINAL BODY... BACK...
KLANK
KLANK
"WHY AM I KILLING PEOPLE WHEN I'M A DOCTOR?"
KLANK...

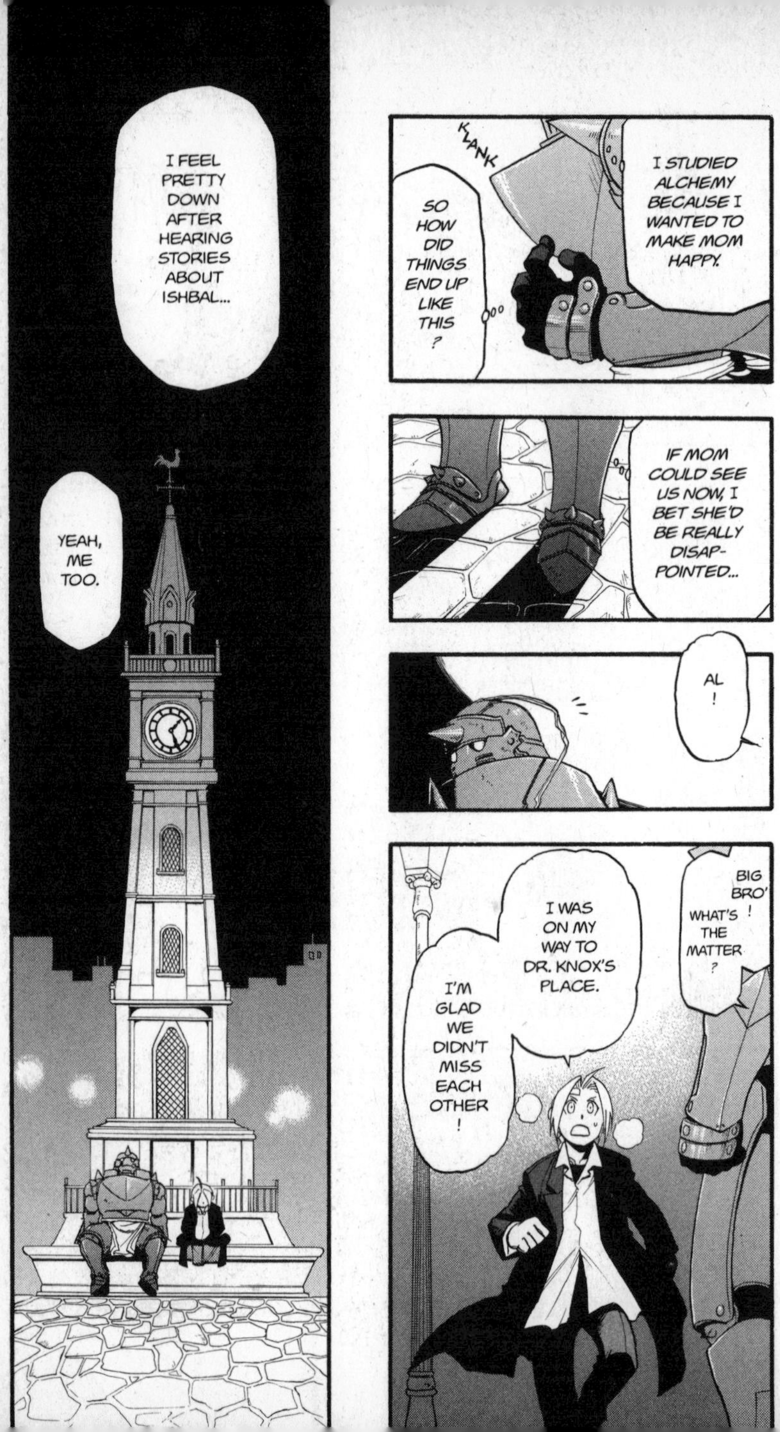
I STUDIED ALCHEMY BECAUSE I WANTED TO MAKE MOM HAPPY.
KLANK
SO HOW DID THINGS END UP LIKE THIS?
IF MOM COULD SEE US NOW, I BET SHE'D BE REALLY DISAPPOINTED...
AL!
BIG BRO'!
WHAT'S THE MATTER?
I WAS ON MY WAY TO DR. KNOX'S PLACE.
I'M GLAD WE DIDN'T MISS EACH OTHER!
I FEEL PRETTY DOWN AFTER HEARING STORIES ABOUT ISHBAL...
YEAH, ME TOO.

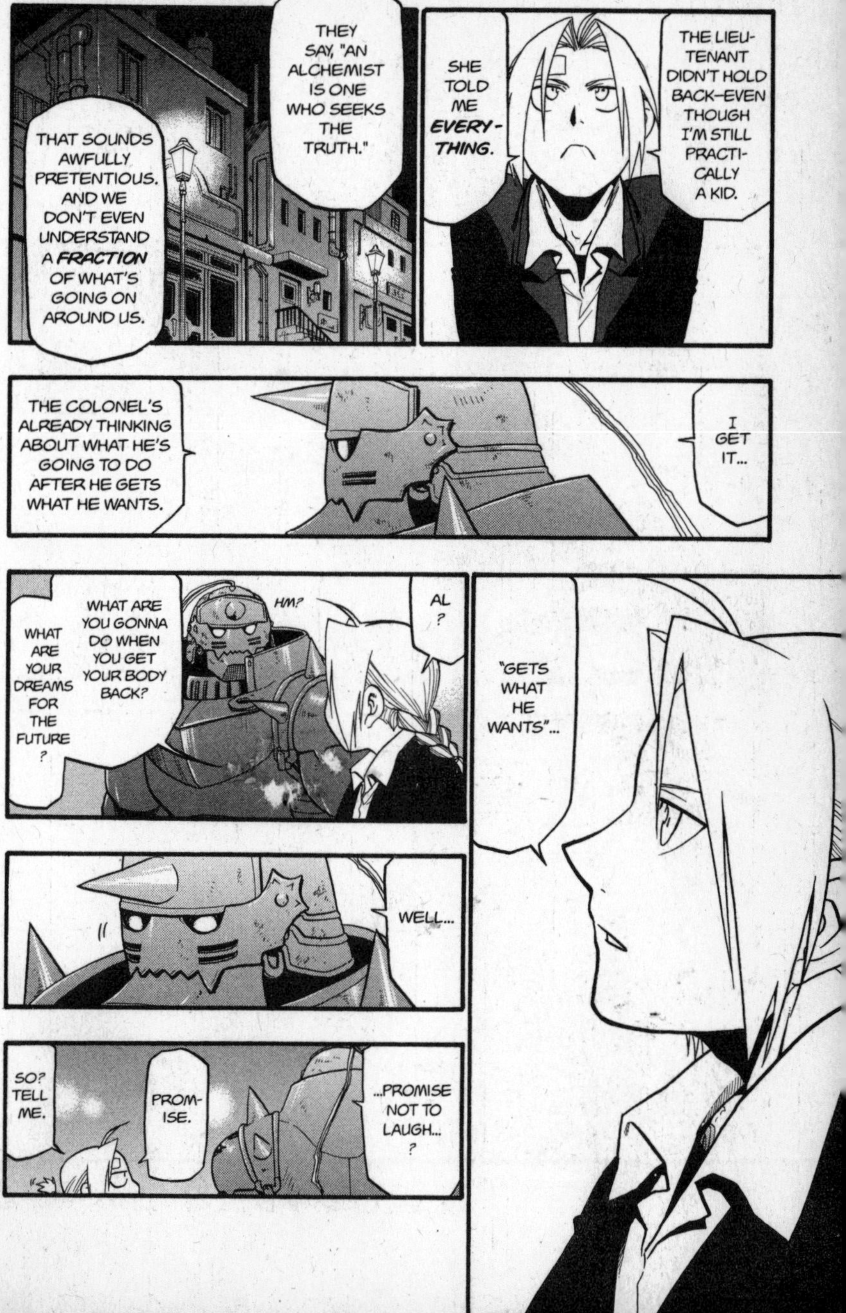
THE LIEU-TENANT DIDN'T HOLD BACK—EVEN THOUGH I'M STILL PRACTI-CALLY A KID.
SHE TOLD ME ***EVERY-THING.***
THEY SAY, "AN ALCHEMIST IS ONE WHO SEEKS THE TRUTH."
THAT SOUNDS AWFULLY PRETENTIOUS. AND WE DON'T EVEN UNDERSTAND A ***FRACTION*** OF WHAT'S GOING ON AROUND US.
I GET IT...
THE COLONEL'S ALREADY THINKING ABOUT WHAT HE'S GOING TO DO AFTER HE GETS WHAT HE WANTS.
"GETS WHAT HE WANTS"...
AL?
HM?
WHAT ARE YOU GONNA DO WHEN YOU GET YOUR BODY BACK?
WHAT ARE YOUR DREAMS FOR THE FUTURE?
WELL...
...PROMISE NOT TO LAUGH...?
PROM-ISE.
SO? TELL ME.

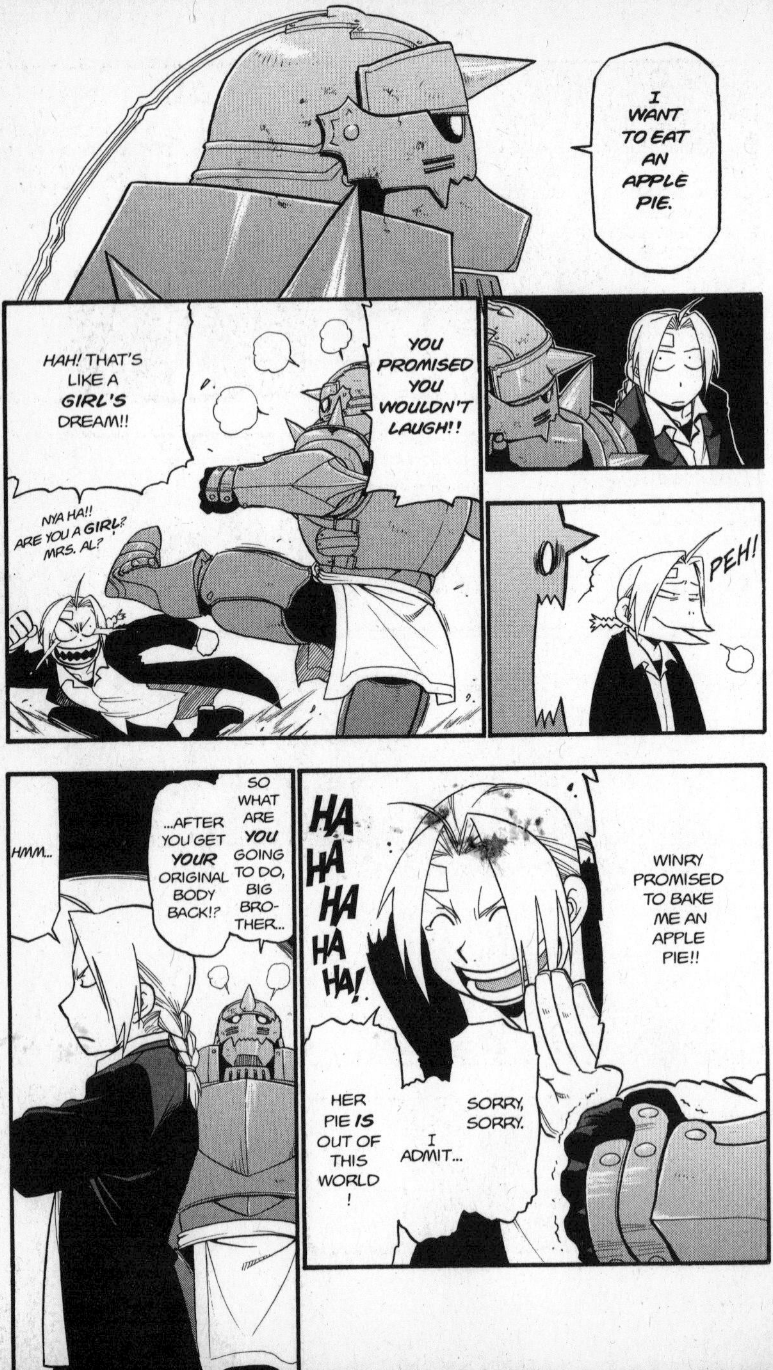
I WANT TO EAT AN APPLE PIE.
PEH!
YOU PROMISED YOU WOULDN'T LAUGH!!
HAH! THAT'S LIKE A GIRL'S DREAM!!
NYA HA!! ARE YOU A GIRL? MRS. AL?
WINRY PROMISED TO BAKE ME AN APPLE PIE!!
HA HA HA HA HA HA!
SORRY, SORRY.
I ADMIT...
HER PIE IS OUT OF THIS WORLD!
SO WHAT ARE YOU GOING TO DO, BIG BROTHER...
...AFTER YOU GET YOUR ORIGINAL BODY BACK!?
HMM...

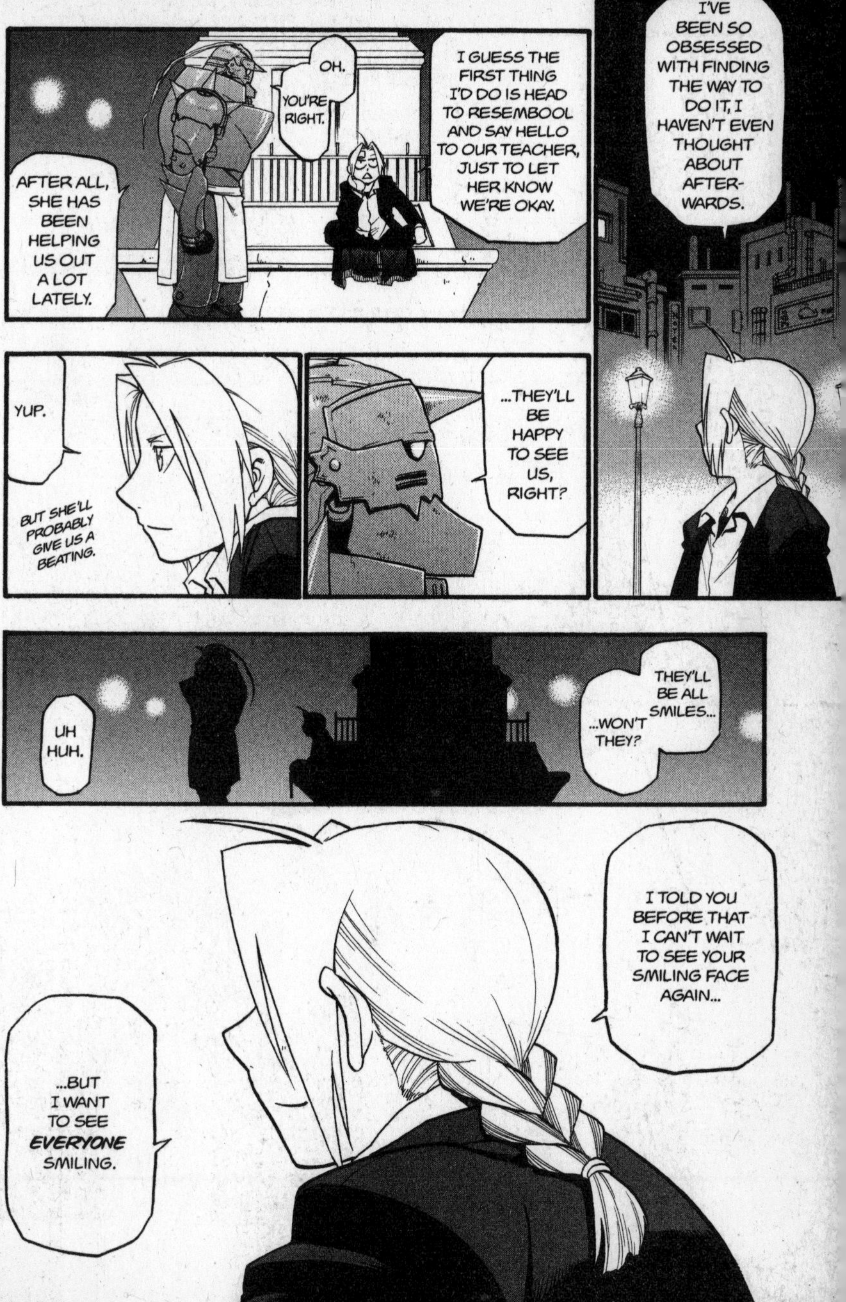
I'VE BEEN SO OBSESSED WITH FINDING THE WAY TO DO IT, I HAVEN'T EVEN THOUGHT ABOUT AFTER-WARDS.
I GUESS THE FIRST THING I'D DO IS HEAD TO RESEMBOOL AND SAY HELLO TO OUR TEACHER, JUST TO LET HER KNOW WE'RE OKAY.
OH.
YOU'RE RIGHT.
AFTER ALL, SHE HAS BEEN HELPING US OUT A LOT LATELY.
...THEY'LL BE HAPPY TO SEE US, RIGHT?
YUP.
BUT SHE'LL PROBABLY GIVE US A BEATING.
THEY'LL BE ALL SMILES...
...WON'T THEY?
UH HUH.
I TOLD YOU BEFORE THAT I CAN'T WAIT TO SEE YOUR SMILING FACE AGAIN...
...BUT I WANT TO SEE EVERYONE SMILING.

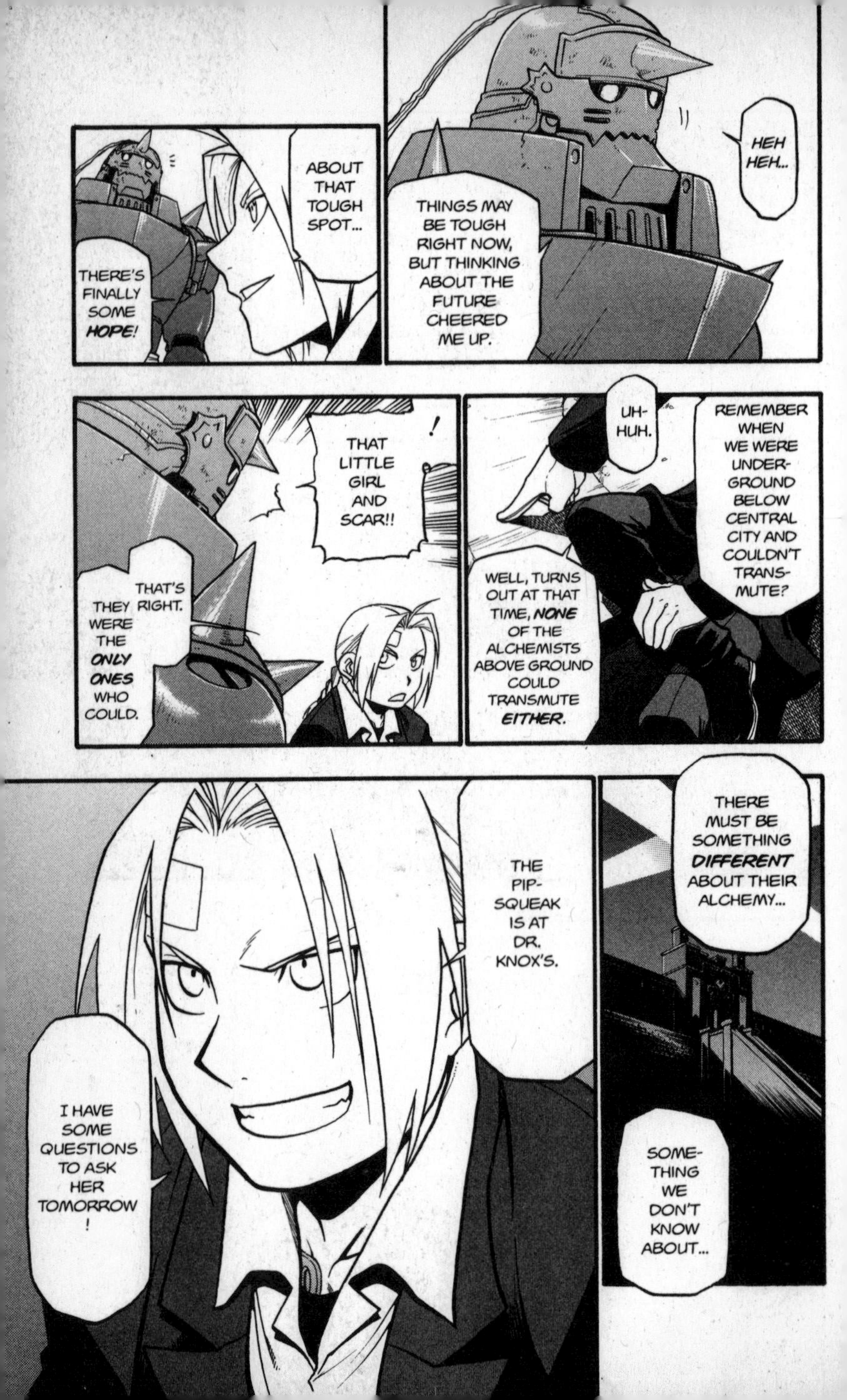
HEH HEH...
THINGS MAY BE TOUGH RIGHT NOW, BUT THINKING ABOUT THE FUTURE CHEERED ME UP.
ABOUT THAT TOUGH SPOT...
THERE'S FINALLY SOME HOPE!
REMEMBER WHEN WE WERE UNDERGROUND BELOW CENTRAL CITY AND COULDN'T TRANSMUTE?
UH-HUH.
WELL, TURNS OUT AT THAT TIME, NONE OF THE ALCHEMISTS ABOVE GROUND COULD TRANSMUTE EITHER.
!
THAT LITTLE GIRL AND SCAR!!
THAT'S RIGHT.
THEY WERE THE ONLY ONES WHO COULD.
THERE MUST BE SOMETHING DIFFERENT ABOUT THEIR ALCHEMY...
SOMETHING WE DON'T KNOW ABOUT...
THE PIPSQUEAK IS AT DR. KNOX'S.
I HAVE SOME QUESTIONS TO ASK HER TOMORROW!

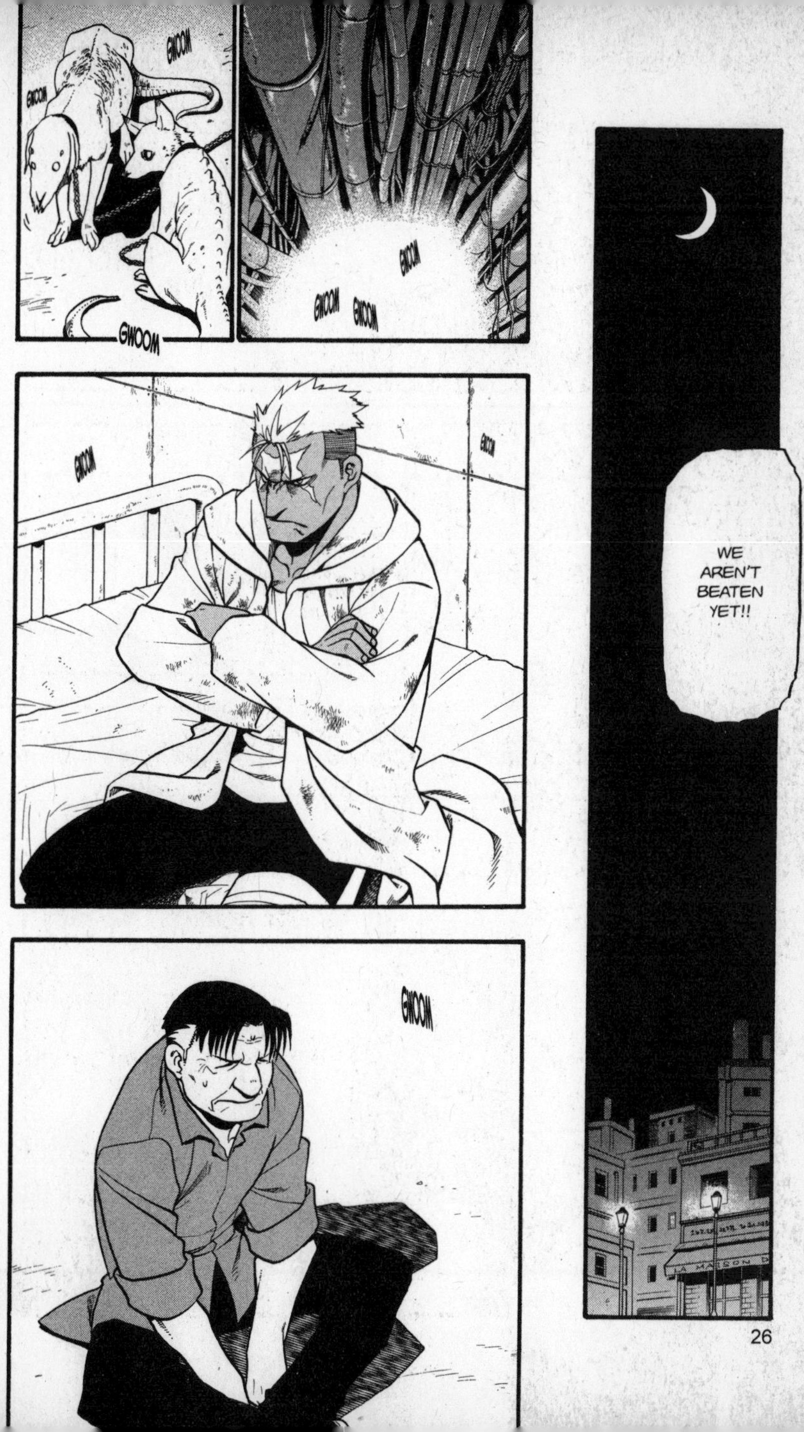
GWOOM
GWOOM
GWOOM
GWOOM
GWOOM
GWOOM
GWOOM
GWOOM
GWOOM
WE AREN'T BEATEN YET!!
LA MAISON D

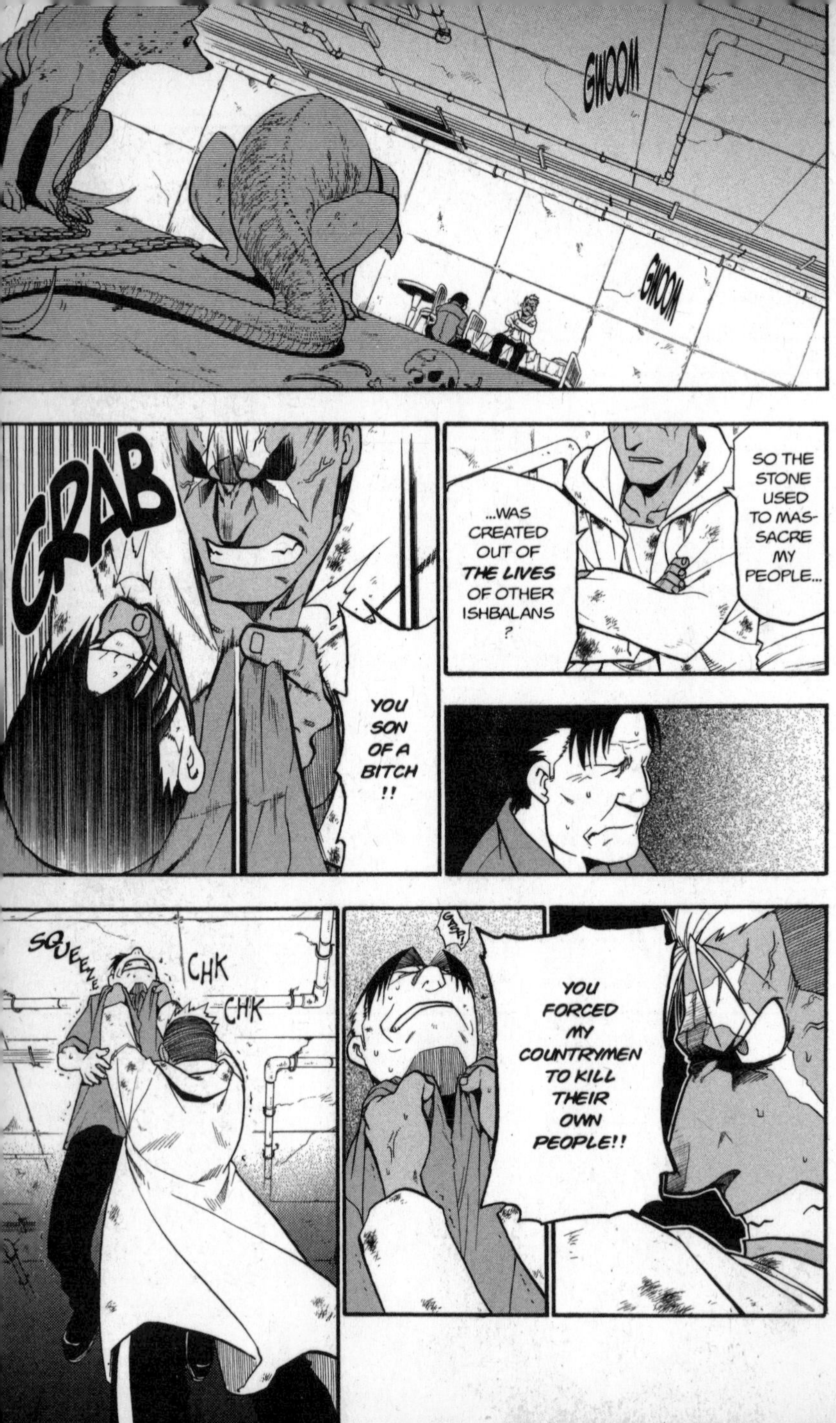
GWOOM
GWOOM
SO THE STONE USED TO MAS-SACRE MY PEOPLE...
...WAS CREATED OUT OF *THE LIVES* OF OTHER ISHBALANS?
GRAB
YOU SON OF A BITCH!!
YOU FORCED MY COUNTRYMEN TO KILL THEIR OWN PEOPLE!!
SQUEEEZE
CHK
CHK

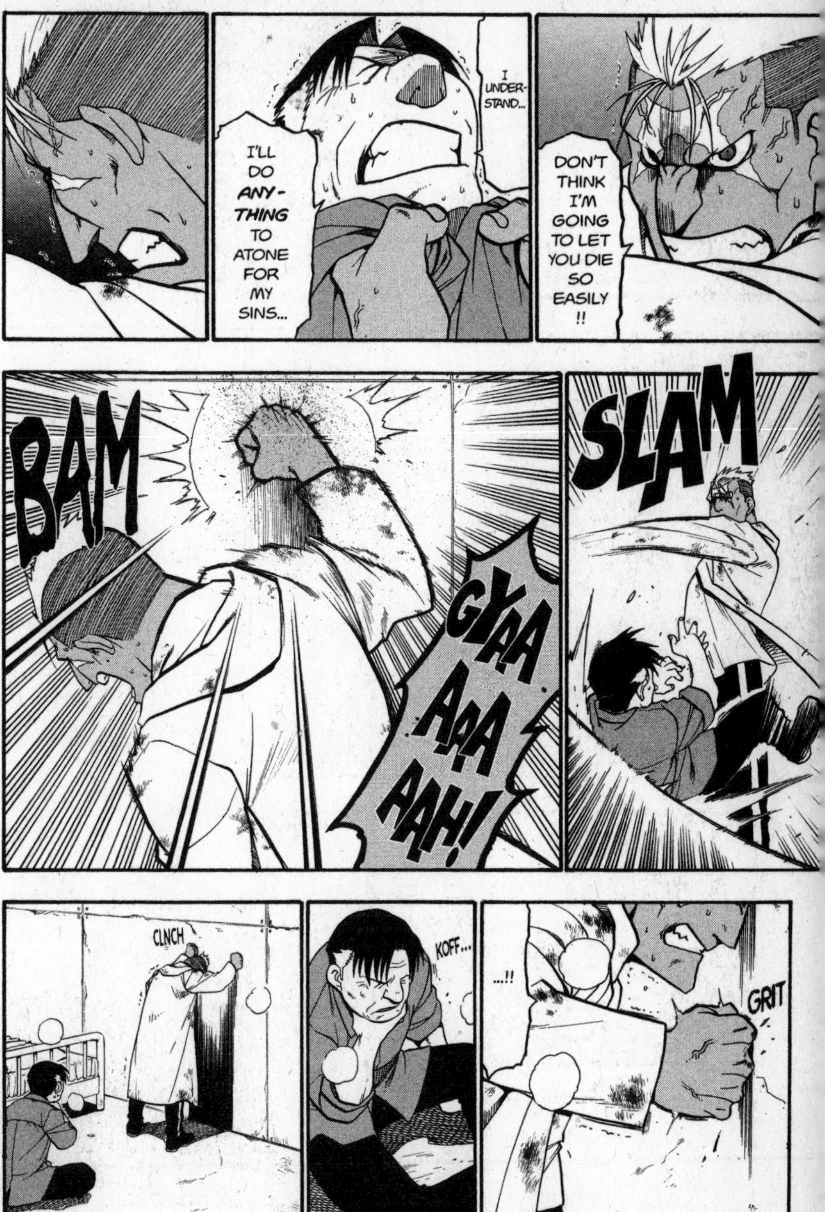
DON'T THINK I'M GOING TO LET YOU DIE SO EASILY !!
I UNDER-STAND...
I'LL DO ANY-THING TO ATONE FOR MY SINS...
SLAM
BAM
GYAAAAAAAH!
GRIT
...!!
KOFF...
CLNCH

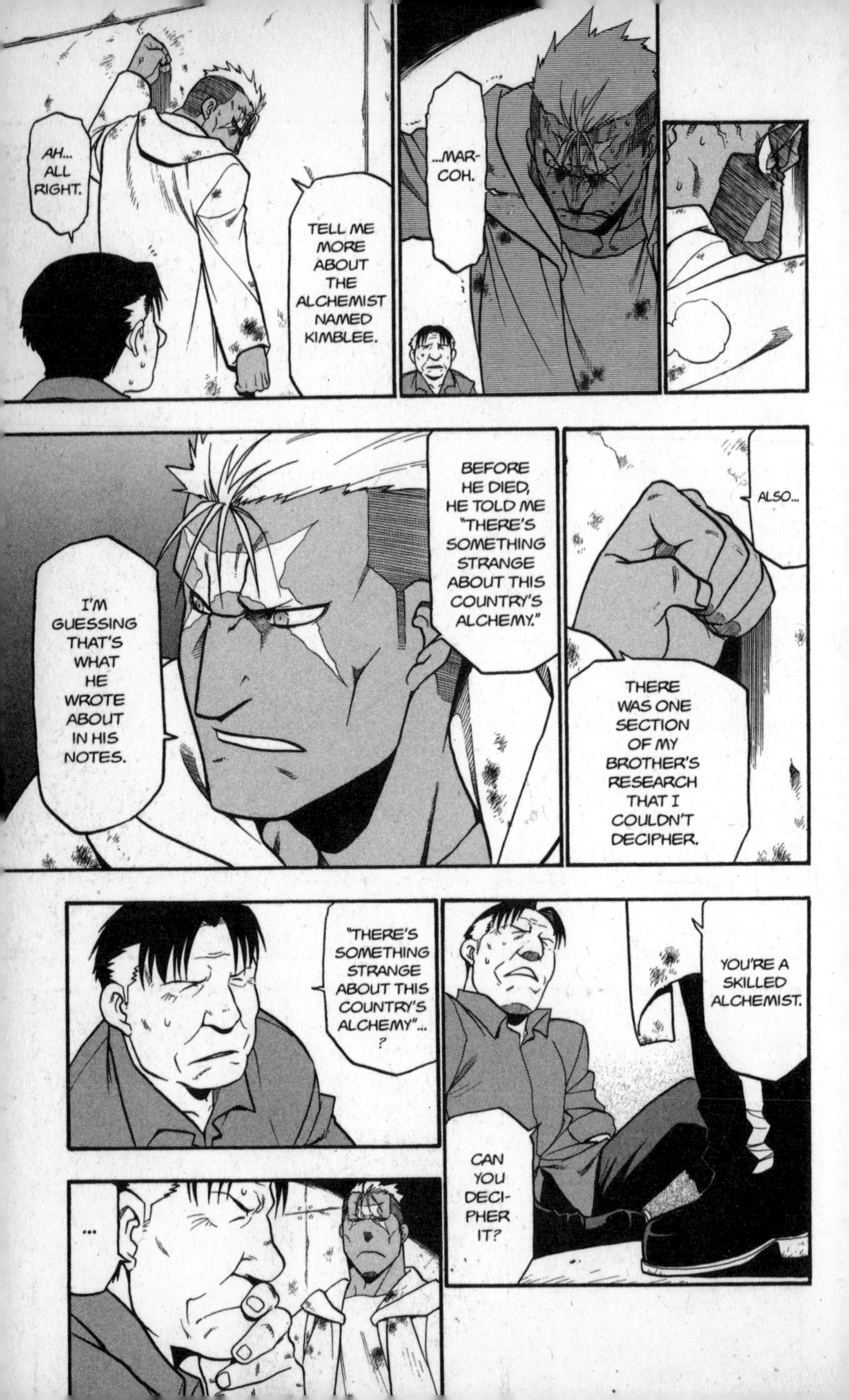
...MAR-COH.
TELL ME MORE ABOUT THE ALCHEMIST NAMED KIMBLEE.
AH... ALL RIGHT.
ALSO...
THERE WAS ONE SECTION OF MY BROTHER'S RESEARCH THAT I COULDN'T DECIPHER.
BEFORE HE DIED, HE TOLD ME "THERE'S SOMETHING STRANGE ABOUT THIS COUNTRY'S ALCHEMY."
I'M GUESSING THAT'S WHAT HE WROTE ABOUT IN HIS NOTES.
YOU'RE A SKILLED ALCHEMIST.
CAN YOU DECI-PHER IT?
"THERE'S SOMETHING STRANGE ABOUT THIS COUNTRY'S ALCHEMY"...?
...

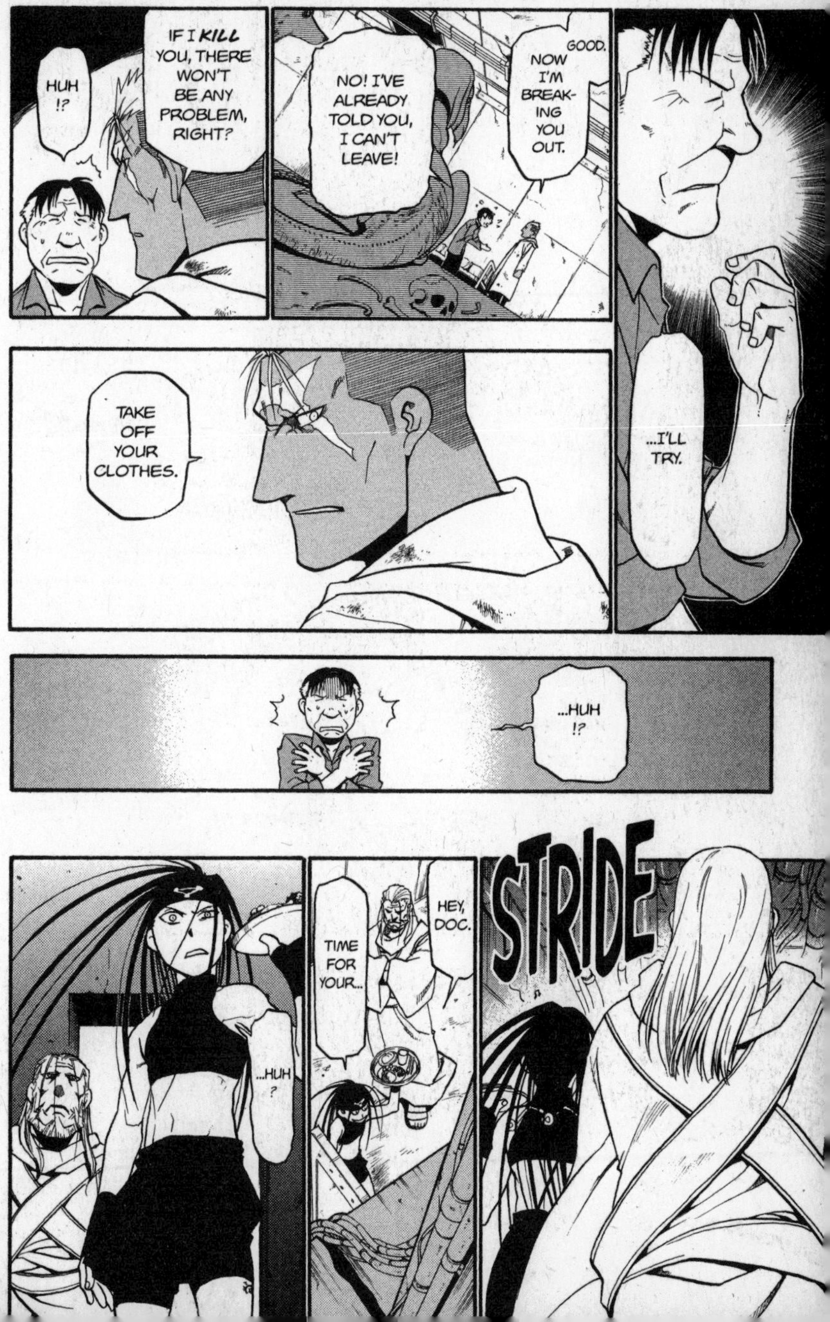
...I'LL TRY.
GOOD. NOW I'M BREAKING YOU OUT.
NO! I'VE ALREADY TOLD YOU, I CAN'T LEAVE!
IF I KILL YOU, THERE WON'T BE ANY PROBLEM, RIGHT?
HUH !?
TAKE OFF YOUR CLOTHES.
...HUH !?
STRIDE
HEY, DOC.
TIME FOR YOUR...
...HUH ?

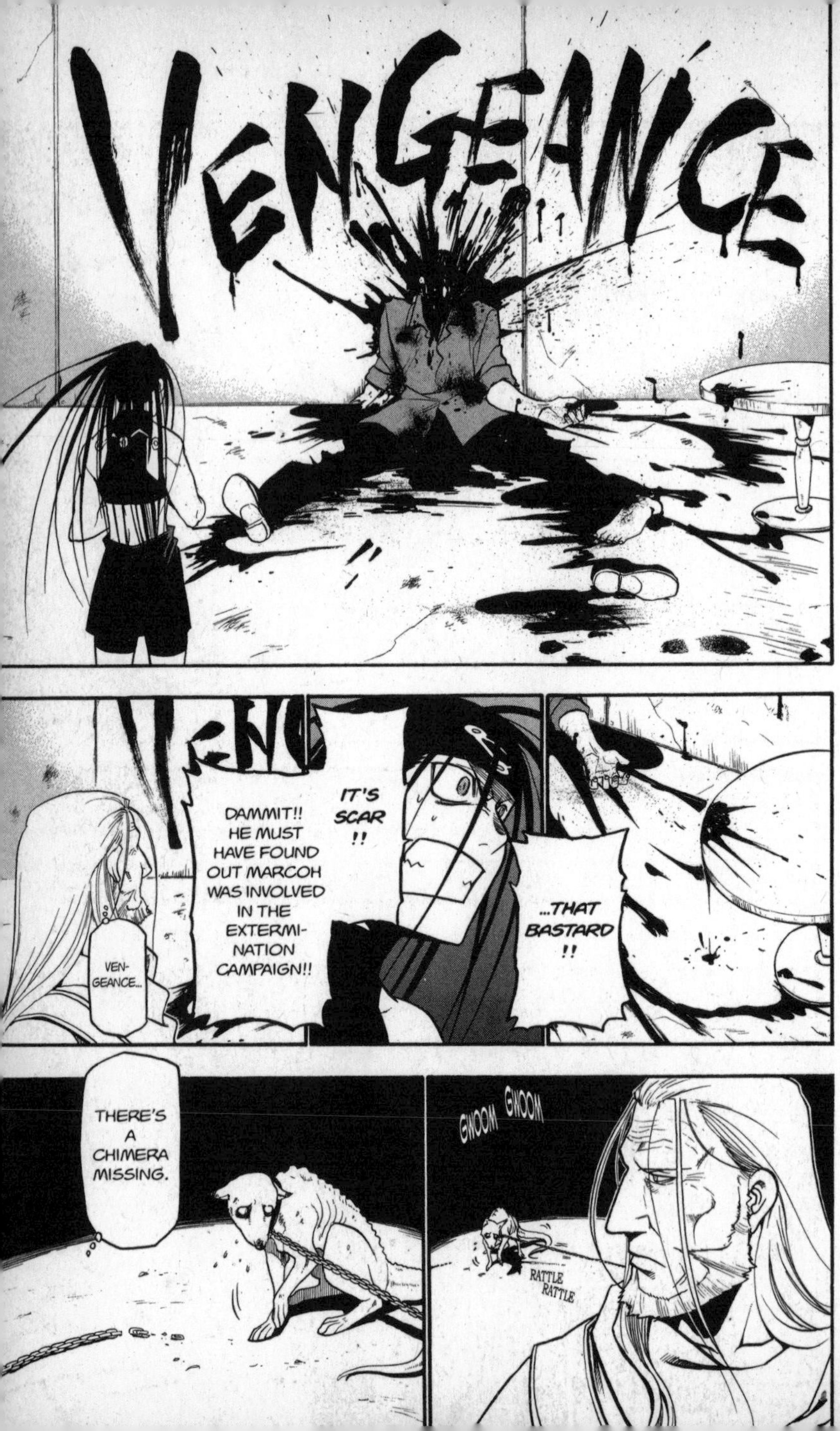
VENGEANCE
...THAT BASTARD!!
IT'S SCAR!!
DAMMIT!! HE MUST HAVE FOUND OUT MARCOH WAS INVOLVED IN THE EXTERMINATION CAMPAIGN!!
VEN-GEANCE...
GWOOM GWOOM
RATTLE RATTLE
THERE'S A CHIMERA MISSING.

HMM...

MARCOH IS AN ALCHEMIST WHO SPECIALIZES IN RESEARCH ON LIVING CREATURES...

EWW... IT'S ALL SQUISHY.

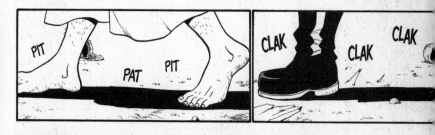

PIT

PAT PIT

CLAK CLAK CLAK

DO YOU THINK THEY'LL FIGURE IT OUT AND COME AFTER US?

HURRY UP IF YOU DON'T WANT THEM TO CATCH YOU.

CLAK

CLAK

CLAK

PIT

PAT

PIT

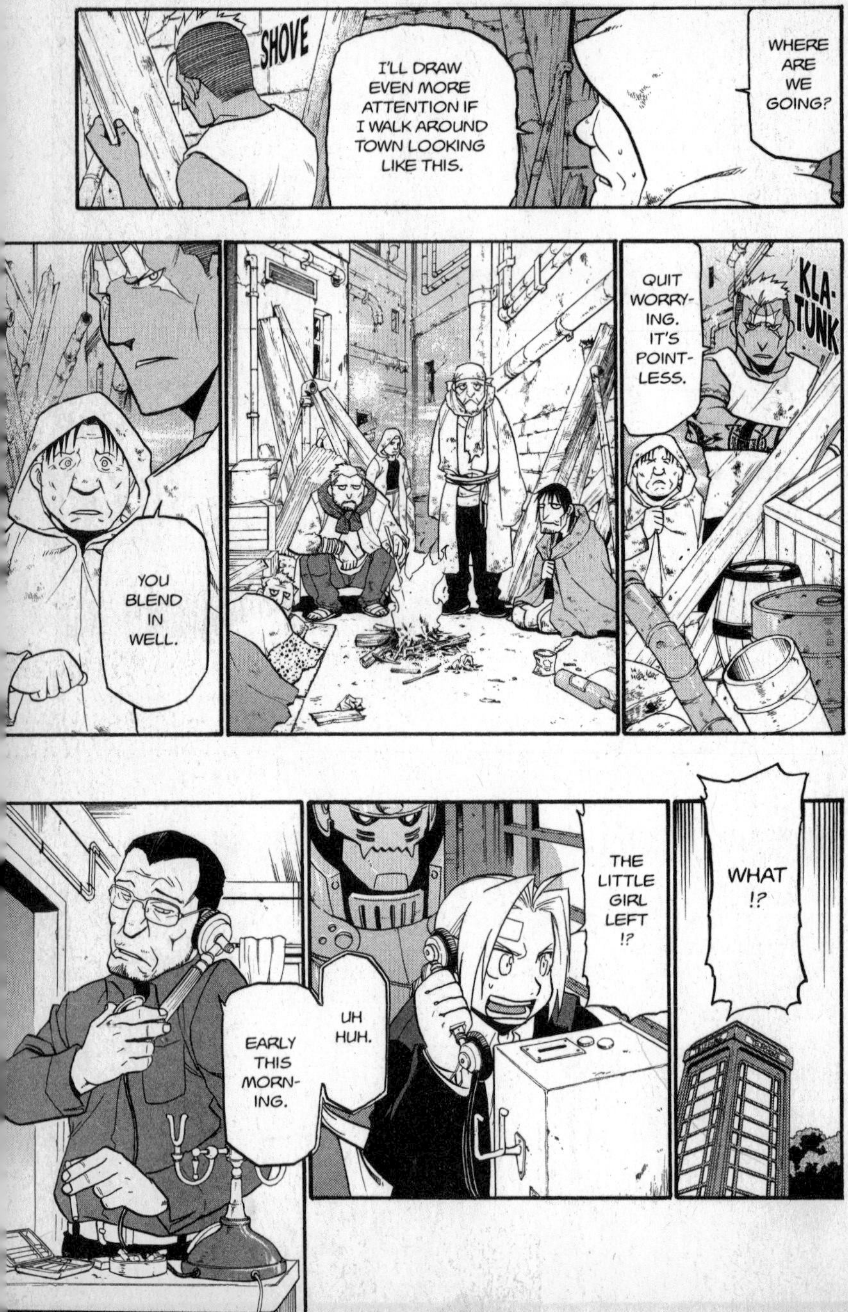
WHERE ARE WE GOING?
I'LL DRAW EVEN MORE ATTENTION IF I WALK AROUND TOWN LOOKING LIKE THIS.
SHOVE
KLA-TUNK
QUIT WORRYING. IT'S POINTLESS.
YOU BLEND IN WELL.
WHAT!?
THE LITTLE GIRL LEFT!?
UH HUH.
EARLY THIS MORNING.

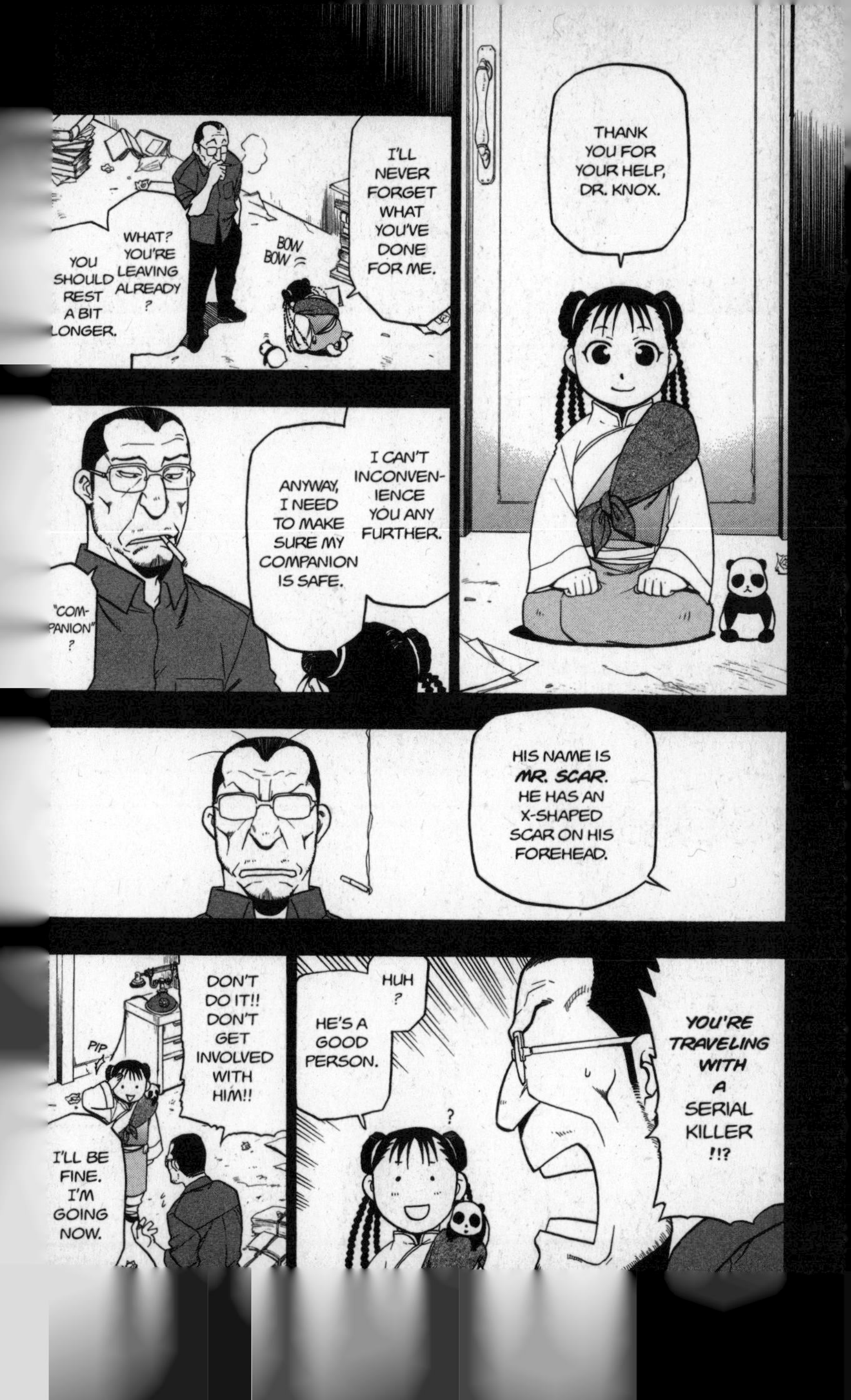
THANK YOU FOR YOUR HELP, DR. KNOX.
I'LL NEVER FORGET WHAT YOU'VE DONE FOR ME.
BOW BOW
WHAT? YOU'RE LEAVING ALREADY?
YOU SHOULD REST A BIT LONGER.
I CAN'T INCONVENIENCE YOU ANY FURTHER.
ANYWAY, I NEED TO MAKE SURE MY COMPANION IS SAFE.
"COMPANION"?
HIS NAME IS **MR. SCAR**. HE HAS AN X-SHAPED SCAR ON HIS FOREHEAD.
YOU'RE TRAVELING WITH A SERIAL KILLER!!?
HUH?
?
HE'S A GOOD PERSON.
DON'T DO IT!! DON'T GET INVOLVED WITH HIM!!
PIP
I'LL BE FINE. I'M GOING NOW.

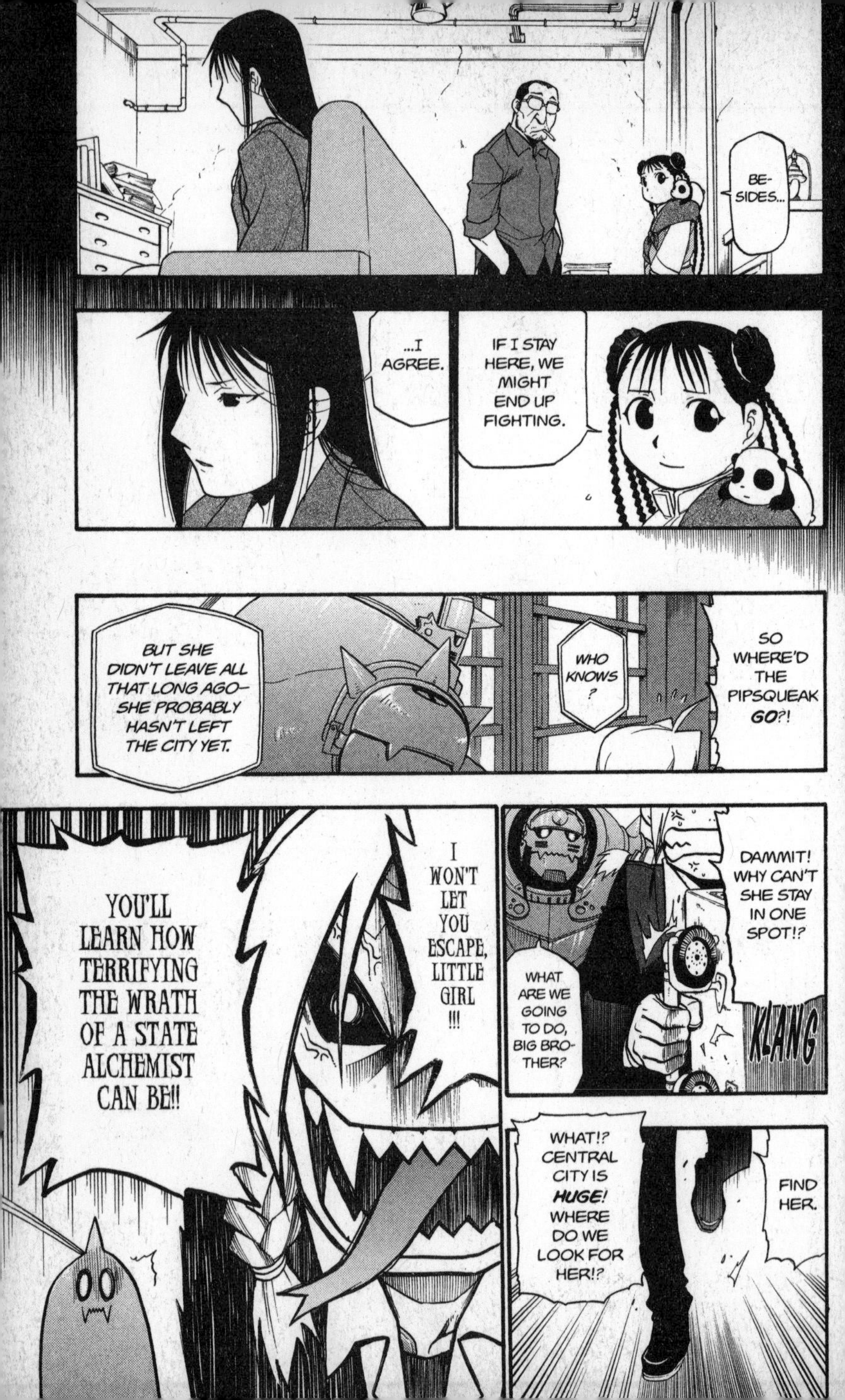
BESIDES...
IF I STAY HERE, WE MIGHT END UP FIGHTING.
...I AGREE.
SO WHERE'D THE PIPSQUEAK GO?!
WHO KNOWS?
BUT SHE DIDN'T LEAVE ALL THAT LONG AGO—SHE PROBABLY HASN'T LEFT THE CITY YET.
DAMMIT! WHY CAN'T SHE STAY IN ONE SPOT!?
KLANG
WHAT ARE WE GOING TO DO, BIG BROTHER?
FIND HER.
WHAT!? CENTRAL CITY IS HUGE! WHERE DO WE LOOK FOR HER!?
I WON'T LET YOU ESCAPE, LITTLE GIRL!!!
YOU'LL LEARN HOW TERRIFYING THE WRATH OF A STATE ALCHEMIST CAN BE!!

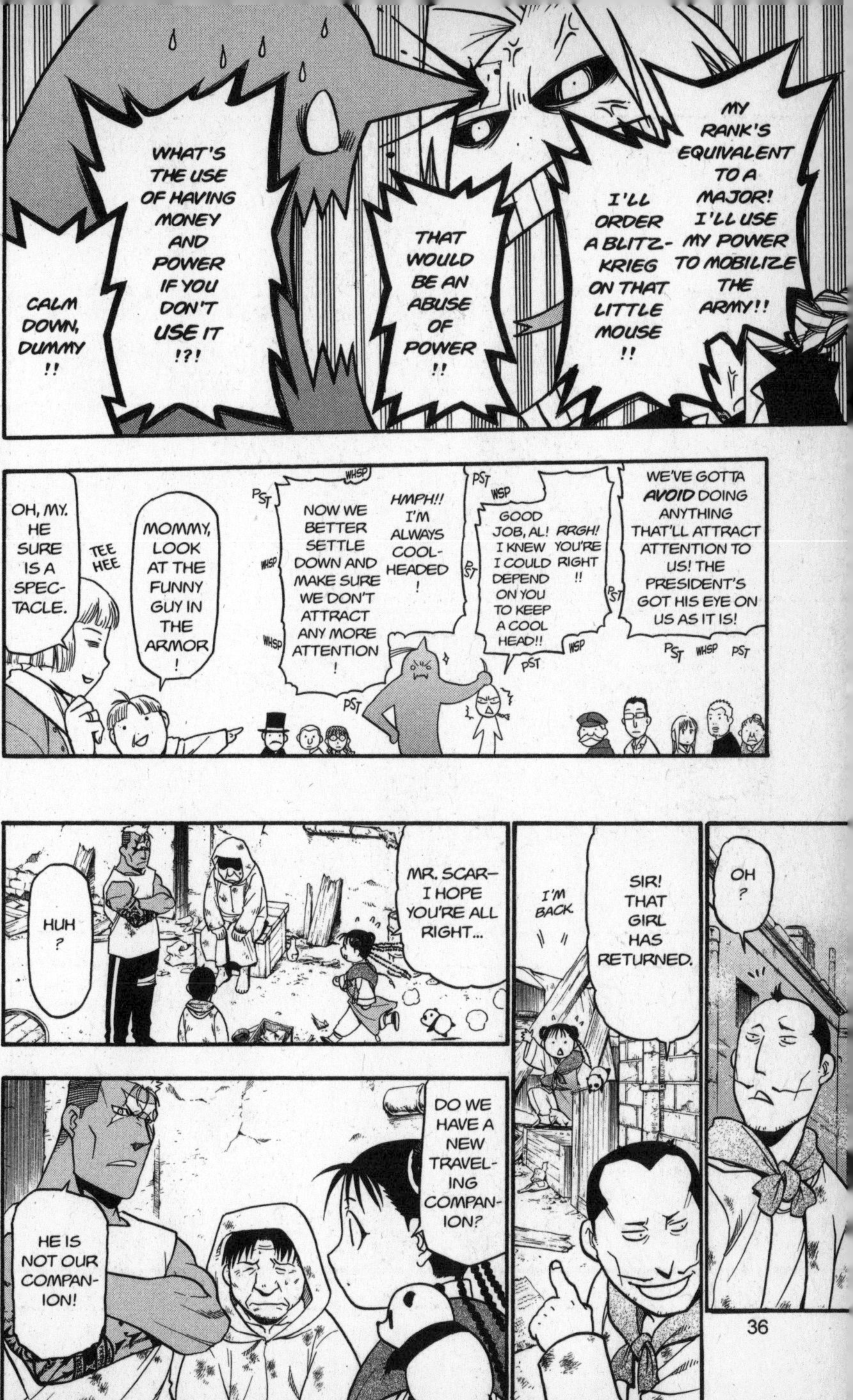
MY RANK'S EQUIVALENT TO A MAJOR! I'LL USE MY POWER TO MOBILIZE THE ARMY!!
I'LL ORDER A BLITZKRIEG ON THAT LITTLE MOUSE!!
THAT WOULD BE AN ABUSE OF POWER!!
WHAT'S THE USE OF HAVING MONEY AND POWER IF YOU DON'T USE IT!?!
CALM DOWN, DUMMY!!
WE'VE GOTTA AVOID DOING ANYTHING THAT'LL ATTRACT ATTENTION TO US! THE PRESIDENT'S GOT HIS EYE ON US AS IT IS!
PST WHSP PST
RRGH! YOU'RE RIGHT!!
GOOD JOB, AL! I KNEW I COULD DEPEND ON YOU TO KEEP A COOL HEAD!!
HMPH!! I'M ALWAYS COOL-HEADED!
NOW WE BETTER SETTLE DOWN AND MAKE SURE WE DON'T ATTRACT ANY MORE ATTENTION!
MOMMY, LOOK AT THE FUNNY GUY IN THE ARMOR!
TEE HEE
OH, MY. HE SURE IS A SPECTACLE.
OH?
SIR! THAT GIRL HAS RETURNED.
I'M BACK.
MR. SCAR–I HOPE YOU'RE ALL RIGHT...
HUH?
DO WE HAVE A NEW TRAVELING COMPANION?
HE IS NOT OUR COMPANION!

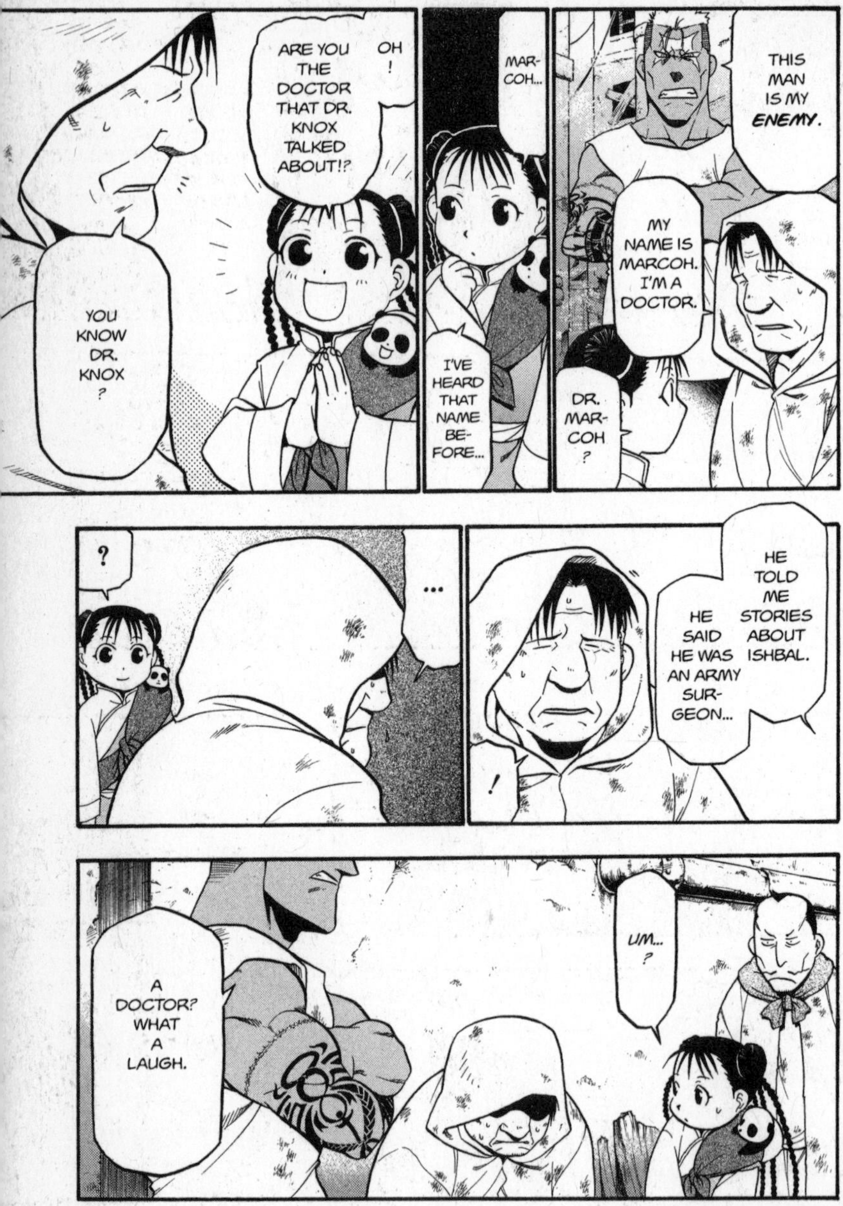
THIS MAN IS MY *ENEMY*.
MY NAME IS MARCOH. I'M A DOCTOR.
DR. MAR-COH?
MAR-COH...
I'VE HEARD THAT NAME BE-FORE...
OH!
ARE YOU THE DOCTOR THAT DR. KNOX TALKED ABOUT!?
YOU KNOW DR. KNOX?
HE TOLD ME STORIES ABOUT ISHBAL.
HE SAID HE WAS AN ARMY SUR-GEON...
!
...
?
UM...?
A DOCTOR? WHAT A LAUGH.

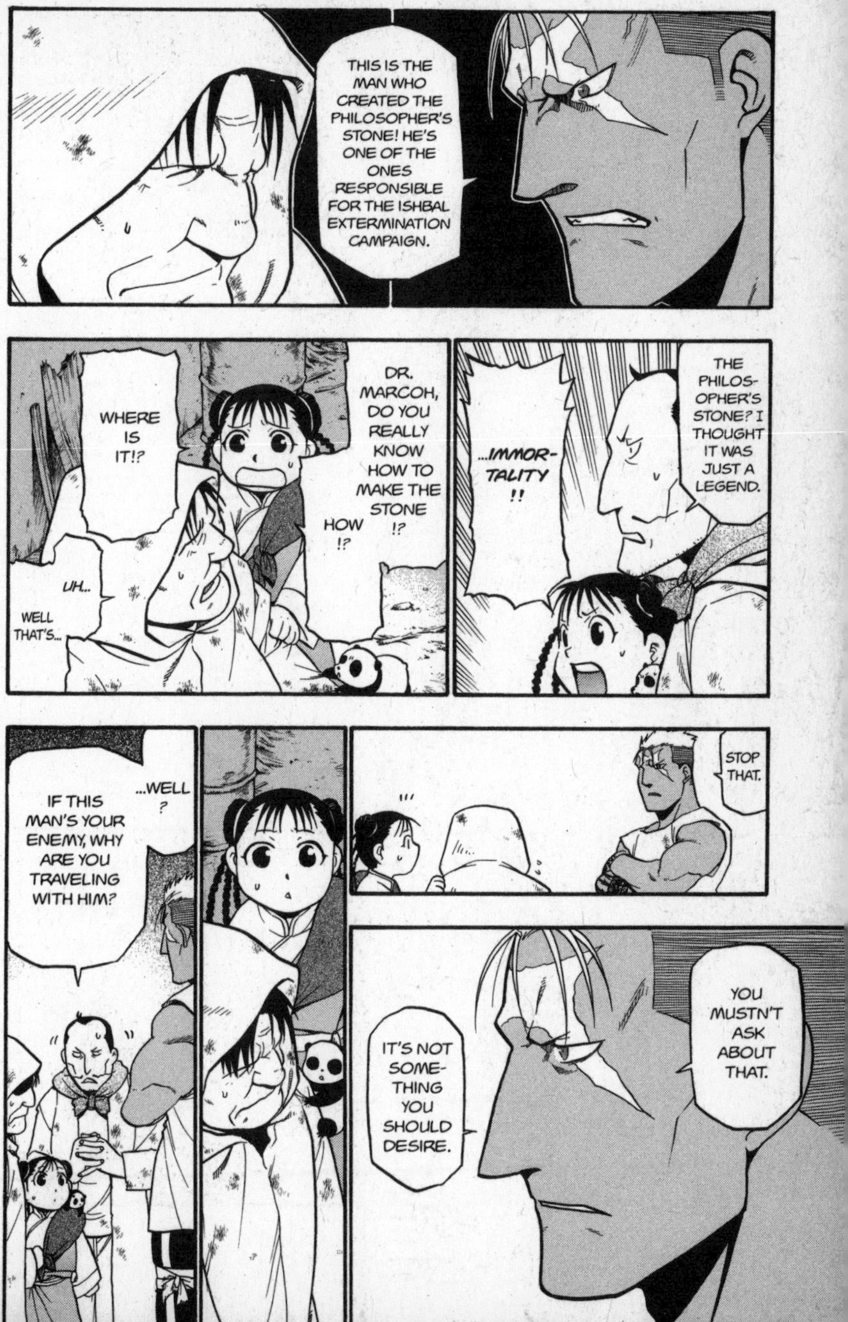
THIS IS THE MAN WHO CREATED THE PHILOSOPHER'S STONE! HE'S ONE OF THE ONES RESPONSIBLE FOR THE ISHBAL EXTERMINATION CAMPAIGN.
THE PHILOSOPHER'S STONE? I THOUGHT IT WAS JUST A LEGEND.
...IMMORTALITY!!
DR. MARCOH, DO YOU REALLY KNOW HOW TO MAKE THE STONE!?
HOW!?
WHERE IS IT!?
UH...
WELL THAT'S...
STOP THAT.
YOU MUSTN'T ASK ABOUT THAT.
IT'S NOT SOMETHING YOU SHOULD DESIRE.
...WELL?
IF THIS MAN'S YOUR ENEMY, WHY ARE YOU TRAVELING WITH HIM?

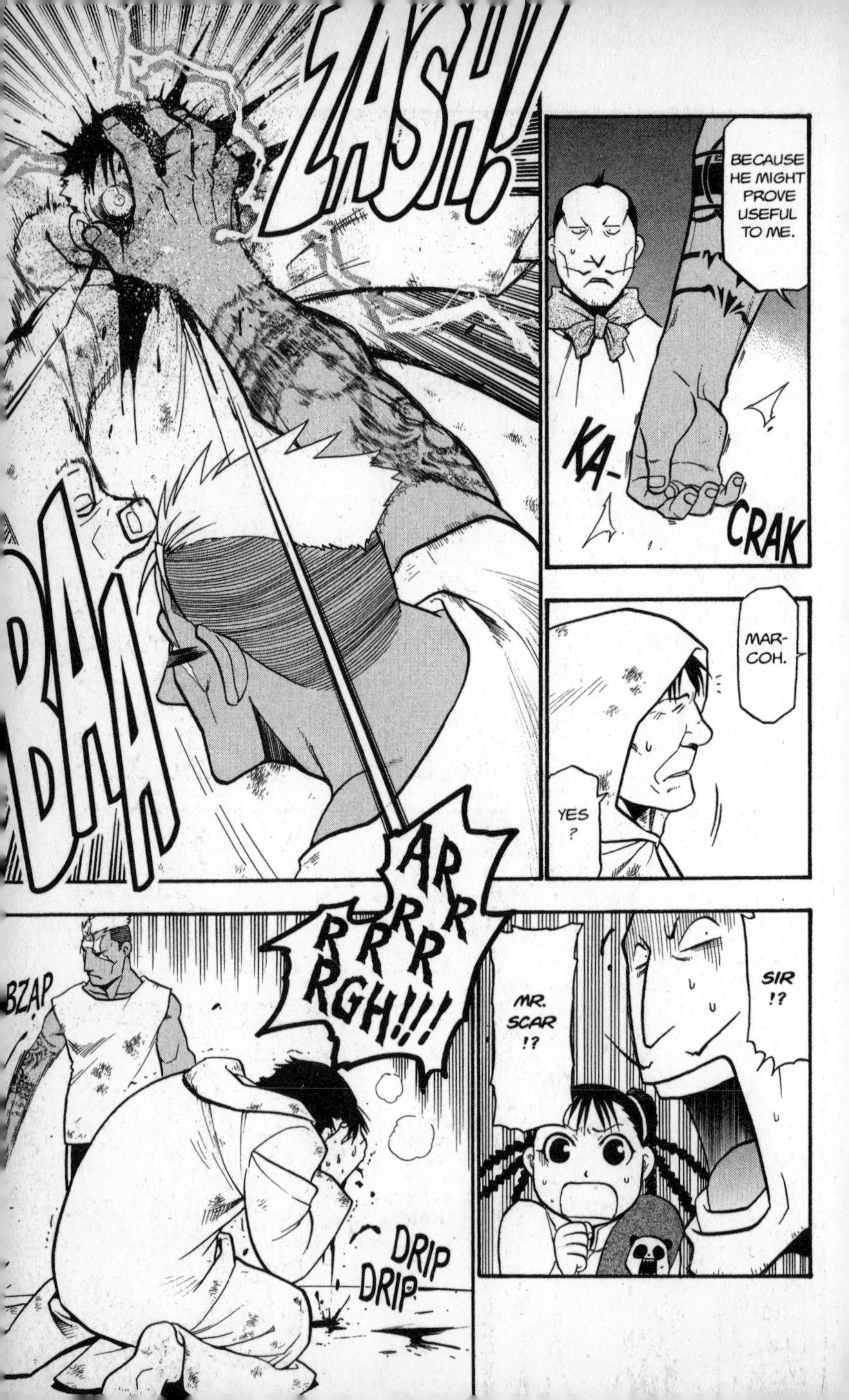
BECAUSE HE MIGHT PROVE USEFUL TO ME.
KA-
CRAK
MAR-COH.
YES?
ZASH!
BAM
ARRRRRRRGH!!!
SIR!?
MR. SCAR!?
BZAP
DRIP
DRIP

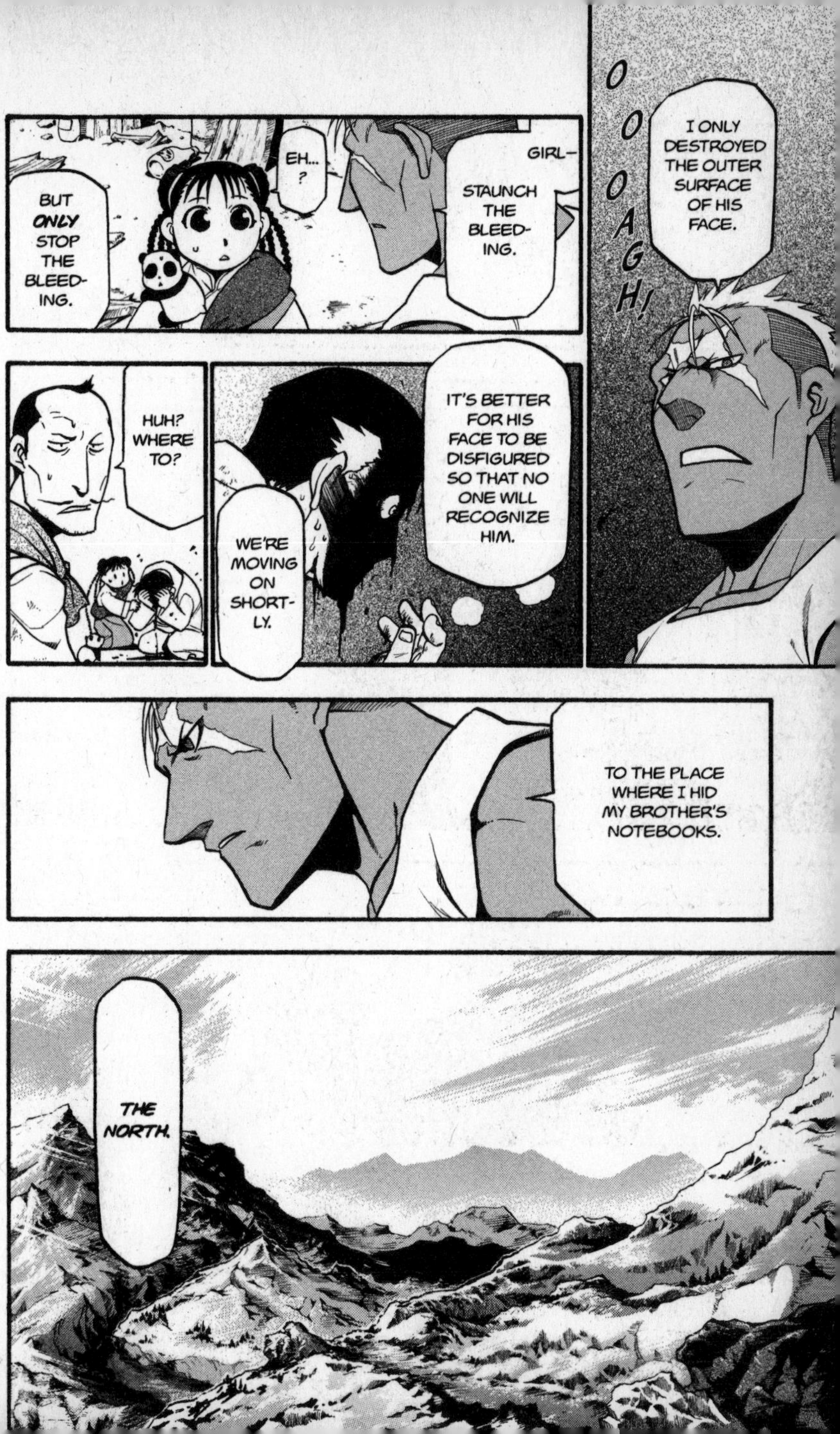
I ONLY DESTROYED THE OUTER SURFACE OF HIS FACE.
OOOAGH!
GIRL—
STAUNCH THE BLEED-ING.
EH...?
BUT ONLY STOP THE BLEED-ING.
IT'S BETTER FOR HIS FACE TO BE DISFIGURED SO THAT NO ONE WILL RECOGNIZE HIM.
WE'RE MOVING ON SHORT-LY.
HUH? WHERE TO?
TO THE PLACE WHERE I HID MY BROTHER'S NOTEBOOKS.
THE NORTH.

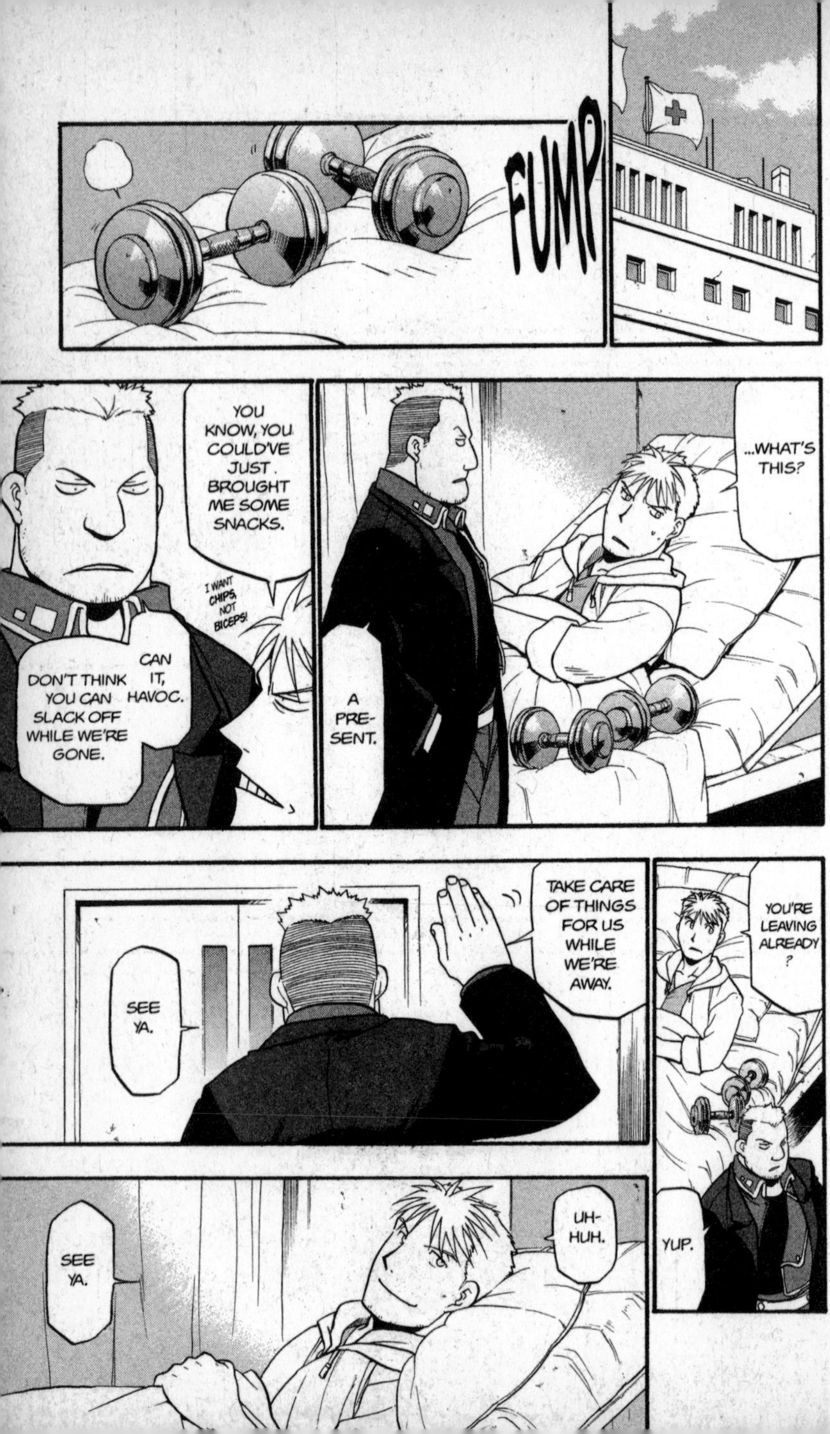
FUMP
...WHAT'S THIS?
A PRESENT.
YOU KNOW, YOU COULD'VE JUST BROUGHT ME SOME SNACKS.
I WANT CHIPS, NOT BICEPS!
CAN IT, HAVOC.
DON'T THINK YOU CAN SLACK OFF WHILE WE'RE GONE.
YOU'RE LEAVING ALREADY?
YUP.
TAKE CARE OF THINGS FOR US WHILE WE'RE AWAY.
SEE YA.
UH-HUH.
SEE YA.

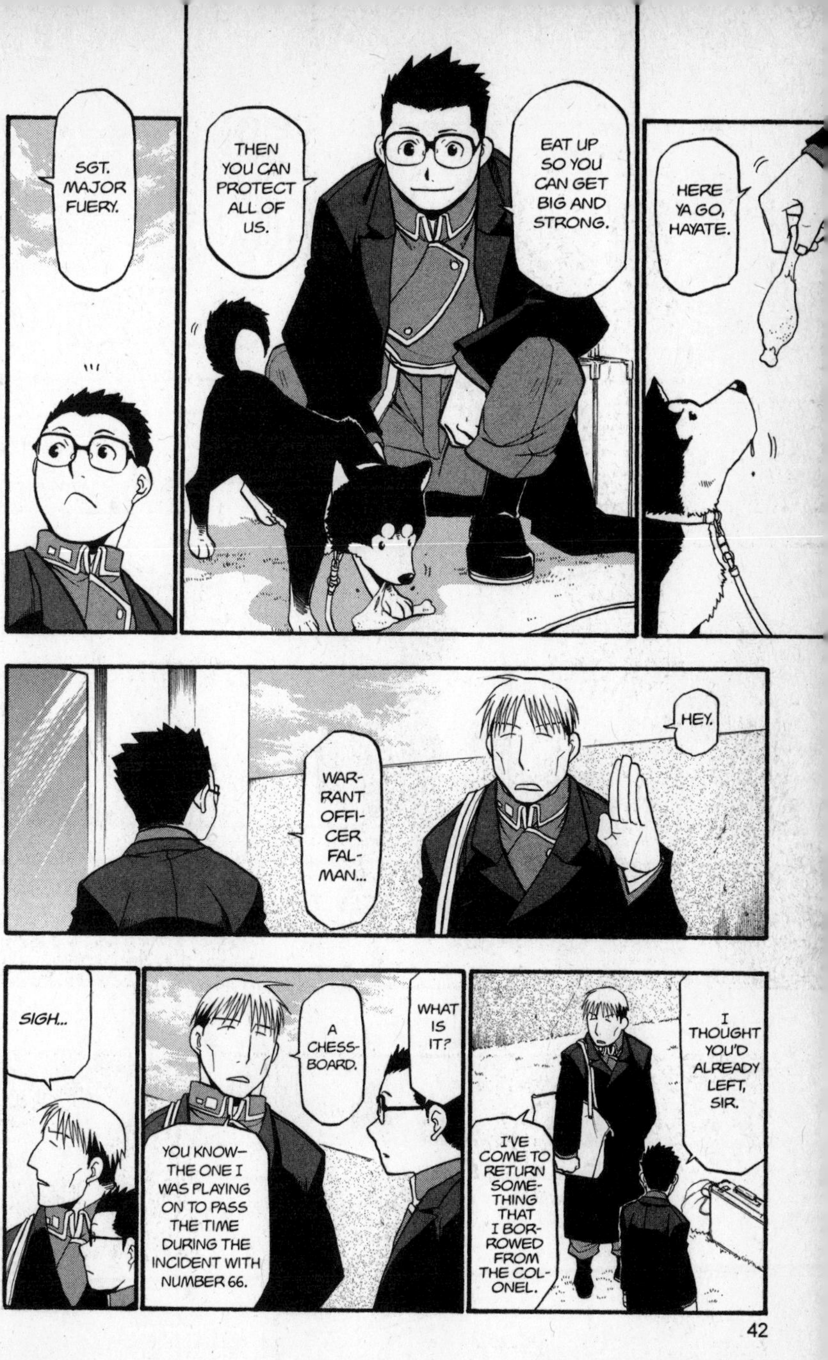
HERE YA GO, HAYATE.
EAT UP SO YOU CAN GET BIG AND STRONG.
THEN YOU CAN PROTECT ALL OF US.
SGT. MAJOR FUERY.
HEY.
WARRANT OFFICER FALMAN...
I THOUGHT YOU'D ALREADY LEFT, SIR.
I'VE COME TO RETURN SOMETHING THAT I BORROWED FROM THE COLONEL.
WHAT IS IT?
A CHESSBOARD.
YOU KNOW— THE ONE I WAS PLAYING ON TO PASS THE TIME DURING THE INCIDENT WITH NUMBER 66.
SIGH...

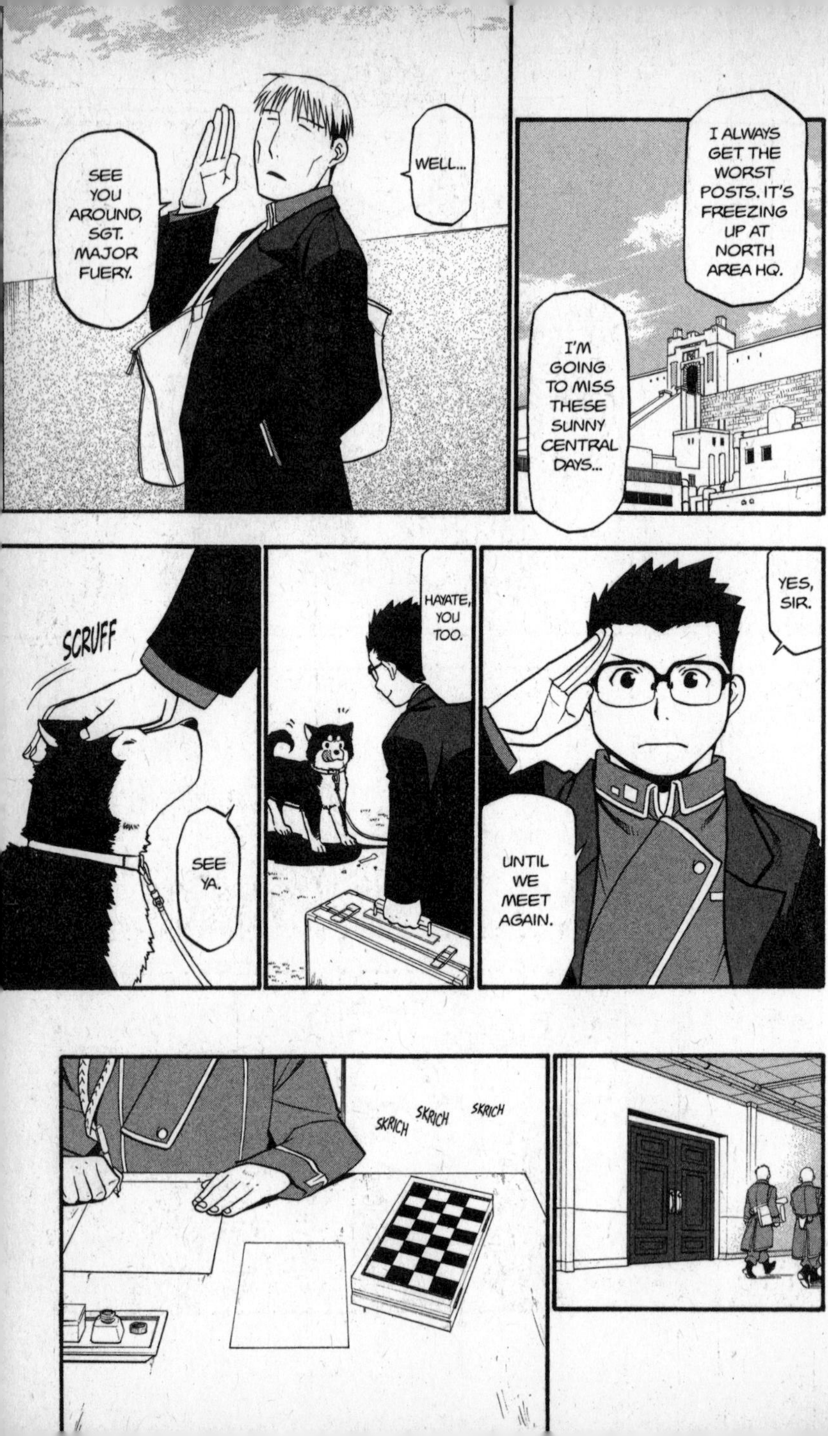
I ALWAYS GET THE WORST POSTS. IT'S FREEZING UP AT NORTH AREA HQ.
I'M GOING TO MISS THESE SUNNY CENTRAL DAYS...
WELL...
SEE YOU AROUND, SGT. MAJOR FUERY.
YES, SIR.
UNTIL WE MEET AGAIN.
HAYATE, YOU TOO.
SCRUFF
SEE YA.
SKRICH
SKRICH
SKRICH

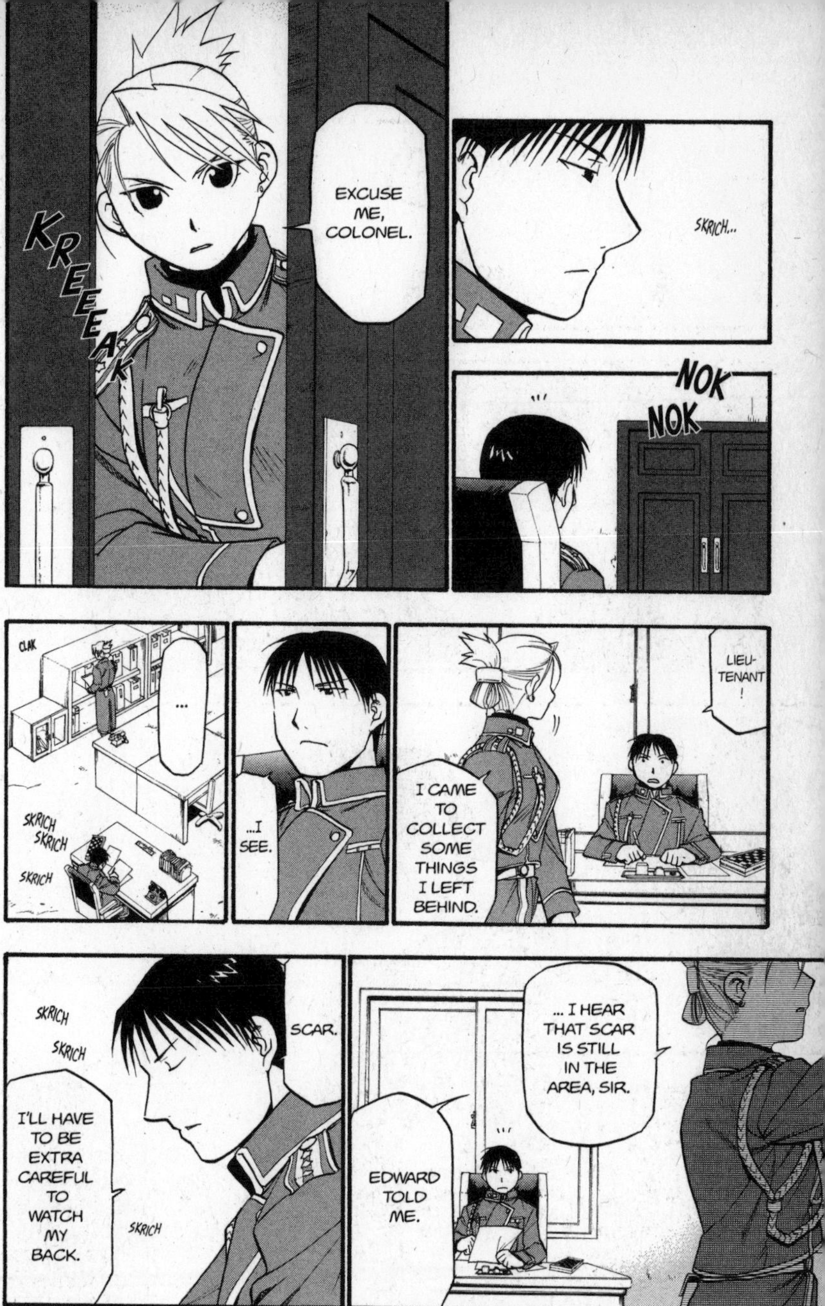
SKRICH...
NOK NOK
KREEEAK
EXCUSE ME, COLONEL.
LIEU-TENANT!
I CAME TO COLLECT SOME THINGS I LEFT BEHIND.
...I SEE.
CLAK
...
SKRICH SKRICH
SKRICH
... I HEAR THAT SCAR IS STILL IN THE AREA, SIR.
EDWARD TOLD ME.
SCAR.
SKRICH
SKRICH
I'LL HAVE TO BE EXTRA CAREFUL TO WATCH MY BACK.
SKRICH

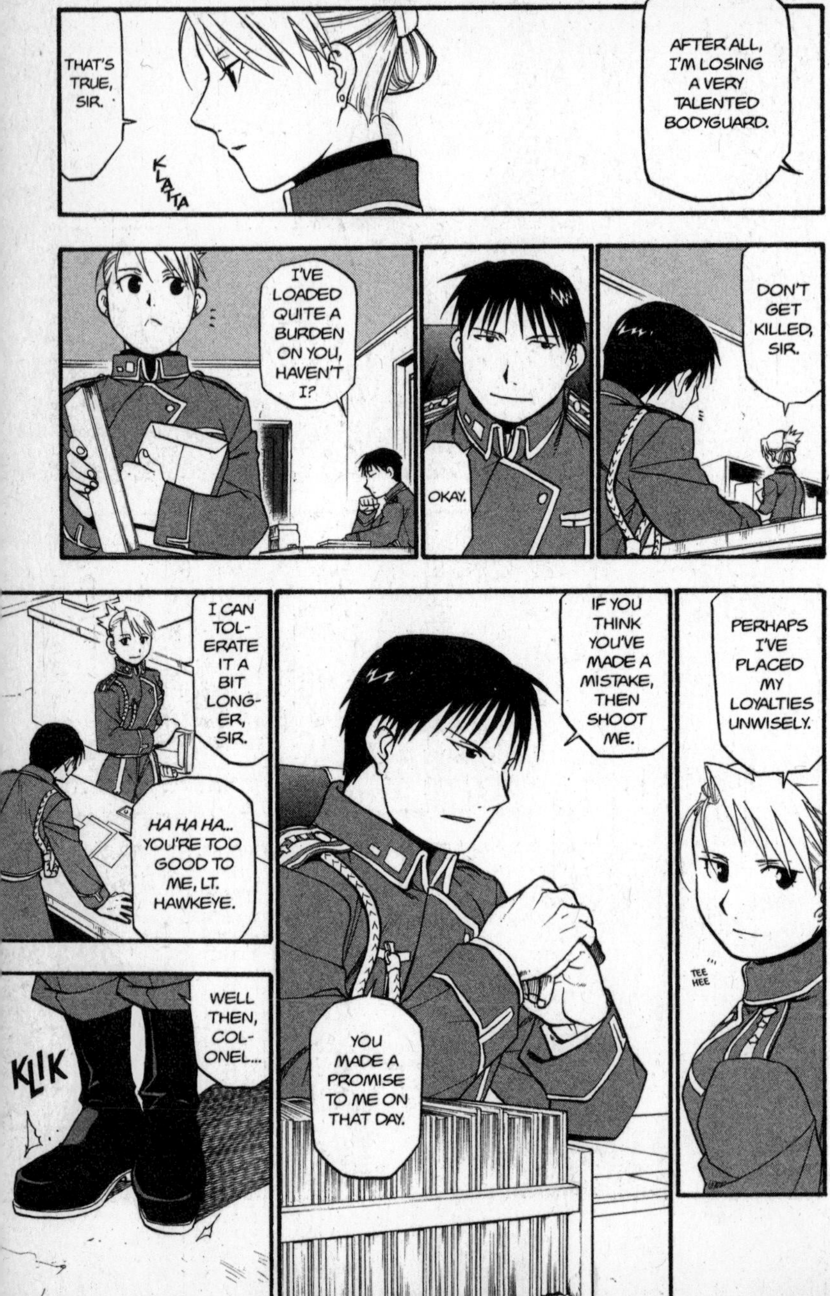
AFTER ALL, I'M LOSING A VERY TALENTED BODYGUARD.
THAT'S TRUE, SIR.
KLAKKA
DON'T GET KILLED, SIR.
OKAY.
I'VE LOADED QUITE A BURDEN ON YOU, HAVEN'T I?
PERHAPS I'VE PLACED MY LOYALTIES UNWISELY.
TEE HEE
IF YOU THINK YOU'VE MADE A MISTAKE, THEN SHOOT ME.
YOU MADE A PROMISE TO ME ON THAT DAY.
I CAN TOL-ERATE IT A BIT LONG-ER, SIR.
HA HA HA... YOU'RE TOO GOOD TO ME, LT. HAWKEYE.
WELL THEN, COL-ONEL...
KLIK

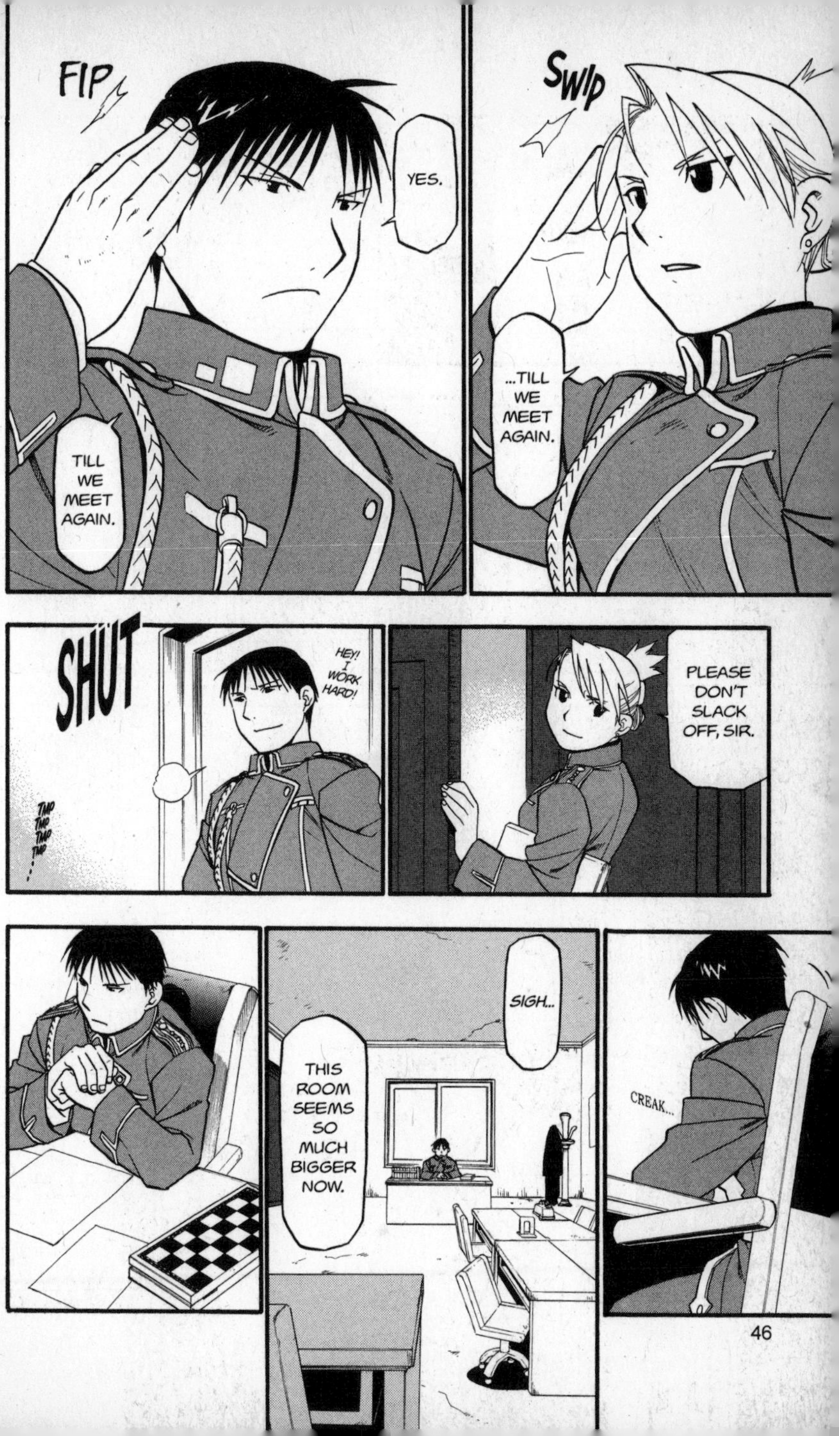
SWIP
...TILL WE MEET AGAIN.
YES.
FIP
TILL WE MEET AGAIN.
PLEASE DON'T SLACK OFF, SIR.
HEY! I WORK HARD!
SHUT
TMP TMP TMP TMP
CREAK...
SIGH...
THIS ROOM SEEMS SO MUCH BIGGER NOW.

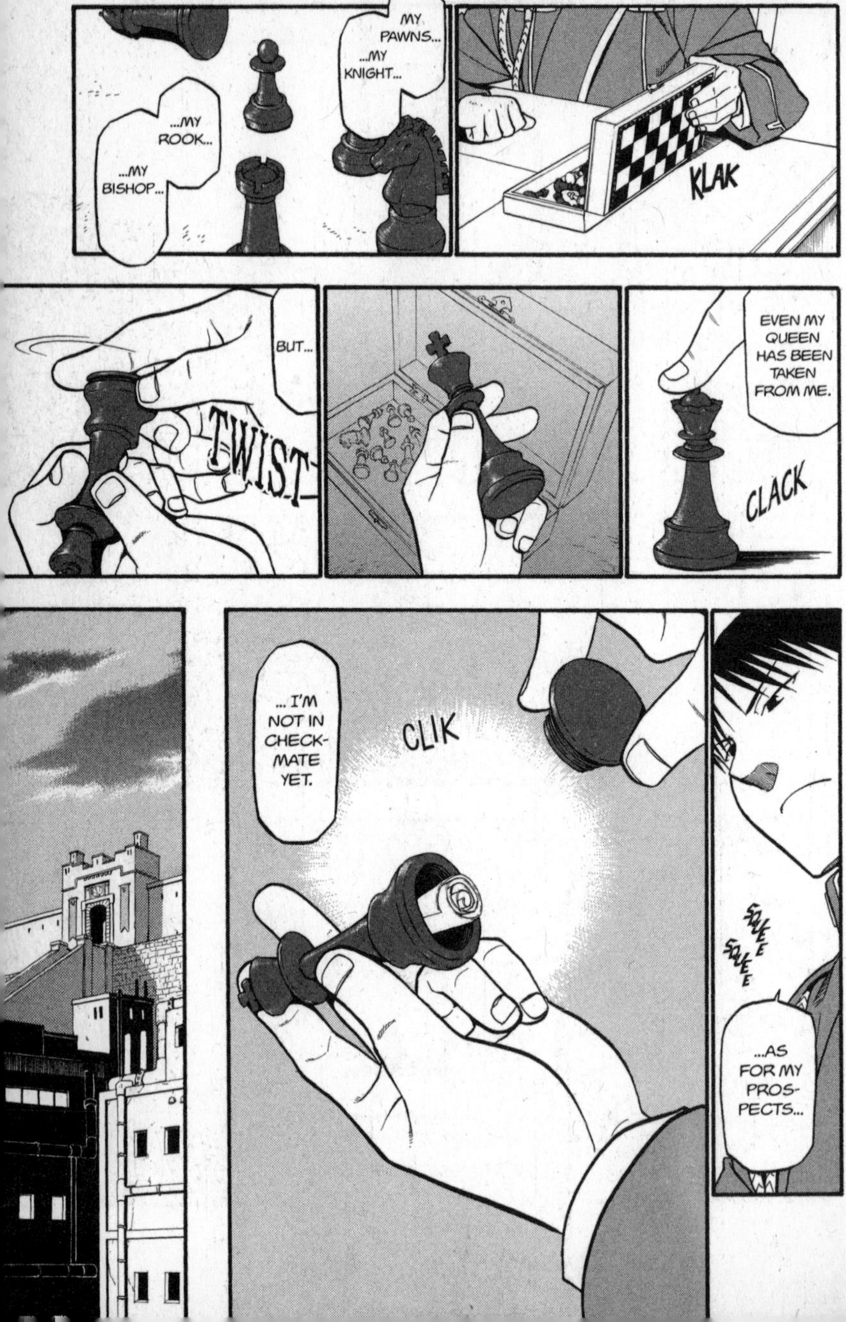
KLAK
MY PAWNS... ...MY KNIGHT...
...MY ROOK...
...MY BISHOP...
EVEN MY QUEEN HAS BEEN TAKEN FROM ME.
CLACK
BUT...
TWIST
SQUEE
SQUEE
...AS FOR MY PROSPECTS...
CLIK
... I'M NOT IN CHECKMATE YET.

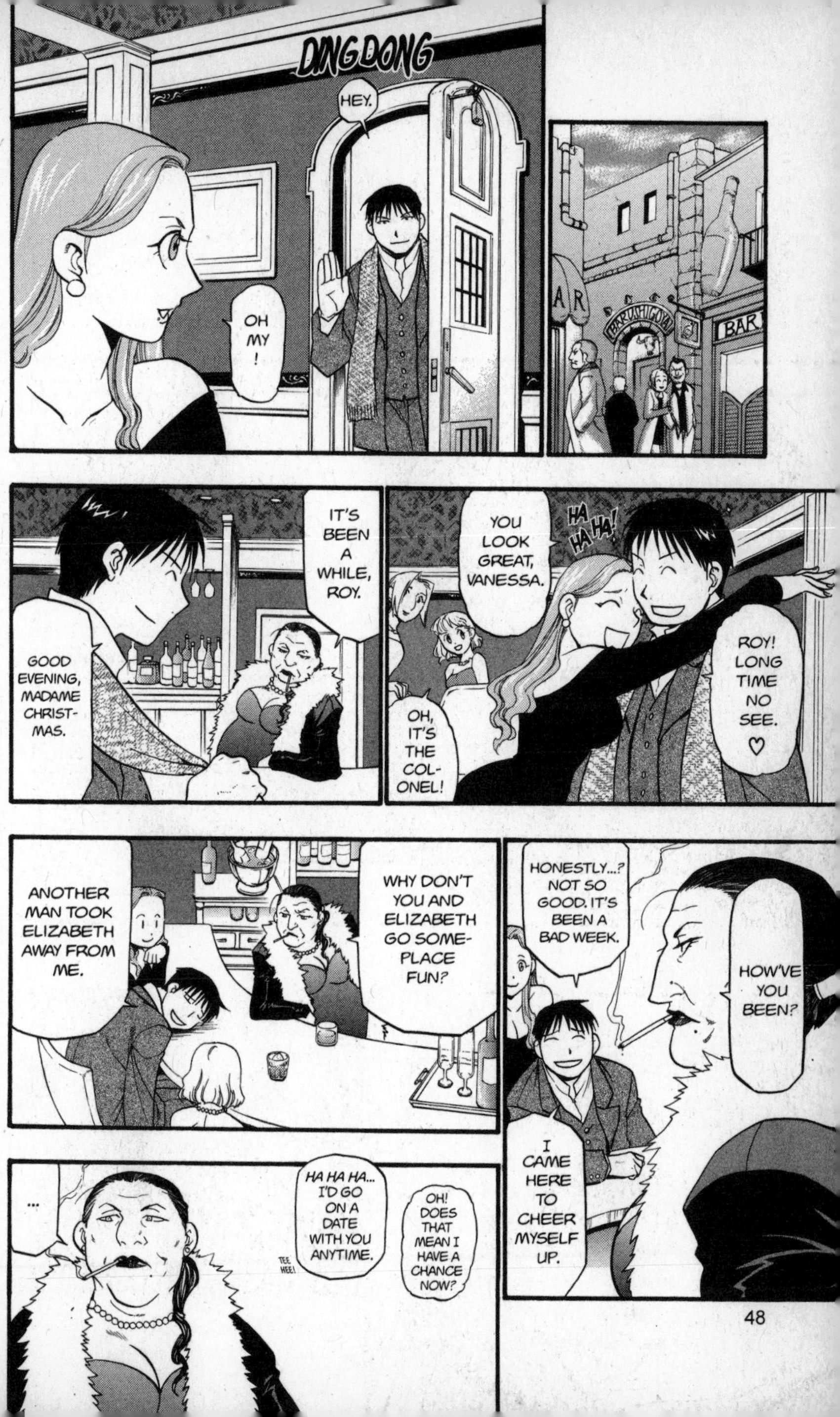
BAR
BAR
DING DONG
HEY.
OH MY !
ROY! LONG TIME NO SEE. ♡
HA HA HA!
YOU LOOK GREAT, VANESSA.
OH, IT'S THE COLONEL!
IT'S BEEN A WHILE, ROY.
GOOD EVENING, MADAME CHRISTMAS.
HOW'VE YOU BEEN?
HONESTLY...? NOT SO GOOD. IT'S BEEN A BAD WEEK.
I CAME HERE TO CHEER MYSELF UP.
WHY DON'T YOU AND ELIZABETH GO SOMEPLACE FUN?
ANOTHER MAN TOOK ELIZABETH AWAY FROM ME.
OH! DOES THAT MEAN I HAVE A CHANCE NOW?
TEE HEE!
HA HA HA... I'D GO ON A DATE WITH YOU ANYTIME.
...

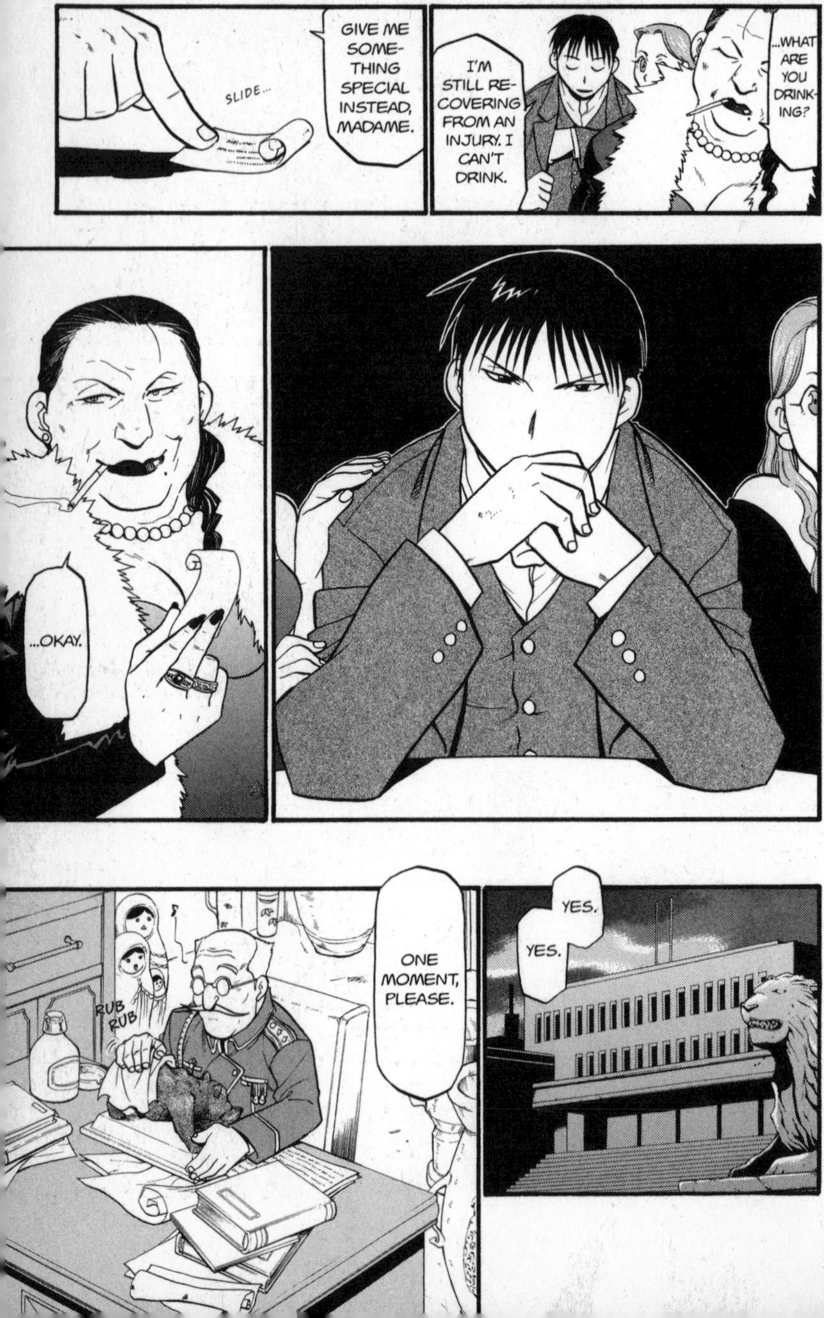
...WHAT ARE YOU DRINKING?
I'M STILL RECOVERING FROM AN INJURY. I CAN'T DRINK.
SLIDE...
GIVE ME SOMETHING SPECIAL INSTEAD, MADAME.
...OKAY.
YES.
YES.
ONE MOMENT, PLEASE.
RUB RUB

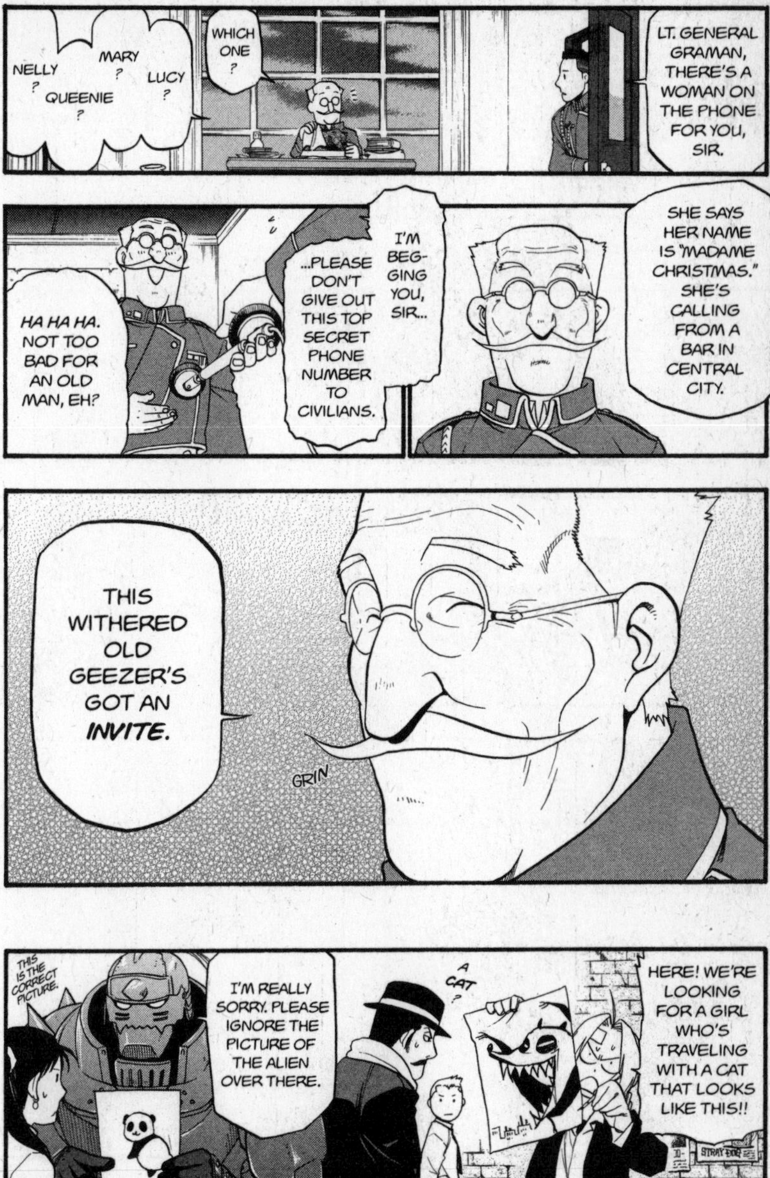
LT. GENERAL GRAMAN, THERE'S A WOMAN ON THE PHONE FOR YOU, SIR.
WHICH ONE?
NELLY? MARY? QUEENIE? LUCY?
SHE SAYS HER NAME IS "MADAME CHRISTMAS." SHE'S CALLING FROM A BAR IN CENTRAL CITY.
I'M BEG-GING YOU, SIR...
...PLEASE DON'T GIVE OUT THIS TOP SECRET PHONE NUMBER TO CIVILIANS.
HA HA HA. NOT TOO BAD FOR AN OLD MAN, EH?
THIS WITHERED OLD GEEZER'S GOT AN INVITE.
GRIN
HERE! WE'RE LOOKING FOR A GIRL WHO'S TRAVELING WITH A CAT THAT LOOKS LIKE THIS!!
STRAY DOG
A CAT?
I'M REALLY SORRY. PLEASE IGNORE THE PICTURE OF THE ALIEN OVER THERE.
THIS IS THE CORRECT PICTURE.

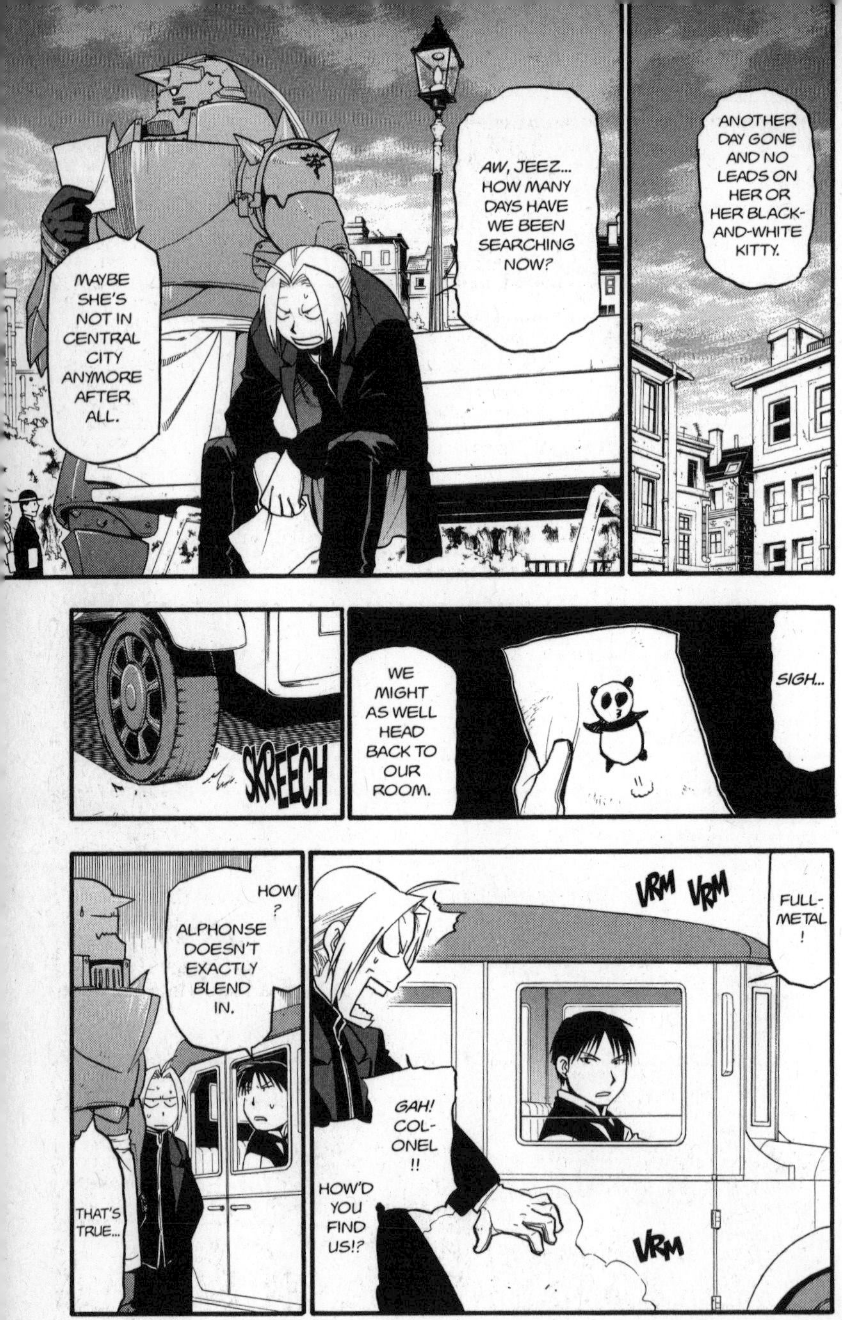
ANOTHER DAY GONE AND NO LEADS ON HER OR HER BLACK-AND-WHITE KITTY.
AW, JEEZ... HOW MANY DAYS HAVE WE BEEN SEARCHING NOW?
MAYBE SHE'S NOT IN CENTRAL CITY ANYMORE AFTER ALL.
SIGH...
WE MIGHT AS WELL HEAD BACK TO OUR ROOM.
SKREECH
FULL-METAL!
VRM VRM
GAH! COL-ONEL!!
HOW'D YOU FIND US!?
VRM
HOW?
ALPHONSE DOESN'T EXACTLY BLEND IN.
THAT'S TRUE...

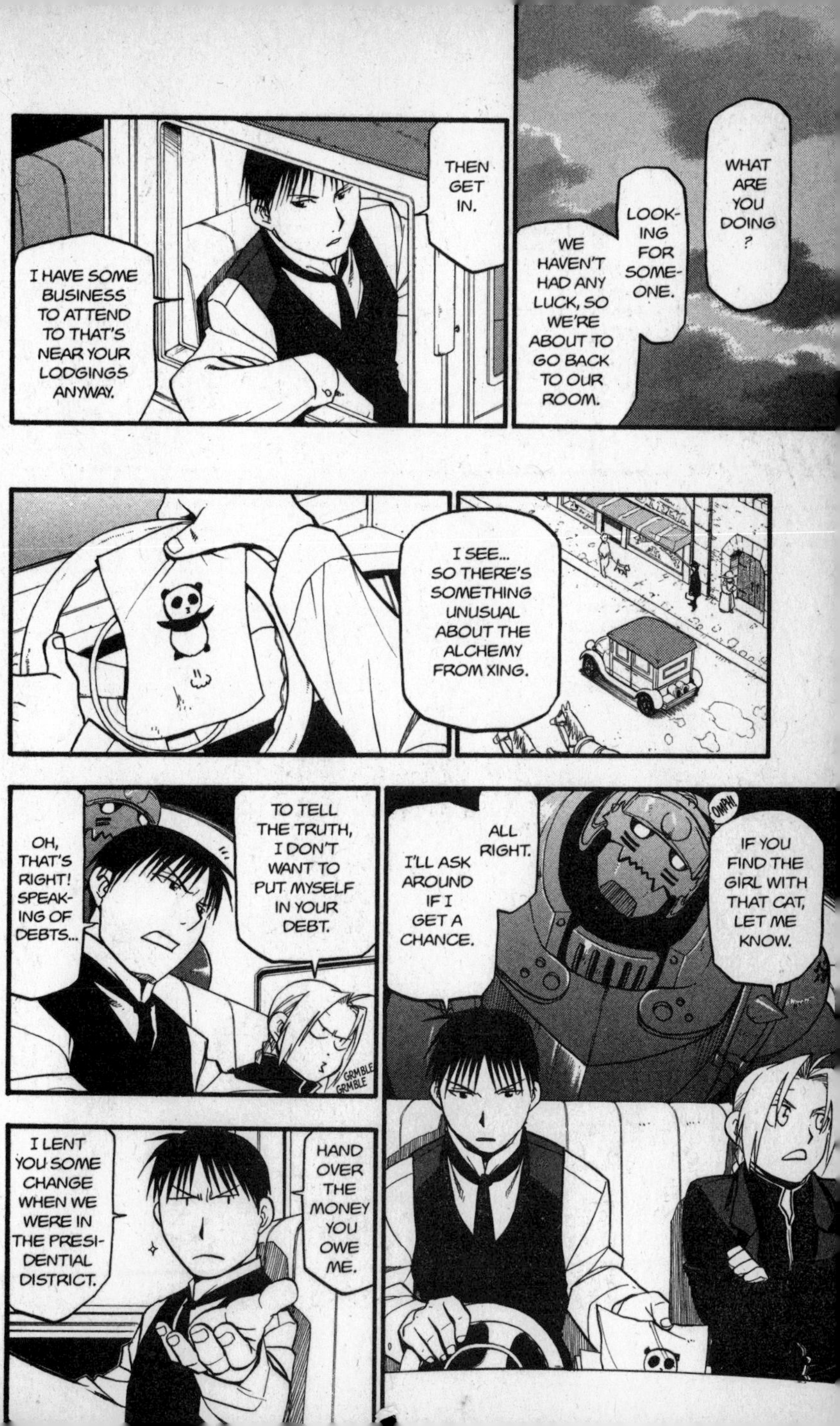
WHAT ARE YOU DOING?
LOOKING FOR SOMEONE.
WE HAVEN'T HAD ANY LUCK, SO WE'RE ABOUT TO GO BACK TO OUR ROOM.
THEN GET IN.
I HAVE SOME BUSINESS TO ATTEND TO THAT'S NEAR YOUR LODGINGS ANYWAY.
I SEE... SO THERE'S SOMETHING UNUSUAL ABOUT THE ALCHEMY FROM XING.
IF YOU FIND THE GIRL WITH THAT CAT, LET ME KNOW.
OMPH!
ALL RIGHT.
I'LL ASK AROUND IF I GET A CHANCE.
TO TELL THE TRUTH, I DON'T WANT TO PUT MYSELF IN YOUR DEBT.
GRMBLE GRMBLE
OH, THAT'S RIGHT! SPEAKING OF DEBTS...
HAND OVER THE MONEY YOU OWE ME.
I LENT YOU SOME CHANGE WHEN WE WERE IN THE PRESIDENTIAL DISTRICT.

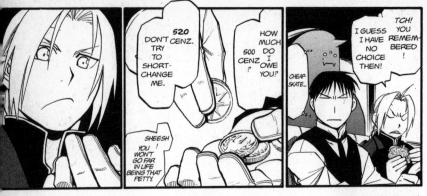

TCH! YOU REMEMBERED!
I GUESS I HAVE NO CHOICE THEN!
CHEAPSKATE...
HOW MUCH DO I OWE YOU?
500 CENZ?
520 CENZ. DON'T TRY TO SHORT-CHANGE ME.
SHEESH! YOU WON'T GO FAR IN LIFE BEING THAT PETTY.
NO, I'M NOT PAYING YOU BACK YET AFTER ALL.
I'LL PAY YOU BACK WHEN YOU BECOME PRESIDENT!

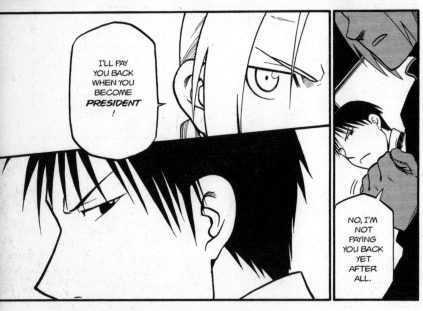

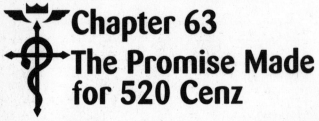

Chapter 63
The Promise Made for 520 Cenz

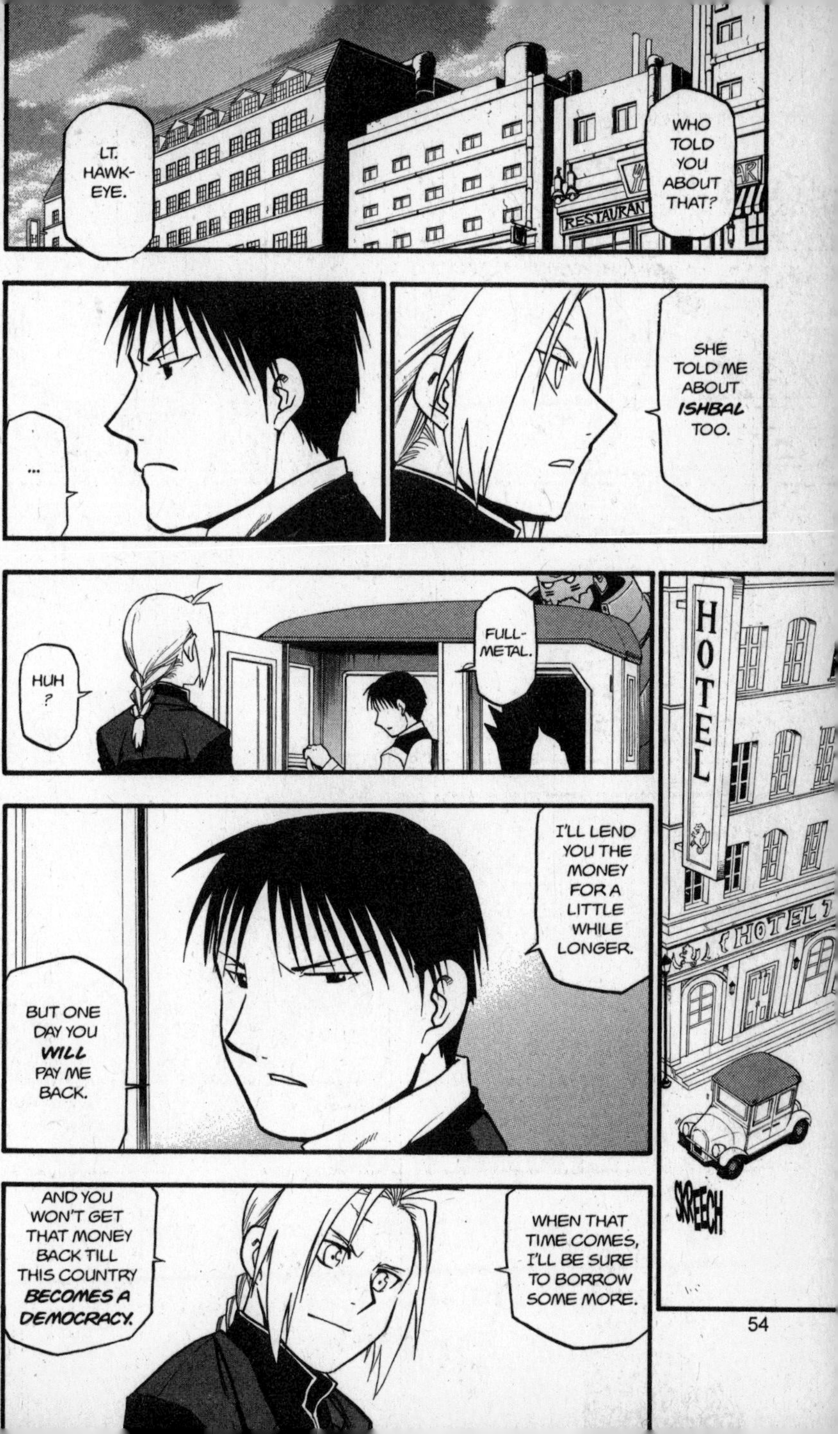
HOTEL
RESTAURANT
WHO TOLD YOU ABOUT THAT?
LT. HAWK-EYE.
SHE TOLD ME ABOUT ISHBAL TOO.
...
HOTEL
HOTEL
SKREECH
FULL-METAL.
HUH?
I'LL LEND YOU THE MONEY FOR A LITTLE WHILE LONGER.
BUT ONE DAY YOU WILL PAY ME BACK.
WHEN THAT TIME COMES, I'LL BE SURE TO BORROW SOME MORE.
AND YOU WON'T GET THAT MONEY BACK TILL THIS COUNTRY BECOMES A DEMOCRACY.

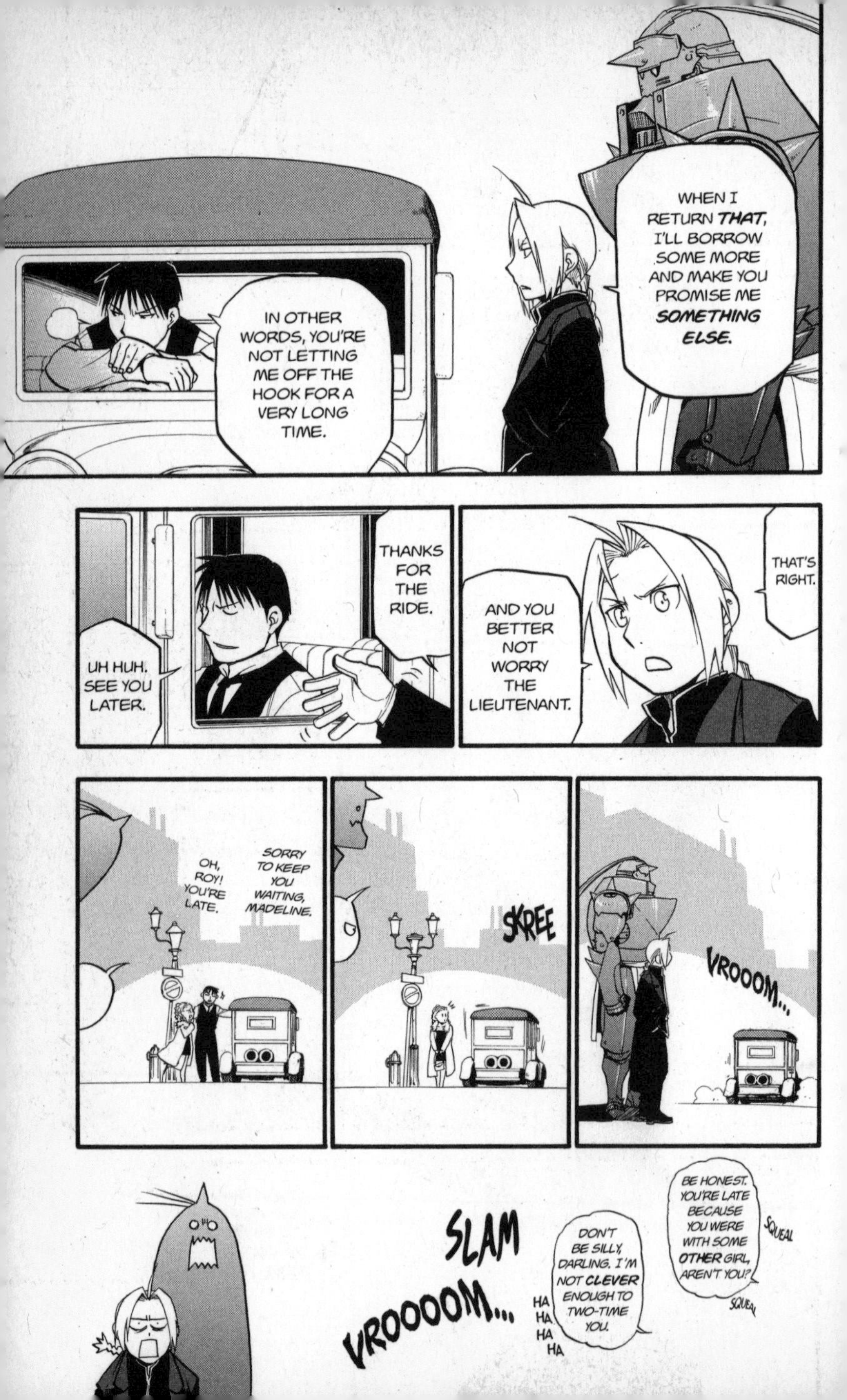
WHEN I RETURN **THAT**, I'LL BORROW SOME MORE AND MAKE YOU PROMISE ME ***SOMETHING ELSE.***
IN OTHER WORDS, YOU'RE NOT LETTING ME OFF THE HOOK FOR A VERY LONG TIME.
THAT'S RIGHT.
AND YOU BETTER NOT WORRY THE LIEUTENANT.
THANKS FOR THE RIDE.
UH HUH. SEE YOU LATER.
VROOOM...
SKREE
SORRY TO KEEP YOU WAITING, MADELINE.
OH, ROY! YOU'RE LATE.
SQUEAL
BE HONEST. YOU'RE LATE BECAUSE YOU WERE WITH SOME **OTHER** GIRL, AREN'T YOU?
SQUEAL
DON'T BE SILLY, DARLING. I'M NOT **CLEVER** ENOUGH TO TWO-TIME YOU.
HA HA HA HA
SLAM
VROOOOM...

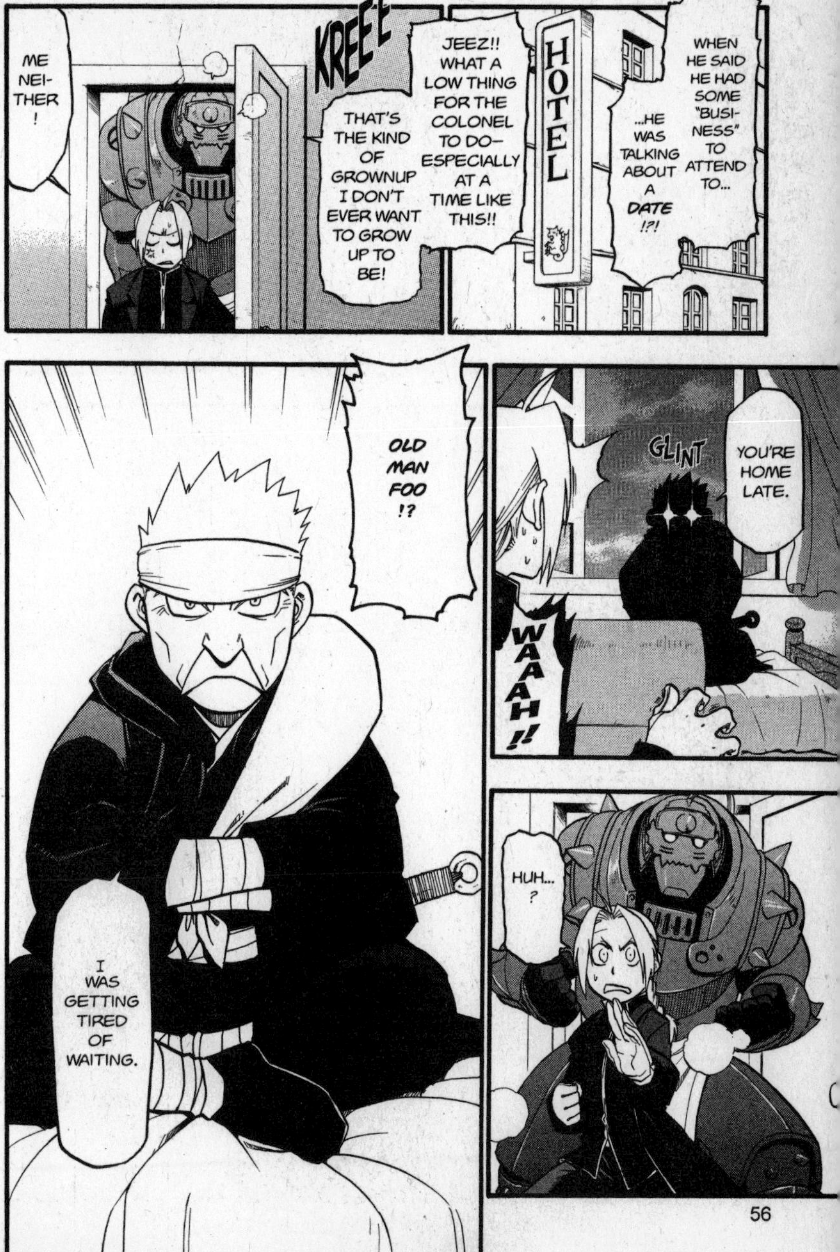
WHEN HE SAID HE HAD SOME "BUSINESS" TO ATTEND TO...
...HE WAS TALKING ABOUT A DATE !?!
KREE-E
JEEZ!! WHAT A LOW THING FOR THE COLONEL TO DO— ESPECIALLY AT A TIME LIKE THIS!!
THAT'S THE KIND OF GROWNUP I DON'T EVER WANT TO GROW UP TO BE!
ME NEITHER!
HOTEL
YOU'RE HOME LATE.
GLINT
WAAAH!!
HUH...?
OLD MAN FOO!?
I WAS GETTING TIRED OF WAITING.

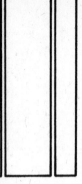

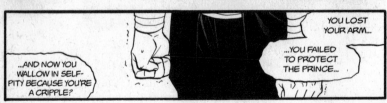

YOU LOST YOUR ARM...

...YOU FAILED TO PROTECT THE PRINCE...

...AND NOW YOU WALLOW IN SELF-PITY BECAUSE YOU'RE A CRIPPLE?

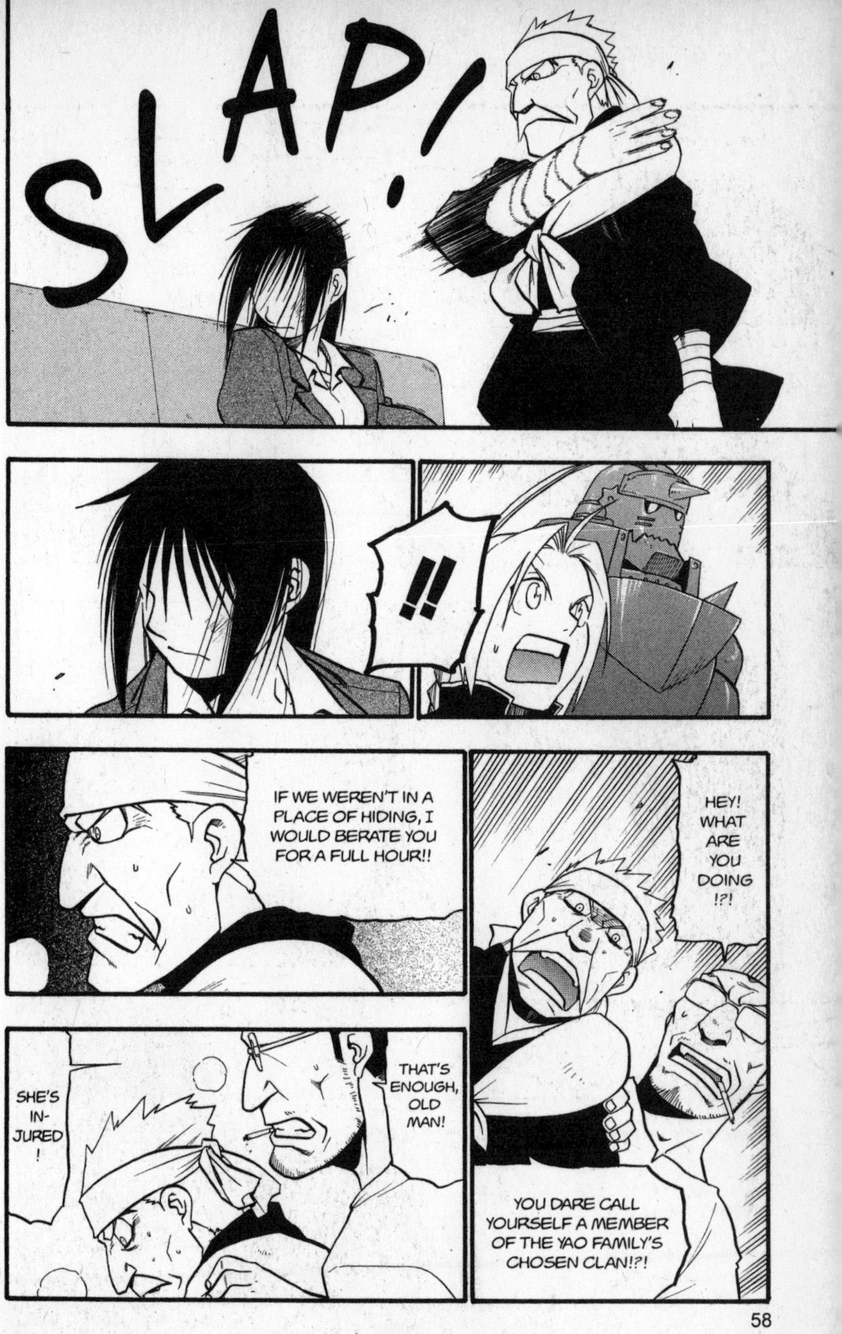
SLAP!
!!
HEY! WHAT ARE YOU DOING !?!
YOU DARE CALL YOURSELF A MEMBER OF THE YAO FAMILY'S CHOSEN CLAN!?!
IF WE WEREN'T IN A PLACE OF HIDING, I WOULD BERATE YOU FOR A FULL HOUR!!
THAT'S ENOUGH, OLD MAN!
SHE'S IN-JURED!

I'M SORRY, GRANDFATHER.

I'M SORRY.

YOU LOST...

...YOUR ARM.

YOUR ARM...

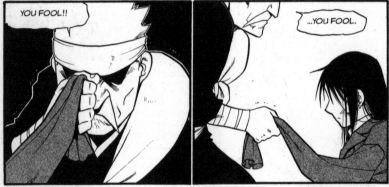

YOU FOOL!!

...YOU FOOL.

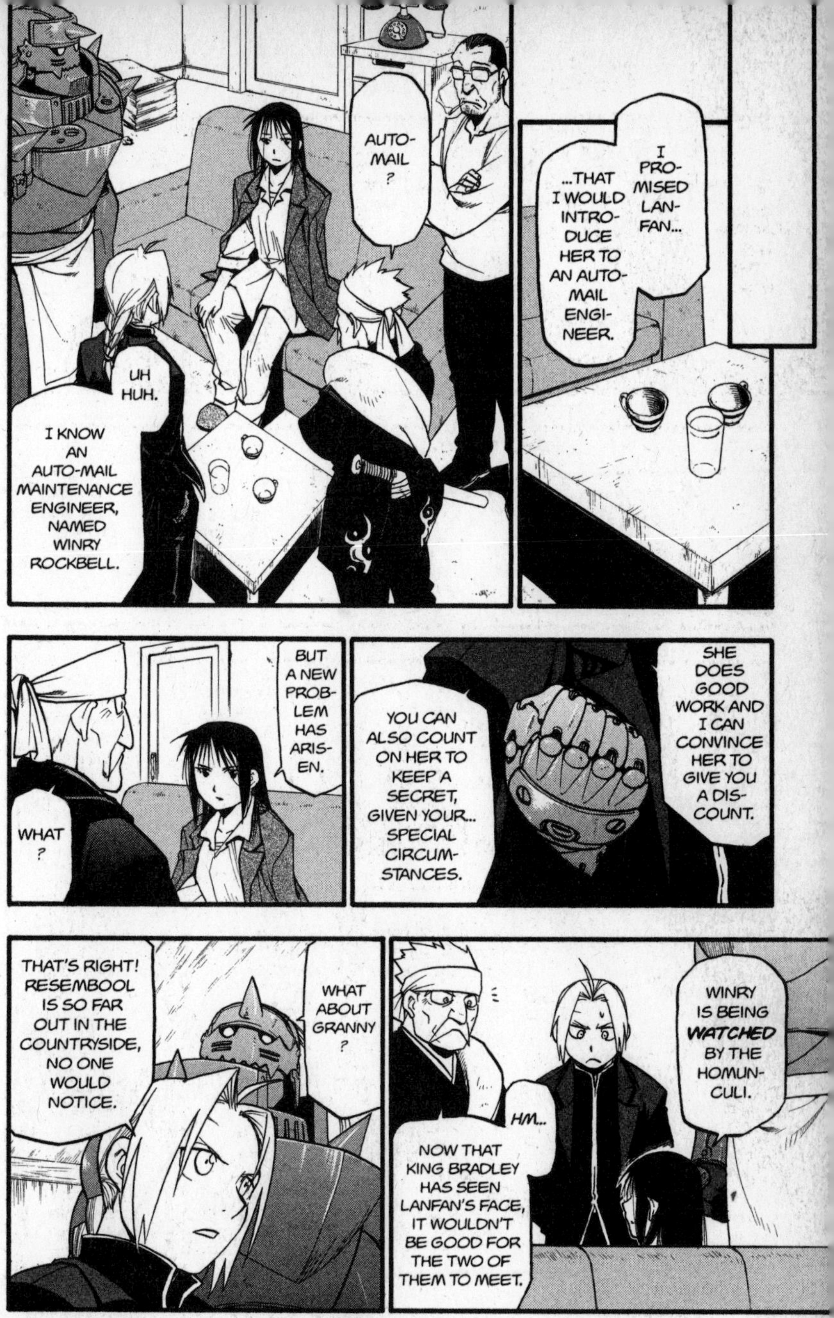
I PROMISED LANFAN...
...THAT I WOULD INTRODUCE HER TO AN AUTO-MAIL ENGINEER.
AUTO-MAIL?
UH HUH.
I KNOW AN AUTO-MAIL MAINTENANCE ENGINEER, NAMED WINRY ROCKBELL.
SHE DOES GOOD WORK AND I CAN CONVINCE HER TO GIVE YOU A DISCOUNT.
YOU CAN ALSO COUNT ON HER TO KEEP A SECRET, GIVEN YOUR... SPECIAL CIRCUMSTANCES.
BUT A NEW PROBLEM HAS ARISEN.
WHAT?
WINRY IS BEING *WATCHED* BY THE HOMUNCULI.
HM...
NOW THAT KING BRADLEY HAS SEEN LANFAN'S FACE, IT WOULDN'T BE GOOD FOR THE TWO OF THEM TO MEET.
WHAT ABOUT GRANNY?
THAT'S RIGHT! RESEMBOOL IS SO FAR OUT IN THE COUNTRYSIDE, NO ONE WOULD NOTICE.

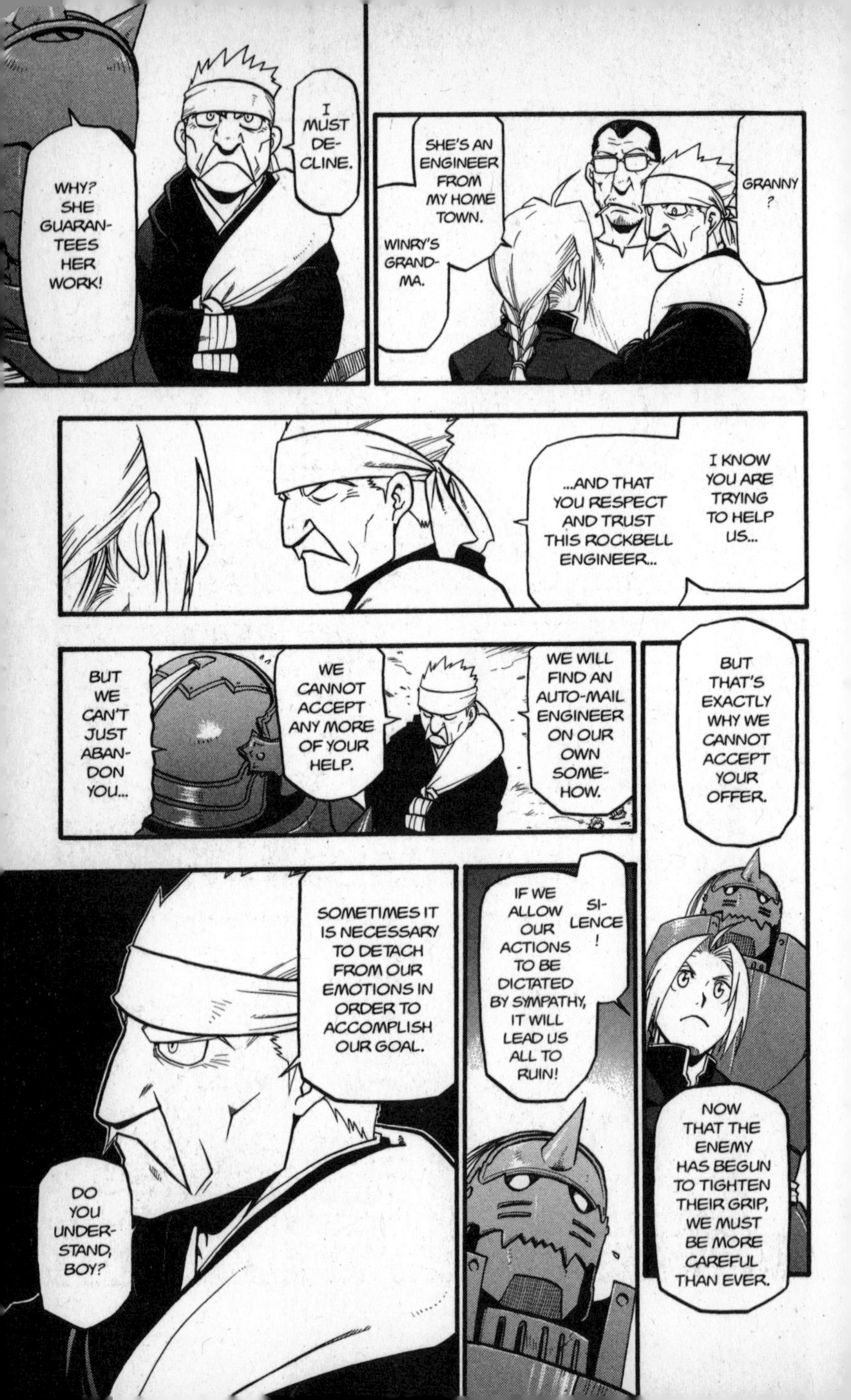
GRANNY?
SHE'S AN ENGINEER FROM MY HOME TOWN.
WINRY'S GRANDMA.
I MUST DECLINE.
WHY? SHE GUARANTEES HER WORK!
I KNOW YOU ARE TRYING TO HELP US...
...AND THAT YOU RESPECT AND TRUST THIS ROCKBELL ENGINEER...
BUT THAT'S EXACTLY WHY WE CANNOT ACCEPT YOUR OFFER.
NOW THAT THE ENEMY HAS BEGUN TO TIGHTEN THEIR GRIP, WE MUST BE MORE CAREFUL THAN EVER.
WE WILL FIND AN AUTO-MAIL ENGINEER ON OUR OWN SOMEHOW.
WE CANNOT ACCEPT ANY MORE OF YOUR HELP.
BUT WE CAN'T JUST ABANDON YOU...
SILENCE!
IF WE ALLOW OUR ACTIONS TO BE DICTATED BY SYMPATHY, IT WILL LEAD US ALL TO RUIN!
SOMETIMES IT IS NECESSARY TO DETACH FROM OUR EMOTIONS IN ORDER TO ACCOMPLISH OUR GOAL.
DO YOU UNDERSTAND, BOY?

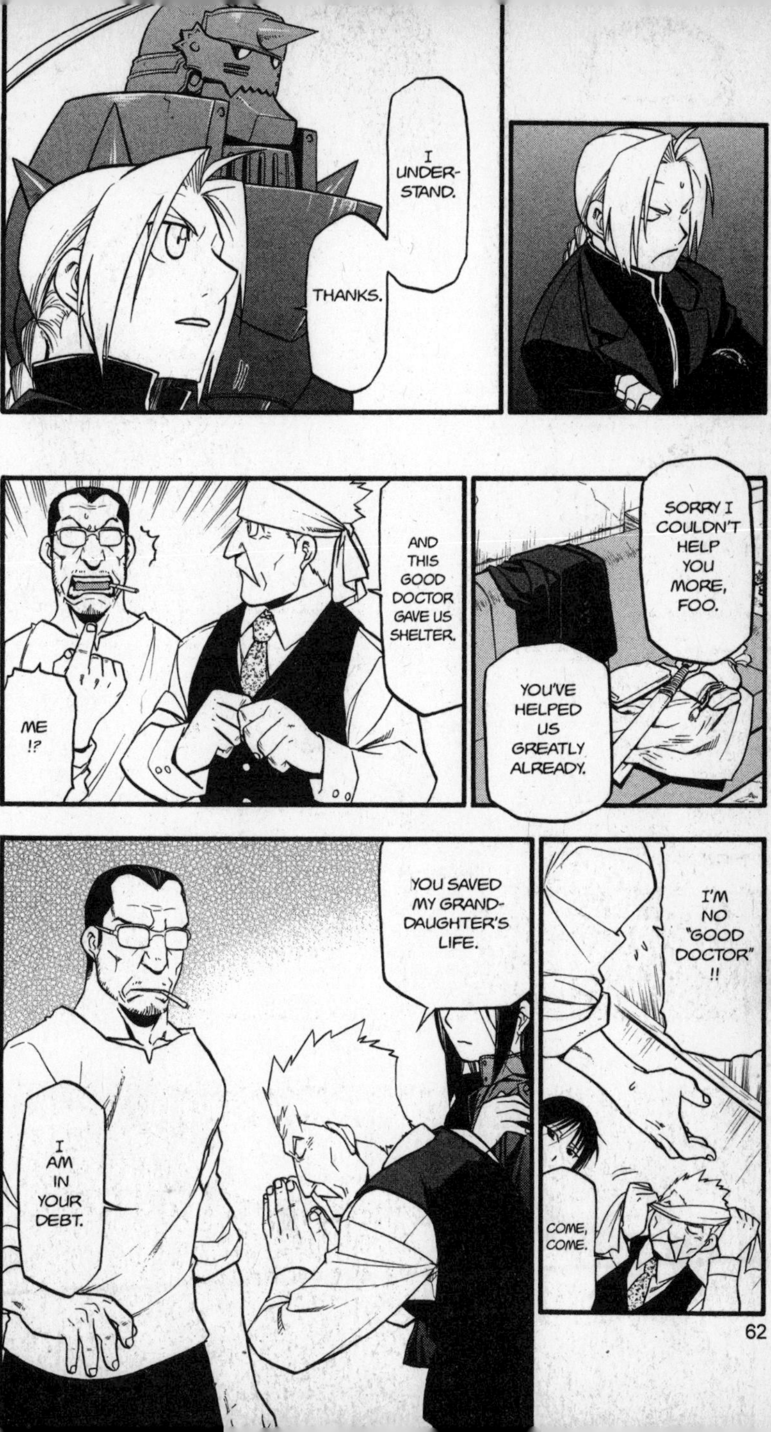
I UNDERSTAND.
THANKS.
SORRY I COULDN'T HELP YOU MORE, FOO.
YOU'VE HELPED US GREATLY ALREADY.
AND THIS GOOD DOCTOR GAVE US SHELTER.
ME !?
I'M NO "GOOD DOCTOR" !!
COME, COME.
YOU SAVED MY GRANDDAUGHTER'S LIFE.
I AM IN YOUR DEBT.

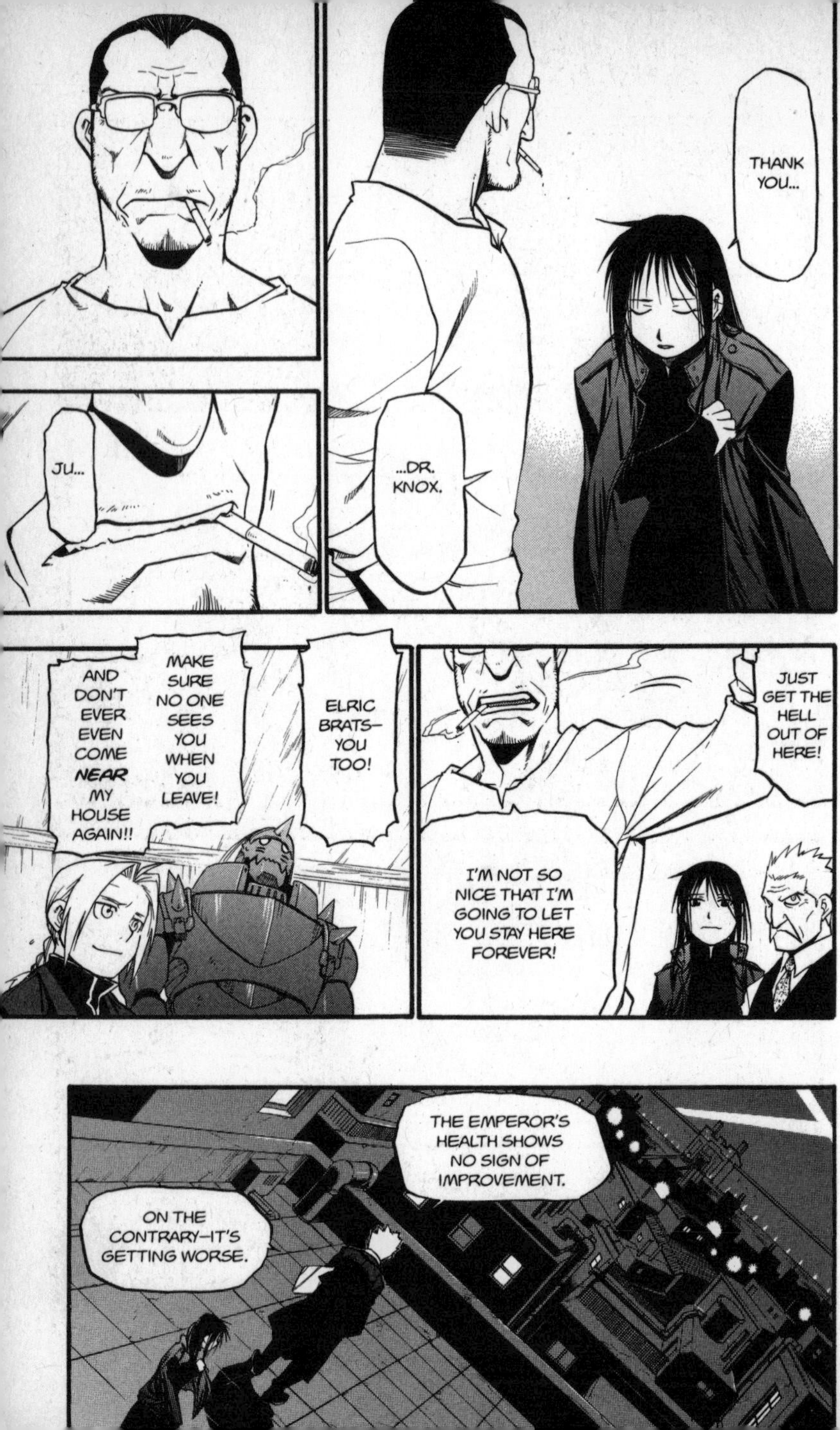
THANK YOU...
...DR. KNOX.
JU...
JUST GET THE HELL OUT OF HERE!
I'M NOT SO NICE THAT I'M GOING TO LET YOU STAY HERE FOREVER!
ELRIC BRATS— YOU TOO!
MAKE SURE NO ONE SEES YOU WHEN YOU LEAVE!
AND DON'T EVER EVEN COME *NEAR* MY HOUSE AGAIN!!
THE EMPEROR'S HEALTH SHOWS NO SIGN OF IMPROVEMENT.
ON THE CONTRARY—IT'S GETTING WORSE.

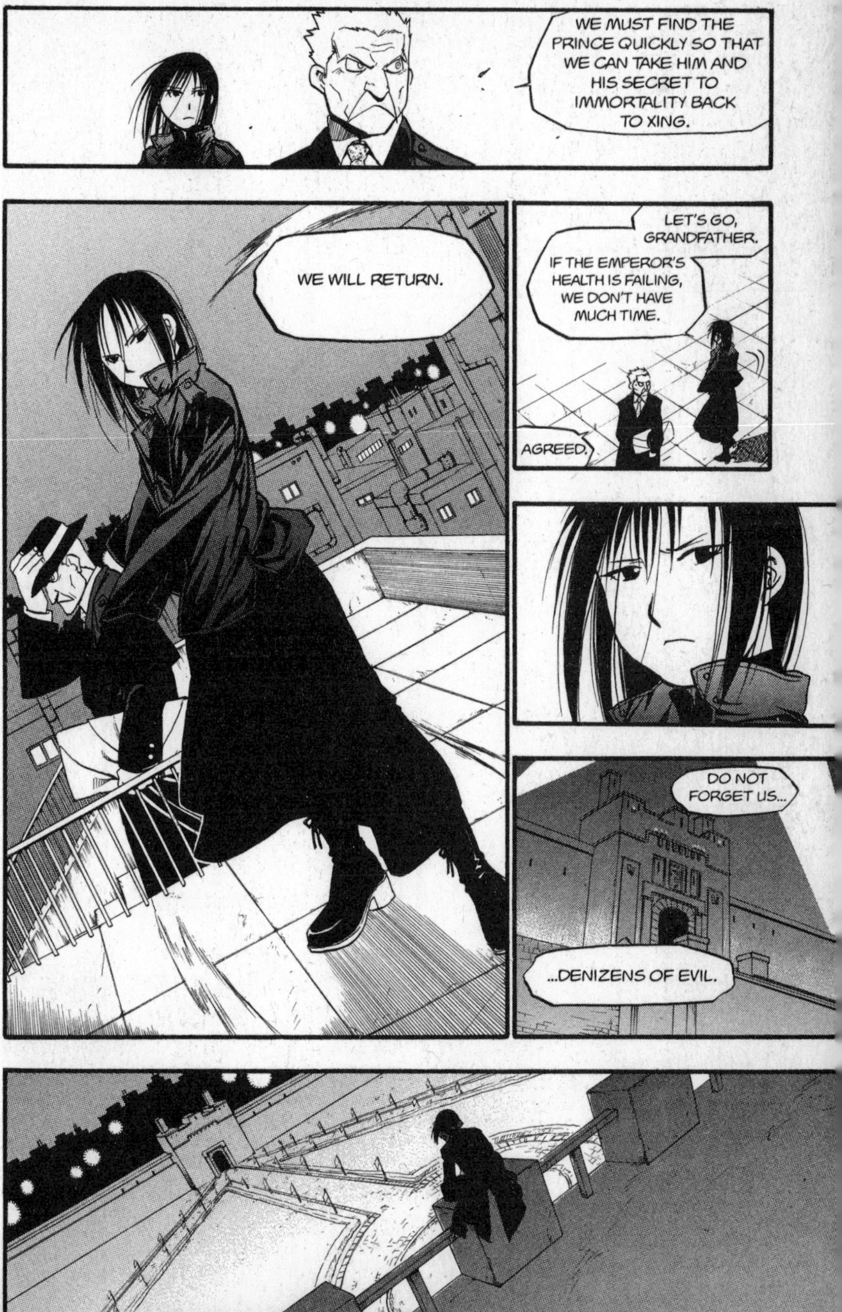
WE MUST FIND THE PRINCE QUICKLY SO THAT WE CAN TAKE HIM AND HIS SECRET TO IMMORTALITY BACK TO XING.
LET'S GO, GRANDFATHER.
IF THE EMPEROR'S HEALTH IS FAILING, WE DON'T HAVE MUCH TIME.
AGREED.
DO NOT FORGET US...
...DENIZENS OF EVIL.
WE WILL RETURN.

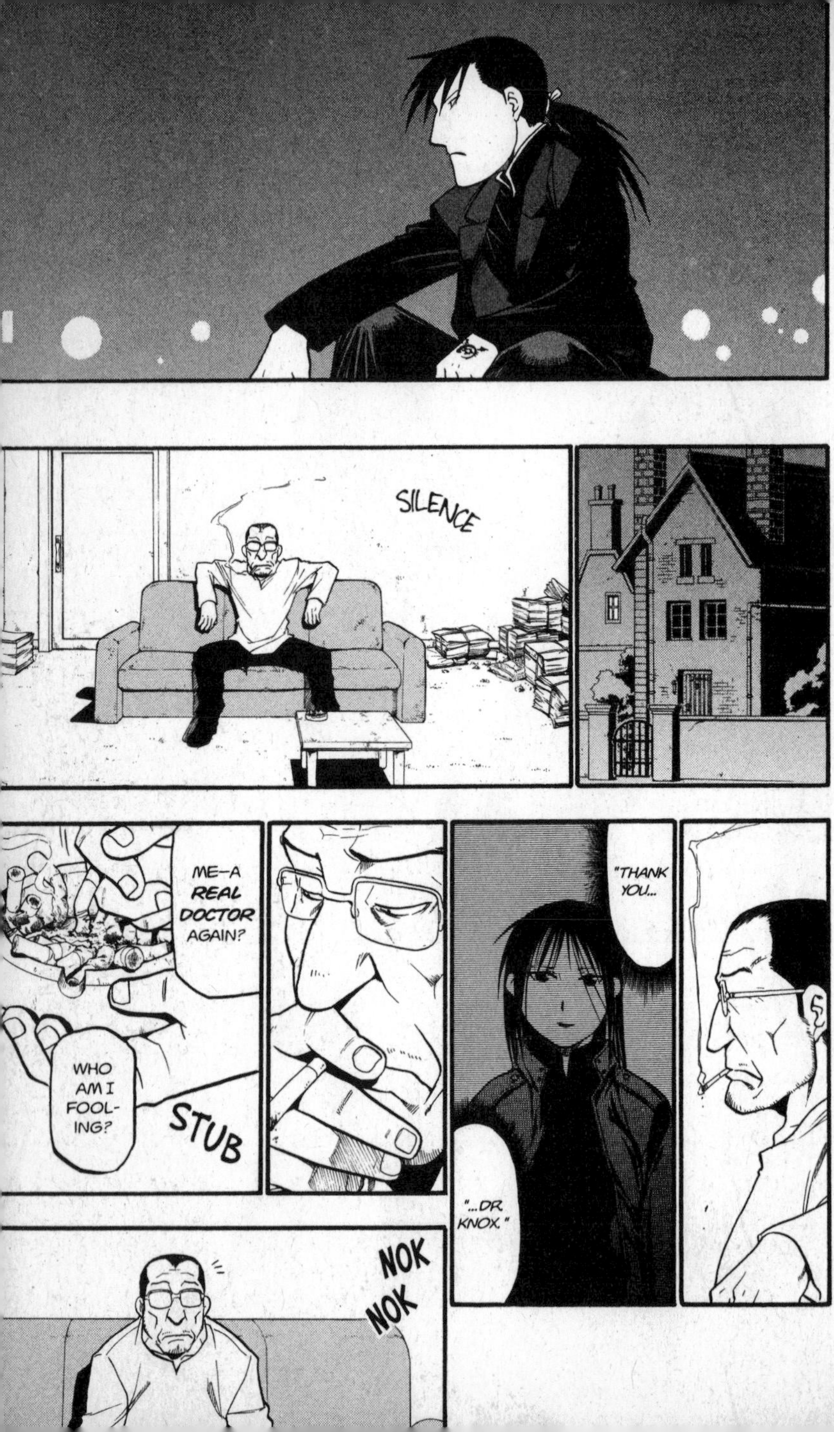
SILENCE
"THANK YOU...
"...DR. KNOX."
ME—A **REAL DOCTOR** AGAIN?
WHO AM I FOOL-ING?
STUB
NOK NOK

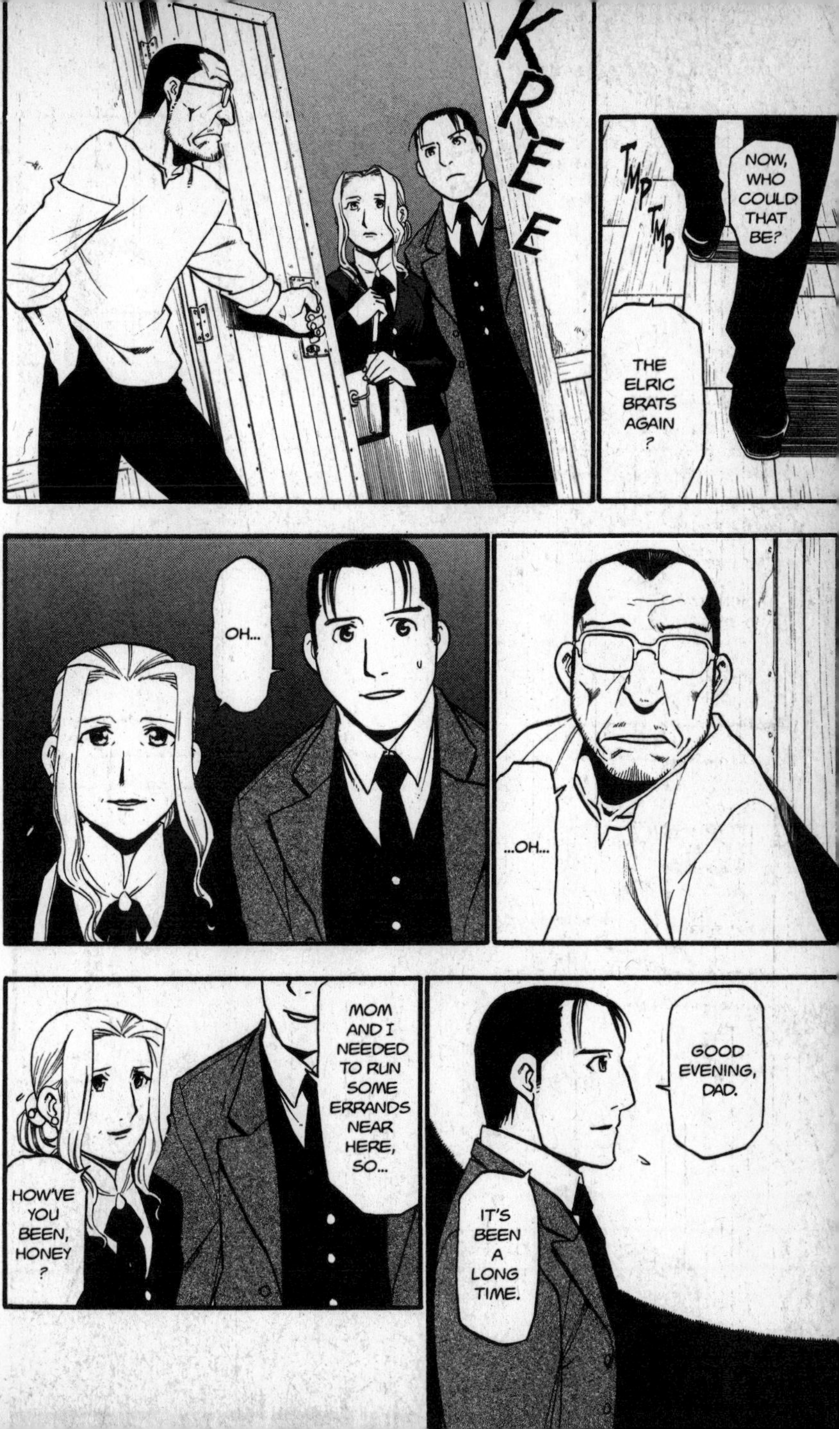
NOW, WHO COULD THAT BE?
TMP TMP
THE ELRIC BRATS AGAIN?
KREE
...OH...
OH...
GOOD EVENING, DAD.
IT'S BEEN A LONG TIME.
MOM AND I NEEDED TO RUN SOME ERRANDS NEAR HERE, SO...
HOW'VE YOU BEEN, HONEY?

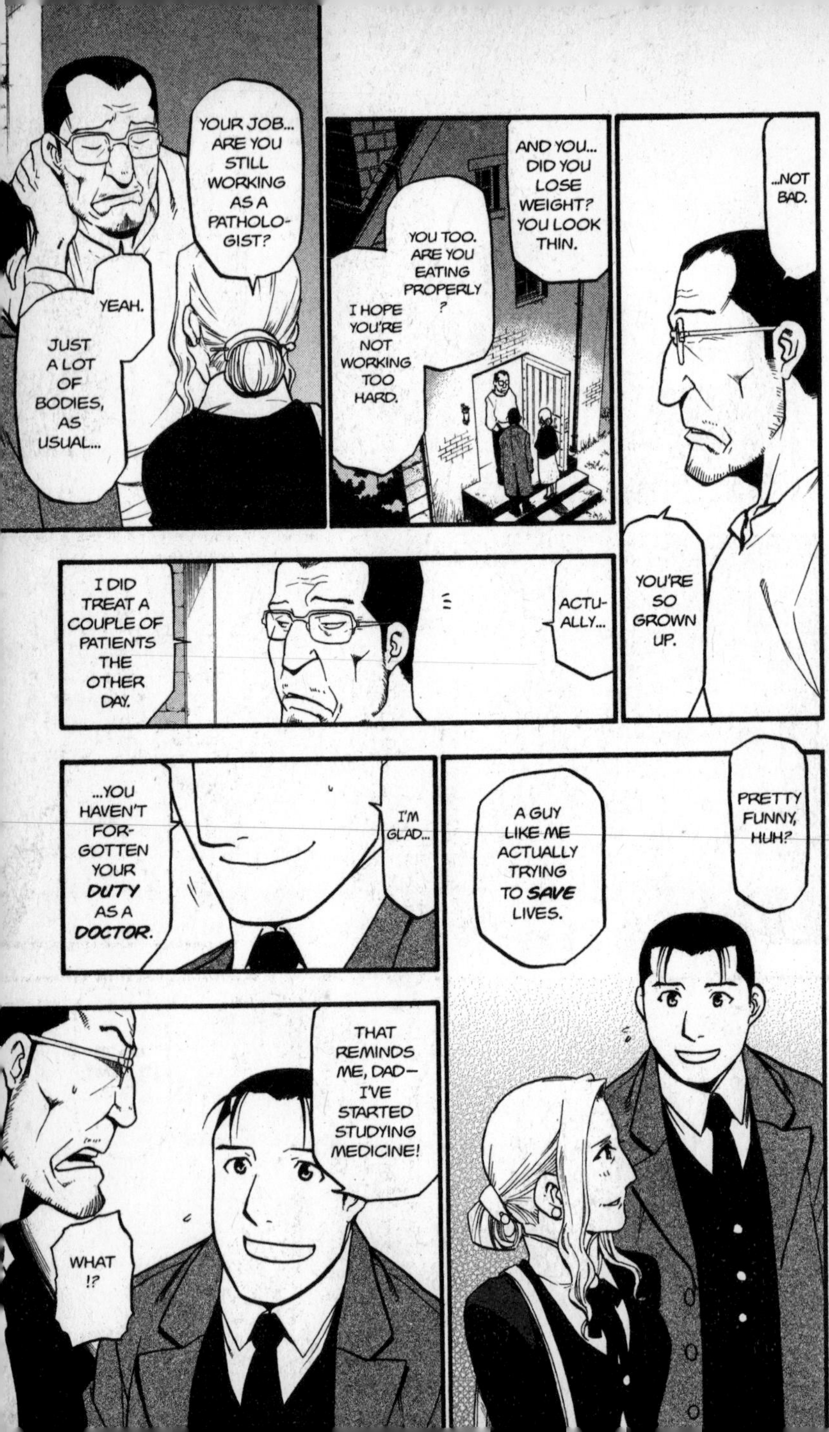
...NOT BAD.
YOU'RE SO GROWN UP.
AND YOU... DID YOU LOSE WEIGHT? YOU LOOK THIN.
YOU TOO. ARE YOU EATING PROPERLY?
I HOPE YOU'RE NOT WORKING TOO HARD.
YOUR JOB... ARE YOU STILL WORKING AS A PATHOLOGIST?
YEAH.
JUST A LOT OF BODIES, AS USUAL...
ACTUALLY...
I DID TREAT A COUPLE OF PATIENTS THE OTHER DAY.
PRETTY FUNNY, HUH?
A GUY LIKE ME ACTUALLY TRYING TO **SAVE** LIVES.
I'M GLAD...
...YOU HAVEN'T FORGOTTEN YOUR **DUTY** AS A **DOCTOR**.
THAT REMINDS ME, DAD— I'VE STARTED STUDYING MEDICINE!
WHAT!?

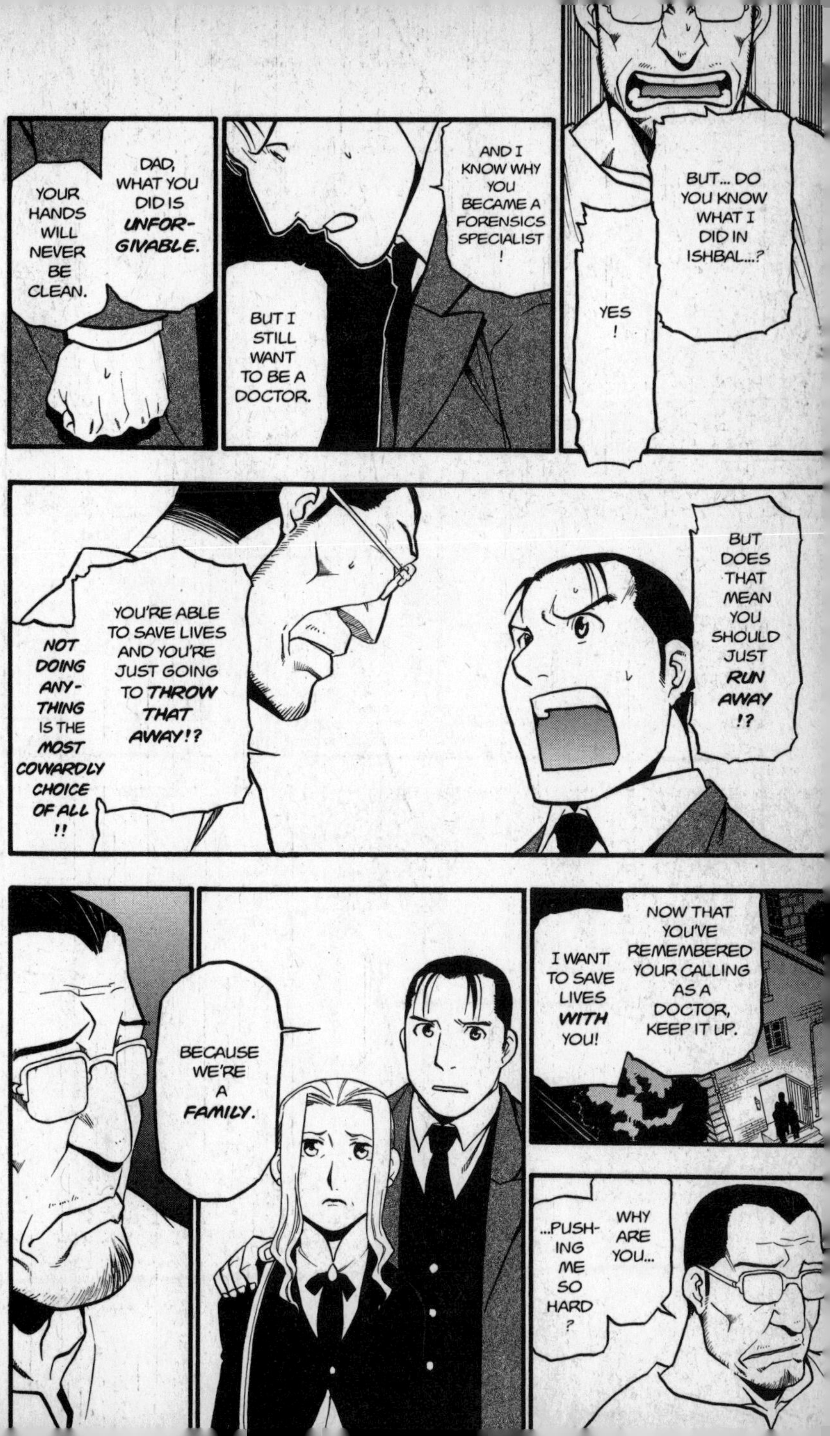
BUT... DO YOU KNOW WHAT I DID IN ISHBAL...?
YES!
AND I KNOW WHY YOU BECAME A FORENSICS SPECIALIST!
BUT I STILL WANT TO BE A DOCTOR.
DAD, WHAT YOU DID IS UNFORGIVABLE.
YOUR HANDS WILL NEVER BE CLEAN.
BUT DOES THAT MEAN YOU SHOULD JUST RUN AWAY!?
YOU'RE ABLE TO SAVE LIVES AND YOU'RE JUST GOING TO THROW THAT AWAY!?
NOT DOING ANYTHING IS THE MOST COWARDLY CHOICE OF ALL!!
NOW THAT YOU'VE REMEMBERED YOUR CALLING AS A DOCTOR, KEEP IT UP.
I WANT TO SAVE LIVES WITH YOU!
WHY ARE YOU...
...PUSHING ME SO HARD?
BECAUSE WE'RE A FAMILY.

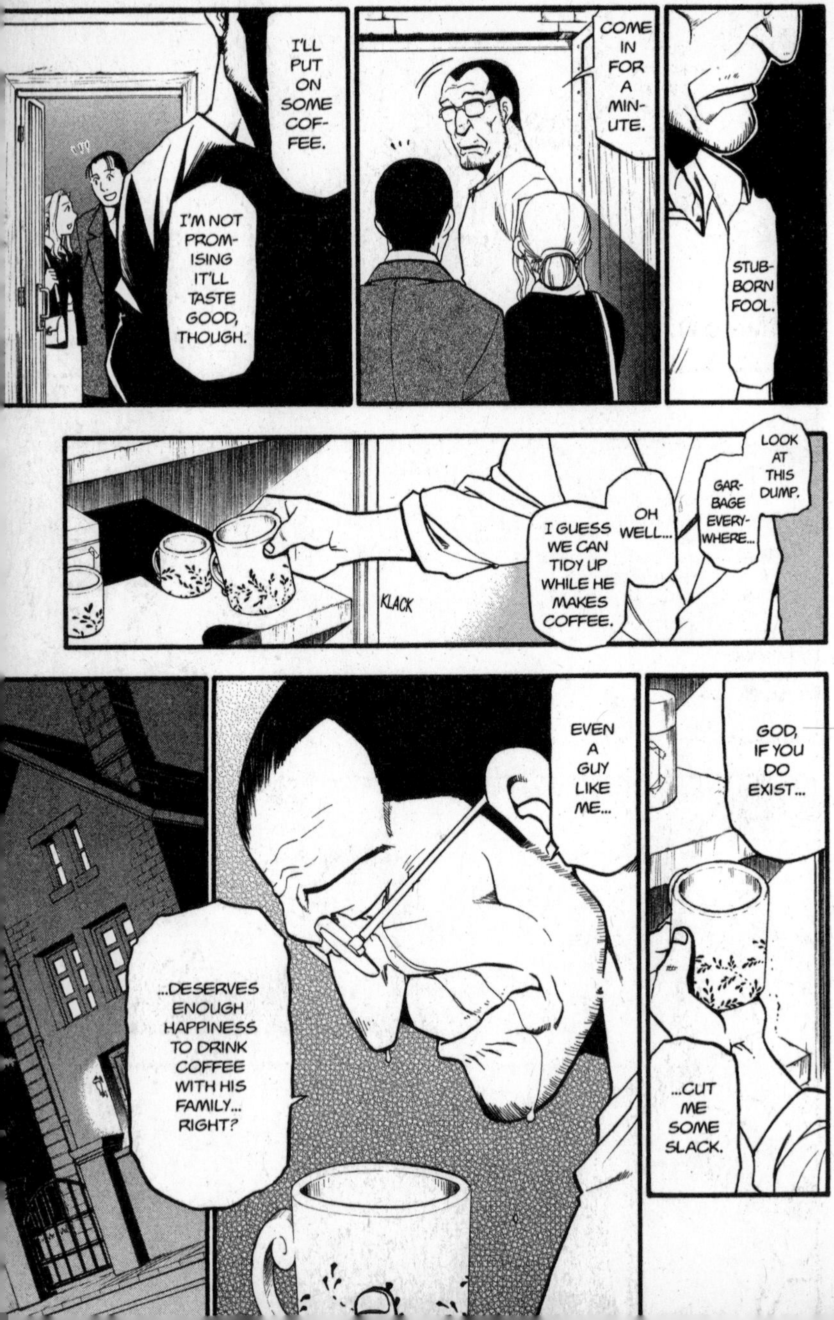
STUBBORN FOOL.
COME IN FOR A MINUTE.
I'LL PUT ON SOME COFFEE.
I'M NOT PROMISING IT'LL TASTE GOOD, THOUGH.
LOOK AT THIS DUMP.
GARBAGE EVERYWHERE...
OH WELL...
I GUESS WE CAN TIDY UP WHILE HE MAKES COFFEE.
KLACK
GOD, IF YOU DO EXIST...
...CUT ME SOME SLACK.
EVEN A GUY LIKE ME...
...DESERVES ENOUGH HAPPINESS TO DRINK COFFEE WITH HIS FAMILY... RIGHT?

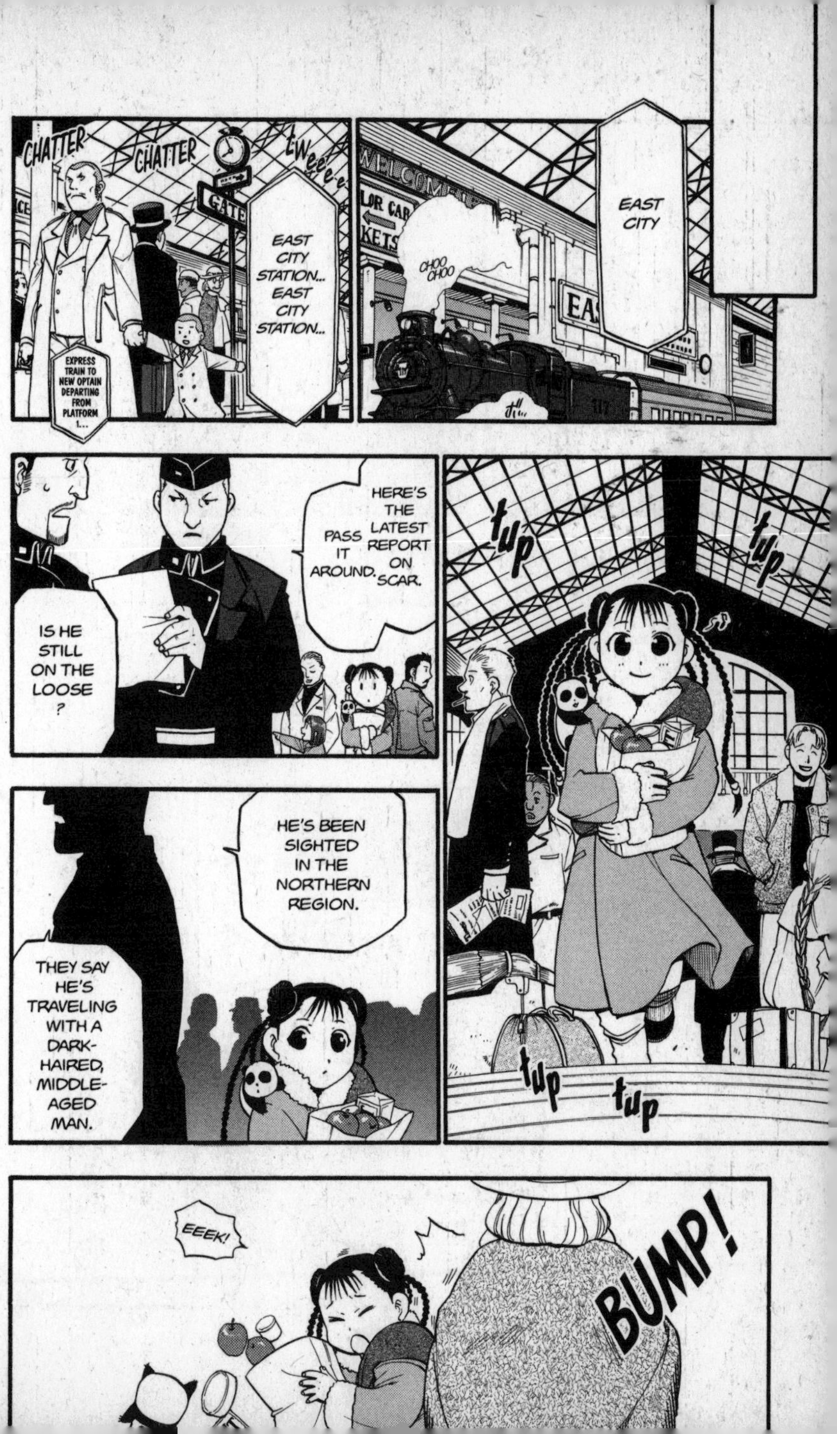
EAST CITY
CHOO CHOO
EAST
WEL
LOR CAR
KETS
CHATTER
CHATTER
TWeeee
EAST CITY STATION... EAST CITY STATION...
GATE
EXPRESS TRAIN TO NEW OPTAIN DEPARTING FROM PLATFORM 1...
tup
tup
tup
tup
HERE'S THE LATEST REPORT ON SCAR.
PASS IT AROUND.
IS HE STILL ON THE LOOSE?
HE'S BEEN SIGHTED IN THE NORTHERN REGION.
THEY SAY HE'S TRAVELING WITH A DARK-HAIRED, MIDDLE-AGED MAN.
BUMP!
EEEK!

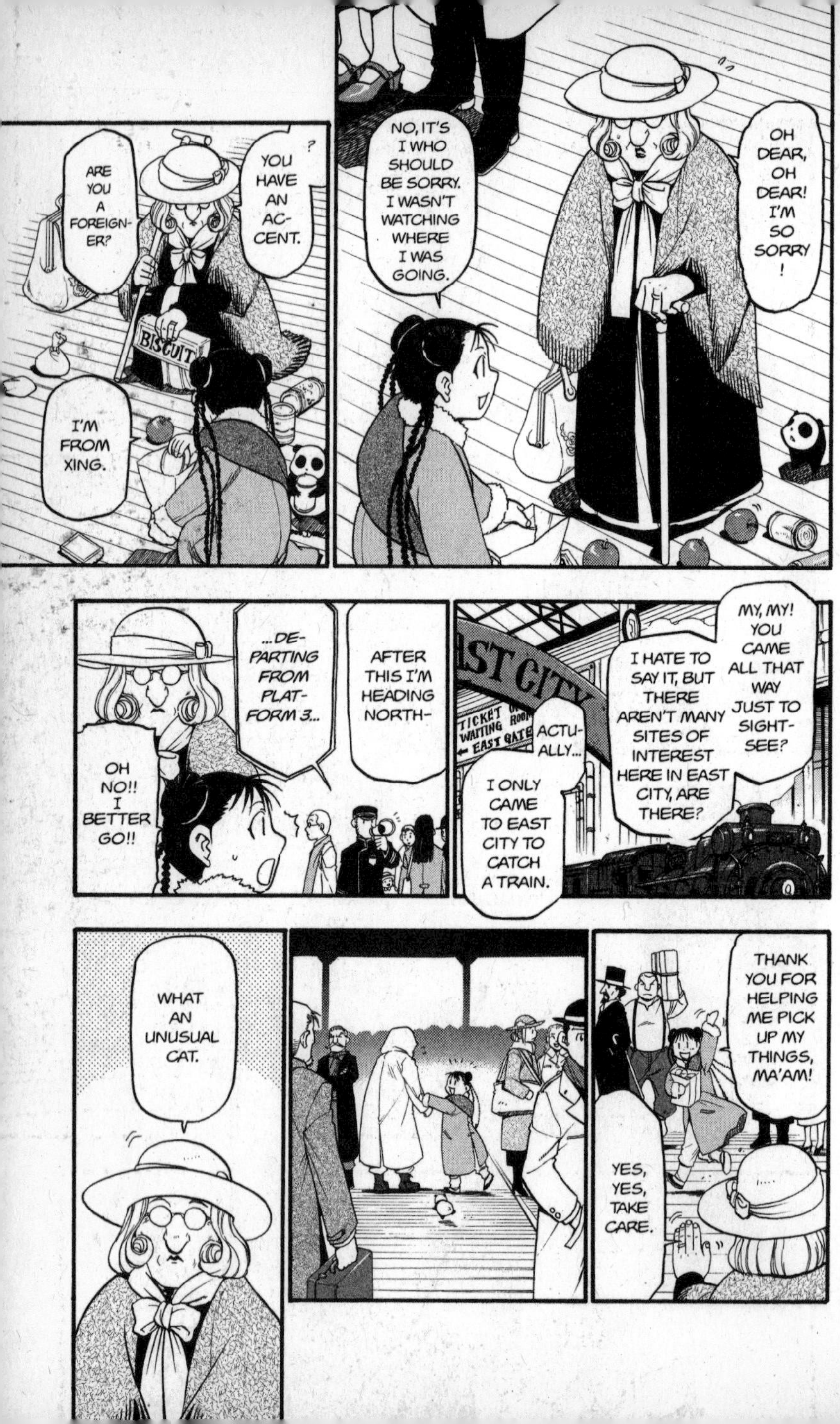
OH DEAR, OH DEAR! I'M SO SORRY!
NO, IT'S I WHO SHOULD BE SORRY. I WASN'T WATCHING WHERE I WAS GOING.
?
YOU HAVE AN ACCENT.
ARE YOU A FOREIGNER?
I'M FROM XING.
MY, MY! YOU CAME ALL THAT WAY JUST TO SIGHTSEE?
I HATE TO SAY IT, BUT THERE AREN'T MANY SITES OF INTEREST HERE IN EAST CITY, ARE THERE?
AST CITY
TICKET
WAITING ROOM
EAST GATE
ACTUALLY...
I ONLY CAME TO EAST CITY TO CATCH A TRAIN.
AFTER THIS I'M HEADING NORTH-
...DEPARTING FROM PLATFORM 3...
OH NO!! I BETTER GO!!
THANK YOU FOR HELPING ME PICK UP MY THINGS, MA'AM!
YES, YES, TAKE CARE.
WHAT AN UNUSUAL CAT.

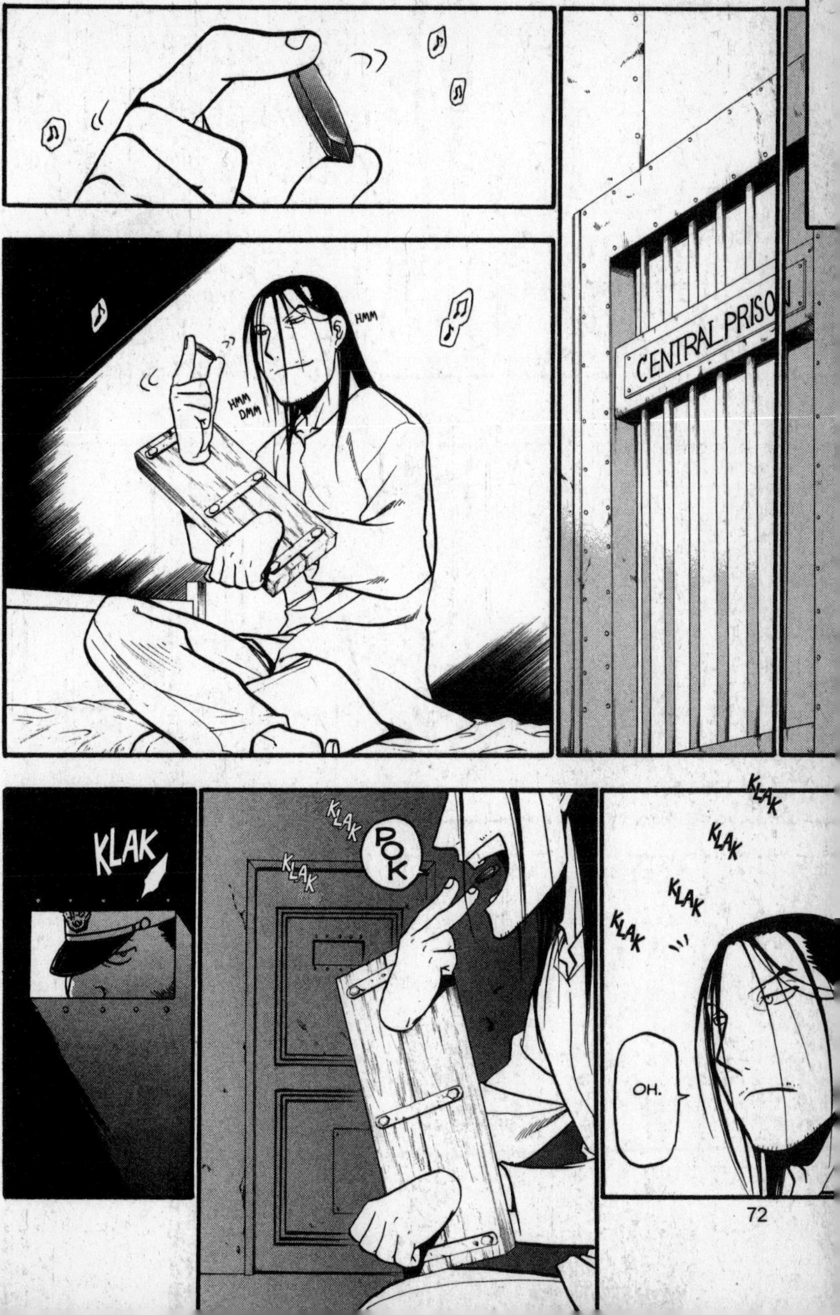
CENTRAL PRISON
HMM
HMM DMM
KLAK
KLAK
KLAK
KLAK
OH.
KLAK
KLAK
POK
KLAK

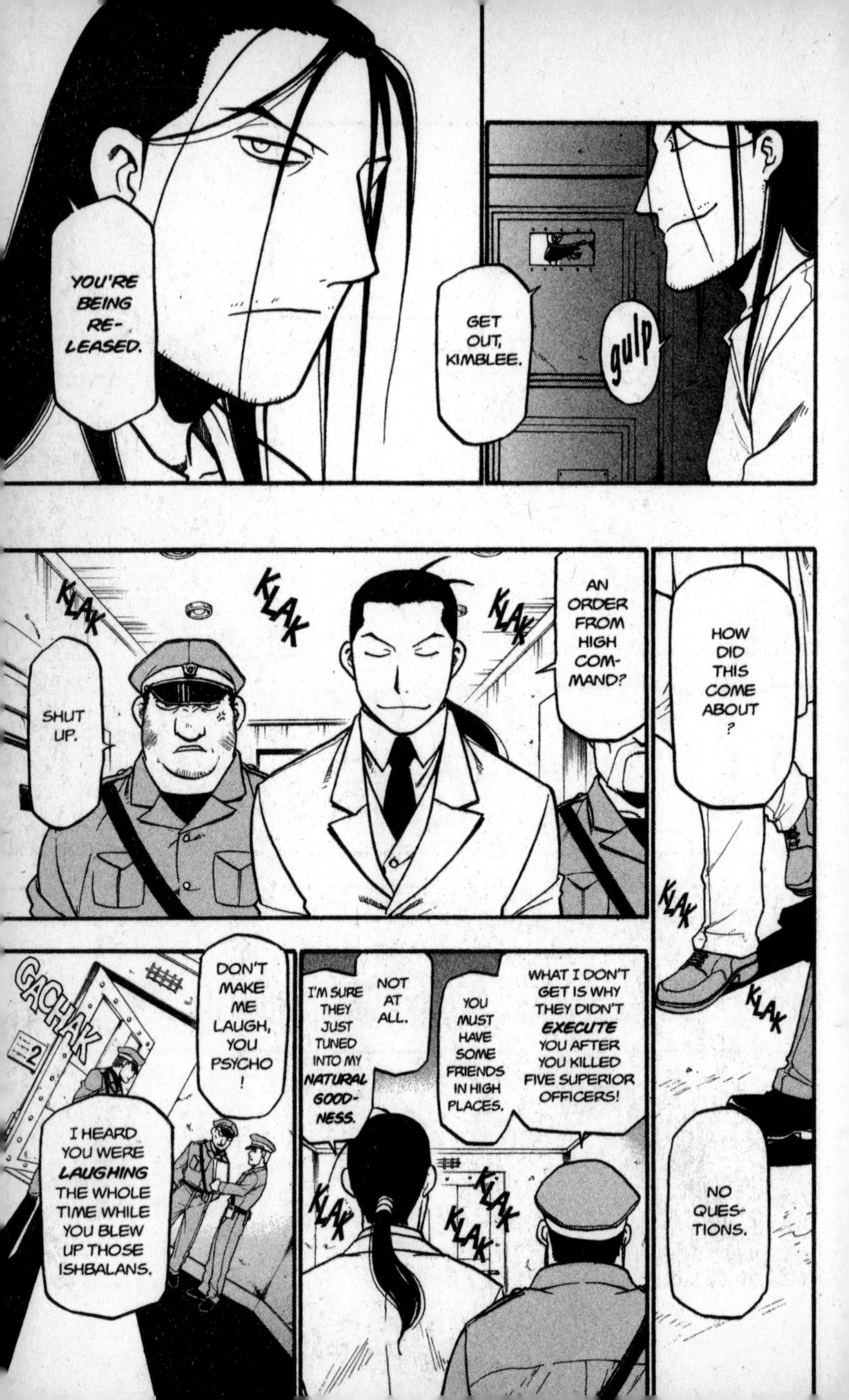
GET OUT, KIMBLEE.
gulp
YOU'RE BEING RE-LEASED.
HOW DID THIS COME ABOUT?
KLAK
KLAK
NO QUES-TIONS.
AN ORDER FROM HIGH COM-MAND?
KLAK
KLAK
KLAK
SHUT UP.
WHAT I DON'T GET IS WHY THEY DIDN'T EXECUTE YOU AFTER YOU KILLED FIVE SUPERIOR OFFICERS!
YOU MUST HAVE SOME FRIENDS IN HIGH PLACES.
NOT AT ALL.
I'M SURE THEY JUST TUNED INTO MY NATURAL GOOD-NESS.
KLAK
KLAK
KLAK
DON'T MAKE ME LAUGH, YOU PSYCHO!
GACHAK
2
I HEARD YOU WERE LAUGHING THE WHOLE TIME WHILE YOU BLEW UP THOSE ISHBALANS.

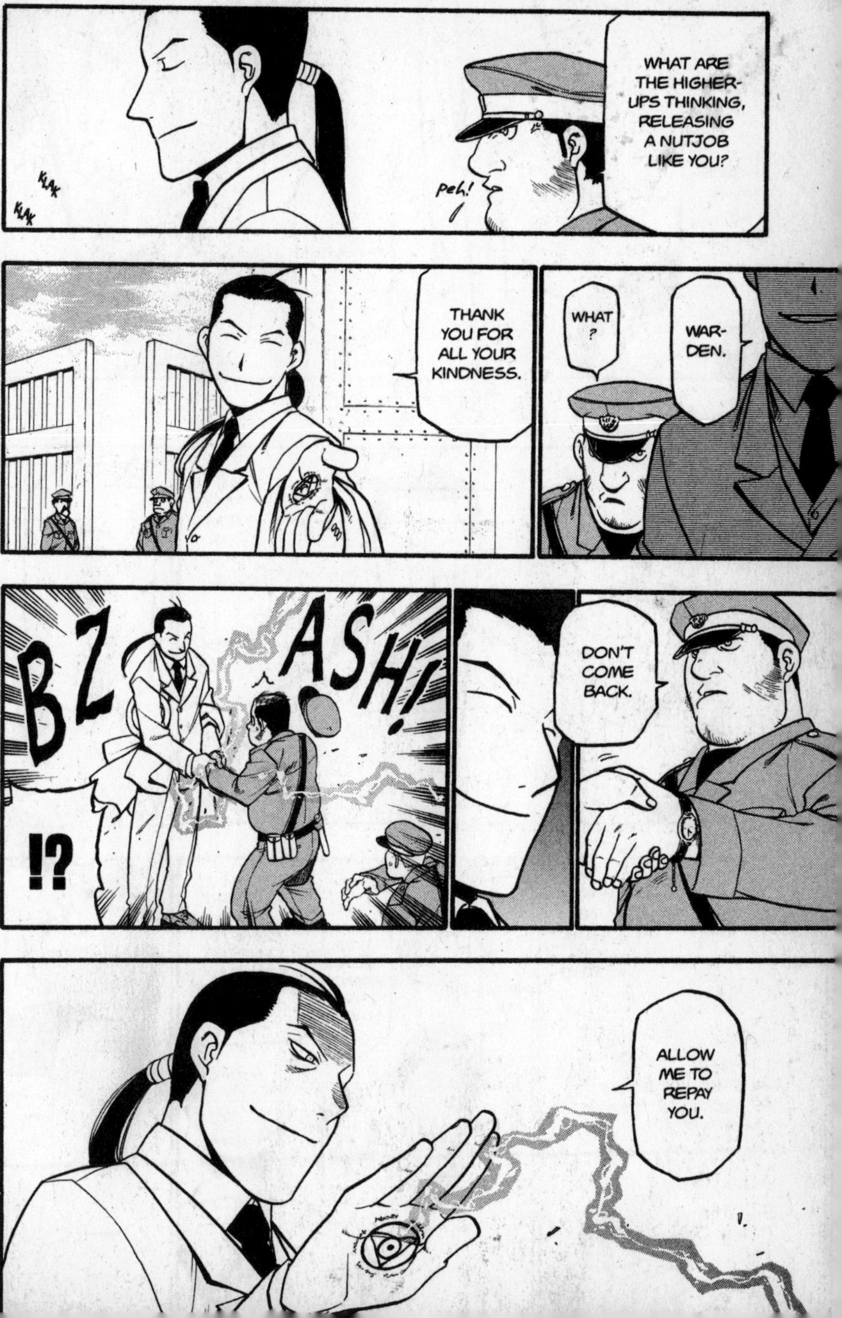
WHAT ARE THE HIGHER-UPS THINKING, RELEASING A NUTJOB LIKE YOU?
peh!
KLAK
KLAK
WAR-DEN.
WHAT ?
THANK YOU FOR ALL YOUR KINDNESS.
DON'T COME BACK.
BZ ASH!
!?
ALLOW ME TO REPAY YOU.

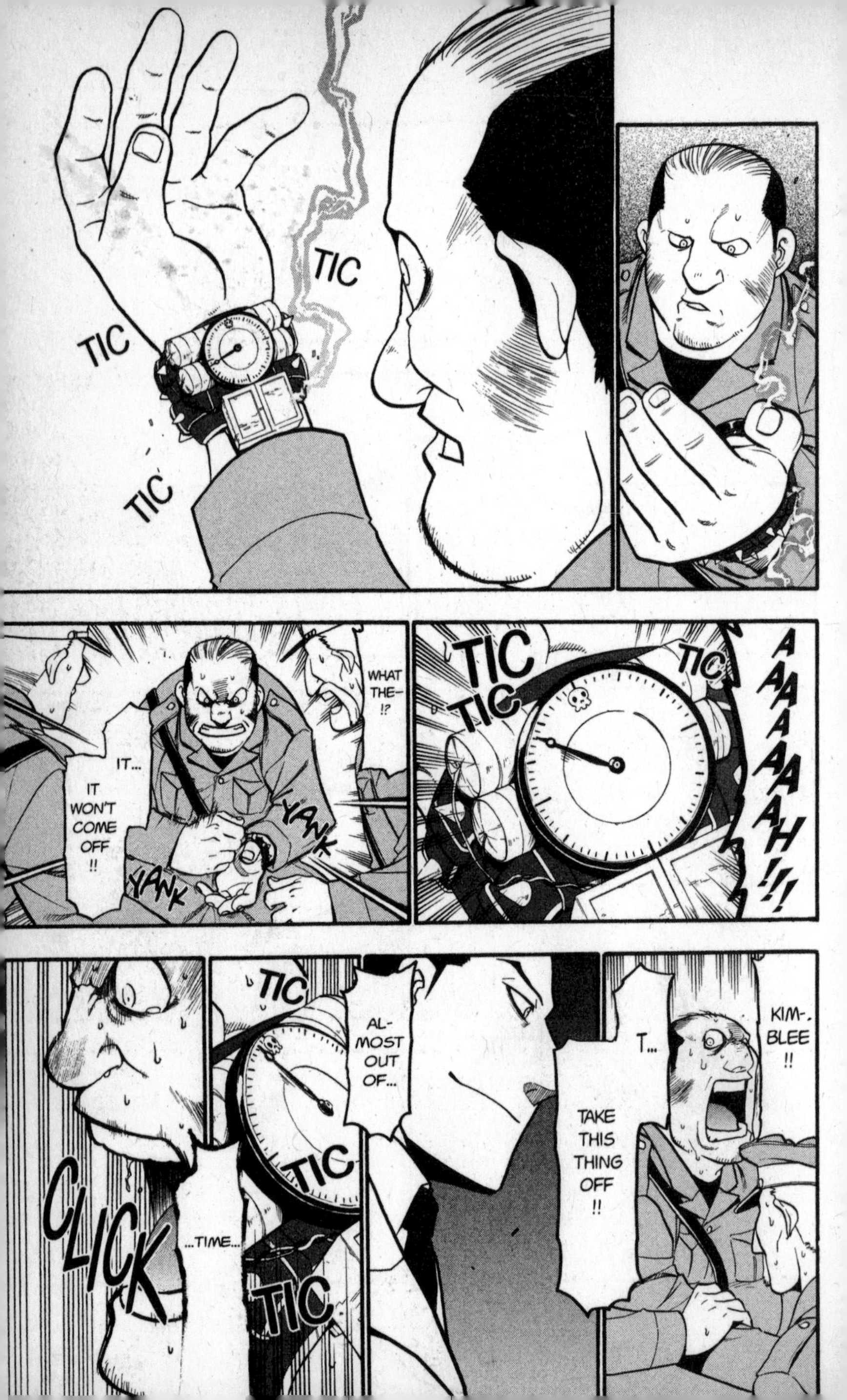
TIC
TIC
TIC
TIC
TIC
TIC
AAAAAAAH!!!
WHAT THE-!?
IT...
IT WON'T COME OFF!!
YANK
YANK
KIM-BLEE!!
T...
TAKE THIS THING OFF!!
TIC
ALMOST OUT OF...
TIC
TIC
...TIME...
CLICK

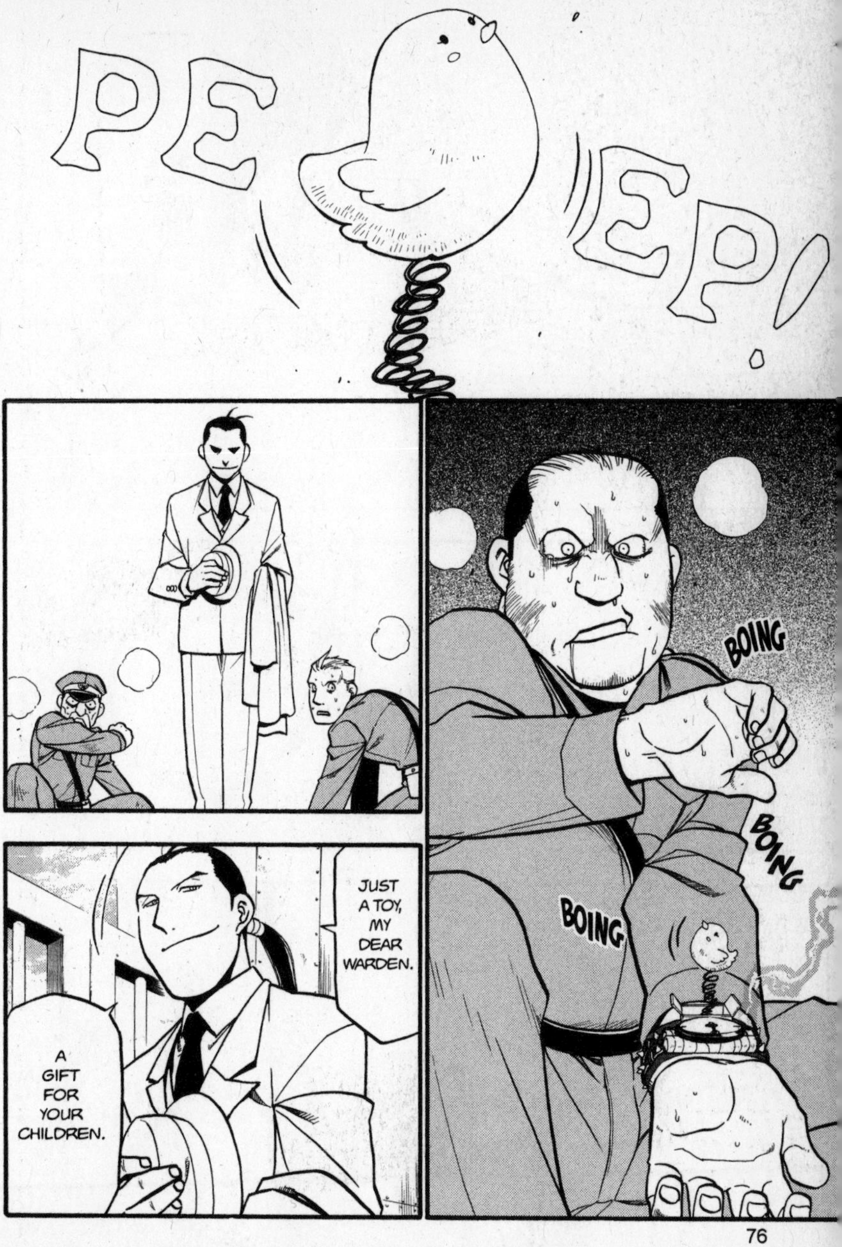
PEEP!
BOING
BOING
BOING
JUST A TOY, MY DEAR WARDEN.
A GIFT FOR YOUR CHILDREN.

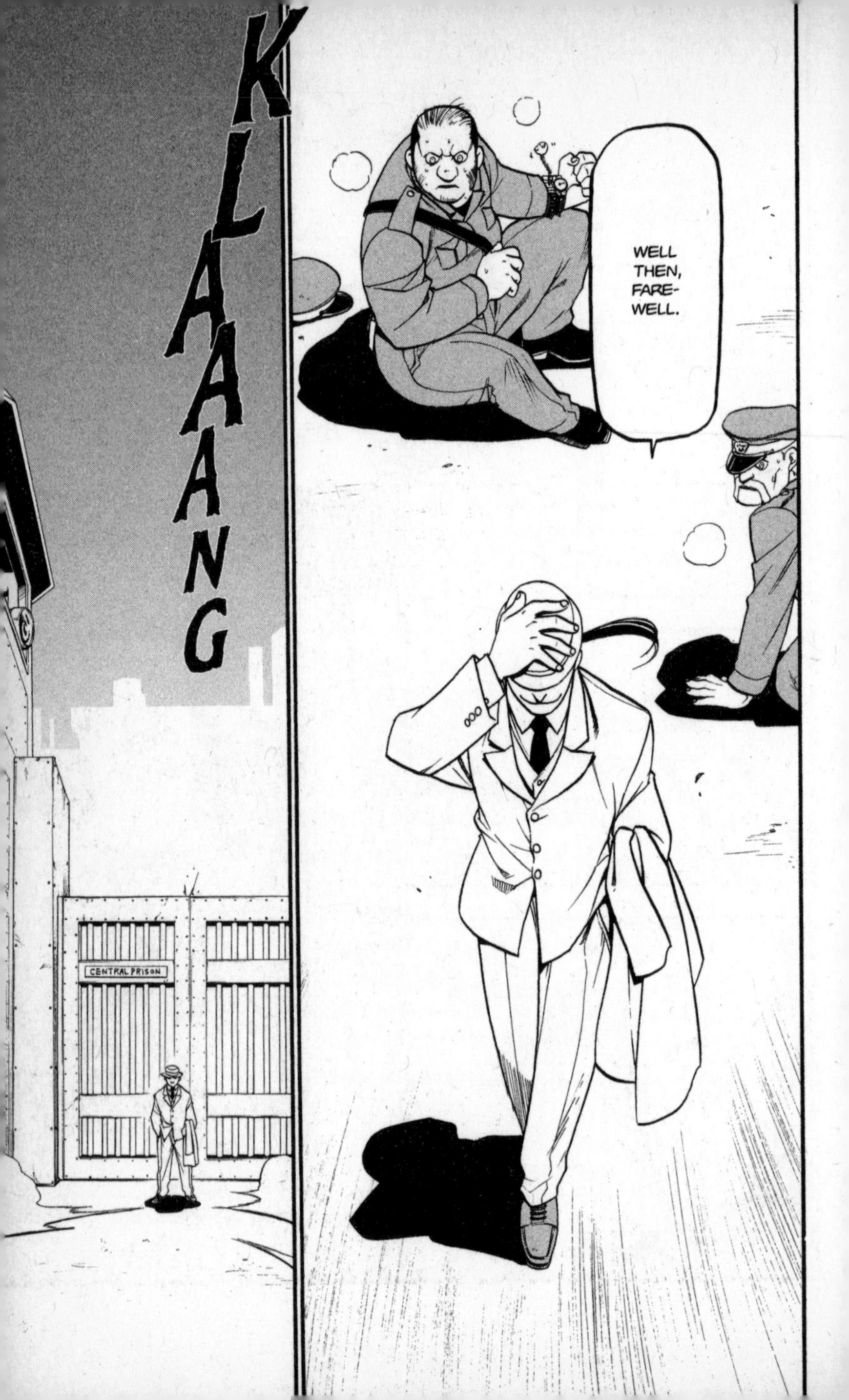
WELL THEN, FARE-WELL.
KLAAAANG
CENTRAL PRISON

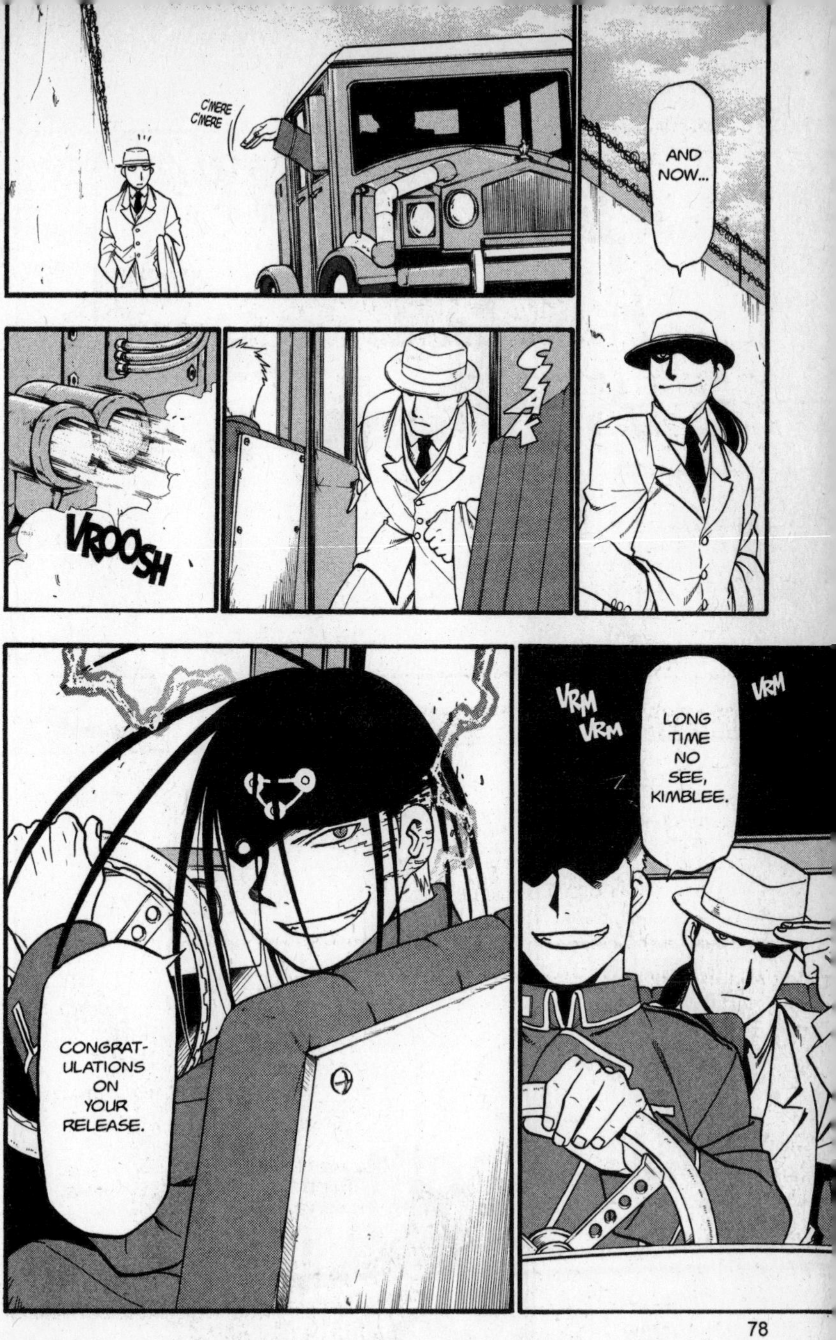
AND NOW...
C'MERE C'MERE
CLAK
VROOSH
VRM
VRM
VRM
LONG TIME NO SEE, KIMBLEE.
CONGRAT-ULATIONS ON YOUR RELEASE.

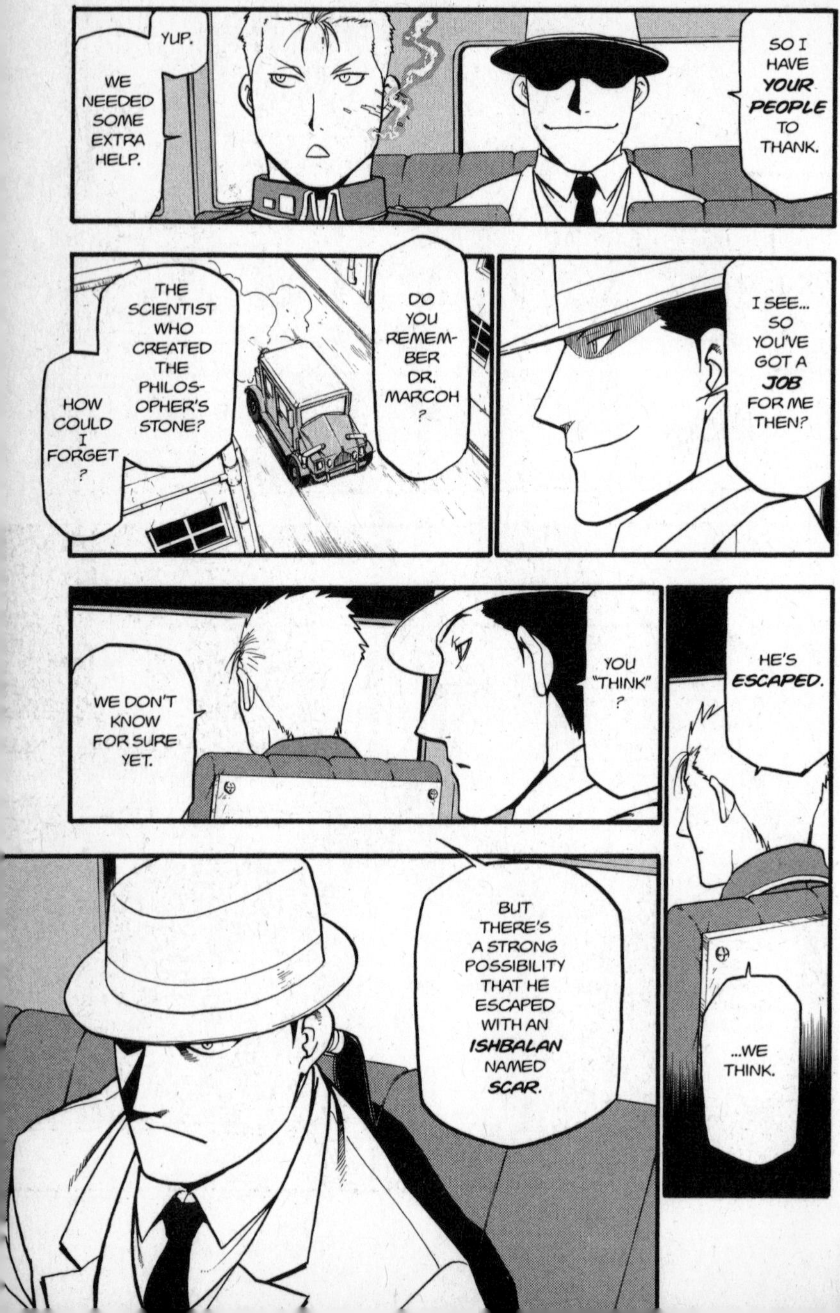
SO I HAVE YOUR PEOPLE TO THANK.
YUP.
WE NEEDED SOME EXTRA HELP.
I SEE... SO YOU'VE GOT A JOB FOR ME THEN?
DO YOU REMEMBER DR. MARCOH?
THE SCIENTIST WHO CREATED THE PHILOSOPHER'S STONE?
HOW COULD I FORGET?
HE'S ESCAPED.
...WE THINK.
YOU "THINK"?
WE DON'T KNOW FOR SURE YET.
BUT THERE'S A STRONG POSSIBILITY THAT HE ESCAPED WITH AN ISHBALAN NAMED SCAR.

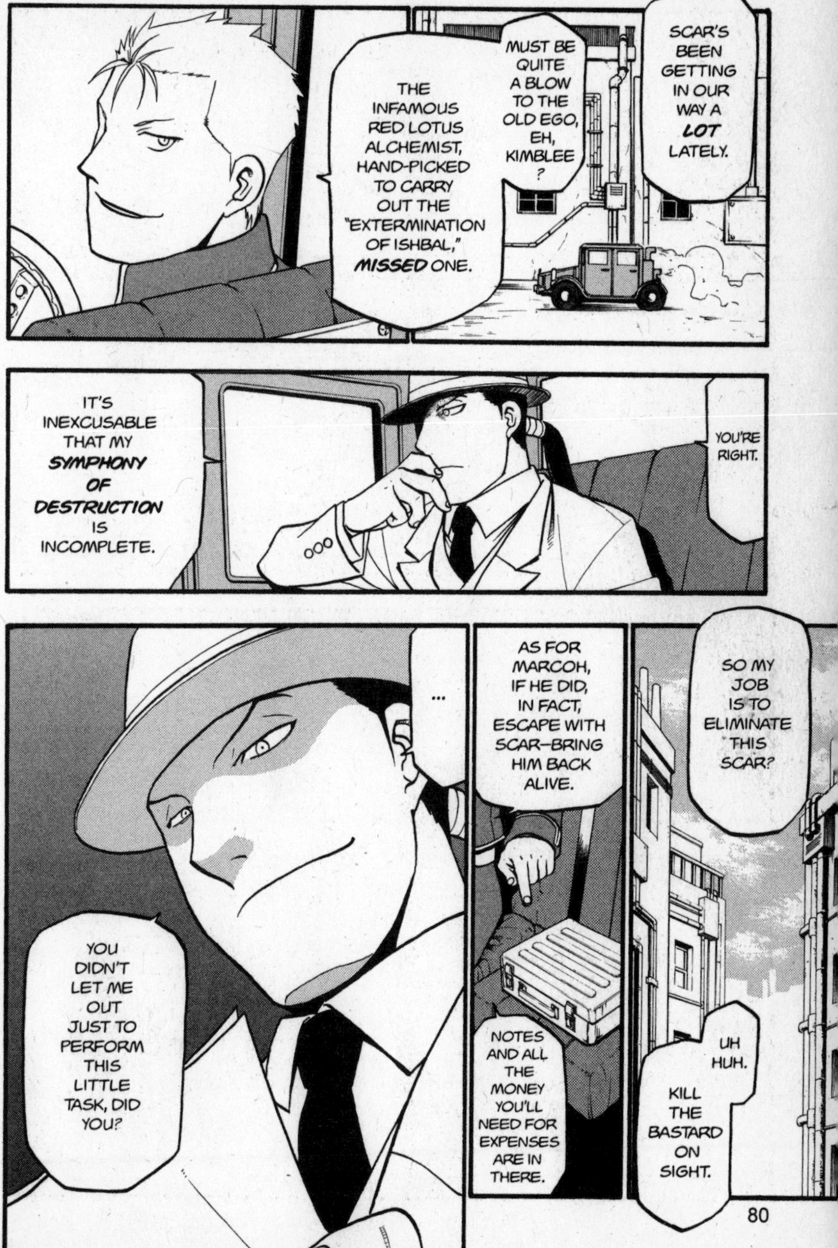
SCAR'S BEEN GETTING IN OUR WAY A **LOT** LATELY.
MUST BE QUITE A BLOW TO THE OLD EGO, EH, KIMBLEE?
THE INFAMOUS RED LOTUS ALCHEMIST, HAND-PICKED TO CARRY OUT THE "EXTERMINATION OF ISHBAL," **MISSED** ONE.
YOU'RE RIGHT.
IT'S INEXCUSABLE THAT MY ***SYMPHONY OF DESTRUCTION*** IS INCOMPLETE.
SO MY JOB IS TO ELIMINATE THIS SCAR?
UH HUH.
KILL THE BASTARD ON SIGHT.
AS FOR MARCOH, IF HE DID, IN FACT, ESCAPE WITH SCAR—BRING HIM BACK ALIVE.
NOTES AND ALL THE MONEY YOU'LL NEED FOR EXPENSES ARE IN THERE.
...
YOU DIDN'T LET ME OUT JUST TO PERFORM THIS LITTLE TASK, DID YOU?

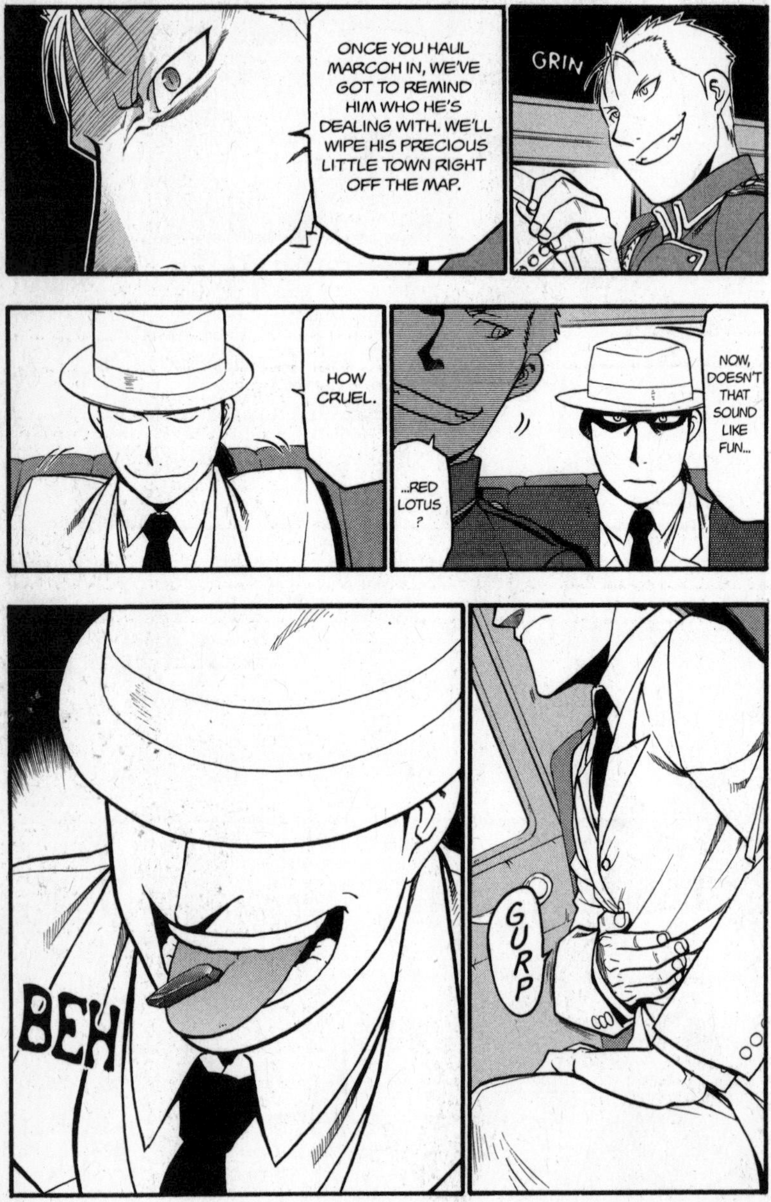
GRIN
ONCE YOU HAUL MARCOH IN, WE'VE GOT TO REMIND HIM WHO HE'S DEALING WITH. WE'LL WIPE HIS PRECIOUS LITTLE TOWN RIGHT OFF THE MAP.
NOW, DOESN'T THAT SOUND LIKE FUN...
...RED LOTUS?
HOW CRUEL.
GURP
BEH

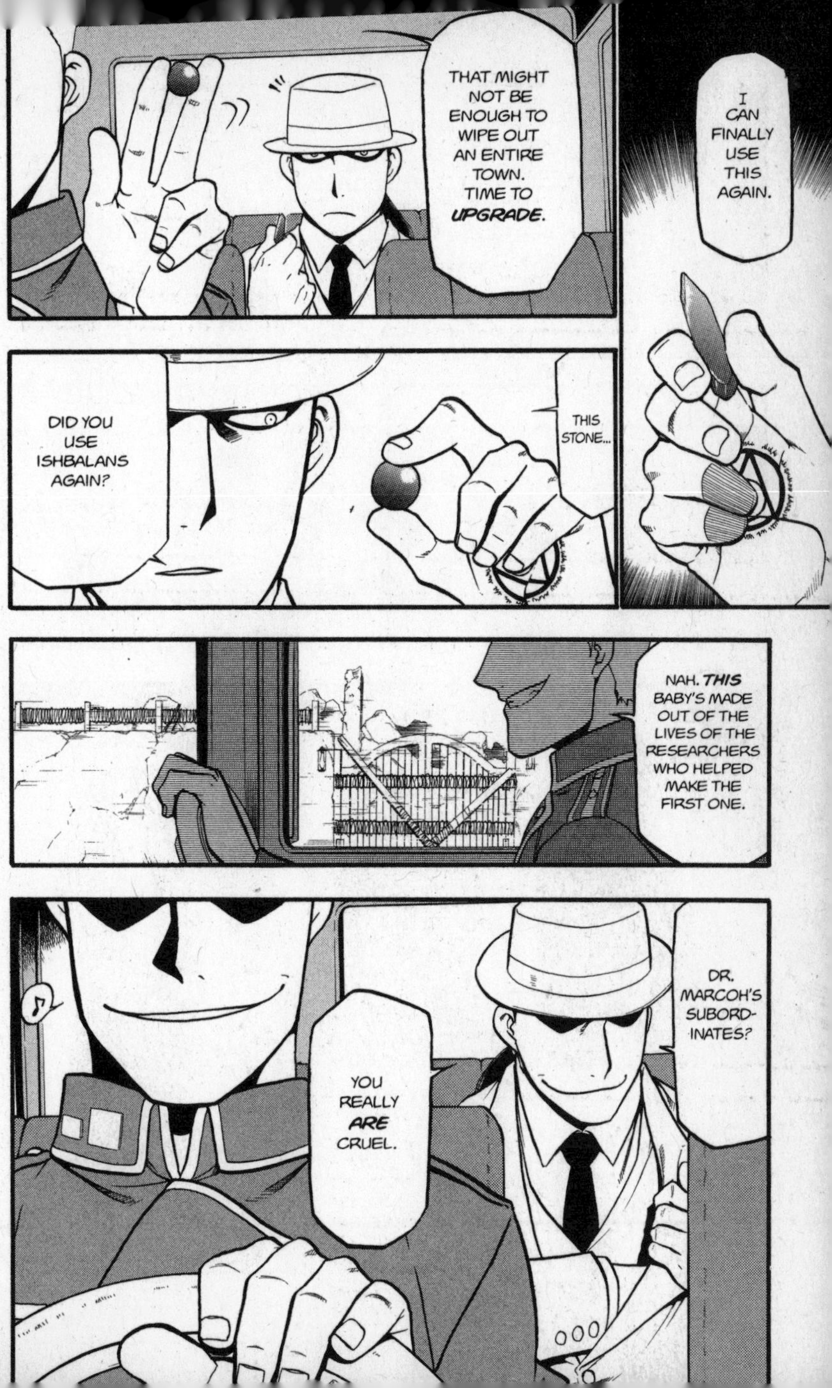
I CAN FINALLY USE THIS AGAIN.
THAT MIGHT NOT BE ENOUGH TO WIPE OUT AN ENTIRE TOWN. TIME TO **UPGRADE**.
THIS STONE...
DID YOU USE ISHBALANS AGAIN?
NAH. **THIS** BABY'S MADE OUT OF THE LIVES OF THE RESEARCHERS WHO HELPED MAKE THE FIRST ONE.
DR. MARCOH'S SUBORD-INATES?
YOU REALLY **ARE** CRUEL.

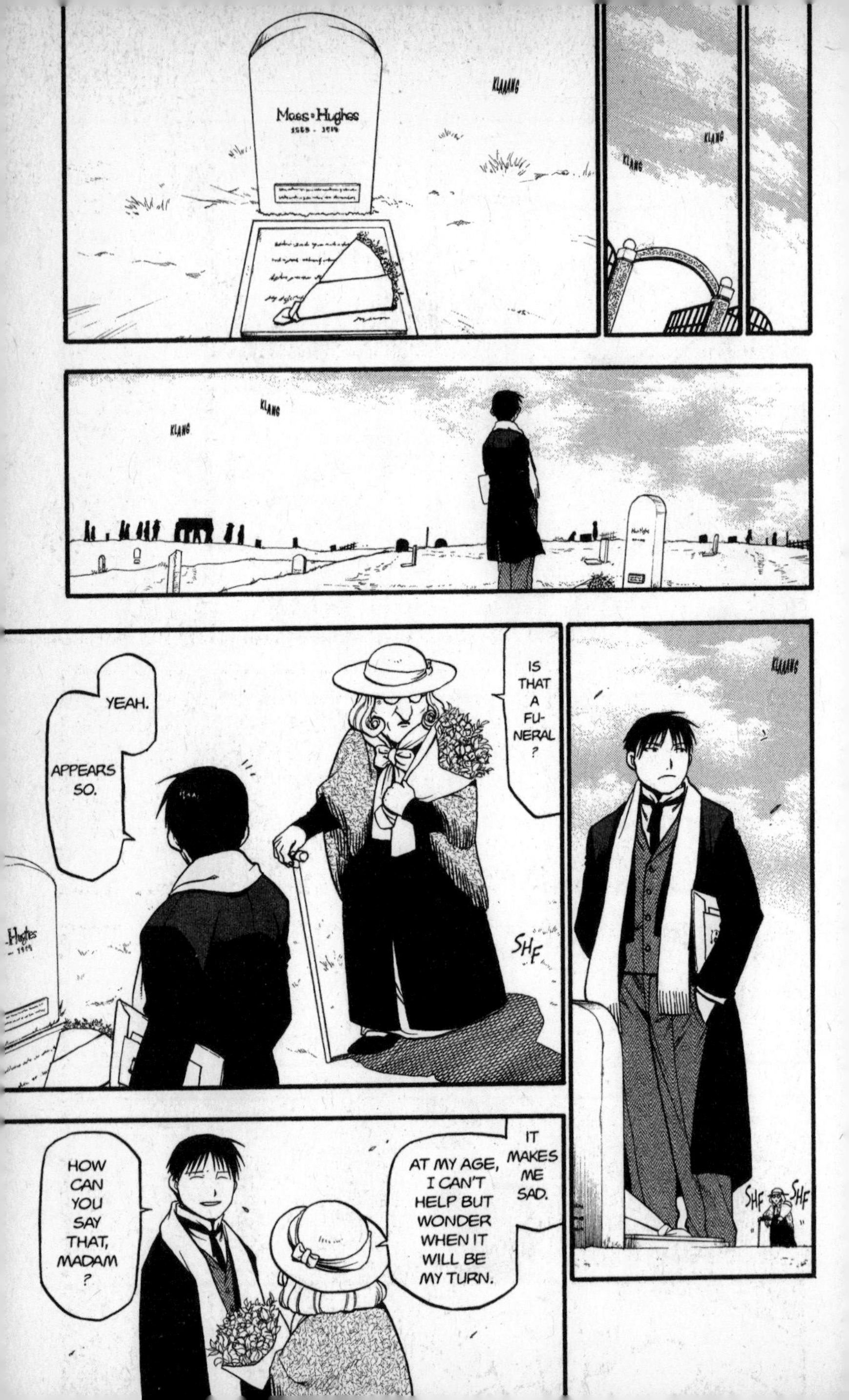
KLANG
KLANG
Maes Hughes
KLAAANG
KLANG
KLANG
KLAAANG
SHF
SHF
IS THAT A FU-NERAL?
SHF
YEAH.
APPEARS SO.
IT MAKES ME SAD.
AT MY AGE, I CAN'T HELP BUT WONDER WHEN IT WILL BE MY TURN.
HOW CAN YOU SAY THAT, MADAM?

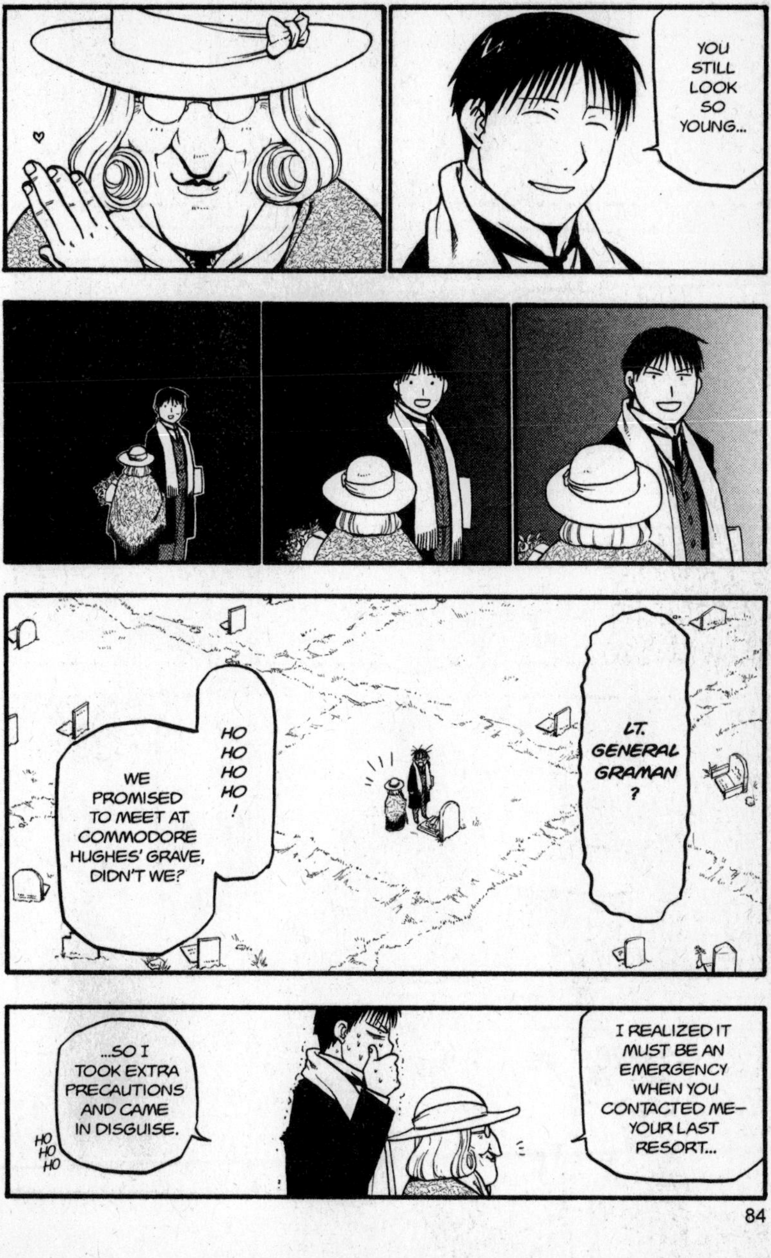
YOU STILL LOOK SO YOUNG...
LT. GENERAL GRAMAN?
HO HO HO HO!
WE PROMISED TO MEET AT COMMODORE HUGHES' GRAVE, DIDN'T WE?
I REALIZED IT MUST BE AN EMERGENCY WHEN YOU CONTACTED ME— YOUR LAST RESORT...
...SO I TOOK EXTRA PRECAUTIONS AND CAME IN DISGUISE.
HO HO HO

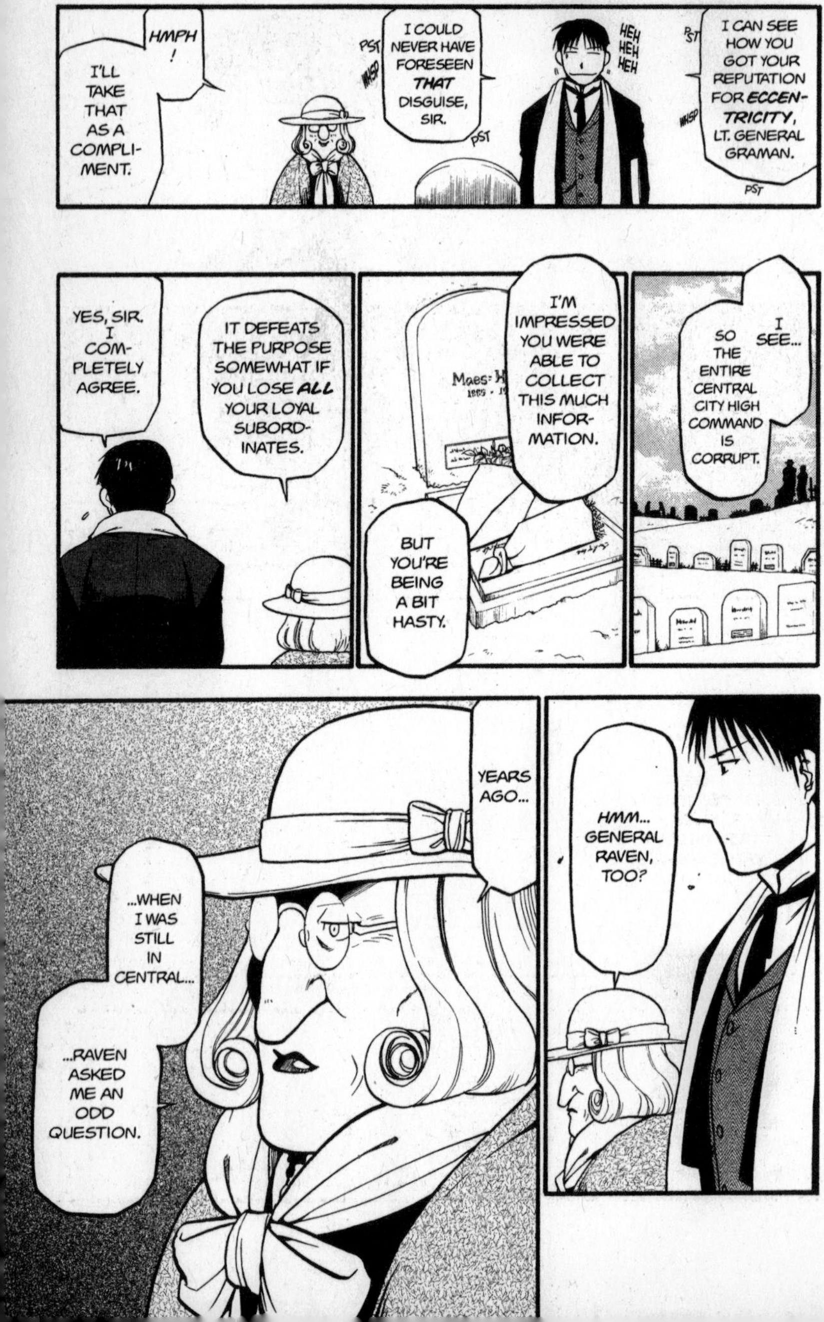
PST
I CAN SEE HOW YOU GOT YOUR REPUTATION FOR ECCENTRICITY, LT. GENERAL GRAMAN.
WHSP
PST
HEH HEH HEH
PST
I COULD NEVER HAVE FORESEEN THAT DISGUISE, SIR.
WHSP
PST
HMPH!
I'LL TAKE THAT AS A COMPLIMENT.
I SEE...
SO THE ENTIRE CENTRAL CITY HIGH COMMAND IS CORRUPT.
I'M IMPRESSED YOU WERE ABLE TO COLLECT THIS MUCH INFORMATION.
BUT YOU'RE BEING A BIT HASTY.
IT DEFEATS THE PURPOSE SOMEWHAT IF YOU LOSE ALL YOUR LOYAL SUBORDINATES.
YES, SIR. I COMPLETELY AGREE.
HMM... GENERAL RAVEN, TOO?
YEARS AGO...
...WHEN I WAS STILL IN CENTRAL...
...RAVEN ASKED ME AN ODD QUESTION.

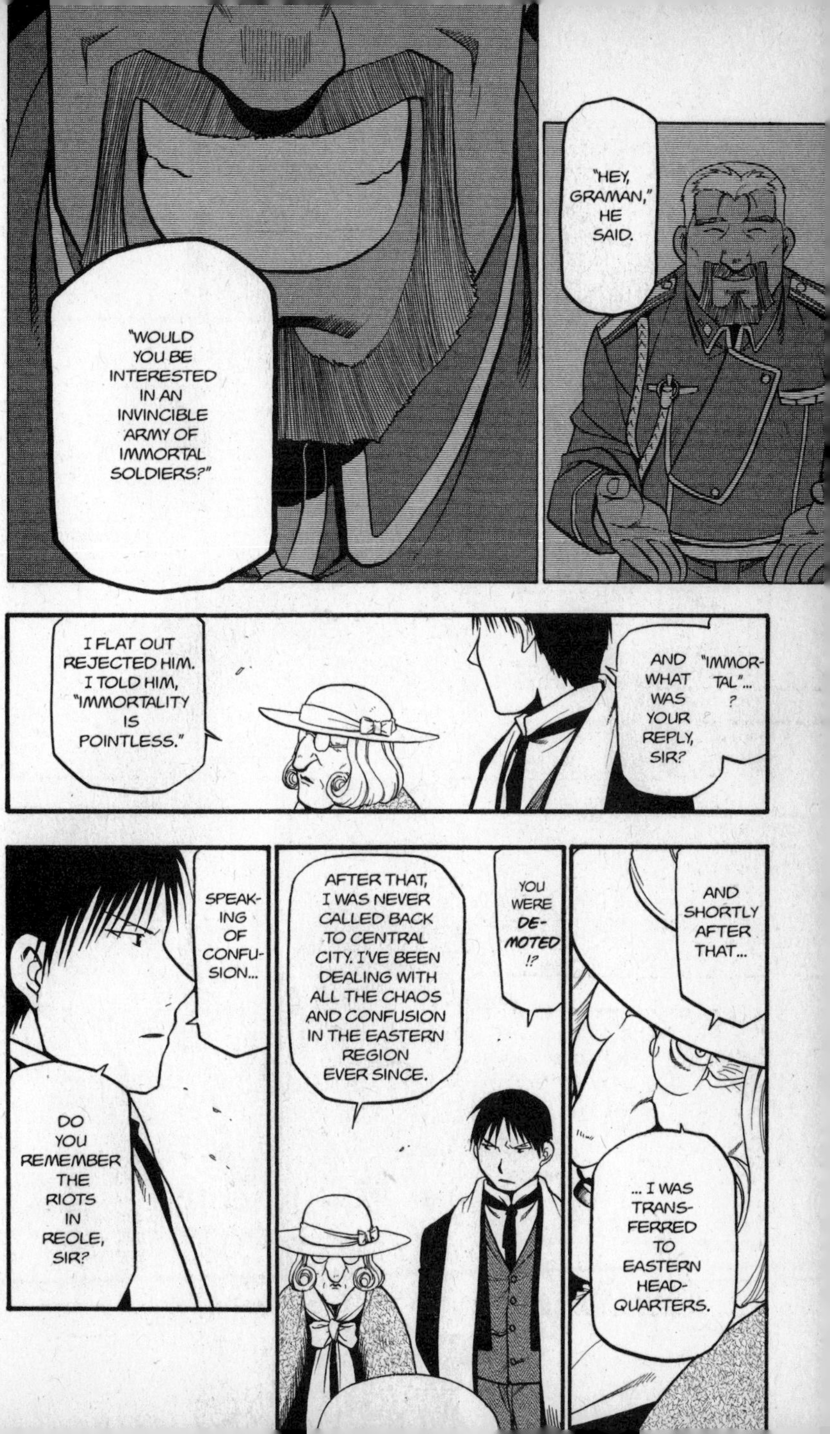
"HEY, GRAMAN," HE SAID.
"WOULD YOU BE INTERESTED IN AN INVINCIBLE ARMY OF IMMORTAL SOLDIERS?"
"IMMORTAL"... ?
AND WHAT WAS YOUR REPLY, SIR?
I FLAT OUT REJECTED HIM. I TOLD HIM, "IMMORTALITY IS POINTLESS."
AND SHORTLY AFTER THAT...
... I WAS TRANSFERRED TO EASTERN HEADQUARTERS.
YOU WERE DEMOTED!?
AFTER THAT, I WAS NEVER CALLED BACK TO CENTRAL CITY. I'VE BEEN DEALING WITH ALL THE CHAOS AND CONFUSION IN THE EASTERN REGION EVER SINCE.
SPEAKING OF CONFUSION...
DO YOU REMEMBER THE RIOTS IN REOLE, SIR?

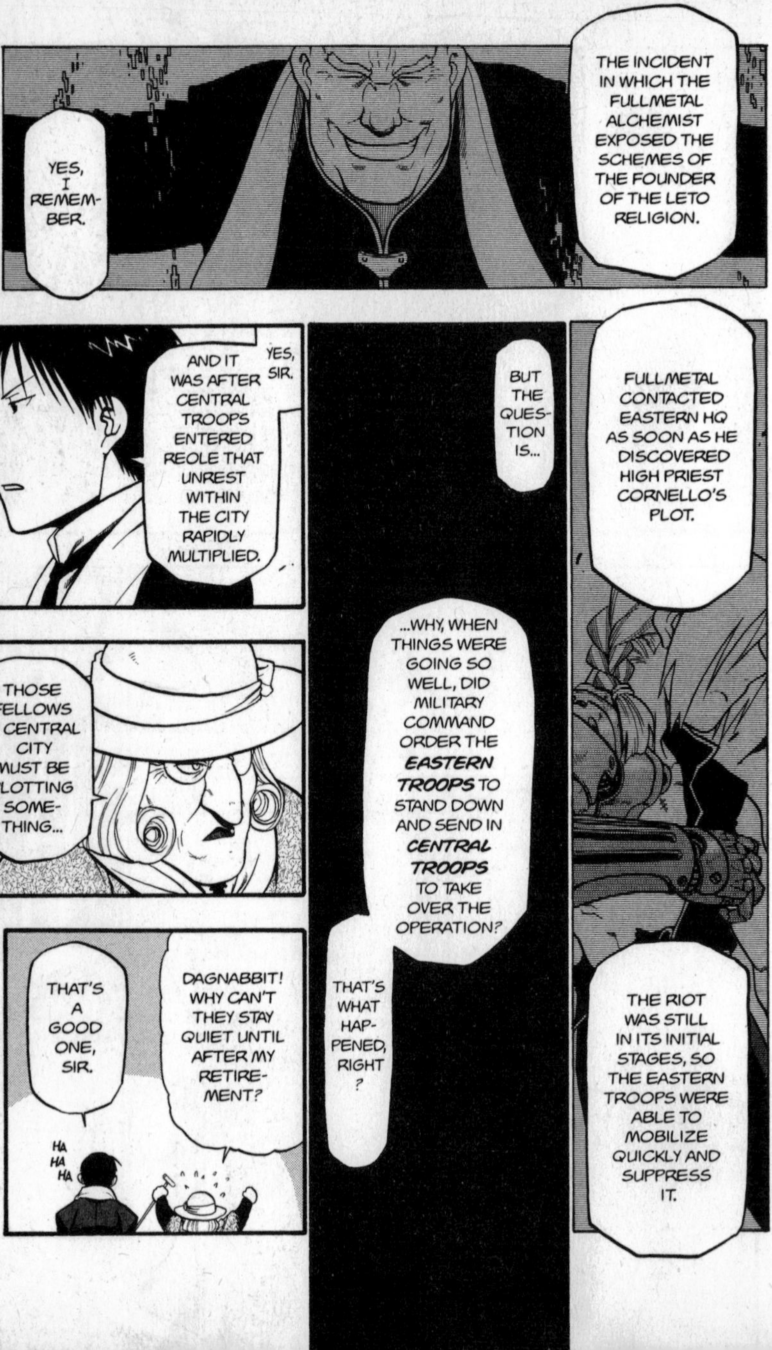
THE INCIDENT IN WHICH THE FULLMETAL ALCHEMIST EXPOSED THE SCHEMES OF THE FOUNDER OF THE LETO RELIGION.
YES, I REMEMBER.
FULLMETAL CONTACTED EASTERN HQ AS SOON AS HE DISCOVERED HIGH PRIEST CORNELLO'S PLOT.
THE RIOT WAS STILL IN ITS INITIAL STAGES, SO THE EASTERN TROOPS WERE ABLE TO MOBILIZE QUICKLY AND SUPPRESS IT.
BUT THE QUESTION IS...
...WHY, WHEN THINGS WERE GOING SO WELL, DID MILITARY COMMAND ORDER THE EASTERN TROOPS TO STAND DOWN AND SEND IN CENTRAL TROOPS TO TAKE OVER THE OPERATION?
THAT'S WHAT HAPPENED, RIGHT?
YES, SIR.
AND IT WAS AFTER CENTRAL TROOPS ENTERED REOLE THAT UNREST WITHIN THE CITY RAPIDLY MULTIPLIED.
THOSE FELLOWS IN CENTRAL CITY MUST BE PLOTTING SOMETHING...
DAGNABBIT! WHY CAN'T THEY STAY QUIET UNTIL AFTER MY RETIREMENT?
THAT'S A GOOD ONE, SIR.
HA HA HA

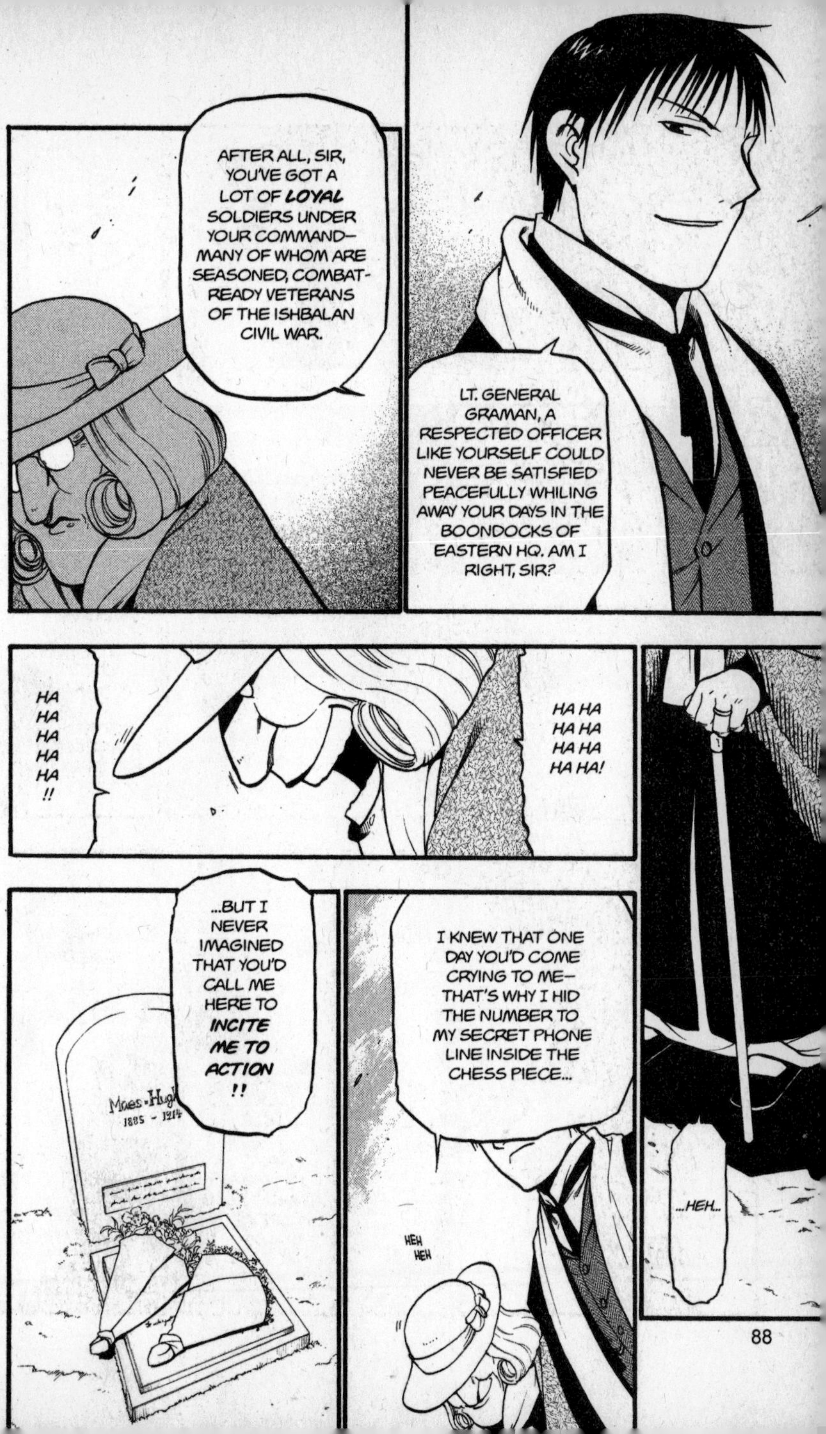
LT. GENERAL GRAMAN, A RESPECTED OFFICER LIKE YOURSELF COULD NEVER BE SATISFIED PEACEFULLY WHILING AWAY YOUR DAYS IN THE BOONDOCKS OF EASTERN HQ. AM I RIGHT, SIR?
AFTER ALL, SIR, YOU'VE GOT A LOT OF LOYAL SOLDIERS UNDER YOUR COMMAND— MANY OF WHOM ARE SEASONED, COMBAT-READY VETERANS OF THE ISHBALAN CIVIL WAR.
...HEH...
HA HA HA HA HA HA HA HA!
HA HA HA HA HA !!
I KNEW THAT ONE DAY YOU'D COME CRYING TO ME— THAT'S WHY I HID THE NUMBER TO MY SECRET PHONE LINE INSIDE THE CHESS PIECE...
HEH HEH
...BUT I NEVER IMAGINED THAT YOU'D CALL ME HERE TO INCITE ME TO ACTION !!

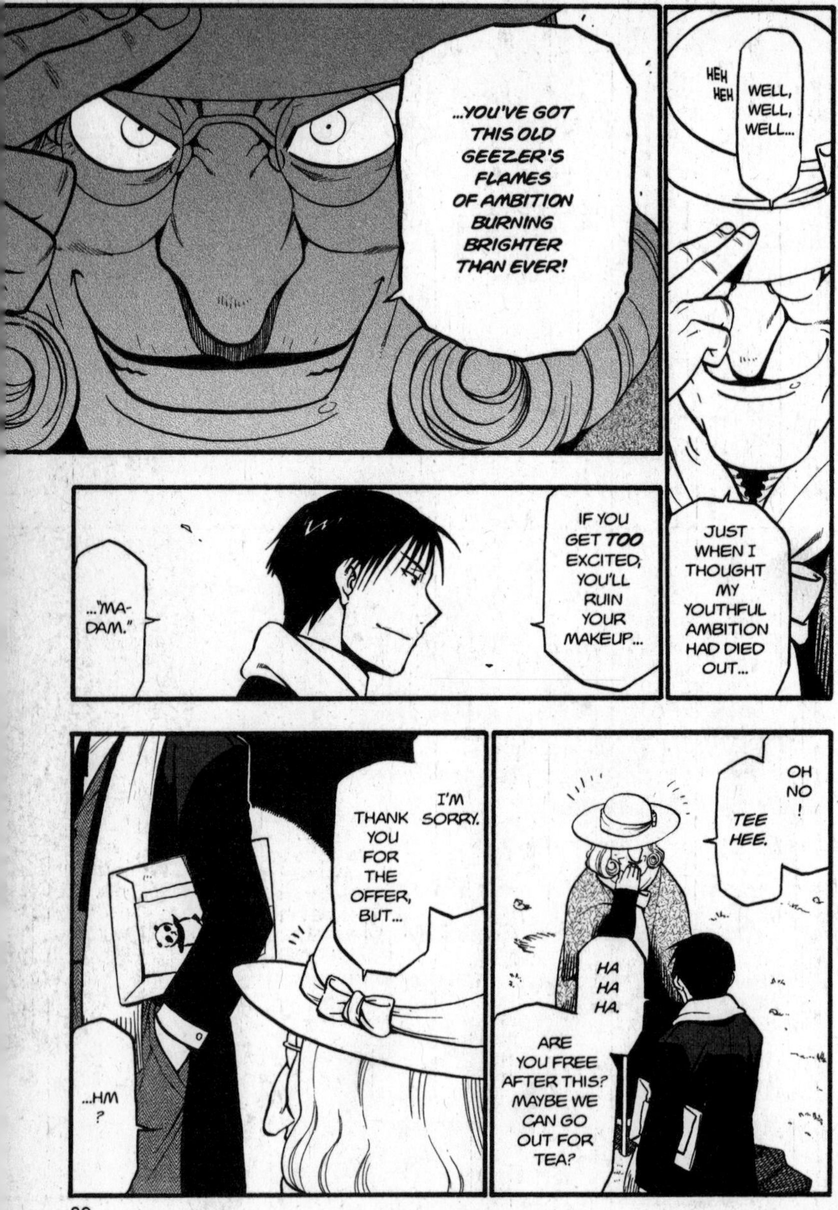
HEH HEH
WELL, WELL, WELL...
JUST WHEN I THOUGHT MY YOUTHFUL AMBITION HAD DIED OUT...
...YOU'VE GOT THIS OLD GEEZER'S FLAMES OF AMBITION BURNING BRIGHTER THAN EVER!
IF YOU GET TOO EXCITED, YOU'LL RUIN YOUR MAKEUP...
..."MADAM."
OH NO!
TEE HEE.
HA HA HA.
ARE YOU FREE AFTER THIS? MAYBE WE CAN GO OUT FOR TEA?
I'M SORRY.
THANK YOU FOR THE OFFER, BUT...
...HM?

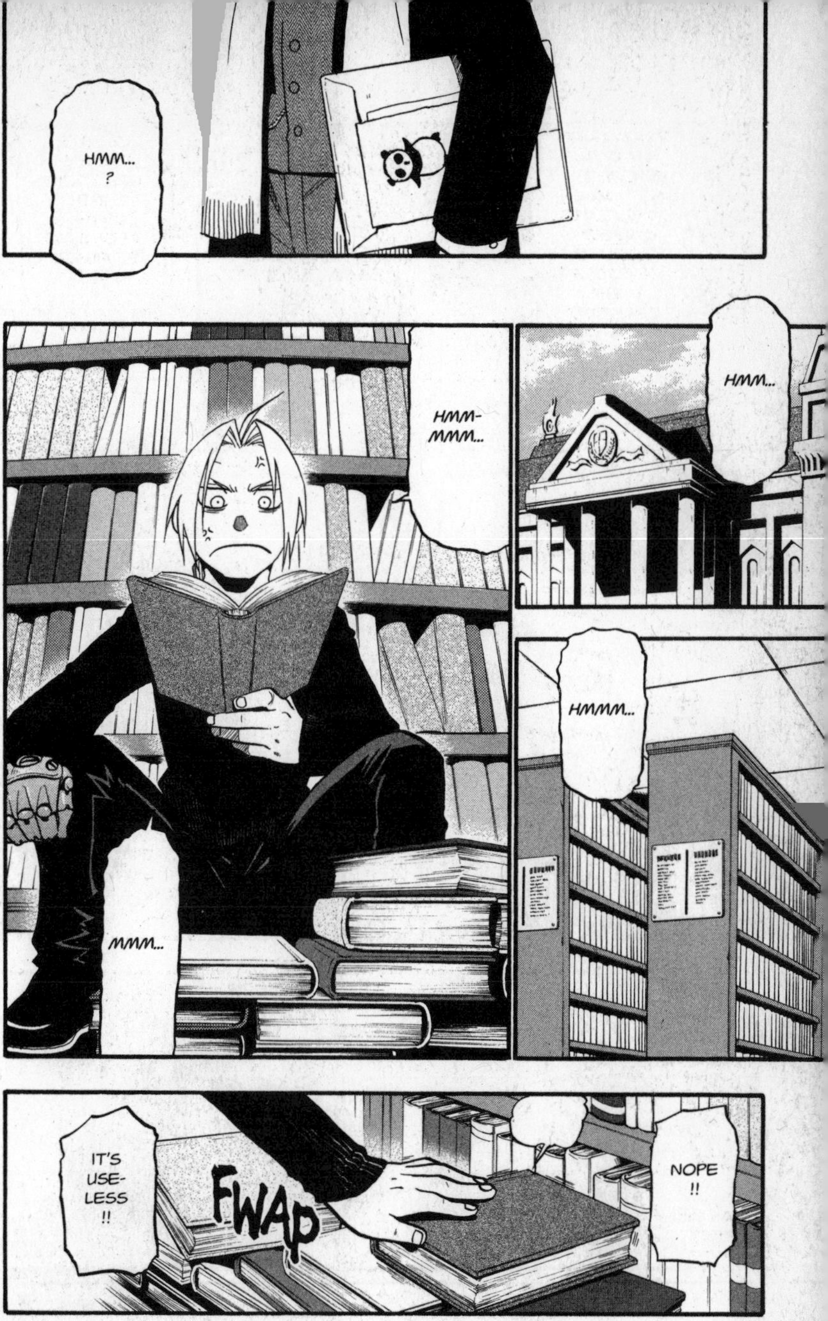
HMM... ?
HMM...
HMMM...
HMM-MMM...
MMM...
NOPE!!
FWAP
IT'S USE-LESS!!

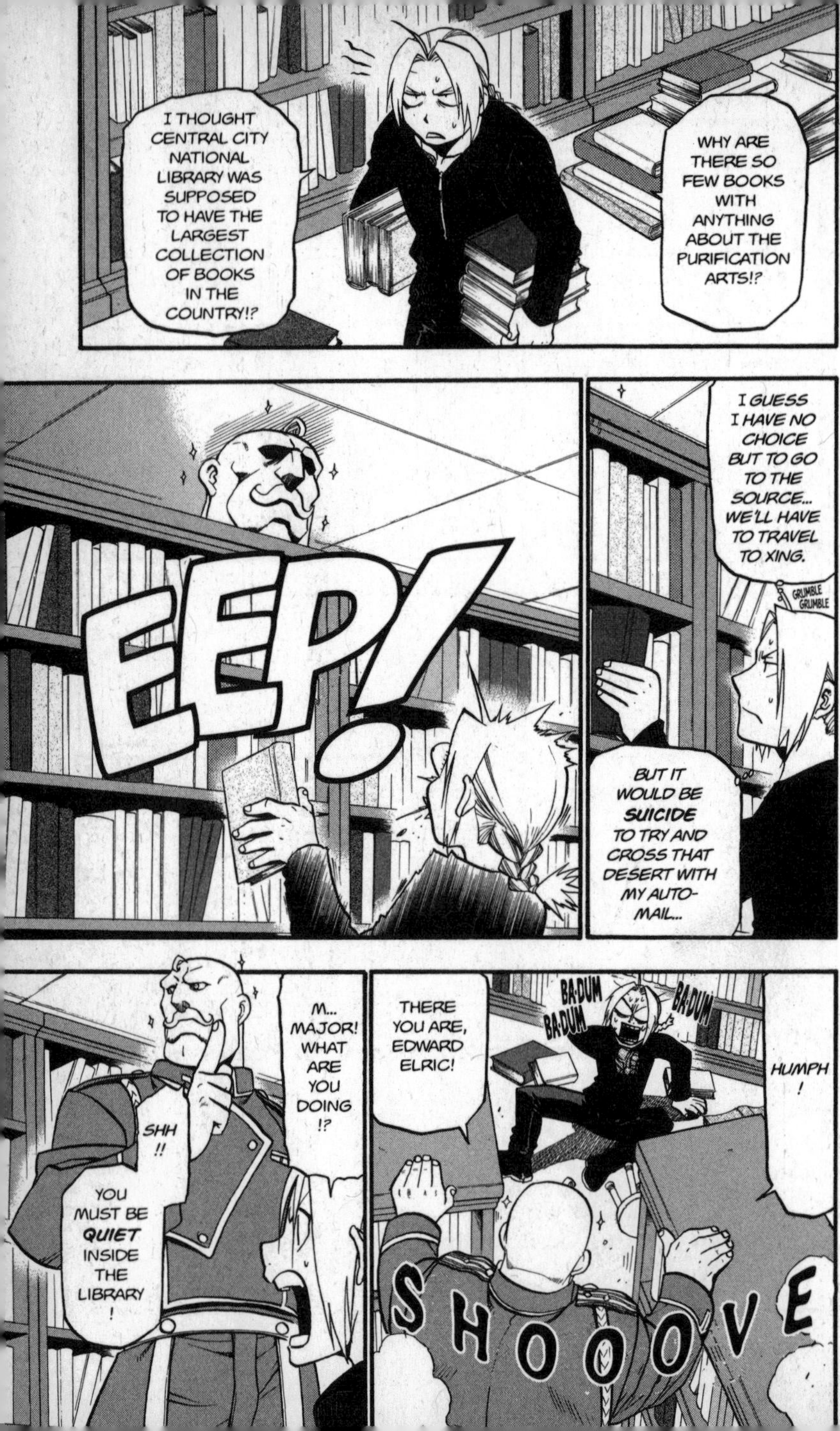
WHY ARE THERE SO FEW BOOKS WITH ANYTHING ABOUT THE PURIFICATION ARTS!?
I THOUGHT CENTRAL CITY NATIONAL LIBRARY WAS SUPPOSED TO HAVE THE LARGEST COLLECTION OF BOOKS IN THE COUNTRY!?
I GUESS I HAVE NO CHOICE BUT TO GO TO THE SOURCE... WE'LL HAVE TO TRAVEL TO XING.
GRUMBLE GRUMBLE
BUT IT WOULD BE SUICIDE TO TRY AND CROSS THAT DESERT WITH MY AUTO-MAIL...
EEP!
HUMPH!
BA-DUM
BA-DUM
BA-DUM
THERE YOU ARE, EDWARD ELRIC!
SHOOOVE
M... MAJOR! WHAT ARE YOU DOING!?
SHH!!
YOU MUST BE QUIET INSIDE THE LIBRARY!

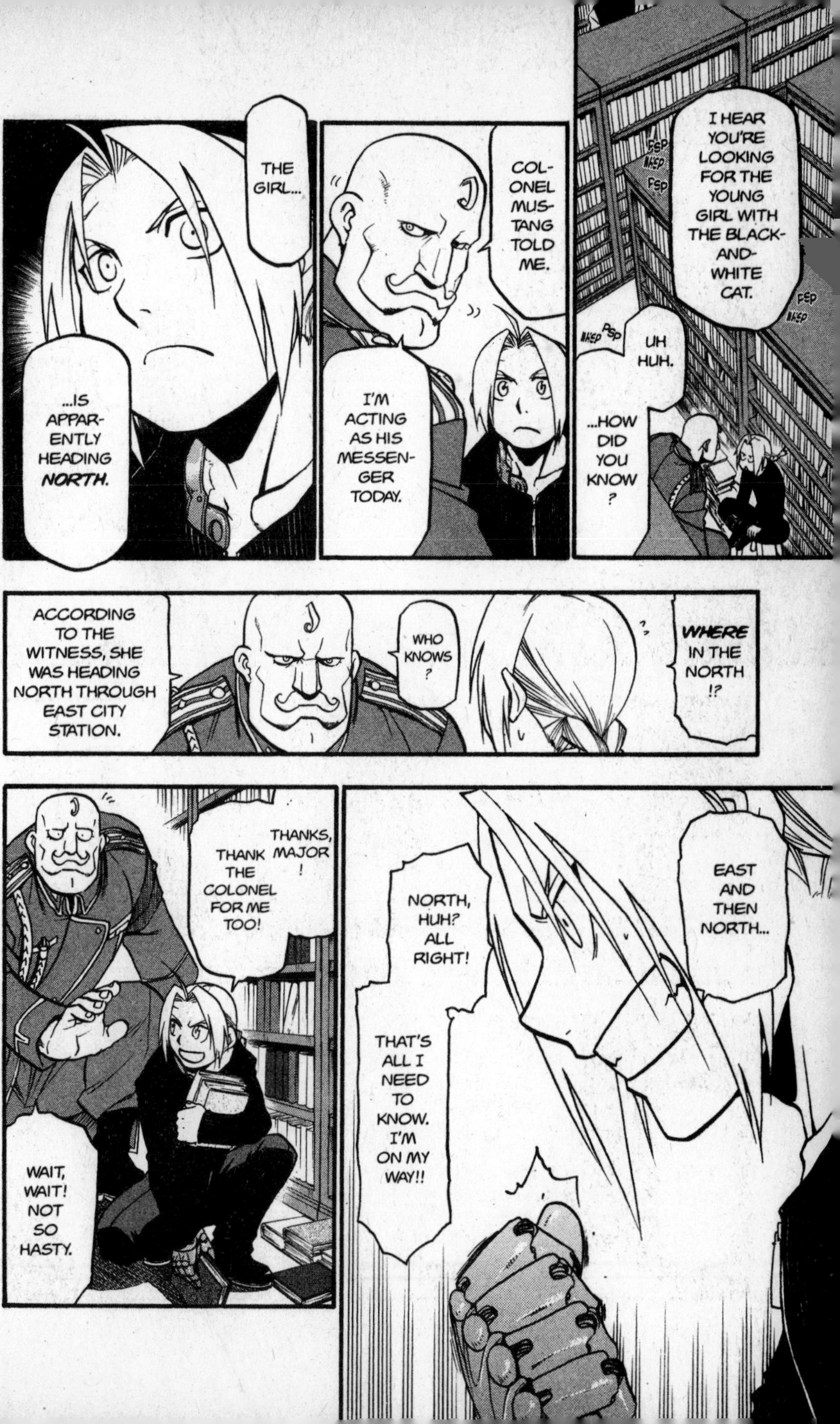
I HEAR YOU'RE LOOKING FOR THE YOUNG GIRL WITH THE BLACK-AND-WHITE CAT.
PSP WHSP PSP
PSP WHSP
WHSP PSP
UH HUH.
...HOW DID YOU KNOW?
COLONEL MUSTANG TOLD ME.
I'M ACTING AS HIS MESSENGER TODAY.
THE GIRL...
...IS APPARENTLY HEADING NORTH.
WHERE IN THE NORTH!?
WHO KNOWS?
ACCORDING TO THE WITNESS, SHE WAS HEADING NORTH THROUGH EAST CITY STATION.
EAST AND THEN NORTH...
NORTH, HUH? ALL RIGHT!
THAT'S ALL I NEED TO KNOW. I'M ON MY WAY!!
THANKS, MAJOR!
THANK THE COLONEL FOR ME TOO!
WAIT, WAIT! NOT SO HASTY.

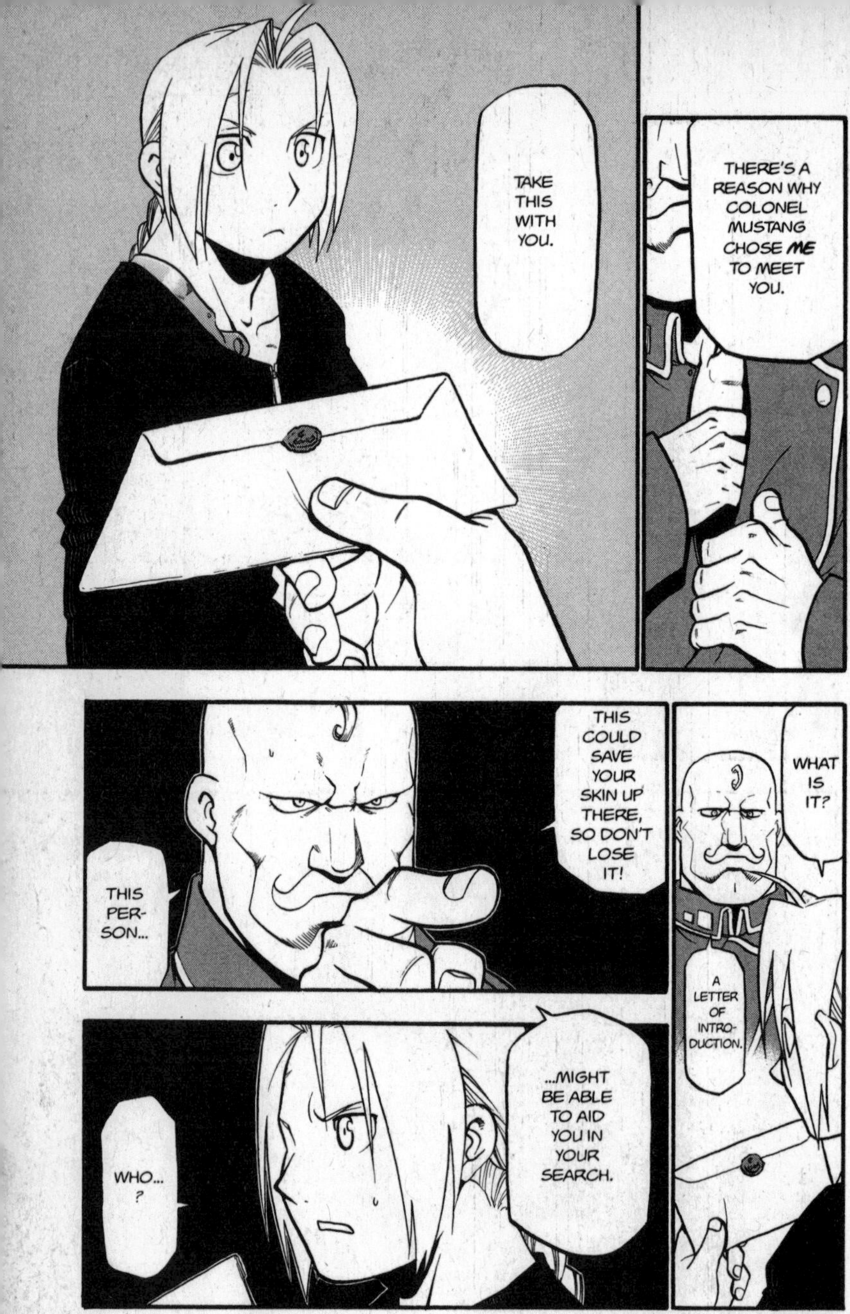
THERE'S A REASON WHY COLONEL MUSTANG CHOSE *ME* TO MEET YOU.
TAKE THIS WITH YOU.
WHAT IS IT?
A LETTER OF INTRODUCTION.
THIS COULD SAVE YOUR SKIN UP THERE, SO DON'T LOSE IT!
THIS PERSON...
...MIGHT BE ABLE TO AID YOU IN YOUR SEARCH.
WHO... ?

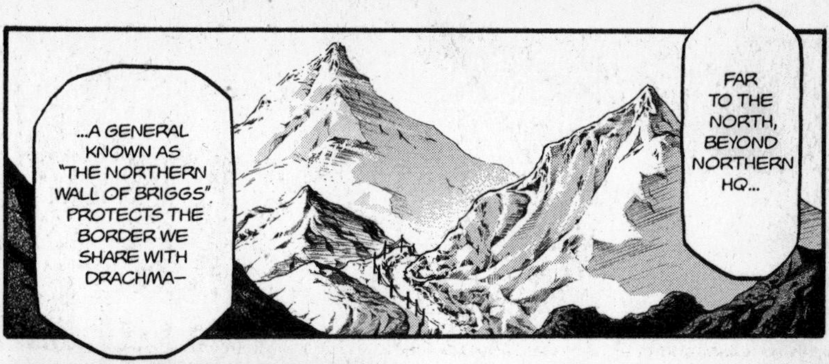
FAR TO THE NORTH, BEYOND NORTHERN HQ...
...A GENERAL KNOWN AS "THE NORTHERN WALL OF BRIGGS" PROTECTS THE BORDER WE SHARE WITH DRACHMA—
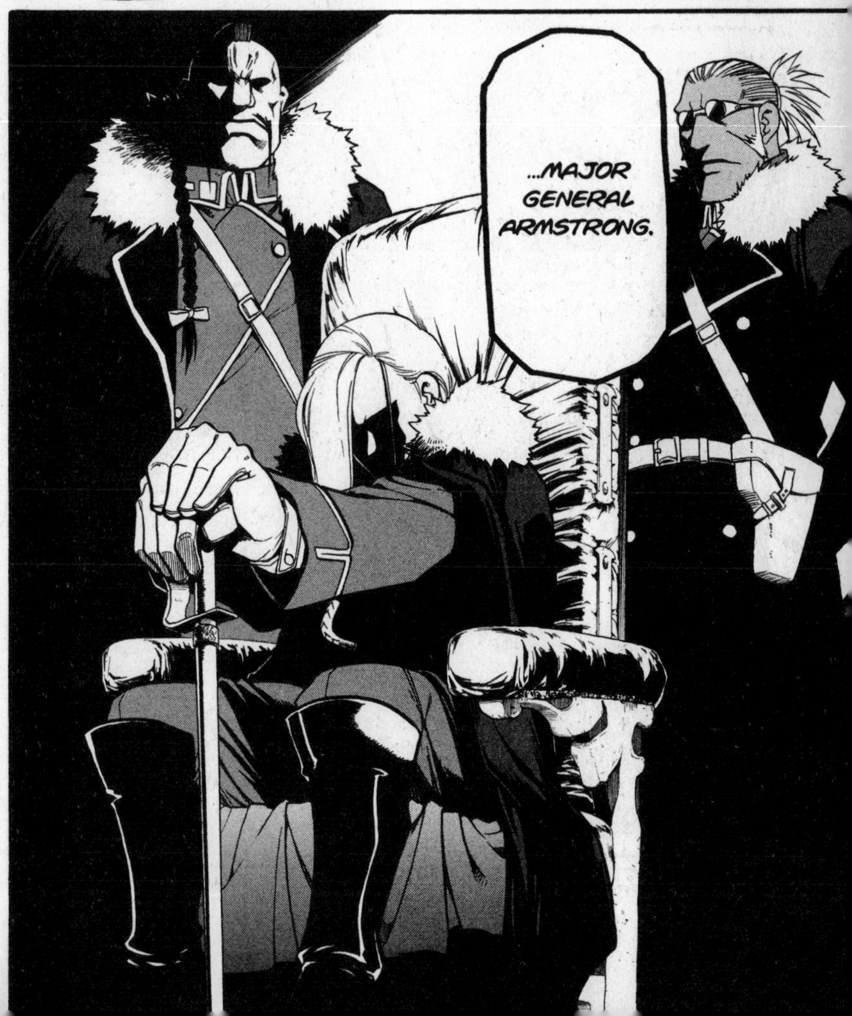
...MAJOR GENERAL ARMSTRONG.

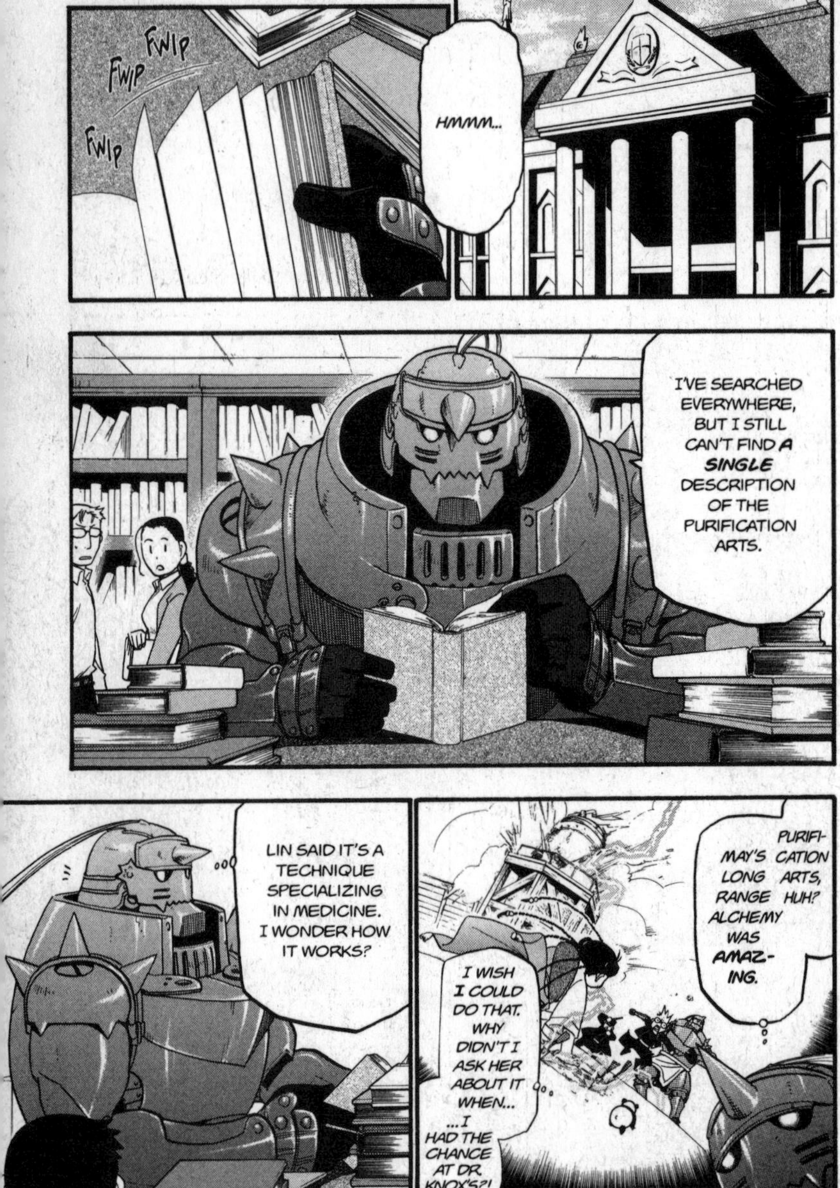
HMMM...
FWIP
FWIP
FWIP
I'VE SEARCHED EVERYWHERE, BUT I STILL CAN'T FIND **A SINGLE** DESCRIPTION OF THE PURIFICATION ARTS.
PURIFICATION ARTS, HUH?
MAY'S LONG RANGE ALCHEMY WAS **AMAZING.**
I WISH **I COULD** DO THAT. WHY DIDN'T I ASK HER ABOUT IT WHEN...
...I HAD THE CHANCE AT DR. KNOX'S?!
LIN SAID IT'S A TECHNIQUE SPECIALIZING IN MEDICINE. I WONDER HOW IT WORKS?

Chapter 64
The Northern Wall of Briggs

UM, EXCUSE ME, MR. ARMOR GUY? AREN'T YOU THE FULLMETAL ALCHEMIST'S BROTHER?!

THAT'S SO COOL! WOW!! I CAN'T BELIEVE IT!!

INFORMATION

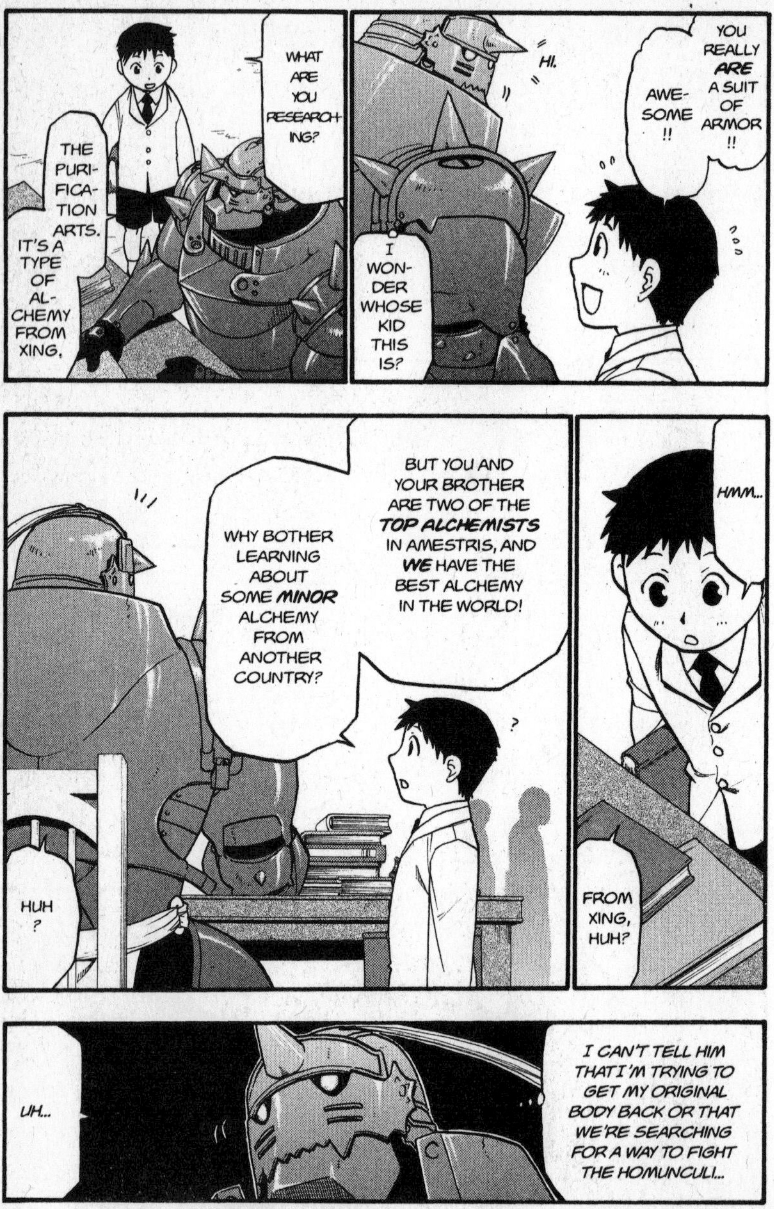
YOU REALLY ARE A SUIT OF ARMOR!!
AWESOME!!
HI.
I WONDER WHOSE KID THIS IS?
WHAT ARE YOU RESEARCHING?
THE PURIFICATION ARTS.
IT'S A TYPE OF ALCHEMY FROM XING.
HMM...
FROM XING, HUH?
BUT YOU AND YOUR BROTHER ARE TWO OF THE TOP ALCHEMISTS IN AMESTRIS, AND WE HAVE THE BEST ALCHEMY IN THE WORLD!
WHY BOTHER LEARNING ABOUT SOME MINOR ALCHEMY FROM ANOTHER COUNTRY?
HUH?
I CAN'T TELL HIM THAT I'M TRYING TO GET MY ORIGINAL BODY BACK OR THAT WE'RE SEARCHING FOR A WAY TO FIGHT THE HOMUNCULI...
UH...

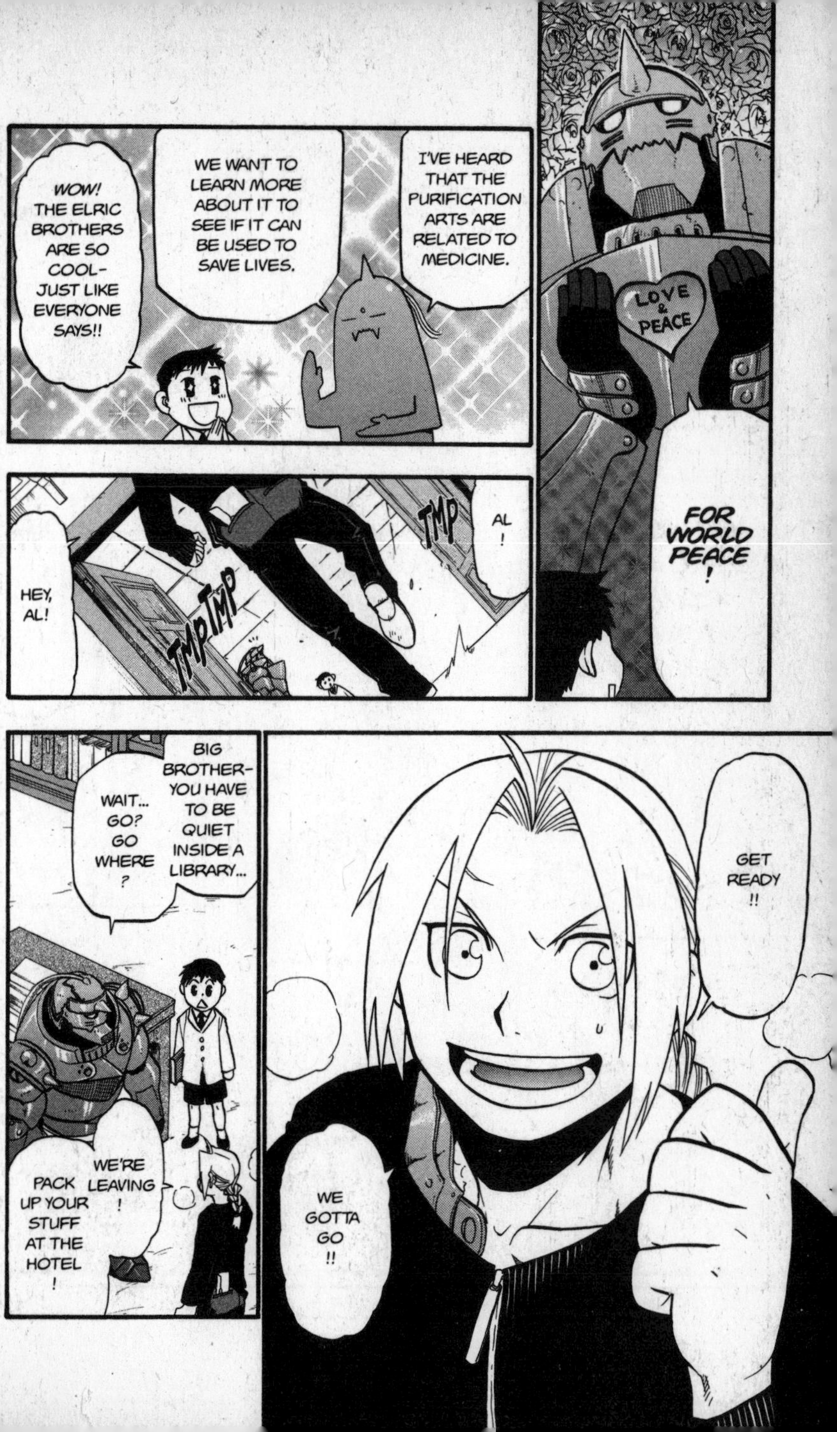
LOVE & PEACE
FOR WORLD PEACE!
I'VE HEARD THAT THE PURIFICATION ARTS ARE RELATED TO MEDICINE.
WE WANT TO LEARN MORE ABOUT IT TO SEE IF IT CAN BE USED TO SAVE LIVES.
WOW! THE ELRIC BROTHERS ARE SO COOL- JUST LIKE EVERYONE SAYS!!
AL!
TMP
TMP TMP
HEY, AL!
GET READY!!
WE GOTTA GO!!
BIG BROTHER- YOU HAVE TO BE QUIET INSIDE A LIBRARY...
WAIT... GO? GO WHERE?
WE'RE LEAVING!
PACK UP YOUR STUFF AT THE HOTEL!

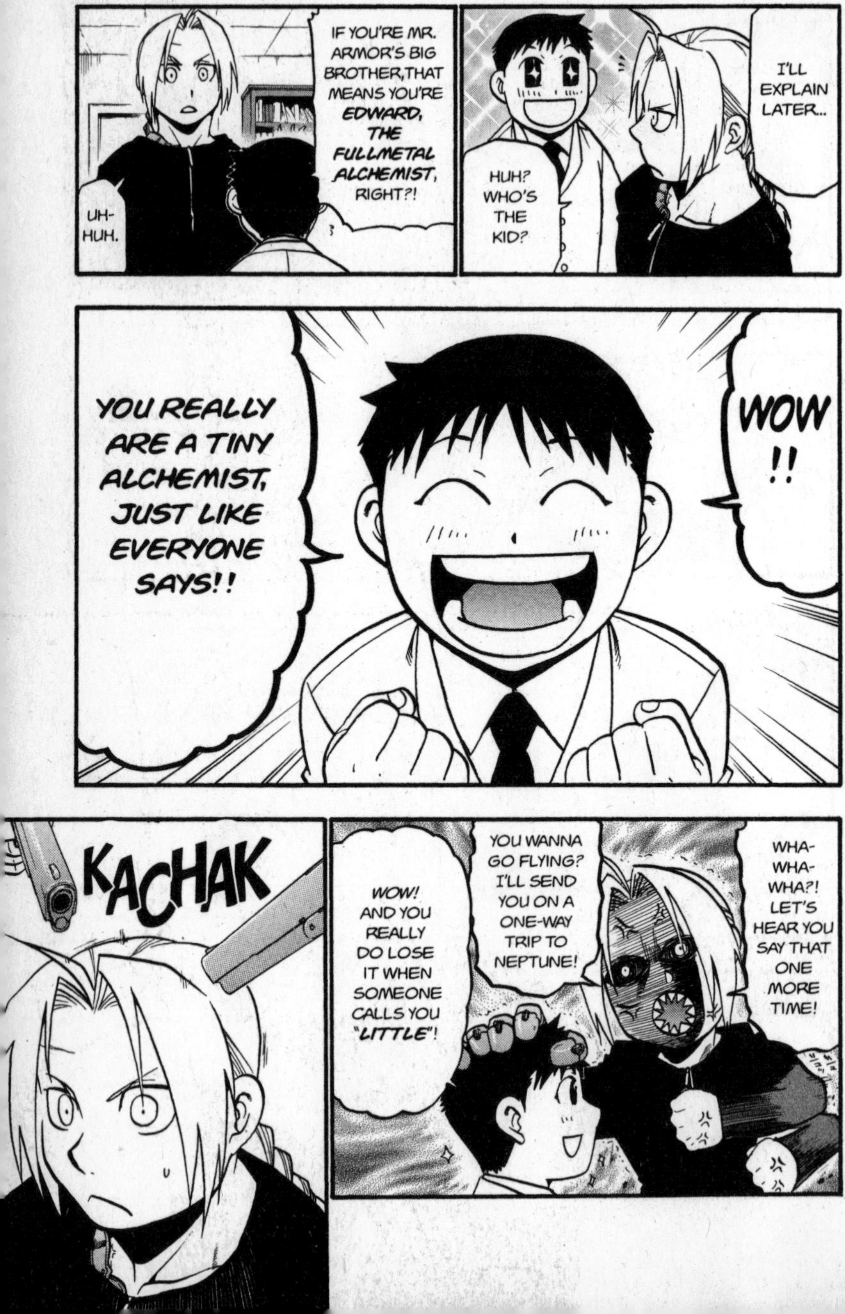
I'LL EXPLAIN LATER...
HUH? WHO'S THE KID?
IF YOU'RE MR. ARMOR'S BIG BROTHER, THAT MEANS YOU'RE ***EDWARD, THE FULLMETAL ALCHEMIST***, RIGHT?!
UH-HUH.
WOW !!
YOU REALLY ARE A TINY ALCHEMIST, JUST LIKE EVERYONE SAYS!!
WHA-WHA-WHA?! LET'S HEAR YOU SAY THAT ONE MORE TIME!
YOU WANNA GO FLYING? I'LL SEND YOU ON A ONE-WAY TRIP TO NEPTUNE!
WOW! AND YOU REALLY DO LOSE IT WHEN SOMEONE CALLS YOU "***LITTLE***"!
KACHAK

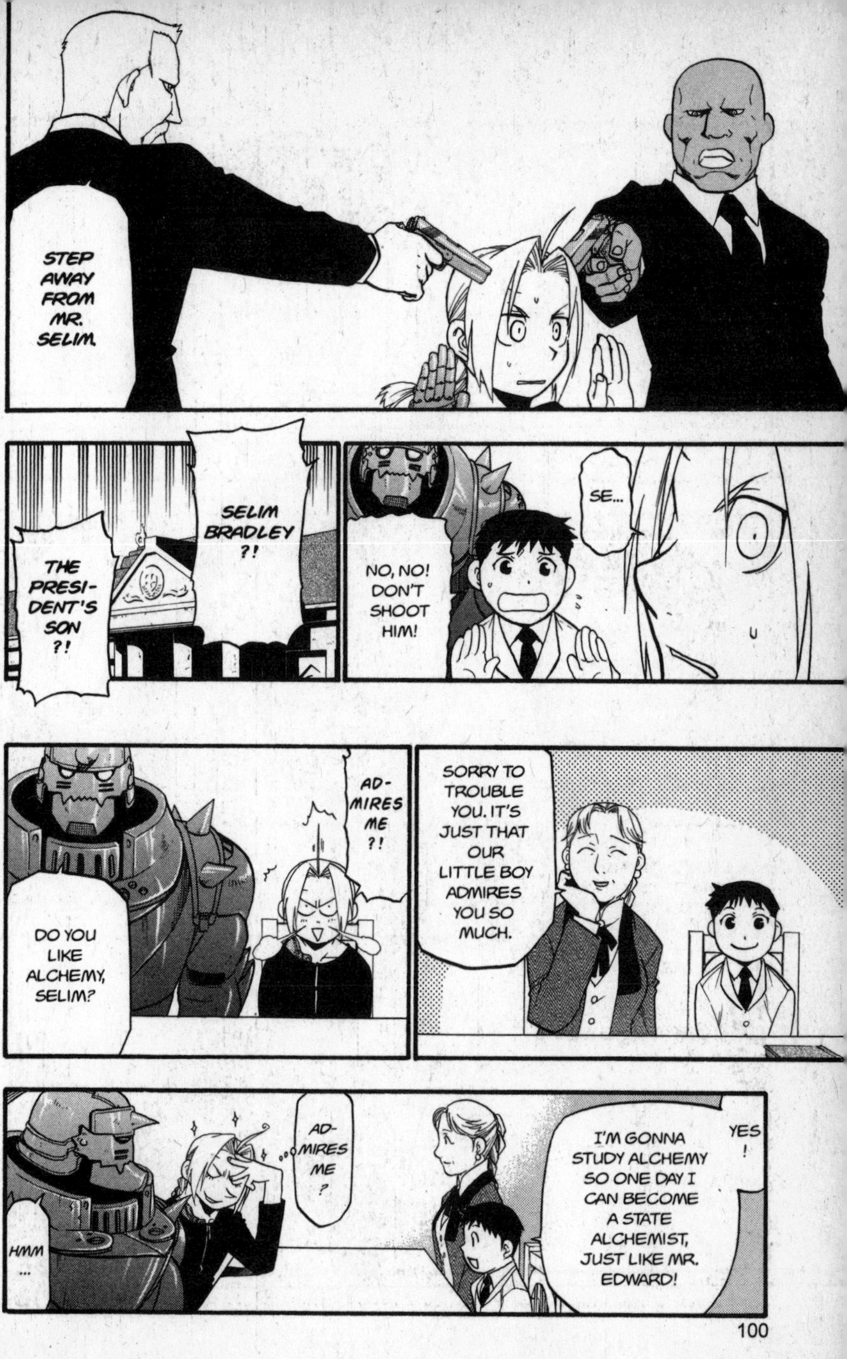
STEP AWAY FROM MR. SELIM.
SE...
NO, NO! DON'T SHOOT HIM!
SELIM BRADLEY?!
THE PRESI-DENT'S SON?!
SORRY TO TROUBLE YOU. IT'S JUST THAT OUR LITTLE BOY ADMIRES YOU SO MUCH.
AD-MIRES ME?!
DO YOU LIKE ALCHEMY, SELIM?
YES!
I'M GONNA STUDY ALCHEMY SO ONE DAY I CAN BECOME A STATE ALCHEMIST, JUST LIKE MR. EDWARD!
AD-MIRES ME?
HMM...

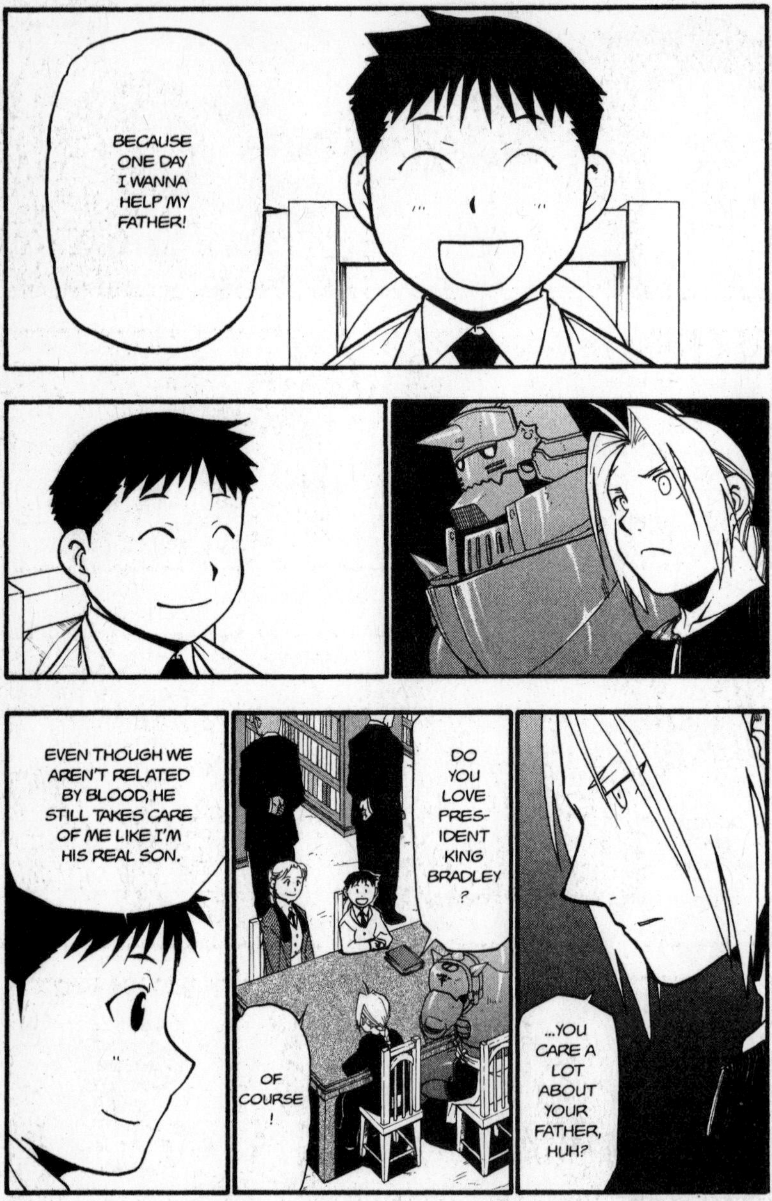
BECAUSE ONE DAY I WANNA HELP MY FATHER!
...YOU CARE A LOT ABOUT YOUR FATHER, HUH?
DO YOU LOVE PRES-IDENT KING BRADLEY?
OF COURSE!
EVEN THOUGH WE AREN'T RELATED BY BLOOD, HE STILL TAKES CARE OF ME LIKE I'M HIS REAL SON.

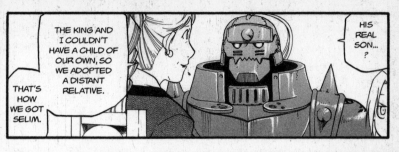

HIS REAL SON...?
THE KING AND I COULDN'T HAVE A CHILD OF OUR OWN, SO WE ADOPTED A DISTANT RELATIVE.
THAT'S HOW WE GOT SELIM.
HE'S GROWN UP TO BE SUCH A GENTLE AND CARING BOY.
MY HUSBAND AND I TREASURE HIM.
HOW HAS THE PRESIDENT BEEN LATELY?
ANY CHANGES IN HIS HEALTH? HE HASN'T FELT...SICK AT ALL, HAS HE?
NOT AT ALL.
HE'S AS ACTIVE AS EVER. I DON'T THINK HE PLANS ON RETIRING ANYTIME SOON.
SOMETIMES I WISH HE WOULD SLOW DOWN, THOUGH. HE'S NOT AS YOUNG AS HE USED TO BE.
MY HUSBAND HAS ALWAYS LIVED FOR HIS WORK.
HE CERTAINLY KNOWS HOW TO WORK HARD... UNFORTUNATELY, HE DOESN'T KNOW A THING ABOUT WOMEN.

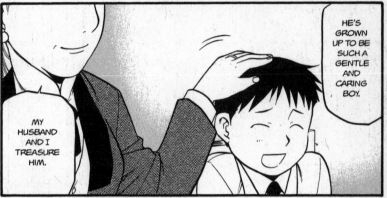

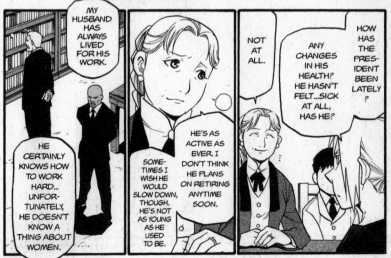

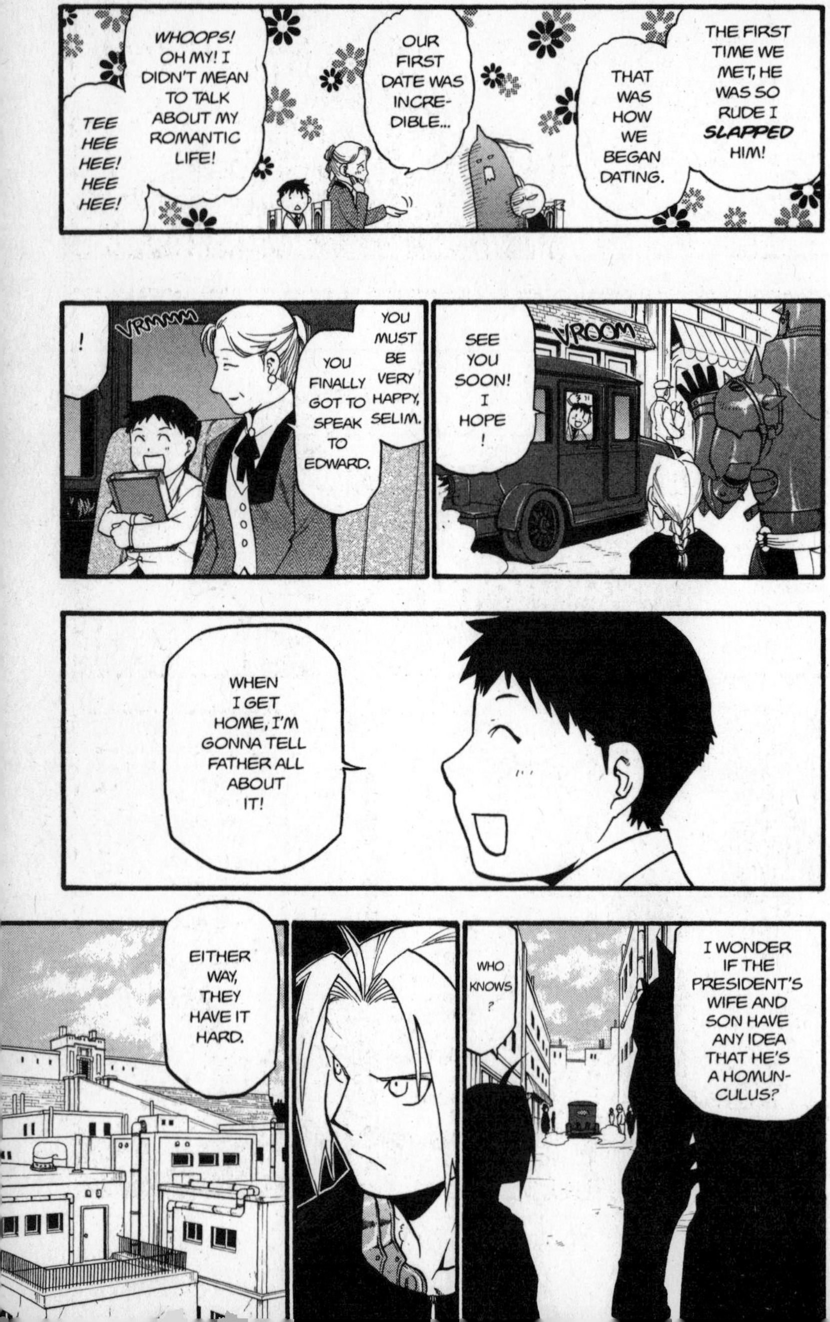
THE FIRST TIME WE MET, HE WAS SO RUDE I *SLAPPED* HIM!
THAT WAS HOW WE BEGAN DATING.
OUR FIRST DATE WAS INCREDIBLE...
WHOOPS! OH MY! I DIDN'T MEAN TO TALK ABOUT MY ROMANTIC LIFE!
TEE HEE HEE! HEE HEE!
VROOM
SEE YOU SOON! I HOPE!
YOU MUST BE VERY HAPPY, SELIM.
YOU FINALLY GOT TO SPEAK TO EDWARD.
VRMMM
!
WHEN I GET HOME, I'M GONNA TELL FATHER ALL ABOUT IT!
I WONDER IF THE PRESIDENT'S WIFE AND SON HAVE ANY IDEA THAT HE'S A HOMUNCULUS?
WHO KNOWS?
EITHER WAY, THEY HAVE IT HARD.

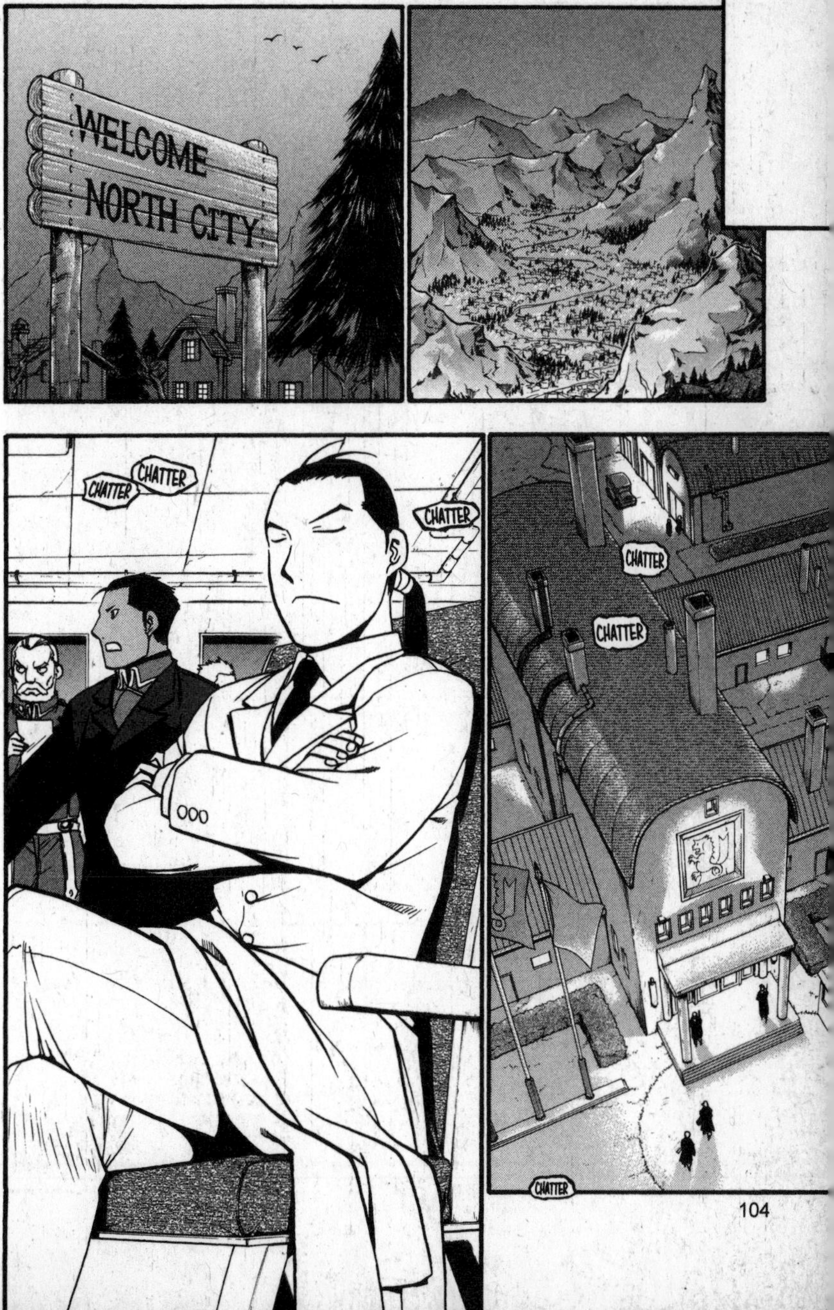
WELCOME
NORTH CITY
CHATTER
CHATTER
CHATTER
CHATTER
CHATTER
CHATTER

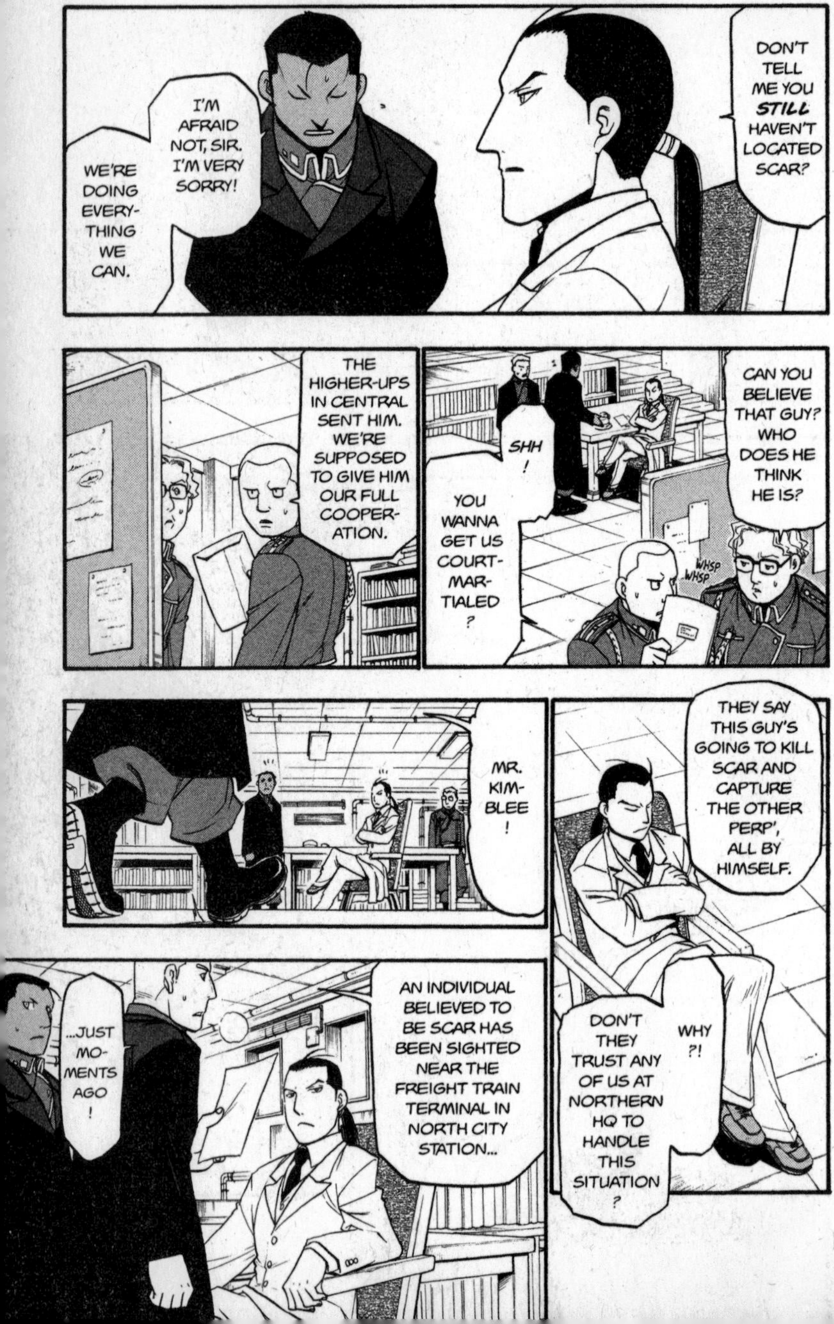
DON'T TELL ME YOU STILL HAVEN'T LOCATED SCAR?
I'M AFRAID NOT, SIR. I'M VERY SORRY!
WE'RE DOING EVERYTHING WE CAN.
CAN YOU BELIEVE THAT GUY? WHO DOES HE THINK HE IS?
WHSP WHSP
SHH!
YOU WANNA GET US COURT-MARTIALED?
THE HIGHER-UPS IN CENTRAL SENT HIM. WE'RE SUPPOSED TO GIVE HIM OUR FULL COOPERATION.
THEY SAY THIS GUY'S GOING TO KILL SCAR AND CAPTURE THE OTHER PERP', ALL BY HIMSELF.
WHY?!
DON'T THEY TRUST ANY OF US AT NORTHERN HQ TO HANDLE THIS SITUATION?
MR. KIMBLEE!
AN INDIVIDUAL BELIEVED TO BE SCAR HAS BEEN SIGHTED NEAR THE FREIGHT TRAIN TERMINAL IN NORTH CITY STATION...
...JUST MOMENTS AGO!

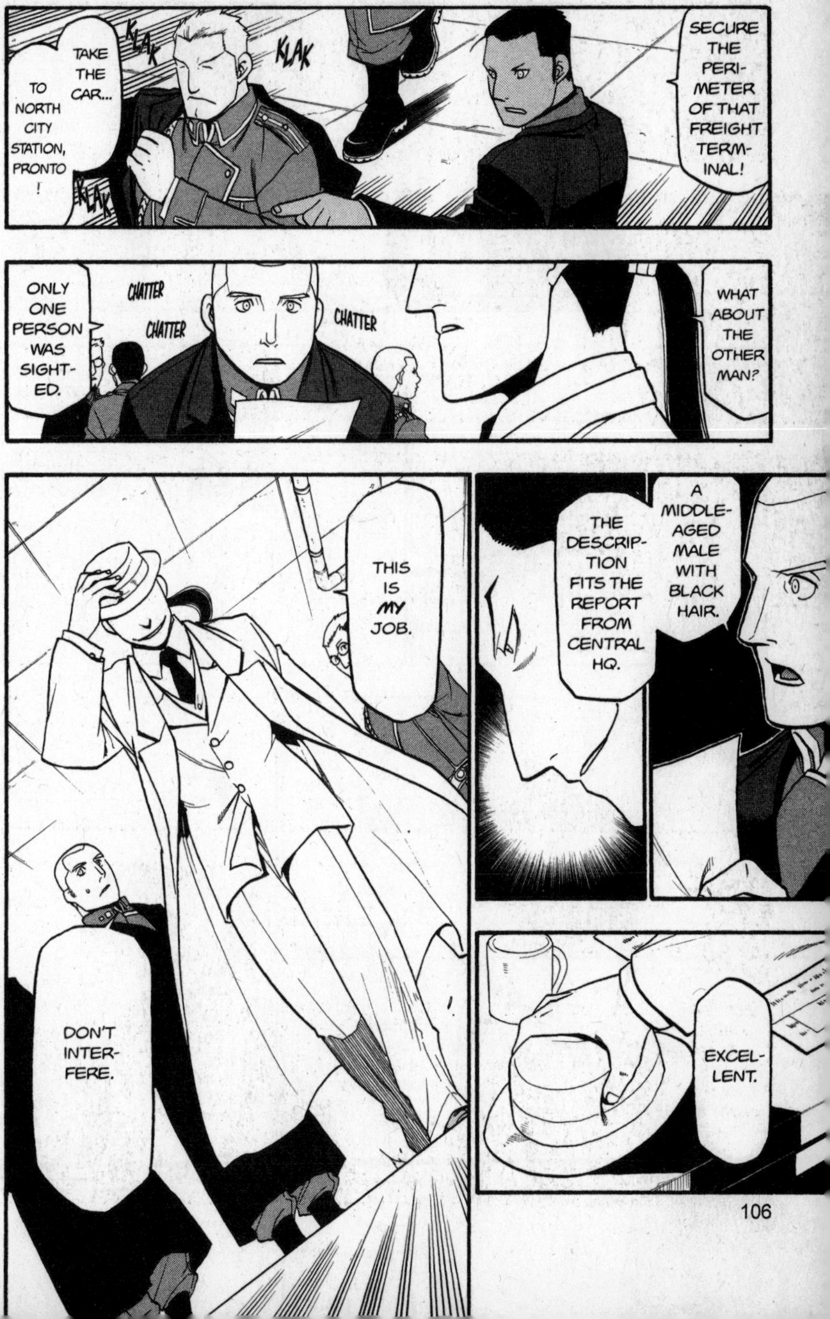
SECURE THE PERIMETER OF THAT FREIGHT TERMINAL!
KLAK
KLAK
KLAK
TAKE THE CAR...
TO NORTH CITY STATION, PRONTO!
WHAT ABOUT THE OTHER MAN?
CHATTER
CHATTER
CHATTER
ONLY ONE PERSON WAS SIGHTED.
A MIDDLE-AGED MALE WITH BLACK HAIR.
THE DESCRIPTION FITS THE REPORT FROM CENTRAL HQ.
EXCELLENT.
THIS IS *MY* JOB.
DON'T INTERFERE.

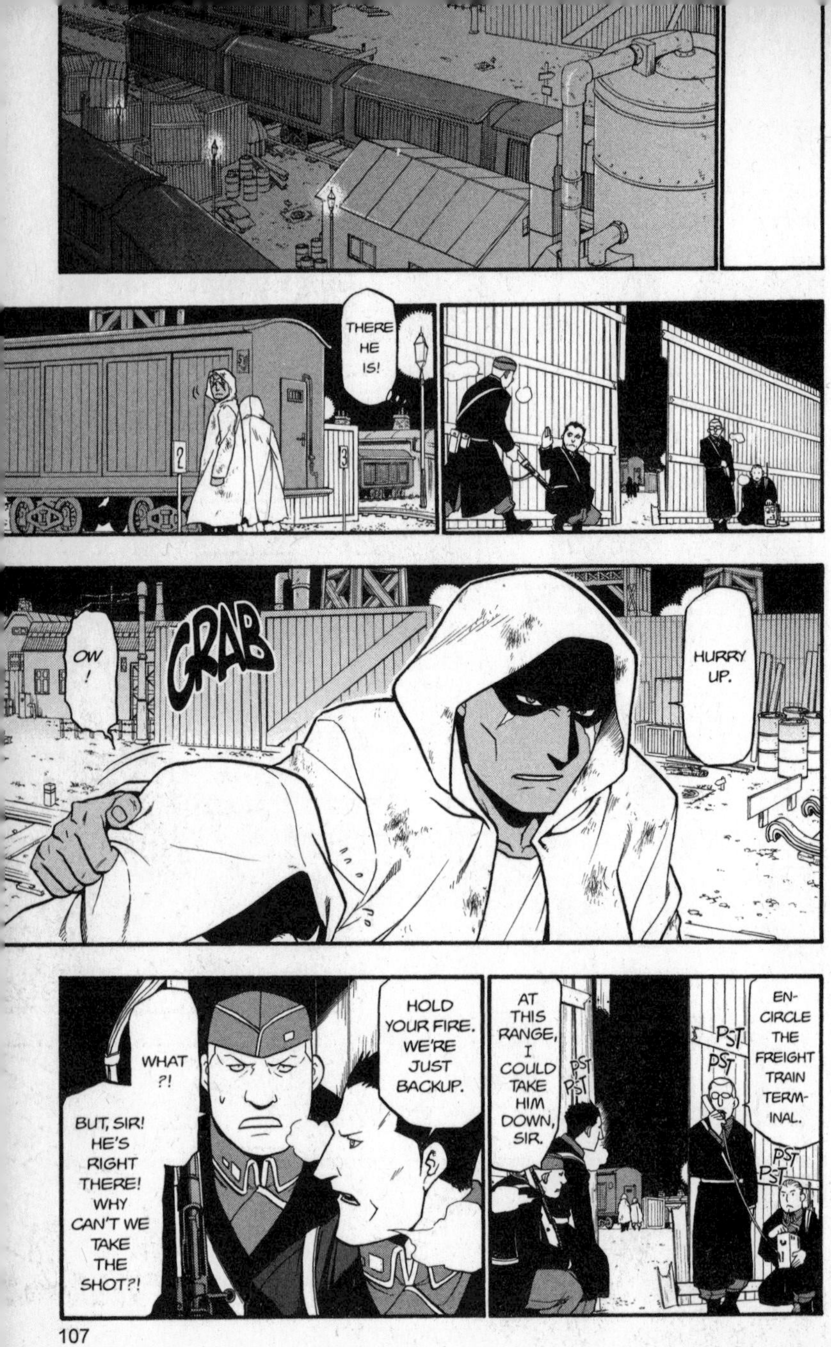
THERE HE IS!
HURRY UP.
GRAB
OW!
ENCIRCLE THE FREIGHT TRAIN TERMINAL.
PST PST
PST PST
AT THIS RANGE, I COULD TAKE HIM DOWN, SIR.
PST PST
HOLD YOUR FIRE. WE'RE JUST BACKUP.
WHAT?!
BUT, SIR! HE'S RIGHT THERE! WHY CAN'T WE TAKE THE SHOT?!

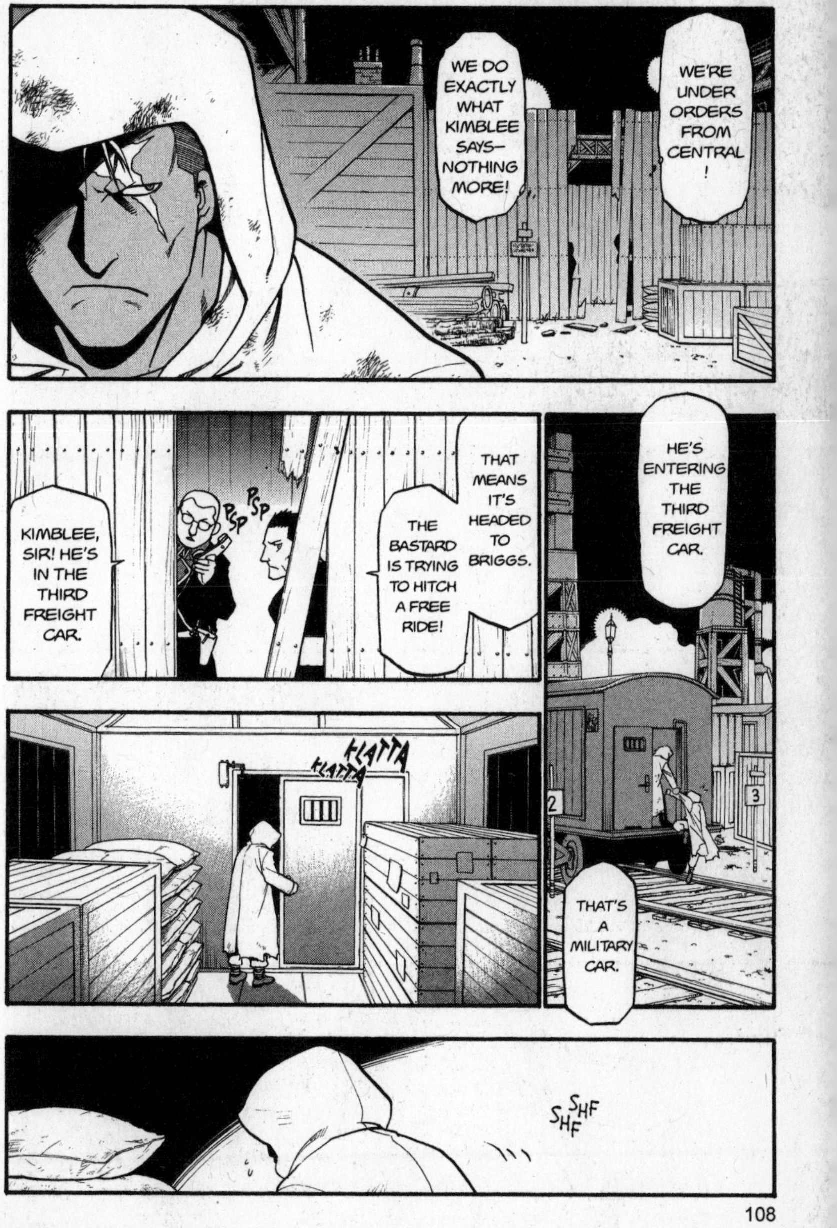
WE'RE UNDER ORDERS FROM CENTRAL!
WE DO EXACTLY WHAT KIMBLEE SAYS— NOTHING MORE!
HE'S ENTERING THE THIRD FREIGHT CAR.
THAT'S A MILITARY CAR.
THAT MEANS IT'S HEADED TO BRIGGS.
THE BASTARD IS TRYING TO HITCH A FREE RIDE!
PSP PSP
KIMBLEE, SIR! HE'S IN THE THIRD FREIGHT CAR.
KLATTA KLATTA
SHF SHF

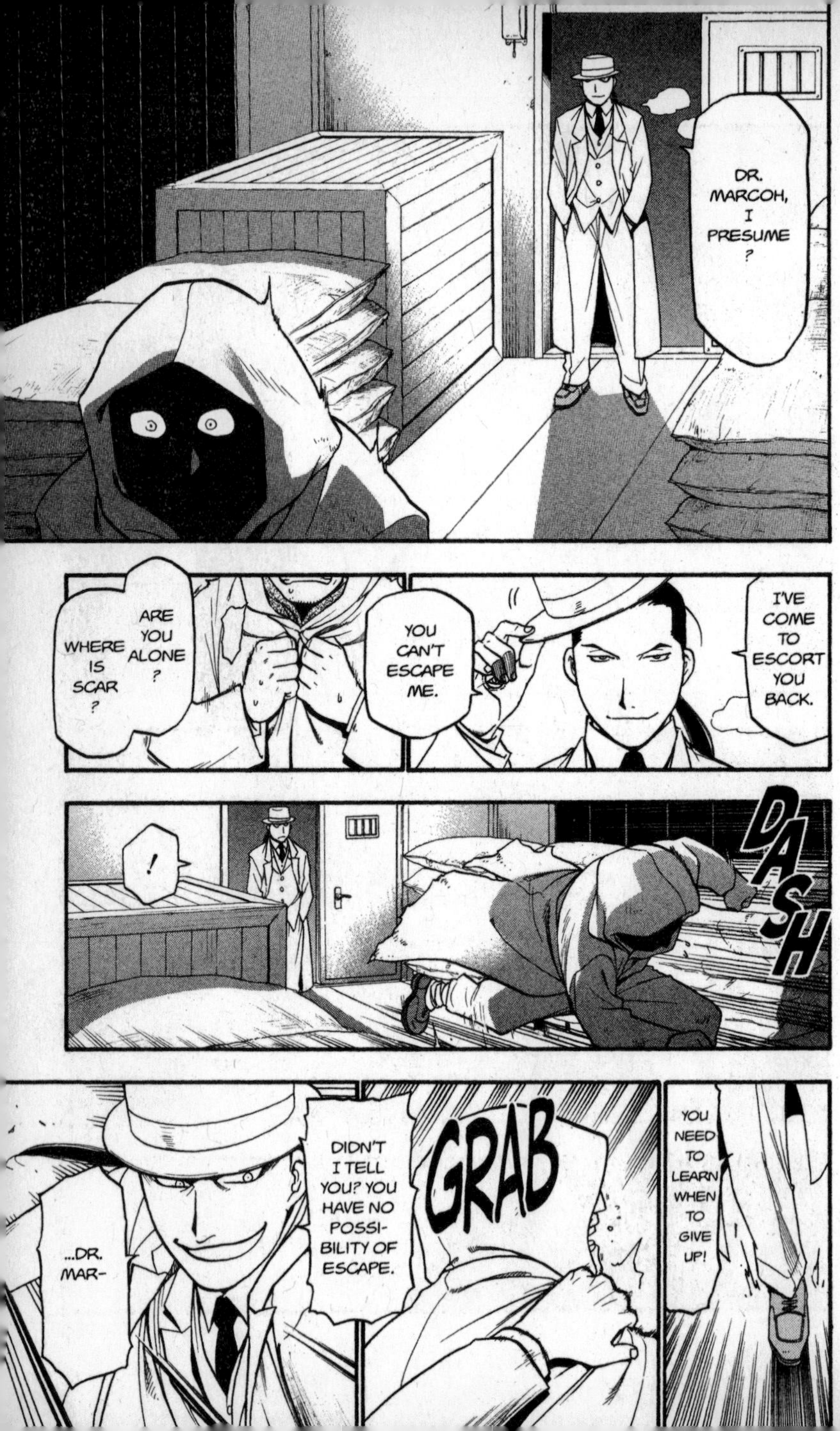
DR. MARCOH, I PRESUME?
I'VE COME TO ESCORT YOU BACK.
YOU CAN'T ESCAPE ME.
ARE YOU ALONE?
WHERE IS SCAR?
DASH
!
YOU NEED TO LEARN WHEN TO GIVE UP!
GRAB
DIDN'T I TELL YOU? YOU HAVE NO POSSIBILITY OF ESCAPE.
...DR. MAR-

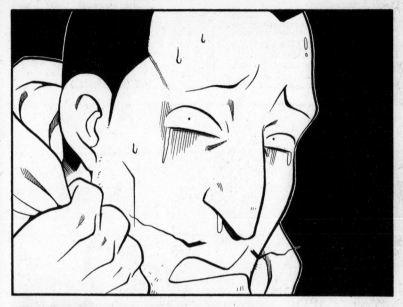

WHO IS THIS?

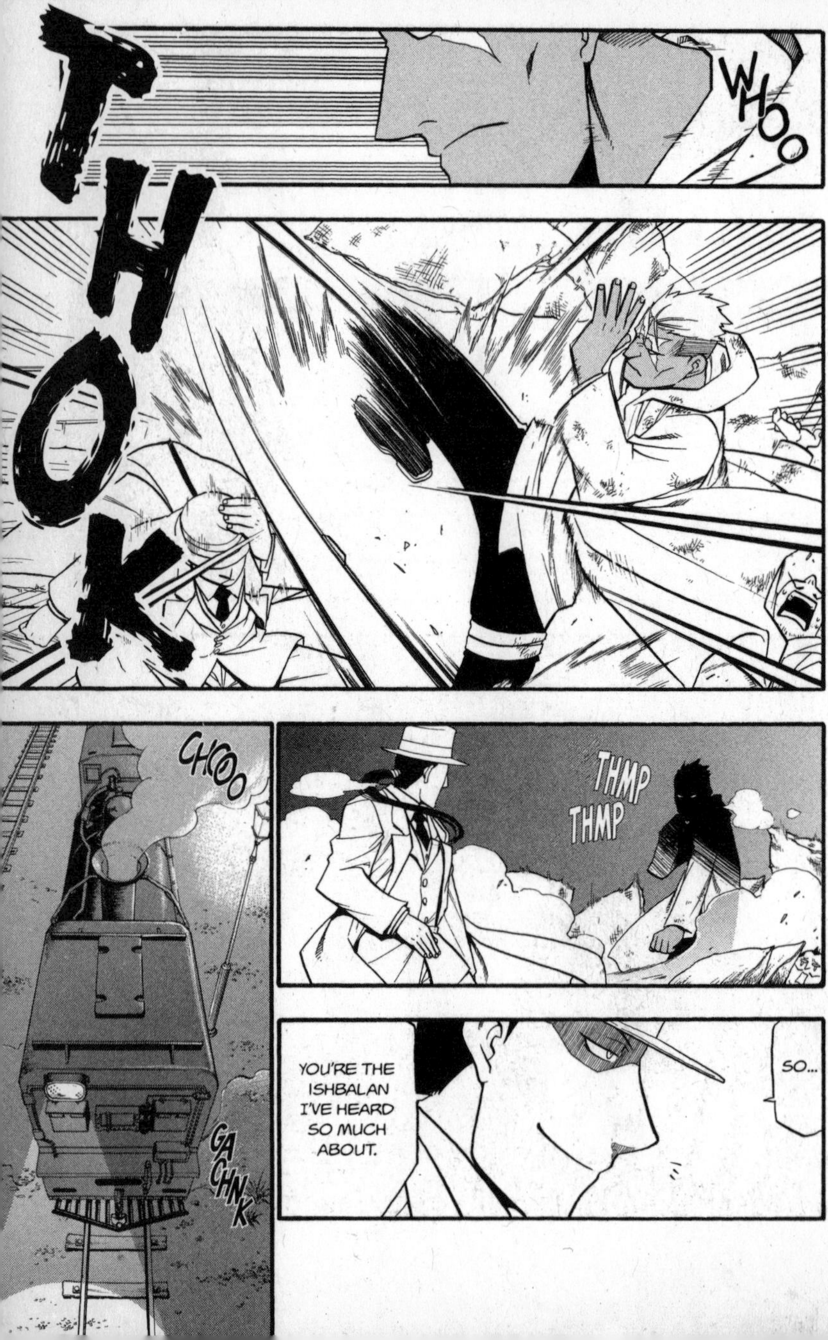
WHOO
THOK
THMP THMP
SO...
YOU'RE THE ISHBALAN I'VE HEARD SO MUCH ABOUT.
CHOOO
GACHNK

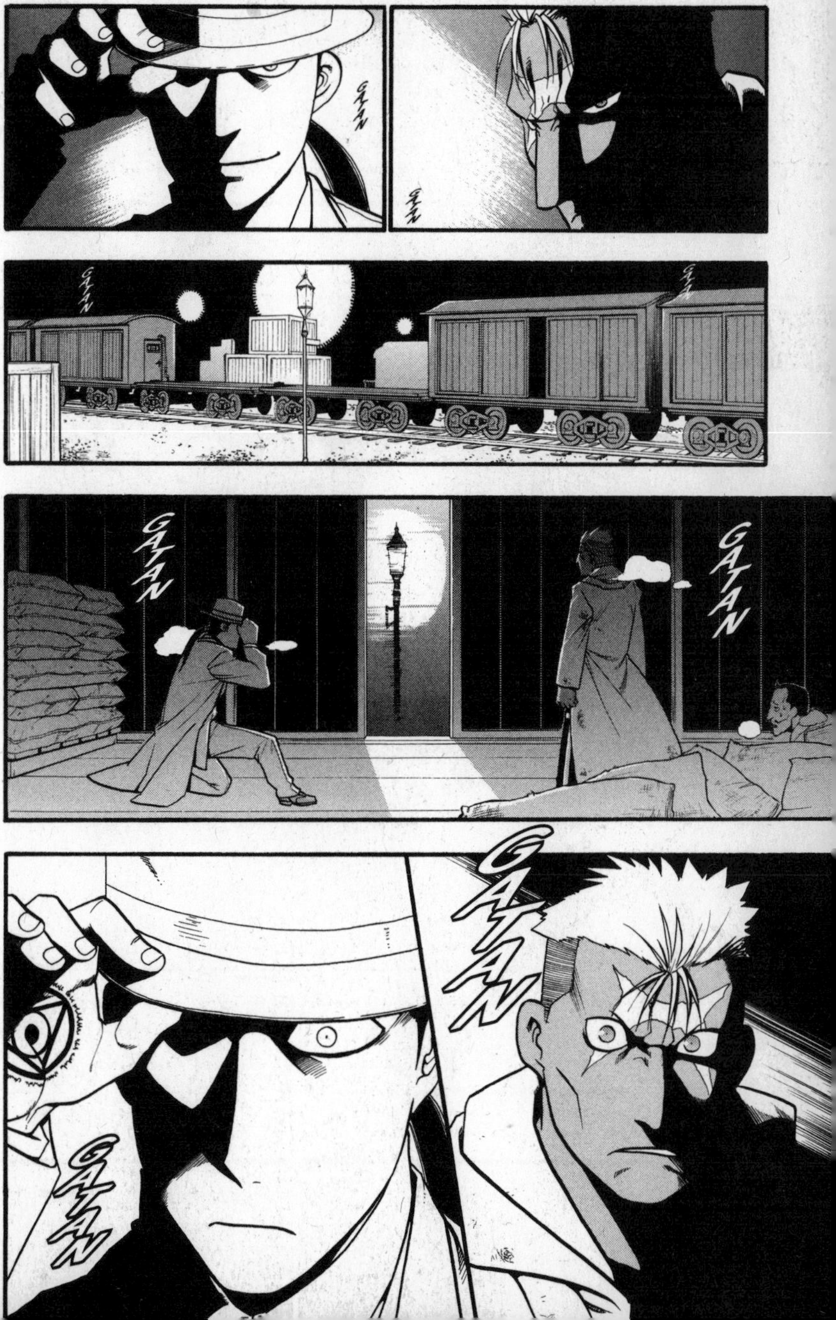
GATAN
GATAN
GATAN
GATAN
GATAN
GATAN
GATAN
GATAN

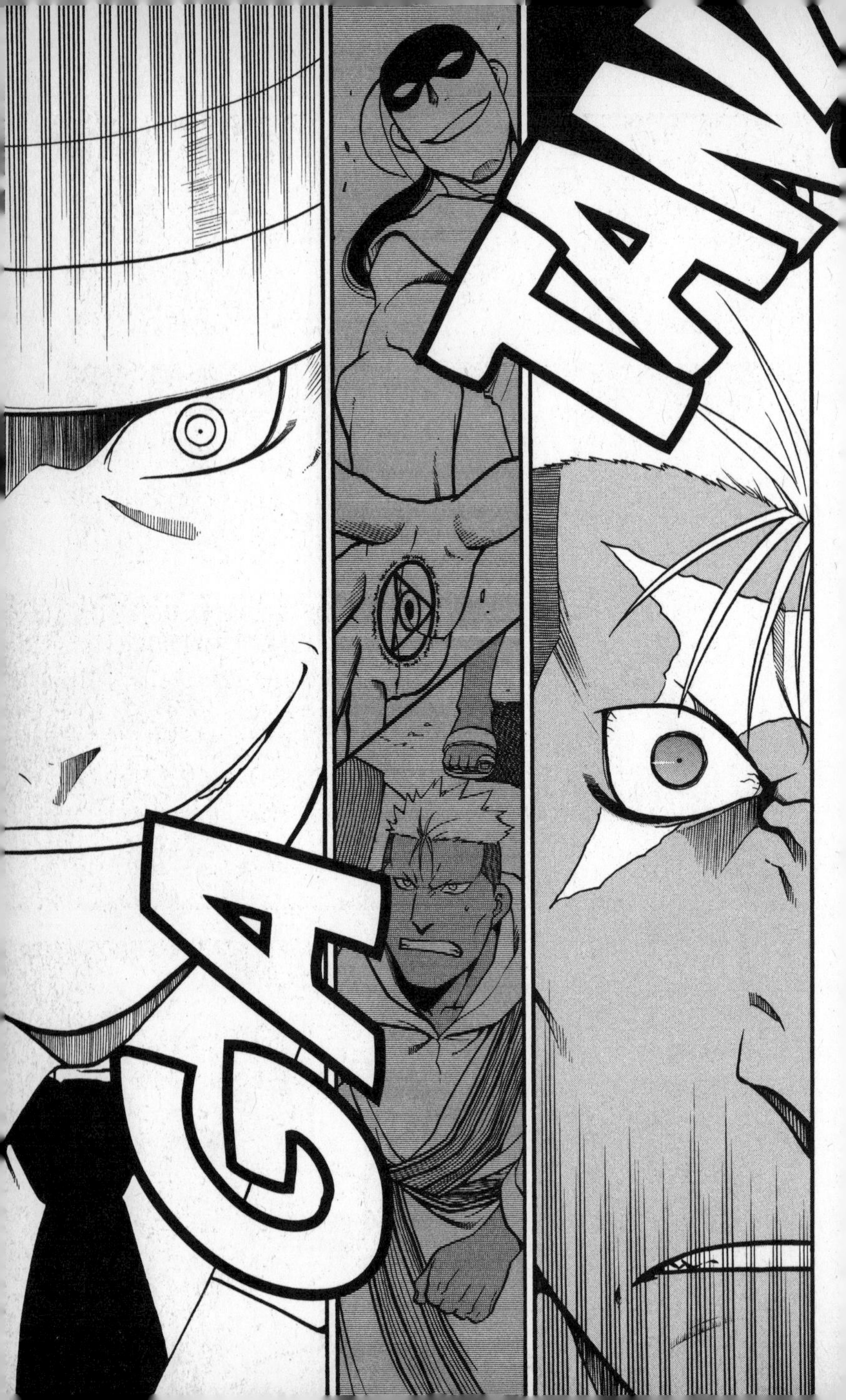
GA
TAN

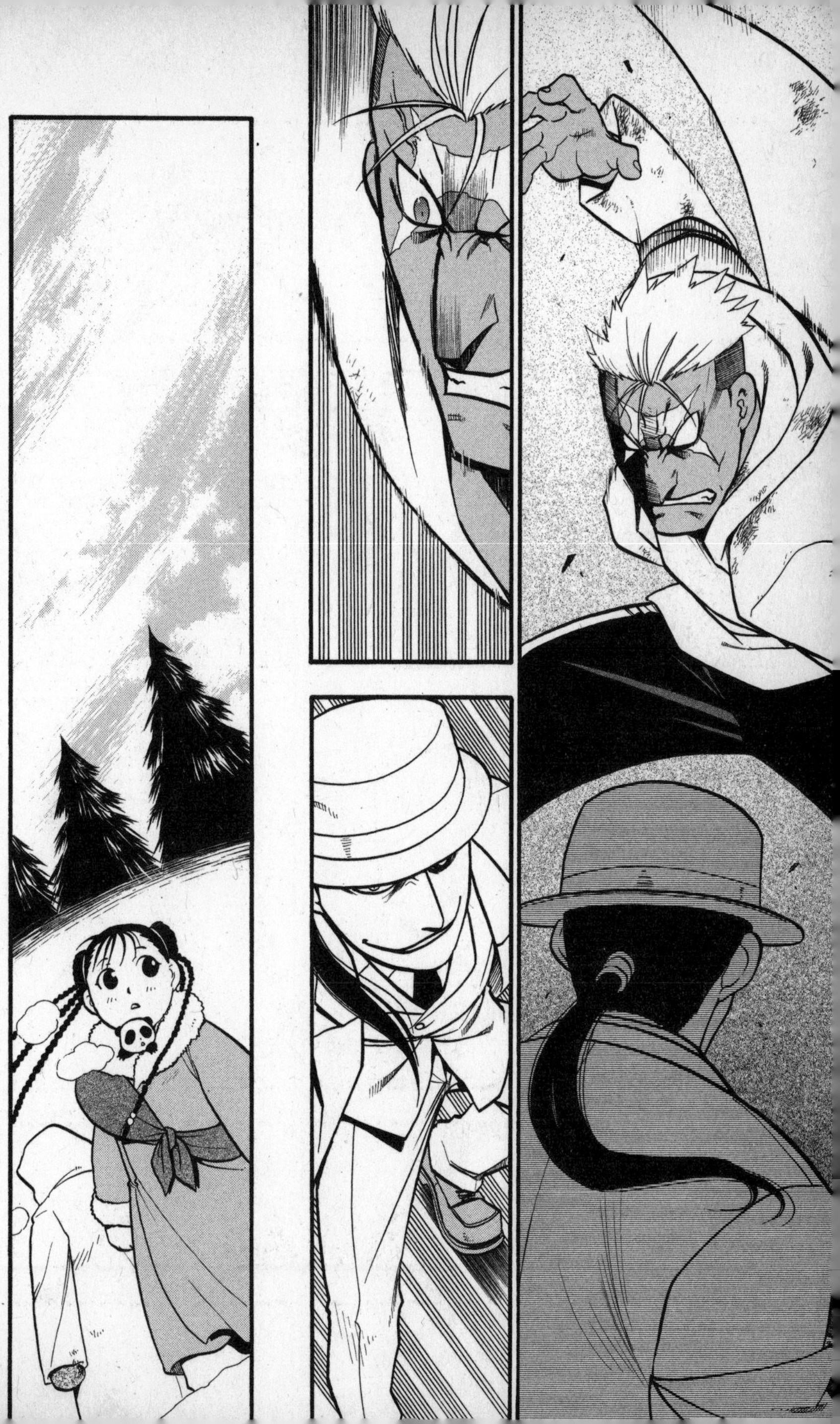

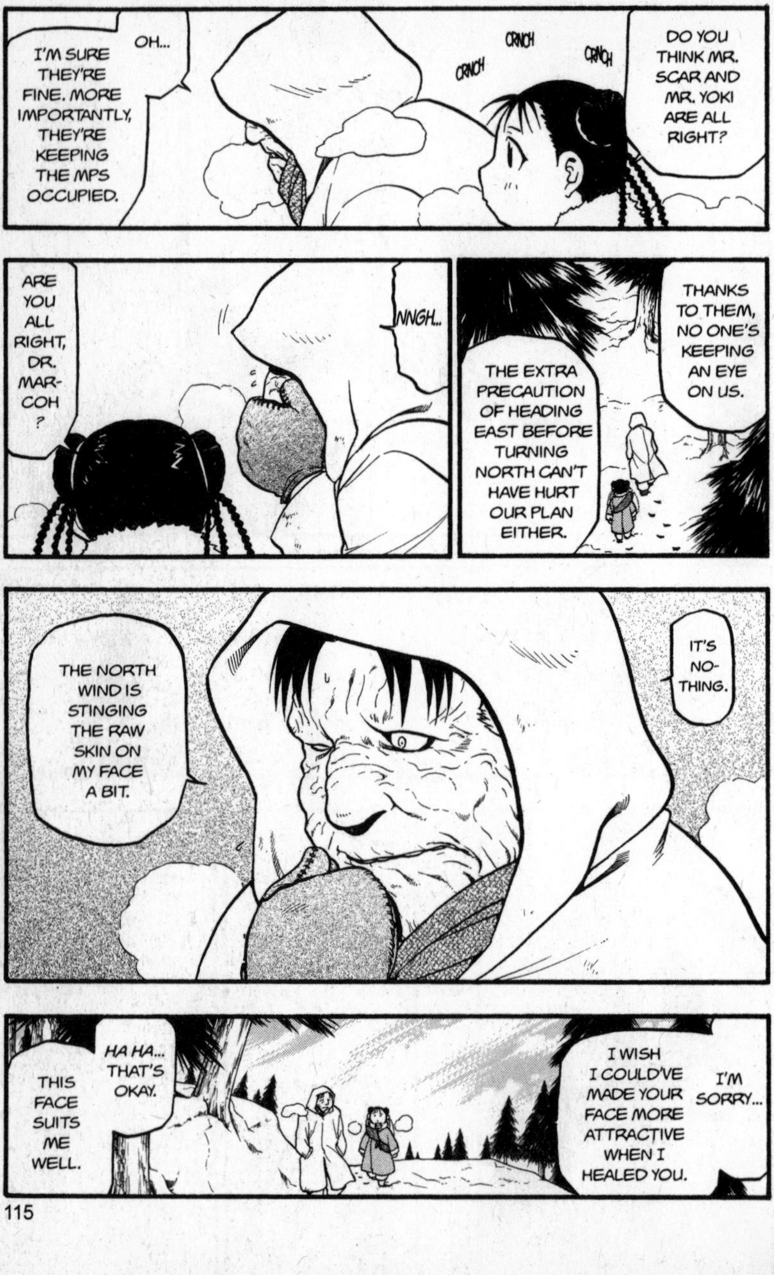
DO YOU THINK MR. SCAR AND MR. YOKI ARE ALL RIGHT?
CRNCH
CRNCH
CRNCH
OH...
I'M SURE THEY'RE FINE. MORE IMPORTANTLY, THEY'RE KEEPING THE MPS OCCUPIED.
THANKS TO THEM, NO ONE'S KEEPING AN EYE ON US.
THE EXTRA PRECAUTION OF HEADING EAST BEFORE TURNING NORTH CAN'T HAVE HURT OUR PLAN EITHER.
NNGH...
ARE YOU ALL RIGHT, DR. MAR-COH?
IT'S NO-THING.
THE NORTH WIND IS STINGING THE RAW SKIN ON MY FACE A BIT.
I'M SORRY...
I WISH I COULD'VE MADE YOUR FACE MORE ATTRACTIVE WHEN I HEALED YOU.
HA HA... THAT'S OKAY.
THIS FACE SUITS ME WELL.

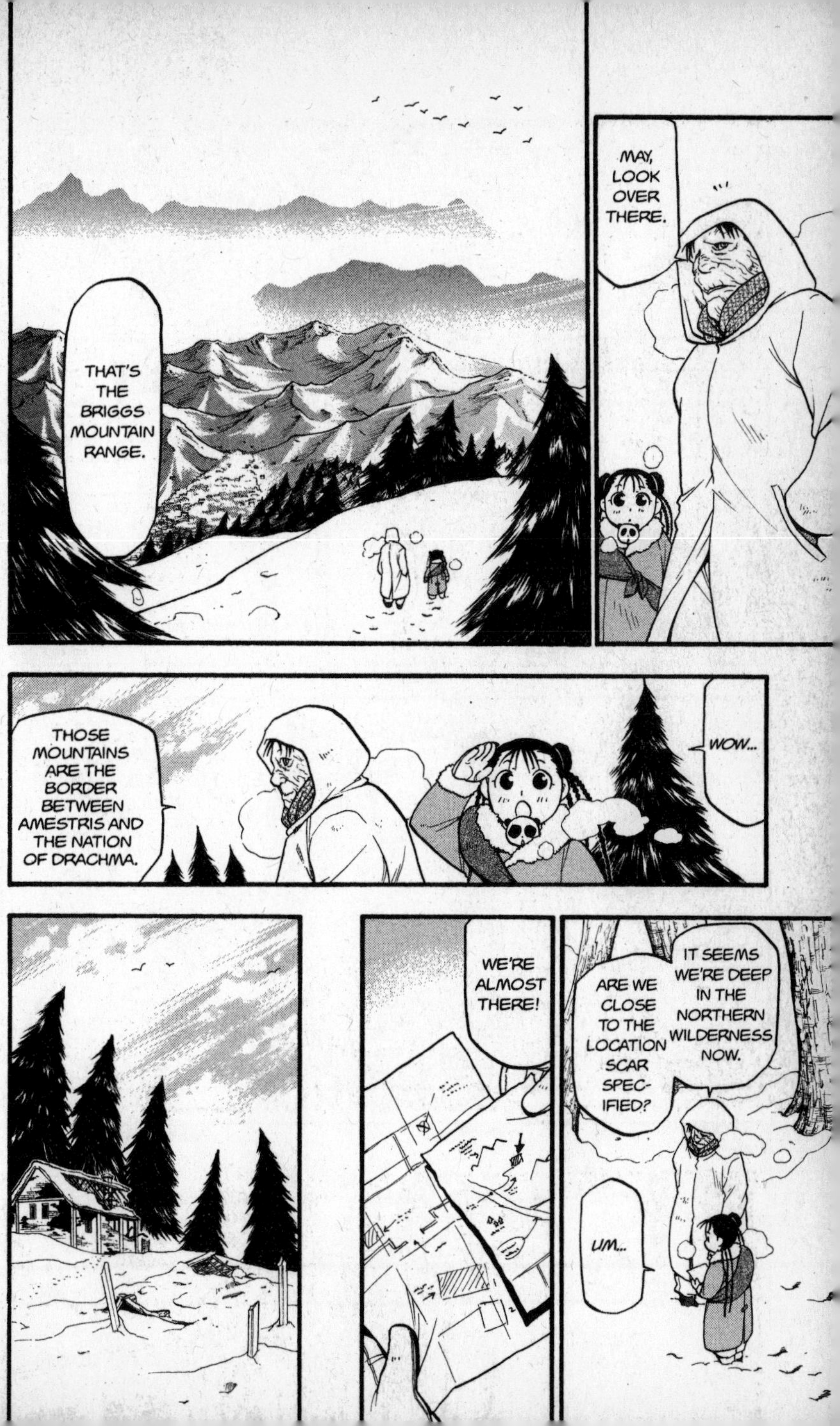
MAY, LOOK OVER THERE.
THAT'S THE BRIGGS MOUNTAIN RANGE.
WOW...
THOSE MOUNTAINS ARE THE BORDER BETWEEN AMESTRIS AND THE NATION OF DRACHMA.
IT SEEMS WE'RE DEEP IN THE NORTHERN WILDERNESS NOW.
ARE WE CLOSE TO THE LOCATION SCAR SPECIFIED?
UM...
WE'RE ALMOST THERE!

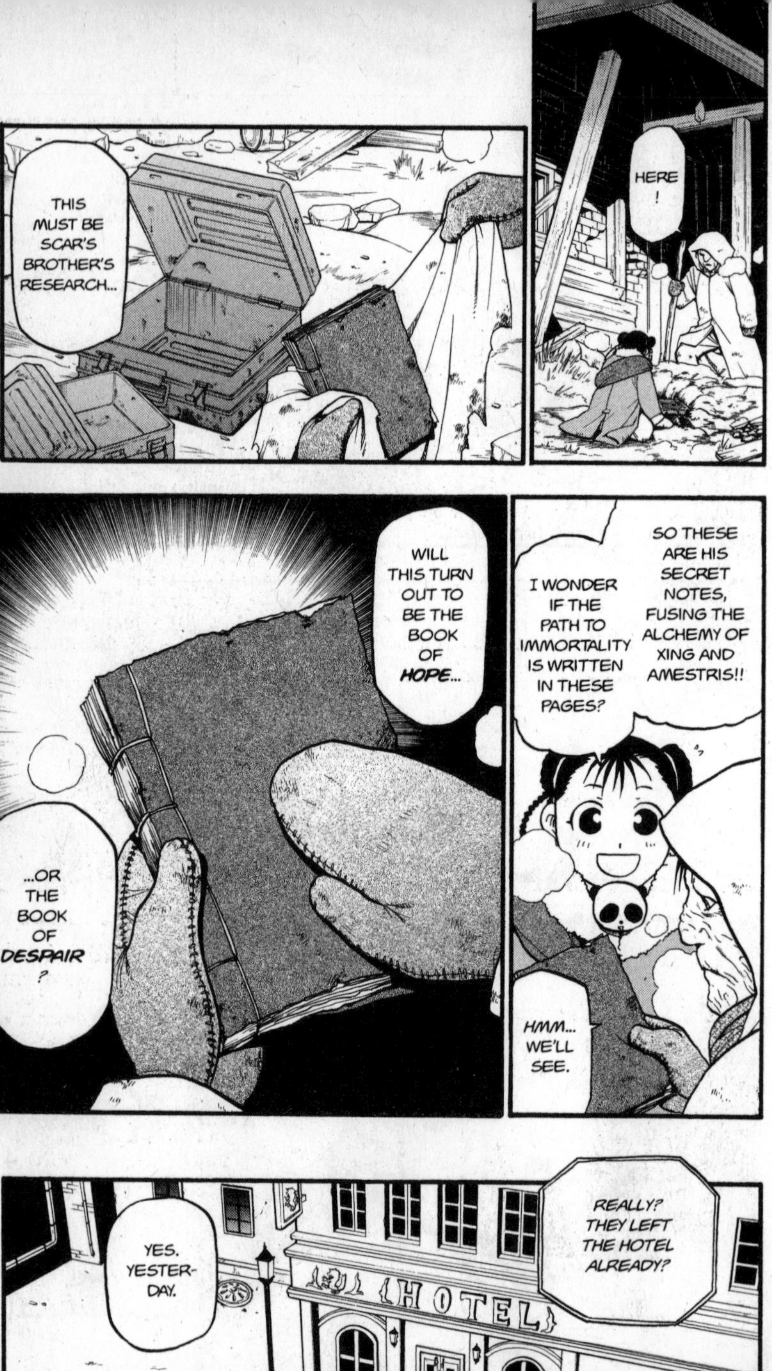
HERE!
THIS MUST BE SCAR'S BROTHER'S RESEARCH...
SO THESE ARE HIS SECRET NOTES, FUSING THE ALCHEMY OF XING AND AMESTRIS!!
I WONDER IF THE PATH TO IMMORTALITY IS WRITTEN IN THESE PAGES?
HMM... WE'LL SEE.
WILL THIS TURN OUT TO BE THE BOOK OF *HOPE*...
...OR THE BOOK OF *DESPAIR*?
REALLY? THEY LEFT THE HOTEL ALREADY?
HOTEL
YES. YESTER-DAY.

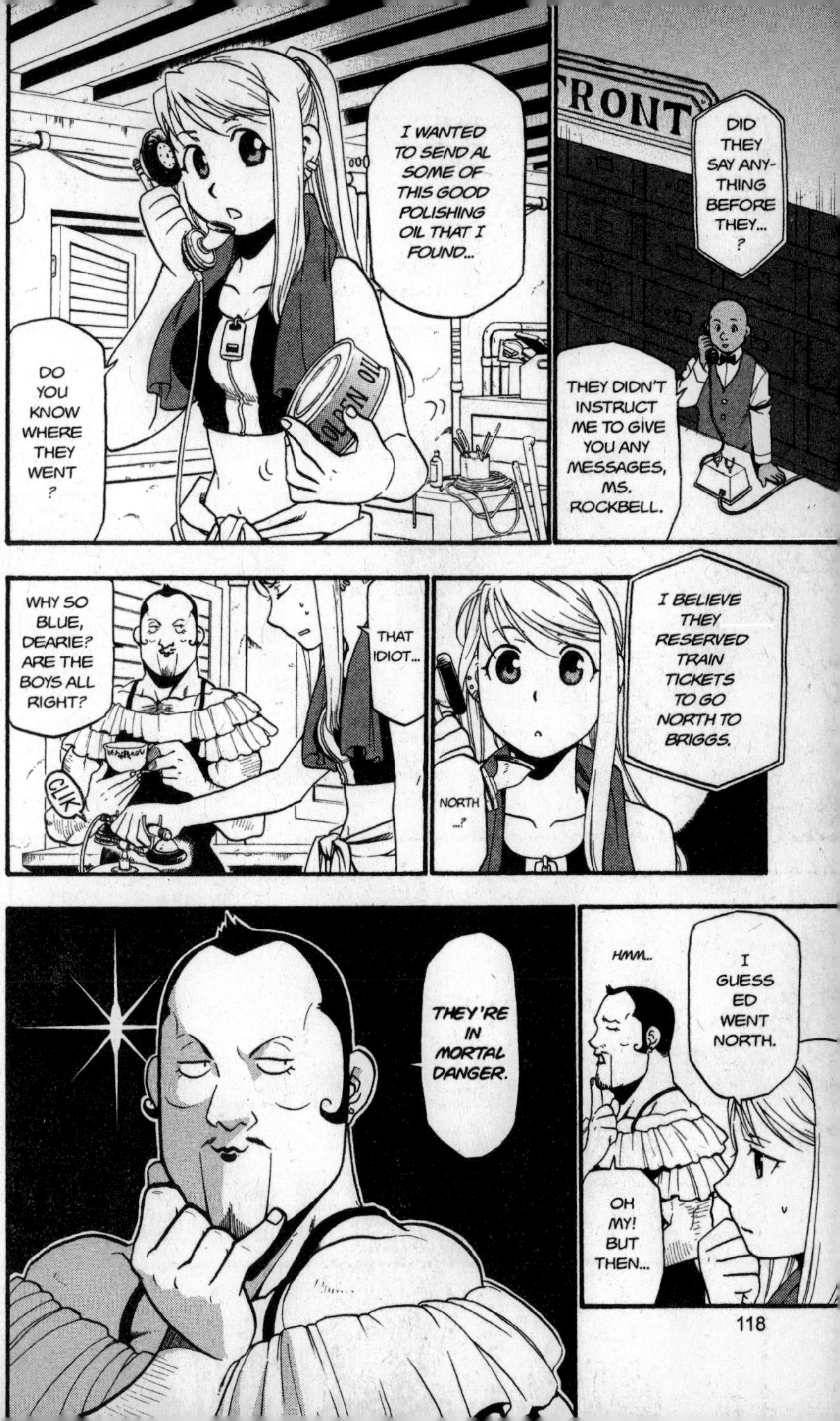
FRONT
DID THEY SAY ANY-THING BEFORE THEY...?
THEY DIDN'T INSTRUCT ME TO GIVE YOU ANY MESSAGES, MS. ROCKBELL.
I WANTED TO SEND AL SOME OF THIS GOOD POLISHING OIL THAT I FOUND...
DO YOU KNOW WHERE THEY WENT?
I BELIEVE THEY RESERVED TRAIN TICKETS TO GO NORTH TO BRIGGS.
NORTH...?
THAT IDIOT...
WHY SO BLUE, DEARIE? ARE THE BOYS ALL RIGHT?
CLIK
I GUESS ED WENT NORTH.
HMM...
OH MY! BUT THEN...
THEY'RE IN MORTAL DANGER.

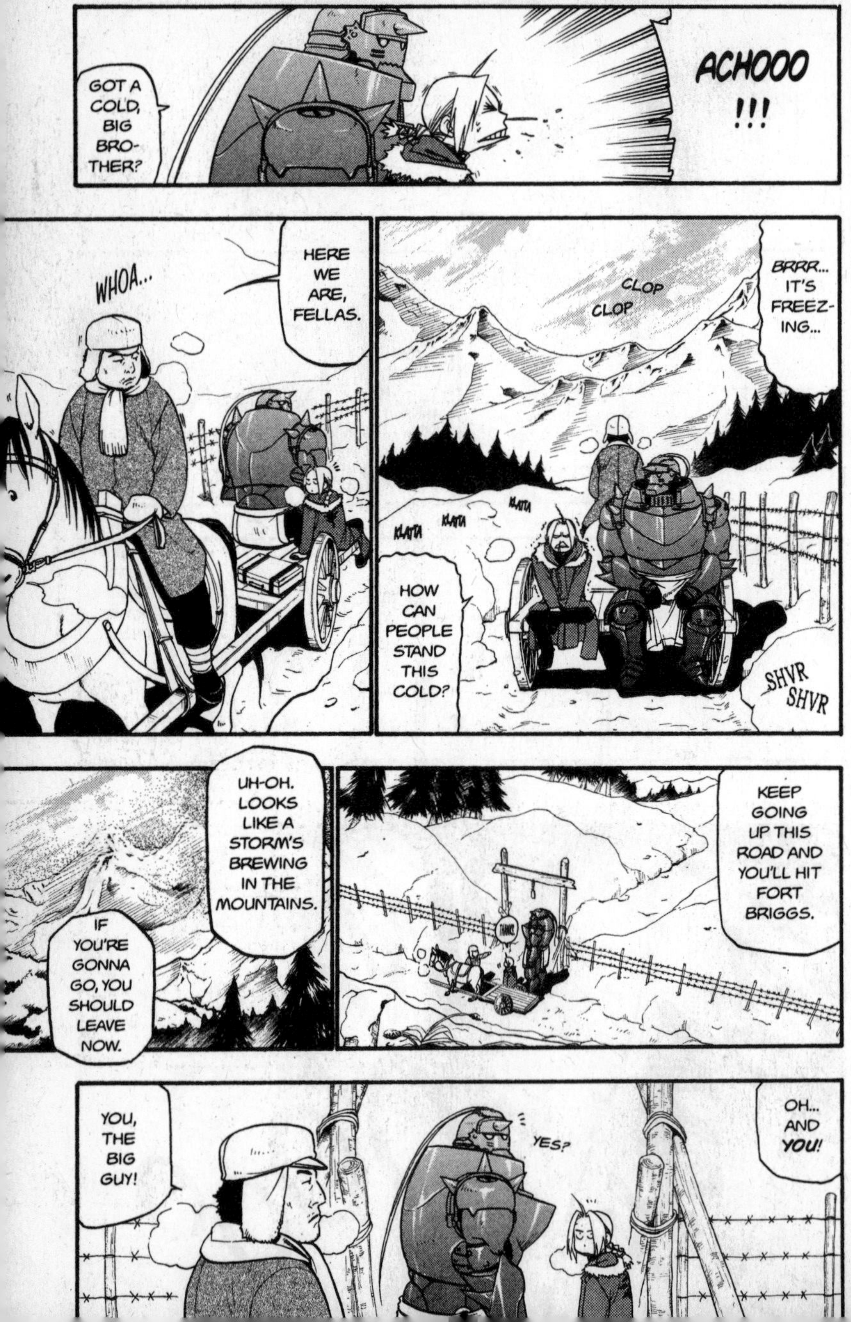
ACHOOO !!!
GOT A COLD, BIG BROTHER?
BRRR... IT'S FREEZING...
CLOP CLOP
KLATTA KLATTA KLATTA
HOW CAN PEOPLE STAND THIS COLD?
SHVR SHVR
HERE WE ARE, FELLAS.
WHOA...
KEEP GOING UP THIS ROAD AND YOU'LL HIT FORT BRIGGS.
UH-OH. LOOKS LIKE A STORM'S BREWING IN THE MOUNTAINS.
IF YOU'RE GONNA GO, YOU SHOULD LEAVE NOW.
OH... AND YOU!
YES?
YOU, THE BIG GUY!

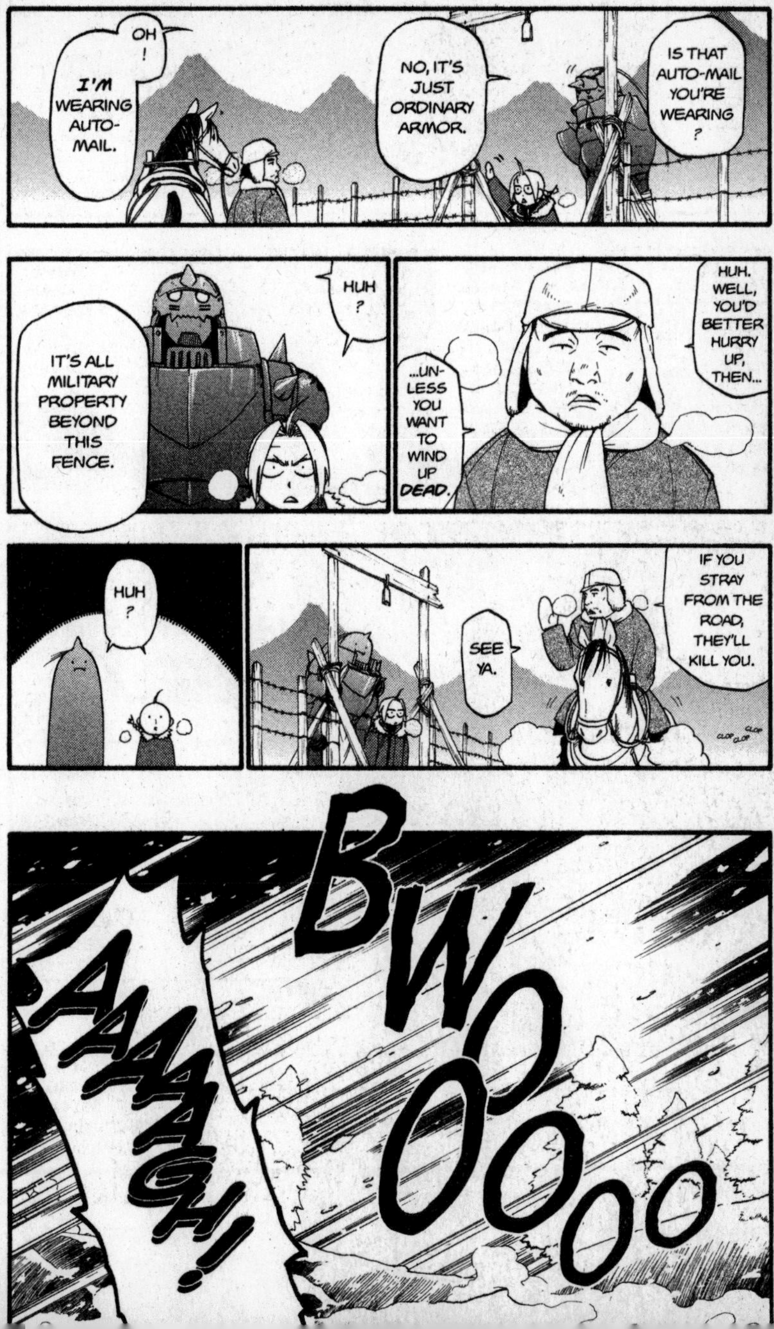
IS THAT AUTO-MAIL YOU'RE WEARING?
NO, IT'S JUST ORDINARY ARMOR.
OH! I'M WEARING AUTO-MAIL.
HUH. WELL, YOU'D BETTER HURRY UP, THEN...
...UNLESS YOU WANT TO WIND UP DEAD.
HUH?
IT'S ALL MILITARY PROPERTY BEYOND THIS FENCE.
IF YOU STRAY FROM THE ROAD, THEY'LL KILL YOU.
SEE YA.
CLOP CLOP CLOP
HUH?
BWOOOOO
AAAAGH!

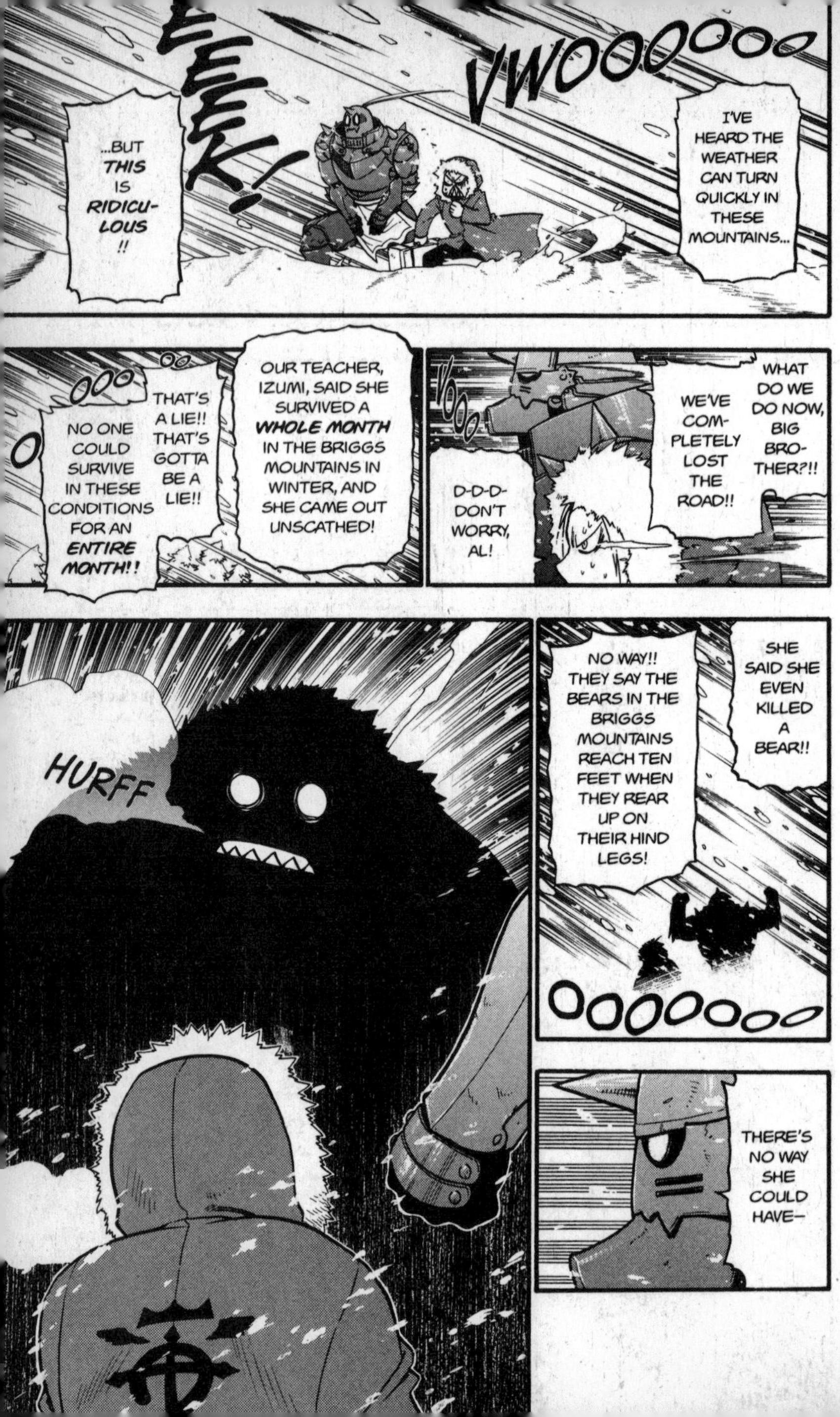
VWOOOOOO
I'VE HEARD THE WEATHER CAN TURN QUICKLY IN THESE MOUNTAINS...
EEEK!
...BUT THIS IS RIDICULOUS!!
WHAT DO WE DO NOW, BIG BROTHER?!!
WE'VE COMPLETELY LOST THE ROAD!!
VOOO
D-D-D-DON'T WORRY, AL!
OUR TEACHER, IZUMI, SAID SHE SURVIVED A WHOLE MONTH IN THE BRIGGS MOUNTAINS IN WINTER, AND SHE CAME OUT UNSCATHED!
THAT'S A LIE!! THAT'S GOTTA BE A LIE!!
OOOO
NO ONE COULD SURVIVE IN THESE CONDITIONS FOR AN ENTIRE MONTH!!
SHE SAID SHE EVEN KILLED A BEAR!!
NO WAY!! THEY SAY THE BEARS IN THE BRIGGS MOUNTAINS REACH TEN FEET WHEN THEY REAR UP ON THEIR HIND LEGS!
OOOOOOOO
THERE'S NO WAY SHE COULD HAVE—
HURFF

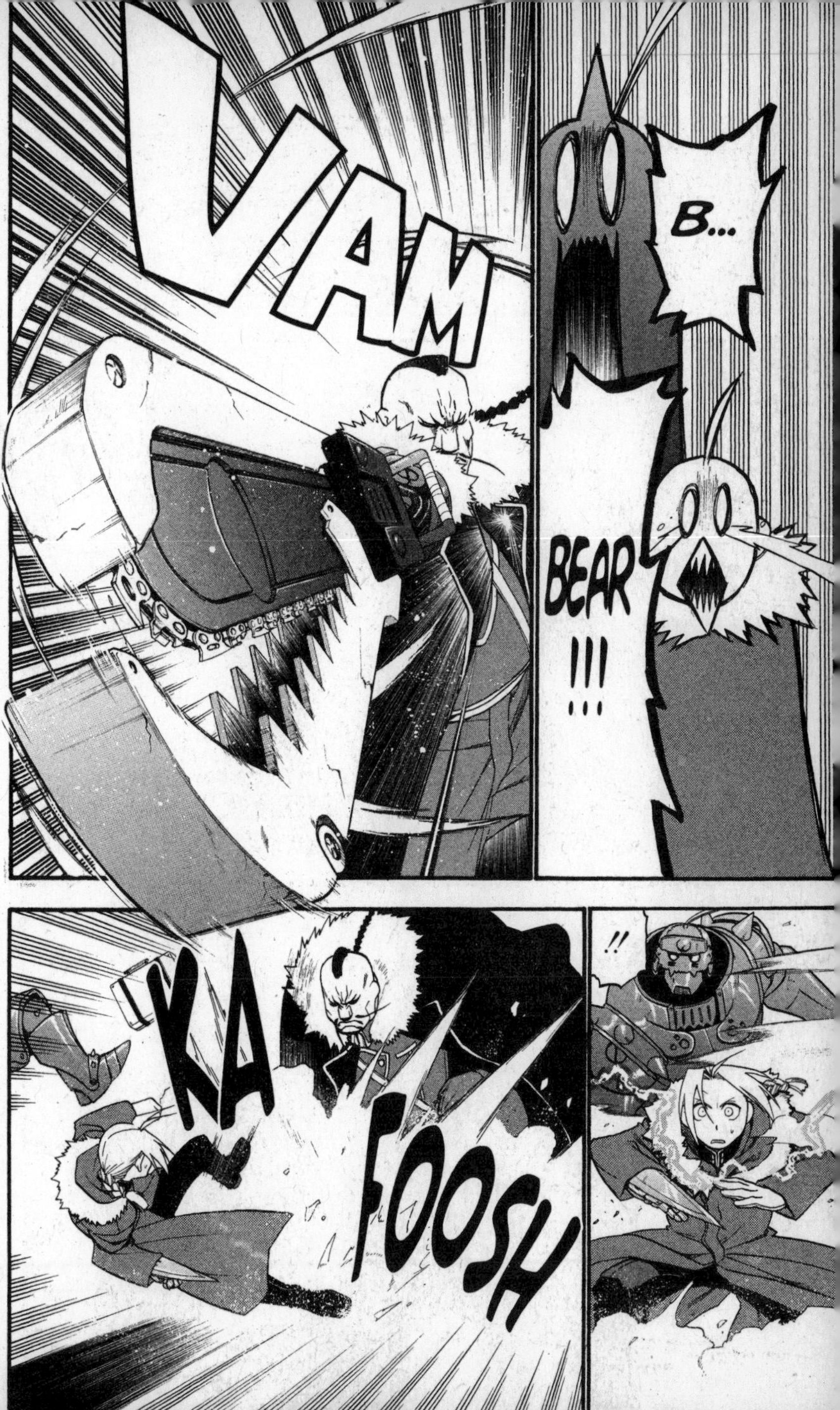
B...
BEAR !!!
VAM
!!
KA
FOOSH

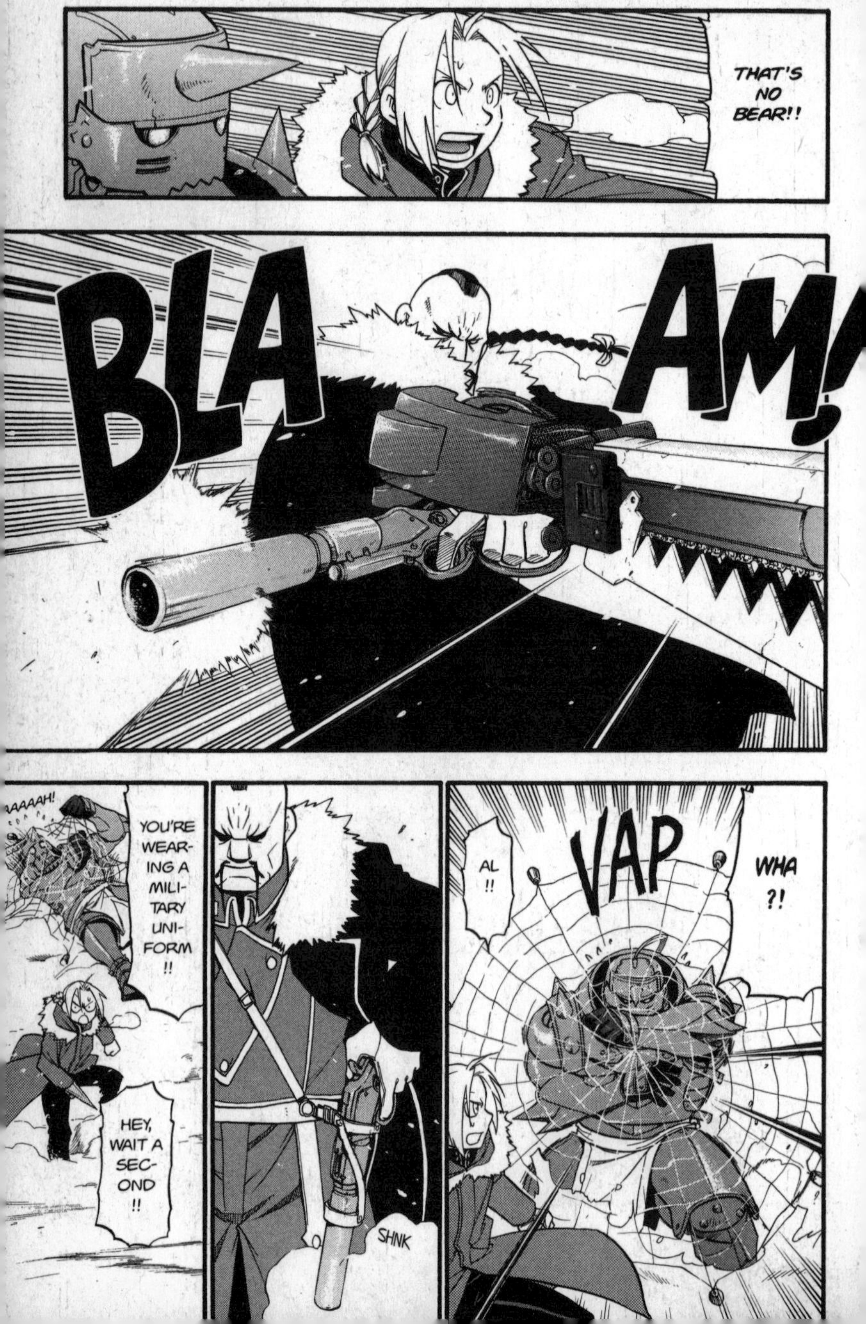
THAT'S NO BEAR!!
BLA AM!!
WHA ?!
VAP
AL !!
SHNK
YOU'RE WEAR-ING A MILI-TARY UNI-FORM !!
HEY, WAIT A SEC-OND !!

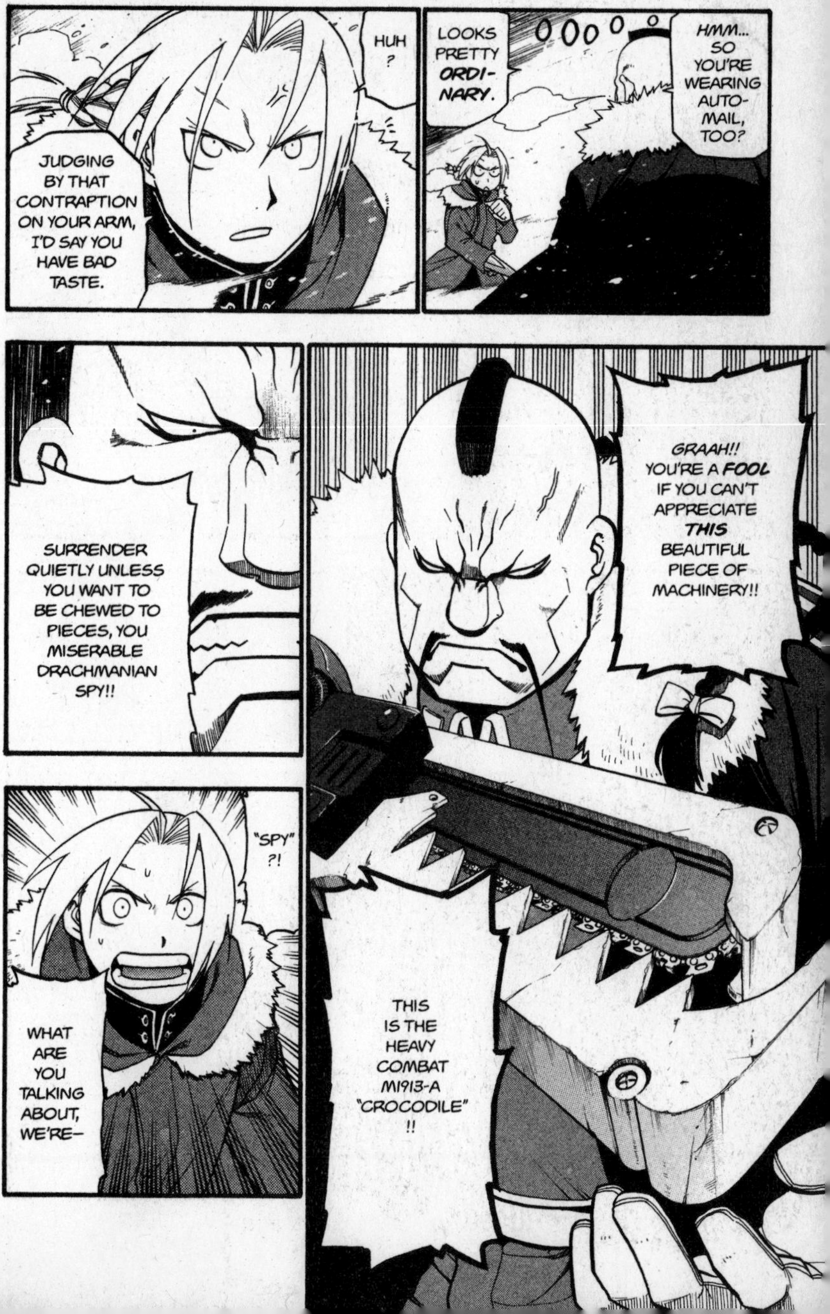
HMM... SO YOU'RE WEARING AUTO-MAIL, TOO?
LOOKS PRETTY **ORDINARY.**
HUH?
JUDGING BY THAT CONTRAPTION ON YOUR ARM, I'D SAY YOU HAVE BAD TASTE.
GRAAH!! YOU'RE A **FOOL** IF YOU CAN'T APPRECIATE **THIS** BEAUTIFUL PIECE OF MACHINERY!!
THIS IS THE HEAVY COMBAT M1913-A "CROCODILE" !!
SURRENDER QUIETLY UNLESS YOU WANT TO BE CHEWED TO PIECES, YOU MISERABLE DRACHMANIAN SPY!!
"SPY" ?!
WHAT ARE YOU TALKING ABOUT, WE'RE-

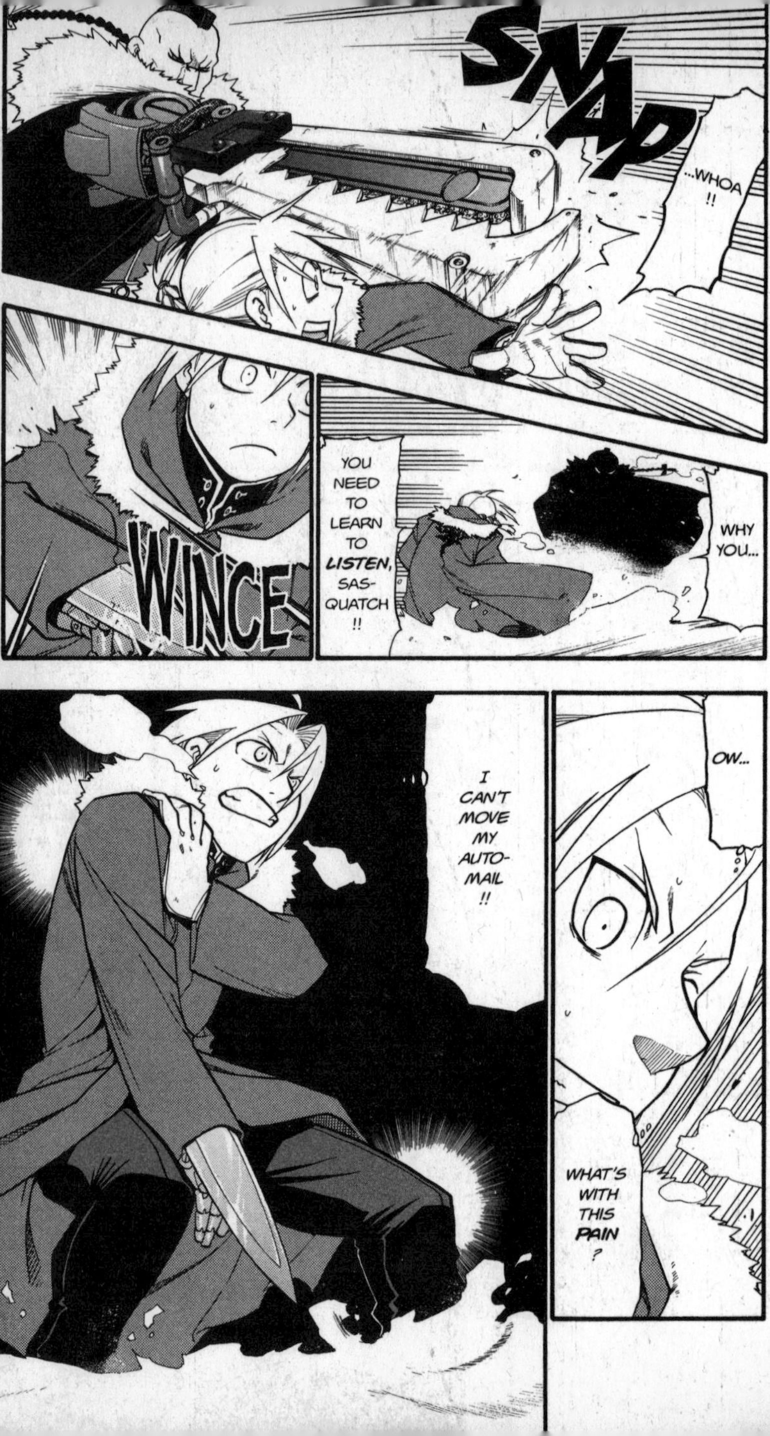
SNAP
...WHOA !!
WHY YOU...
YOU NEED TO LEARN TO LISTEN, SASQUATCH !!
WINCE
OW...
WHAT'S WITH THIS PAIN ?
I CAN'T MOVE MY AUTO-MAIL !!

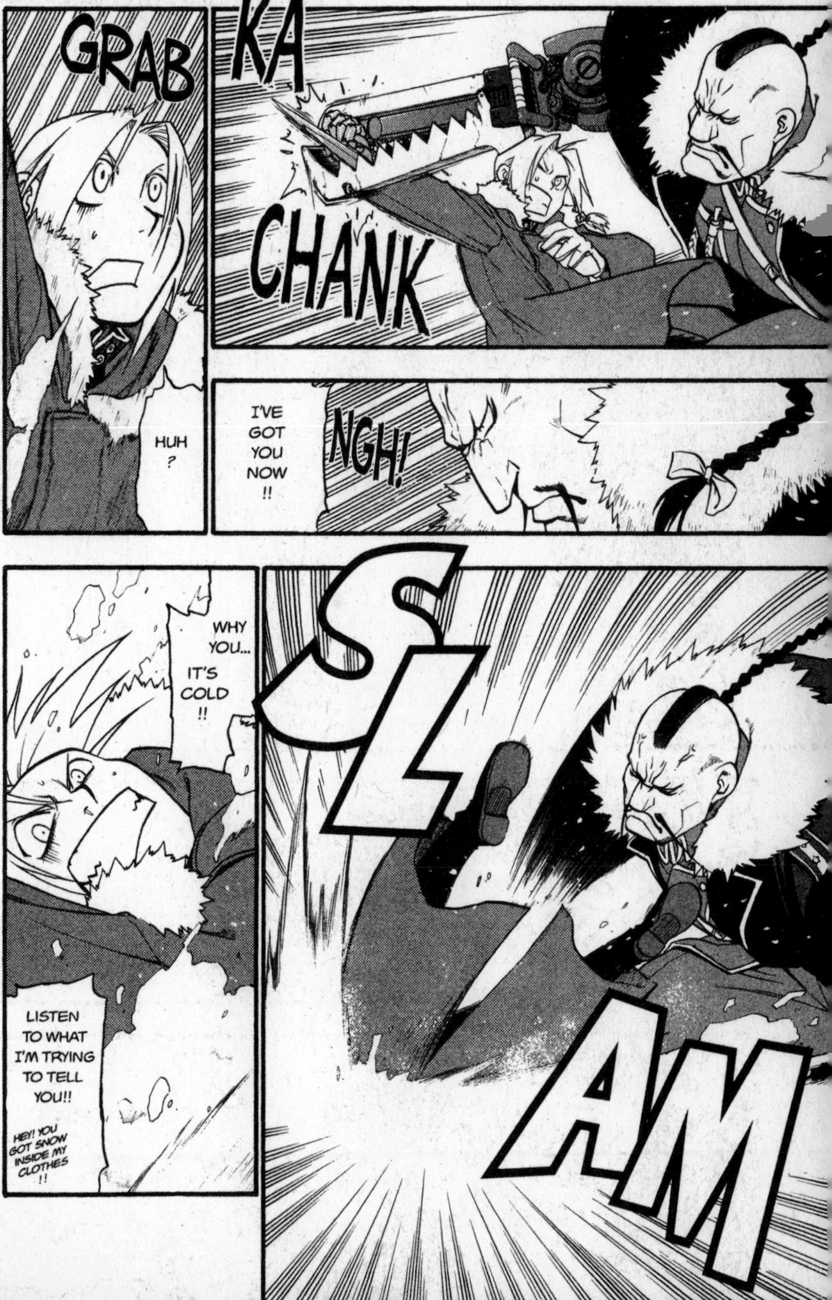
KA
CHANK
I'VE GOT YOU NOW!!
NGH!
GRAB
HUH?
SL
AM
WHY YOU...
IT'S COLD!!
LISTEN TO WHAT I'M TRYING TO TELL YOU!!
HEY! YOU GOT SNOW INSIDE MY CLOTHES!!

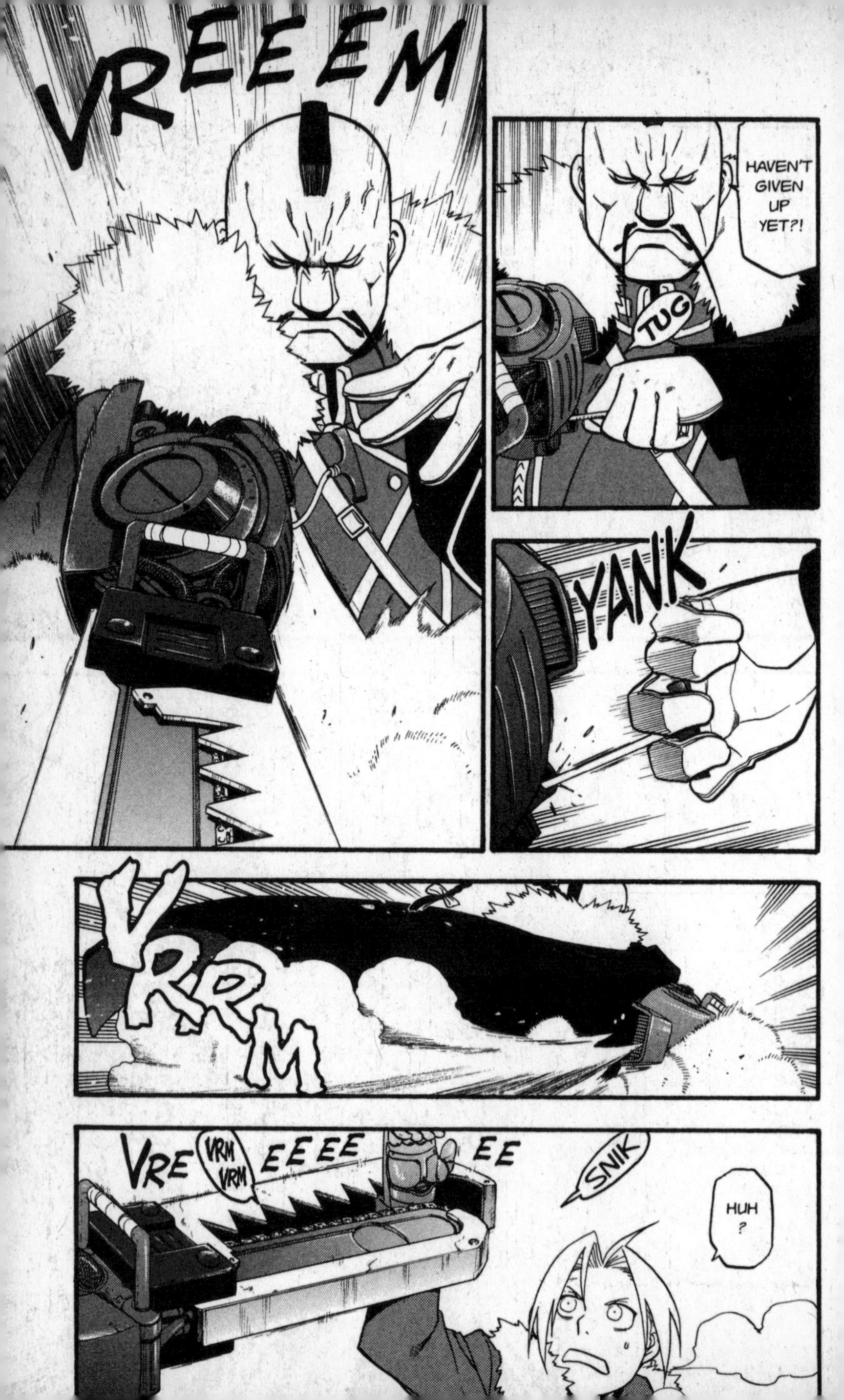
HAVEN'T GIVEN UP YET?!
TUG
YANK
VREEEM
VRRM
HUH?
SNIK
VRE EEEE EE
VRM VRM

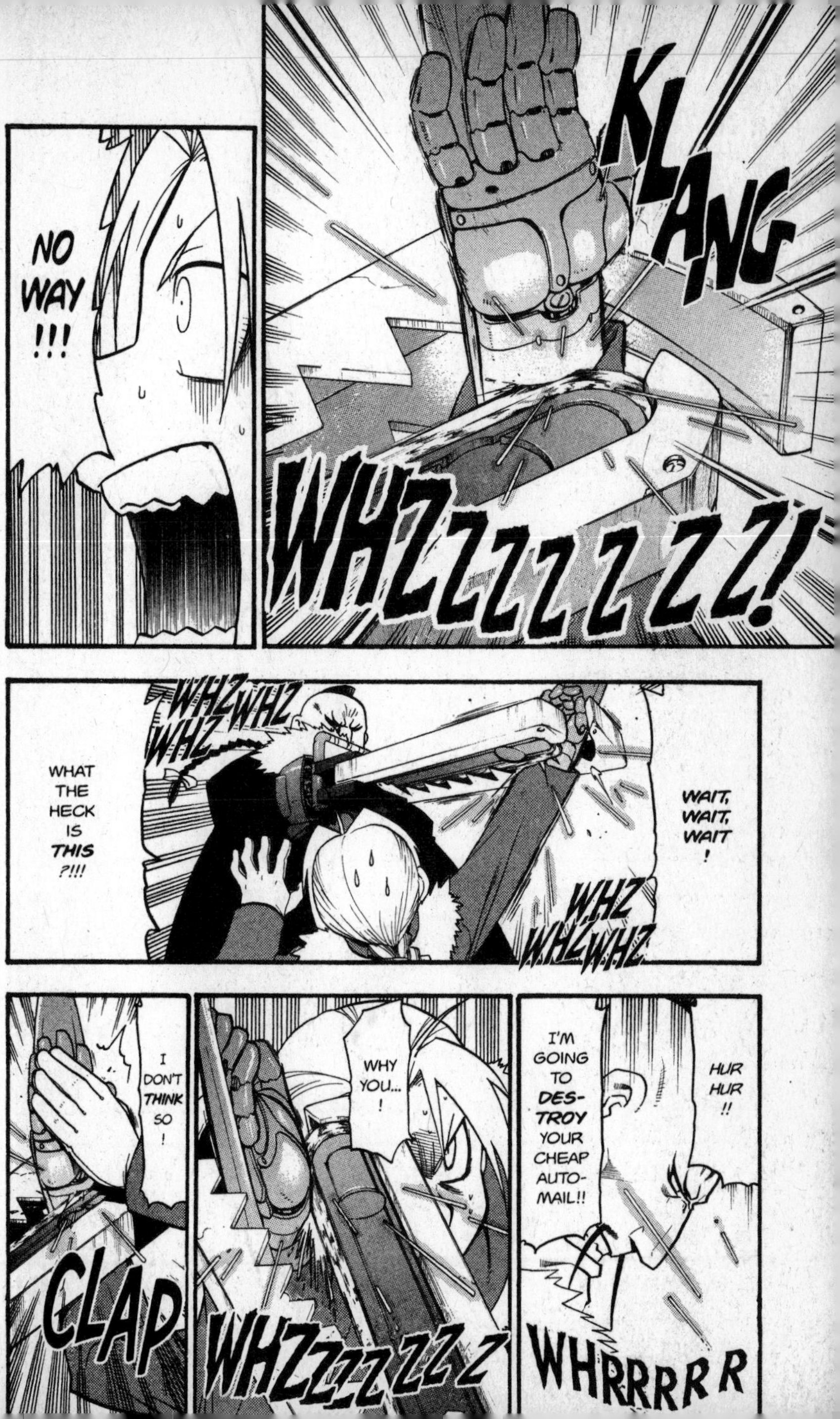
KLANG
WHZZZZZ!
NO WAY!!!
WAIT, WAIT, WAIT!
WHZ WHZ WHZ
WHAT THE HECK IS THIS?!!!
WHZ WHZ WHZ
HUR HUR!!
I'M GOING TO DESTROY YOUR CHEAP AUTO-MAIL!!
WHRRRRR
WHY YOU...!
WHZZZZZZ
I DON'T THINK SO!
CLAP

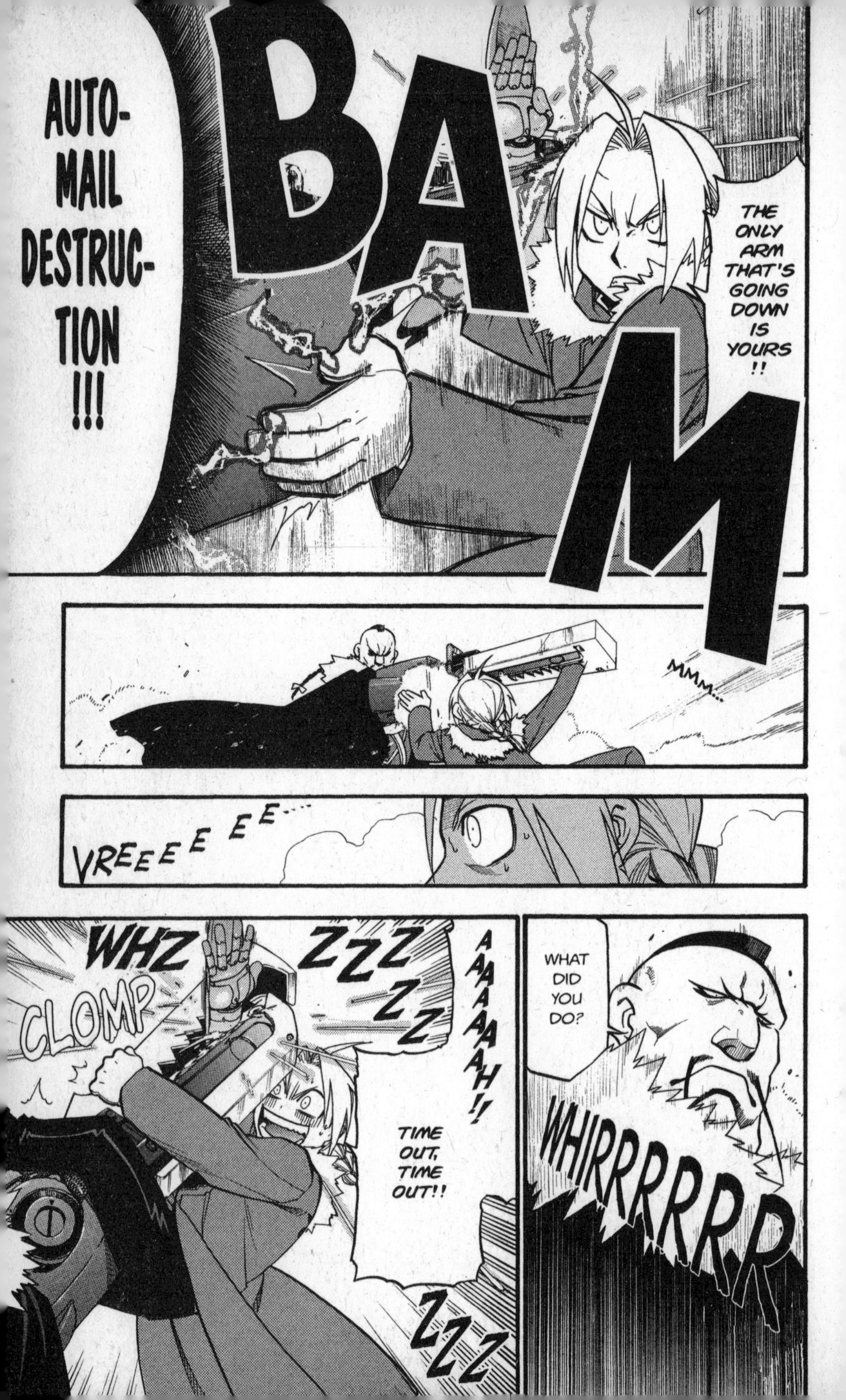
AUTO-MAIL DESTRUCTION!!!
BAM
THE ONLY ARM THAT'S GOING DOWN IS YOURS!!
MMM...
VREEEEEE...
WHAT DID YOU DO?
WHIRRRRRRR
AAAAAAAH!!
TIME OUT, TIME OUT!!
WHZ
ZZZZZ
CLOMP
ZZZ

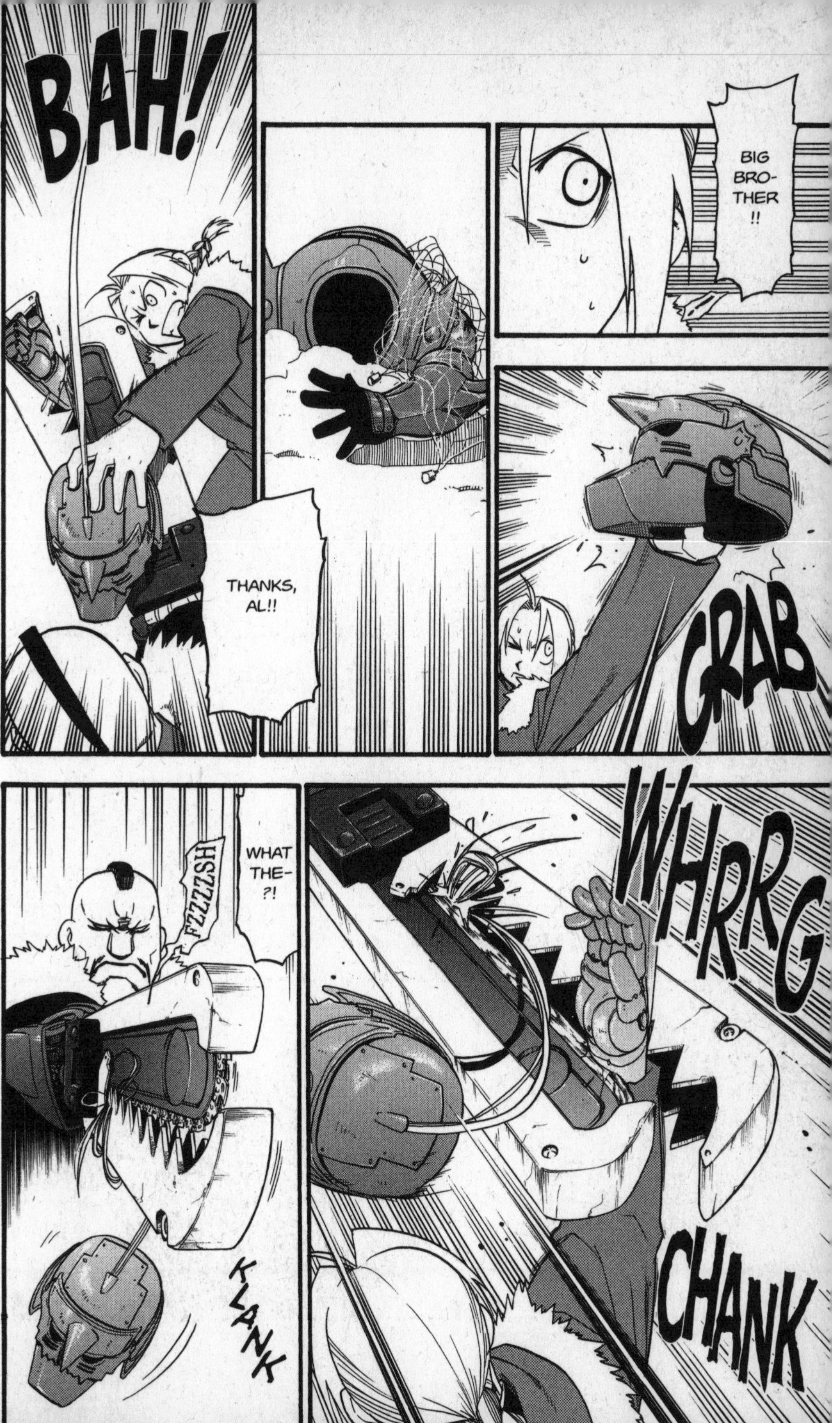
BIG BROTHER!!
GRAB
THANKS, AL!!
BAH!
WHRRG
CHANK
WHAT THE-?!
FZZZZSH
KLANK

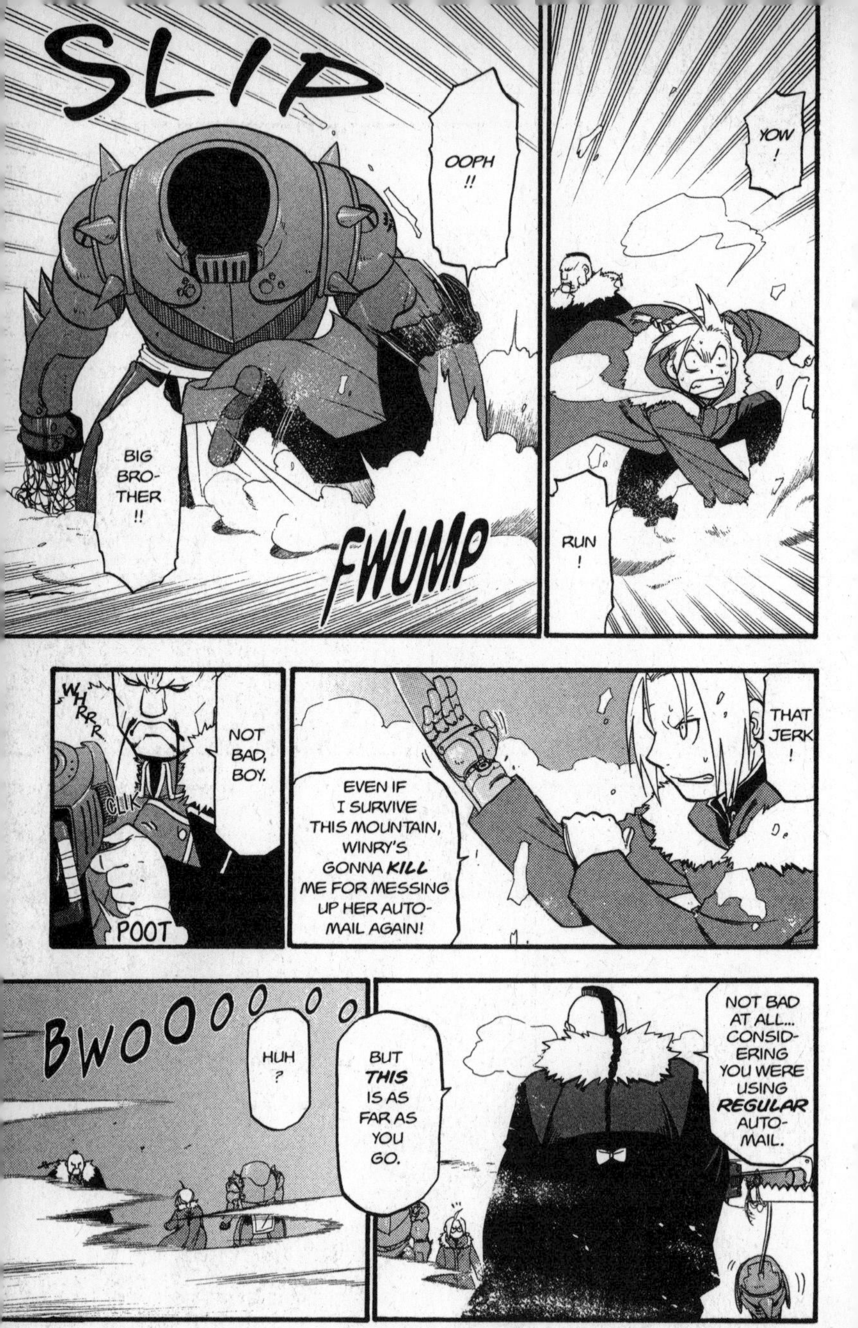

YOW!
RUN!
SLIP
OOPH!!
BIG BROTHER!!
FWUMP
THAT JERK!
EVEN IF I SURVIVE THIS MOUNTAIN, WINRY'S GONNA **KILL** ME FOR MESSING UP HER AUTOMAIL AGAIN!
WHRRR
NOT BAD, BOY.
CLIK
POOT
NOT BAD AT ALL... CONSIDERING YOU WERE USING **REGULAR** AUTOMAIL.
BUT **THIS** IS AS FAR AS YOU GO.
BWOOOOOO
HUH?

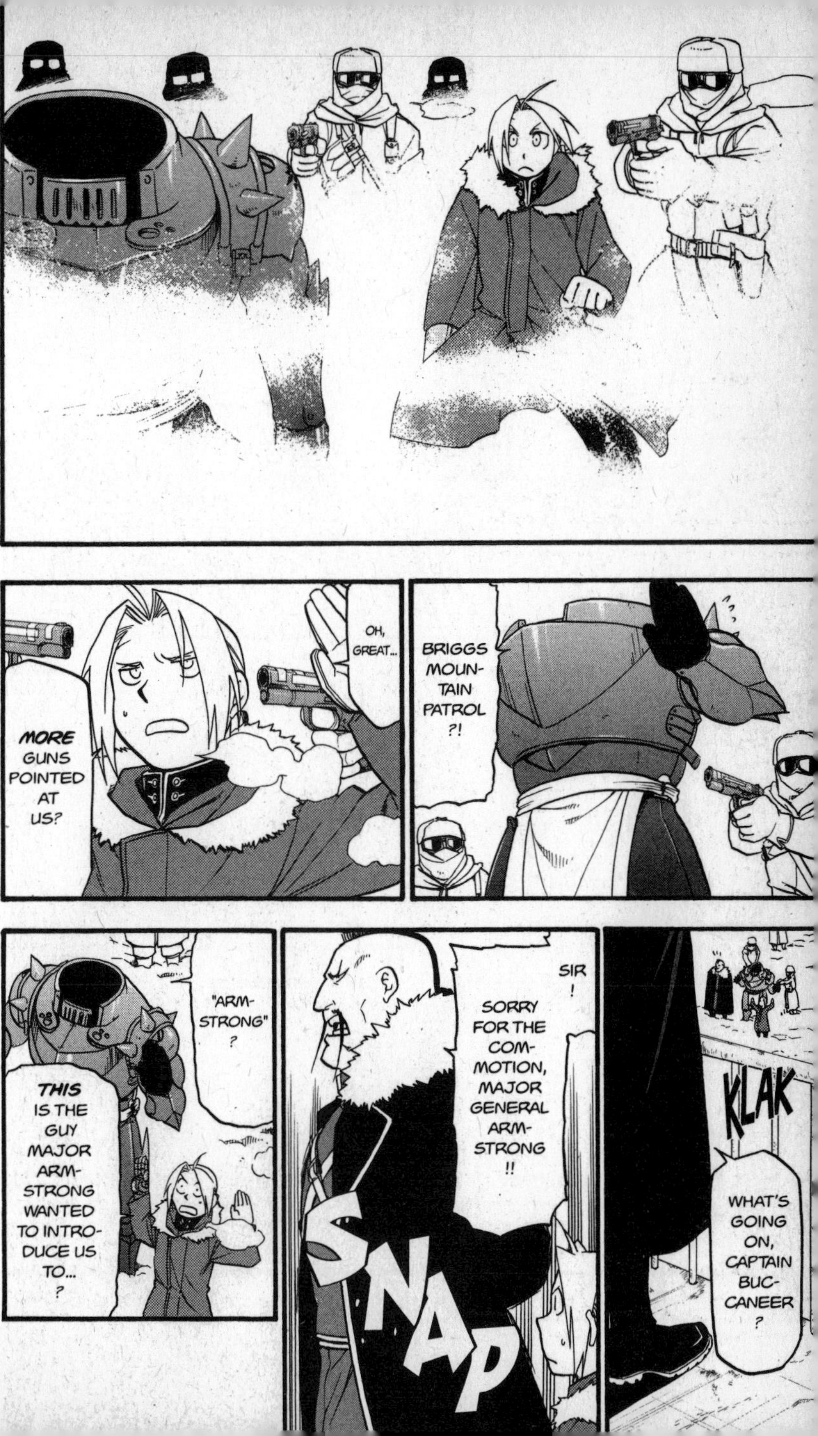
BRIGGS MOUNTAIN PATROL ?!
OH, GREAT...
MORE GUNS POINTED AT US?
KLAK
WHAT'S GOING ON, CAPTAIN BUCCANEER ?
SIR !
SORRY FOR THE COMMOTION, MAJOR GENERAL ARMSTRONG !!
SNAP
"ARMSTRONG" ?
THIS IS THE GUY MAJOR ARMSTRONG WANTED TO INTRODUCE US TO... ?

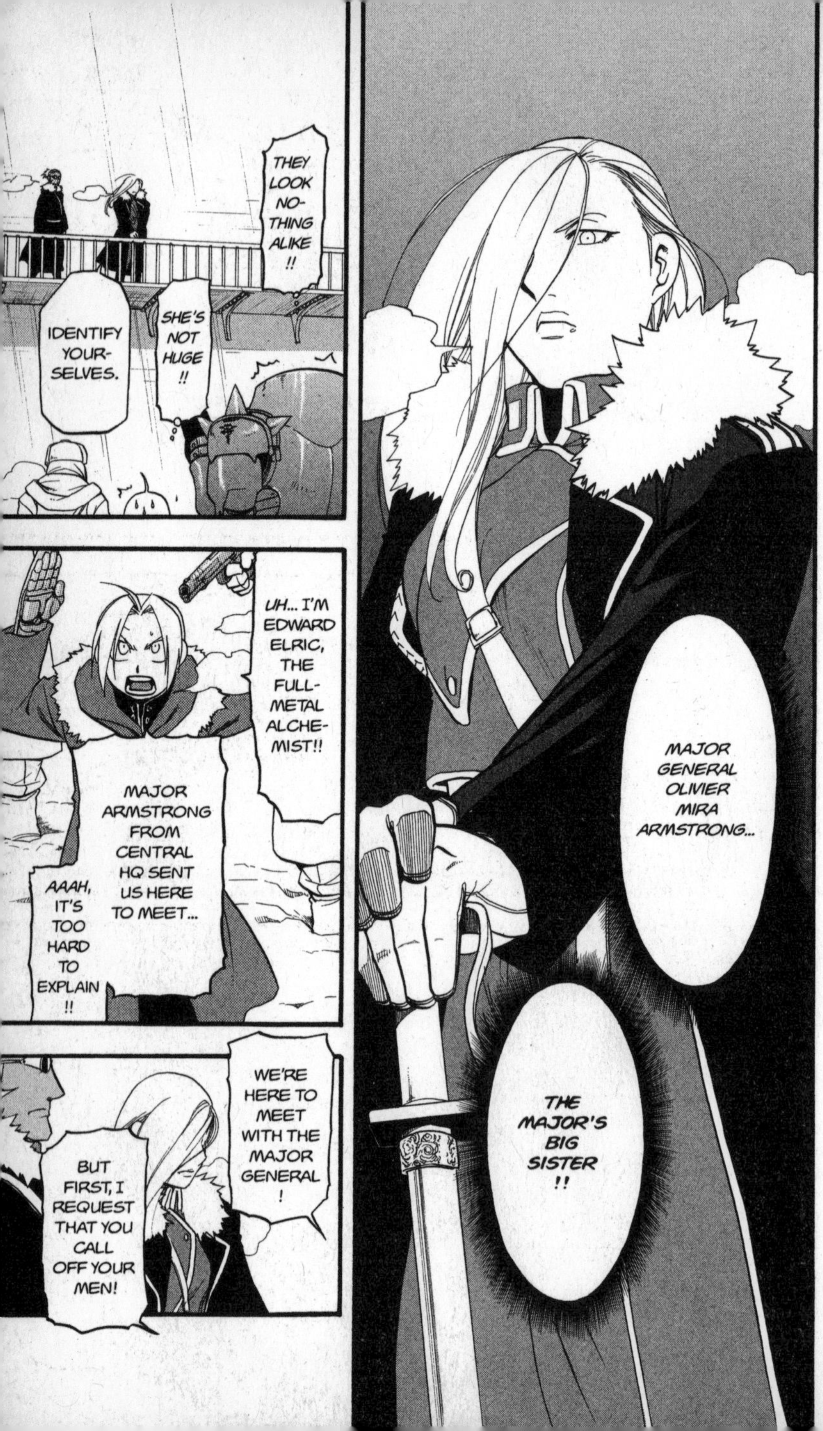
MAJOR GENERAL OLIVIER MIRA ARMSTRONG...
THE MAJOR'S BIG SISTER!!
THEY LOOK NO-THING ALIKE!!
SHE'S NOT HUGE!!
IDENTIFY YOUR-SELVES.
UH... I'M EDWARD ELRIC, THE FULL-METAL ALCHE-MIST!!
MAJOR ARMSTRONG FROM CENTRAL HQ SENT US HERE TO MEET...
AAAH, IT'S TOO HARD TO EXPLAIN!!
WE'RE HERE TO MEET WITH THE MAJOR GENERAL!
BUT FIRST, I REQUEST THAT YOU CALL OFF YOUR MEN!

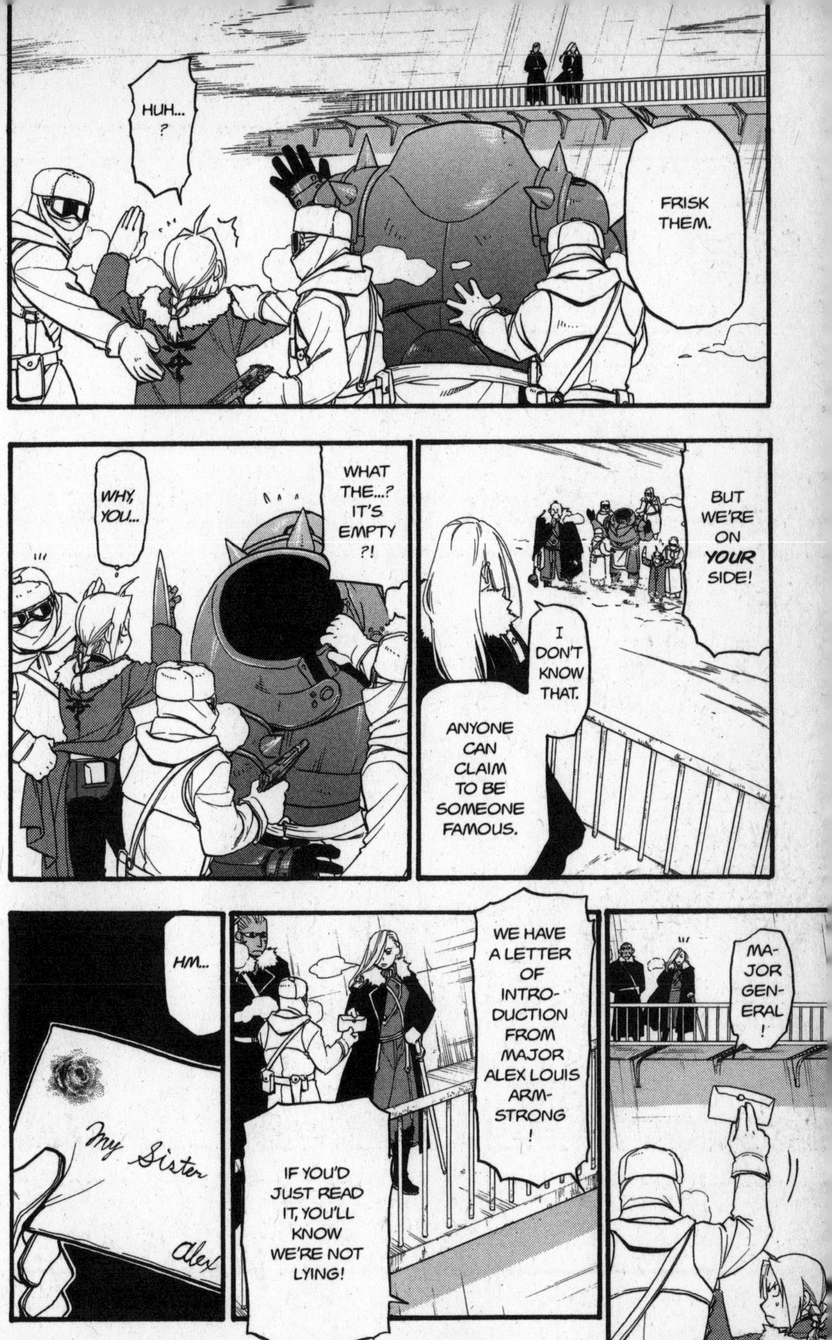
FRISK THEM.
HUH...?
BUT WE'RE ON YOUR SIDE!
I DON'T KNOW THAT.
ANYONE CAN CLAIM TO BE SOMEONE FAMOUS.
WHAT THE...? IT'S EMPTY?!
WHY, YOU...
MAJOR GENERAL!
WE HAVE A LETTER OF INTRODUCTION FROM MAJOR ALEX LOUIS ARMSTRONG!
IF YOU'D JUST READ IT, YOU'LL KNOW WE'RE NOT LYING!
HM...
My Sister
Alex

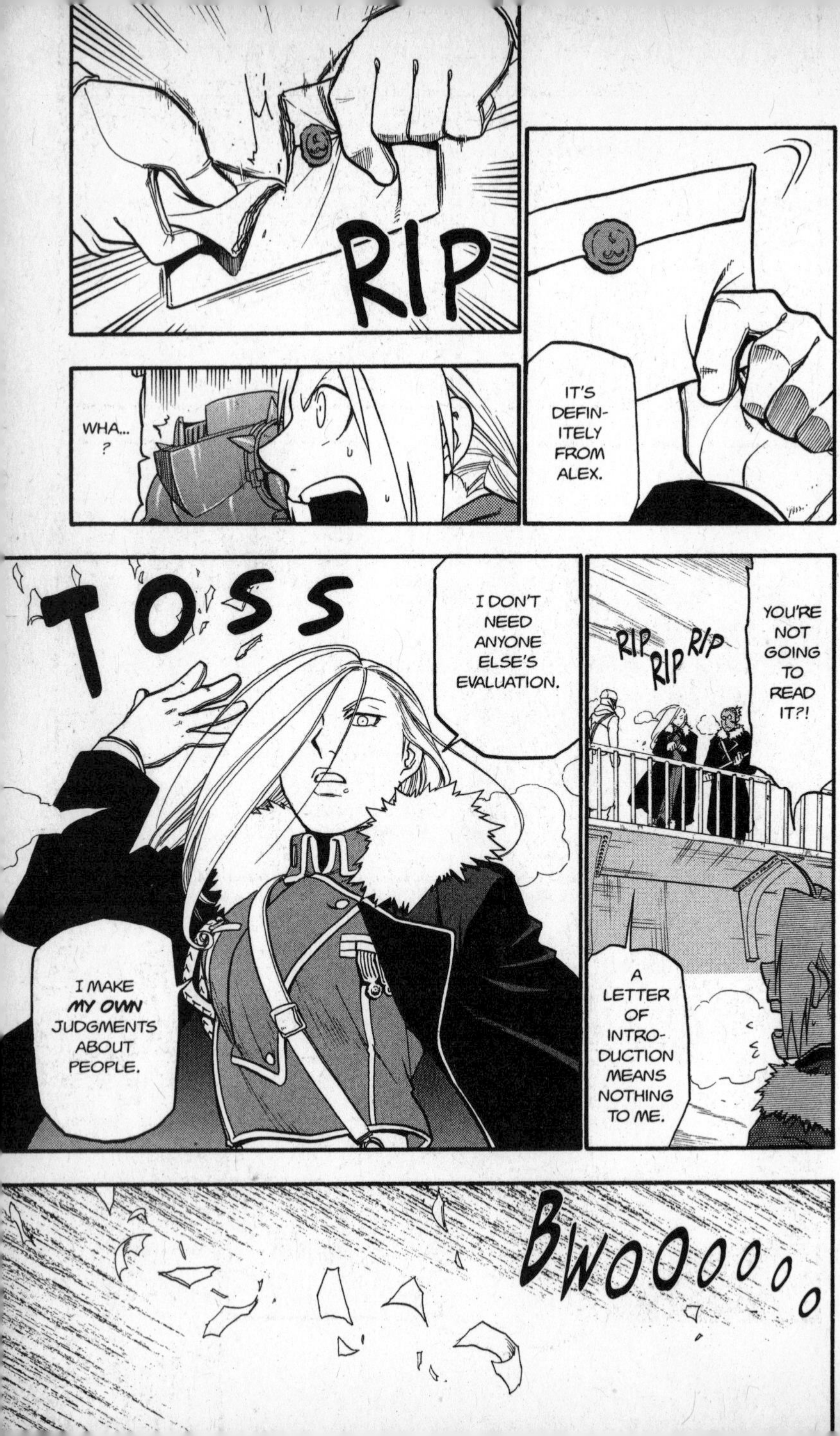

IT'S DEFIN-ITELY FROM ALEX.
RIP
WHA... ?
RIP RIP RIP
YOU'RE NOT GOING TO READ IT?!
A LETTER OF INTRO-DUCTION MEANS NOTHING TO ME.
I DON'T NEED ANYONE ELSE'S EVALUATION.
TOSS
I MAKE *MY OWN* JUDGMENTS ABOUT PEOPLE.
BWOOOOOOO

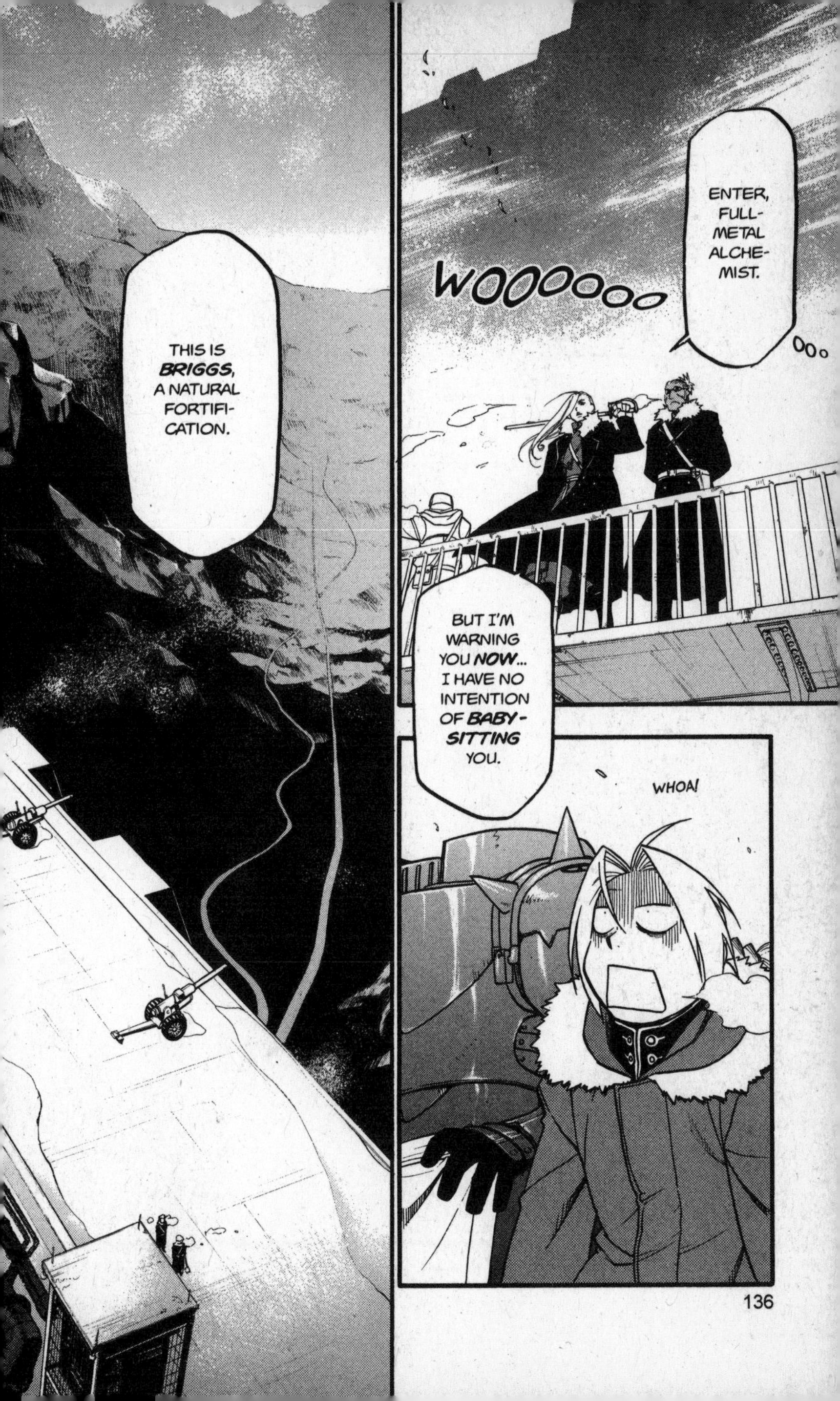
ENTER, FULL-METAL ALCHE-MIST.
WOOOOOOOOOo
BUT I'M WARNING YOU *NOW*... I HAVE NO INTENTION OF *BABY-SITTING* YOU.
WHOA!
THIS IS *BRIGGS*, A NATURAL FORTIFI-CATION.

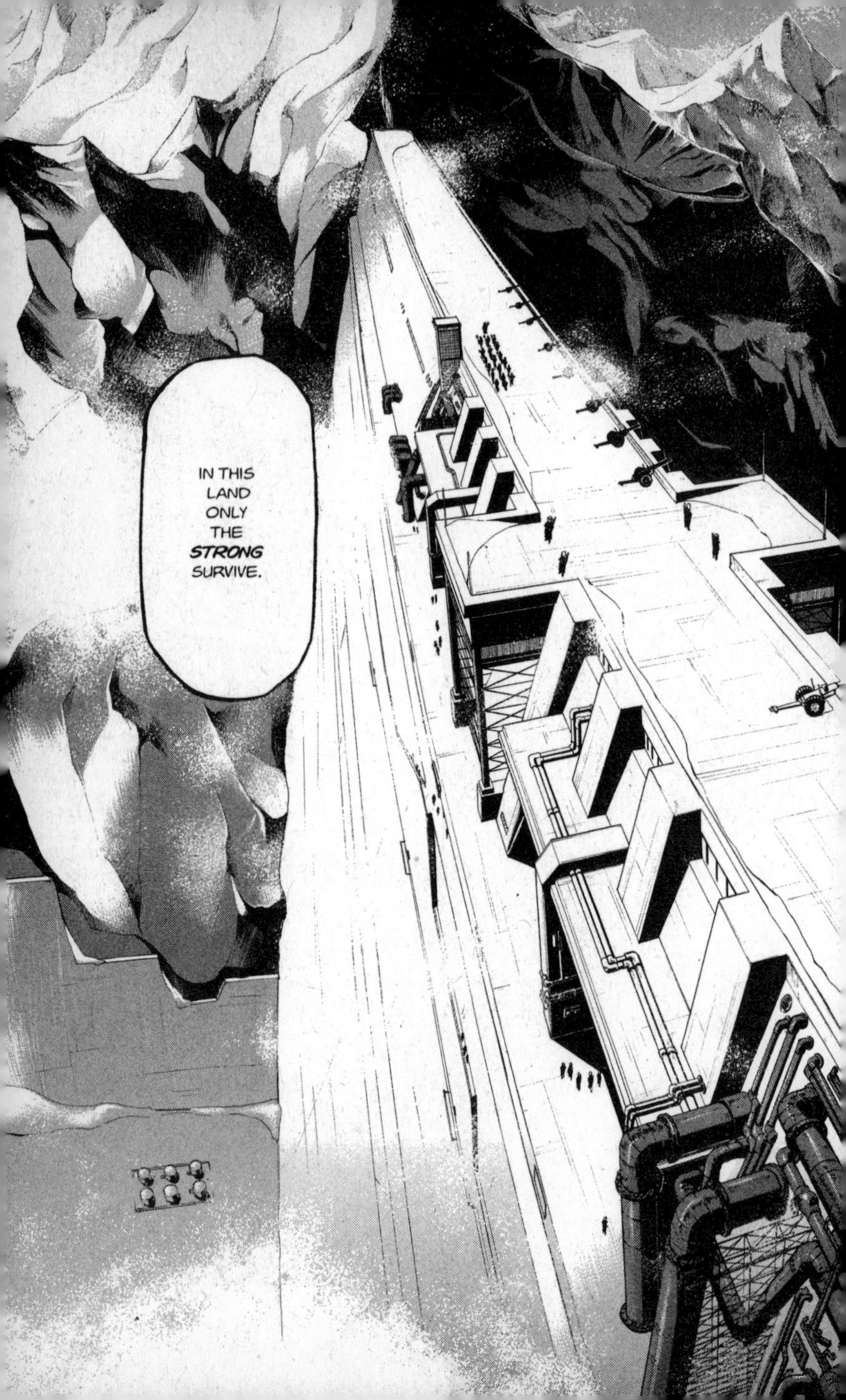
IN THIS LAND ONLY THE **STRONG** SURVIVE.

FULLMETAL
ALCHEMIST

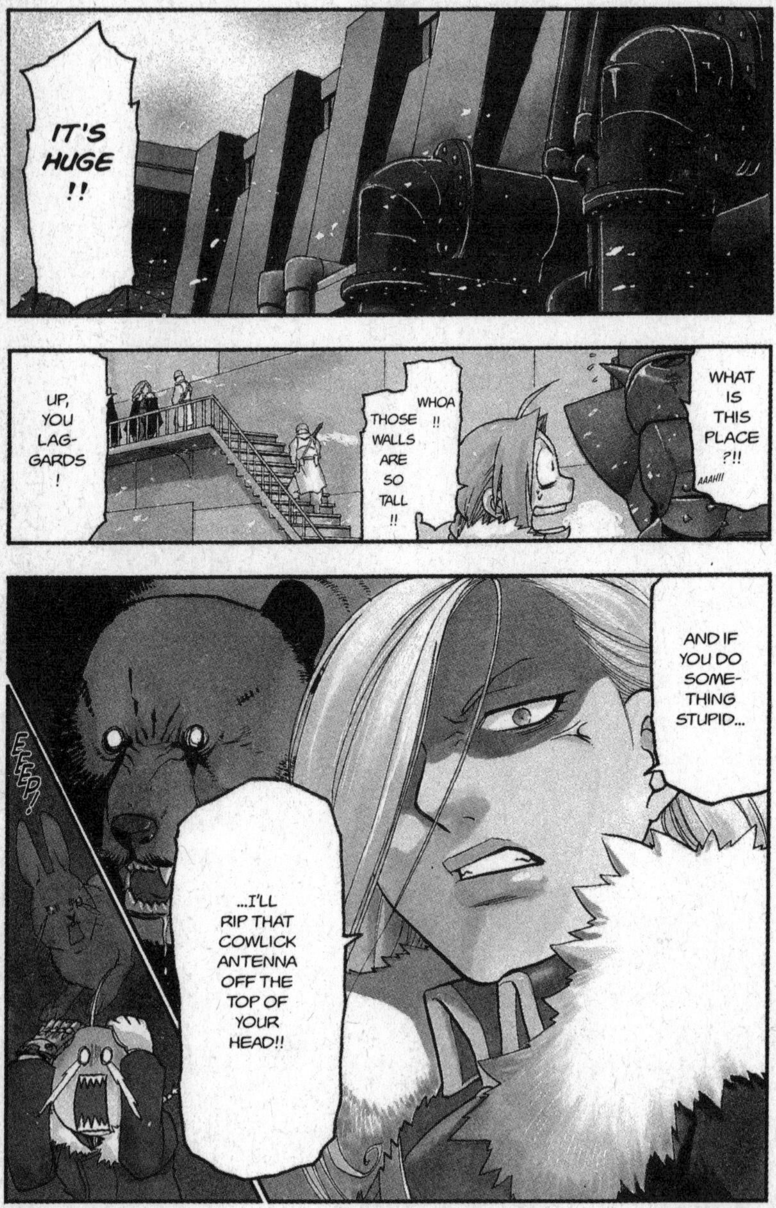
IT'S HUGE !!
WHAT IS THIS PLACE ?!!
AAAH!!
WHOA !! THOSE WALLS ARE SO TALL !!
UP, YOU LAG-GARDS !
AND IF YOU DO SOME-THING STUPID...
...I'LL RIP THAT COWLICK ANTENNA OFF THE TOP OF YOUR HEAD!!
EEEP!

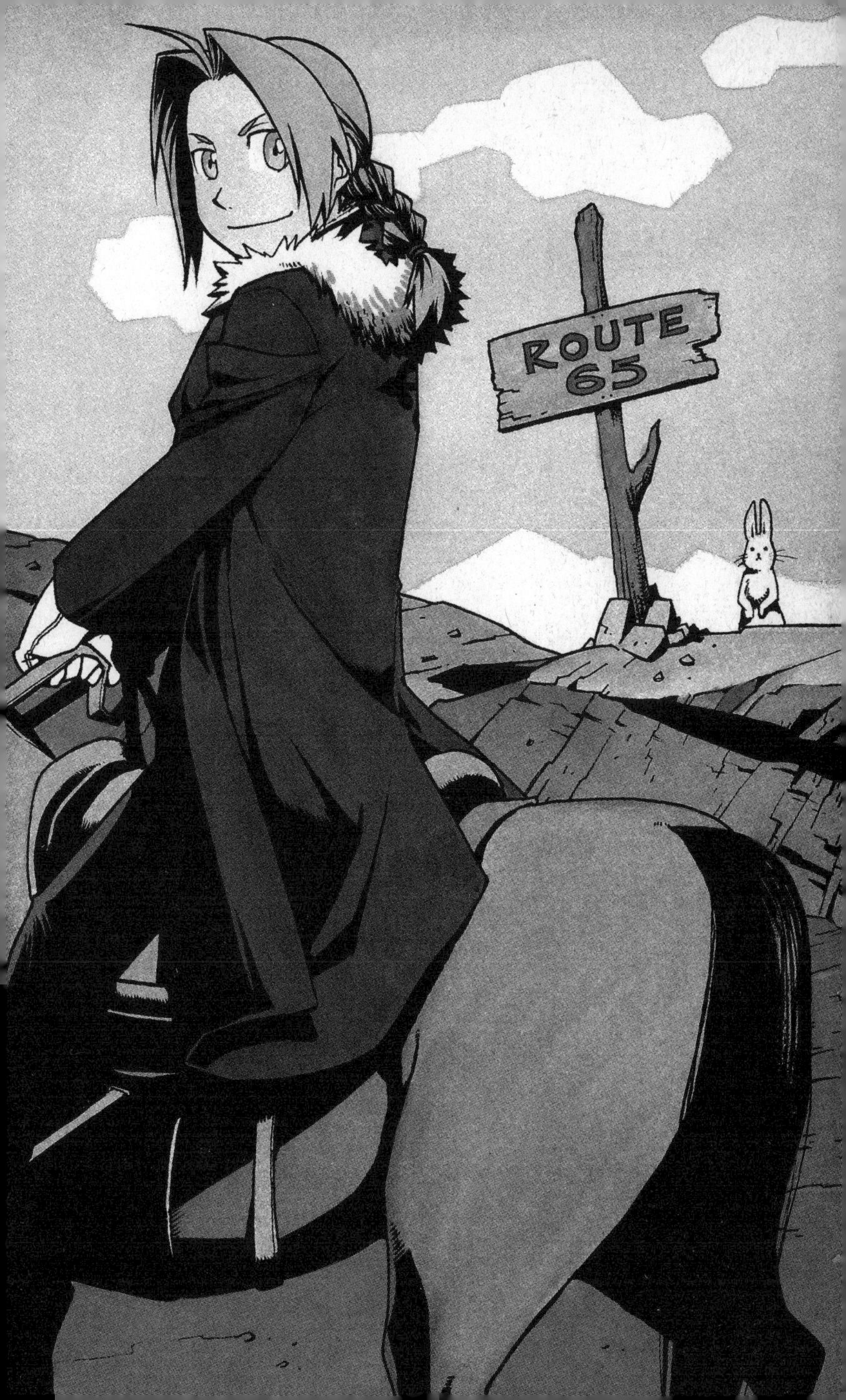
ROUTE 65

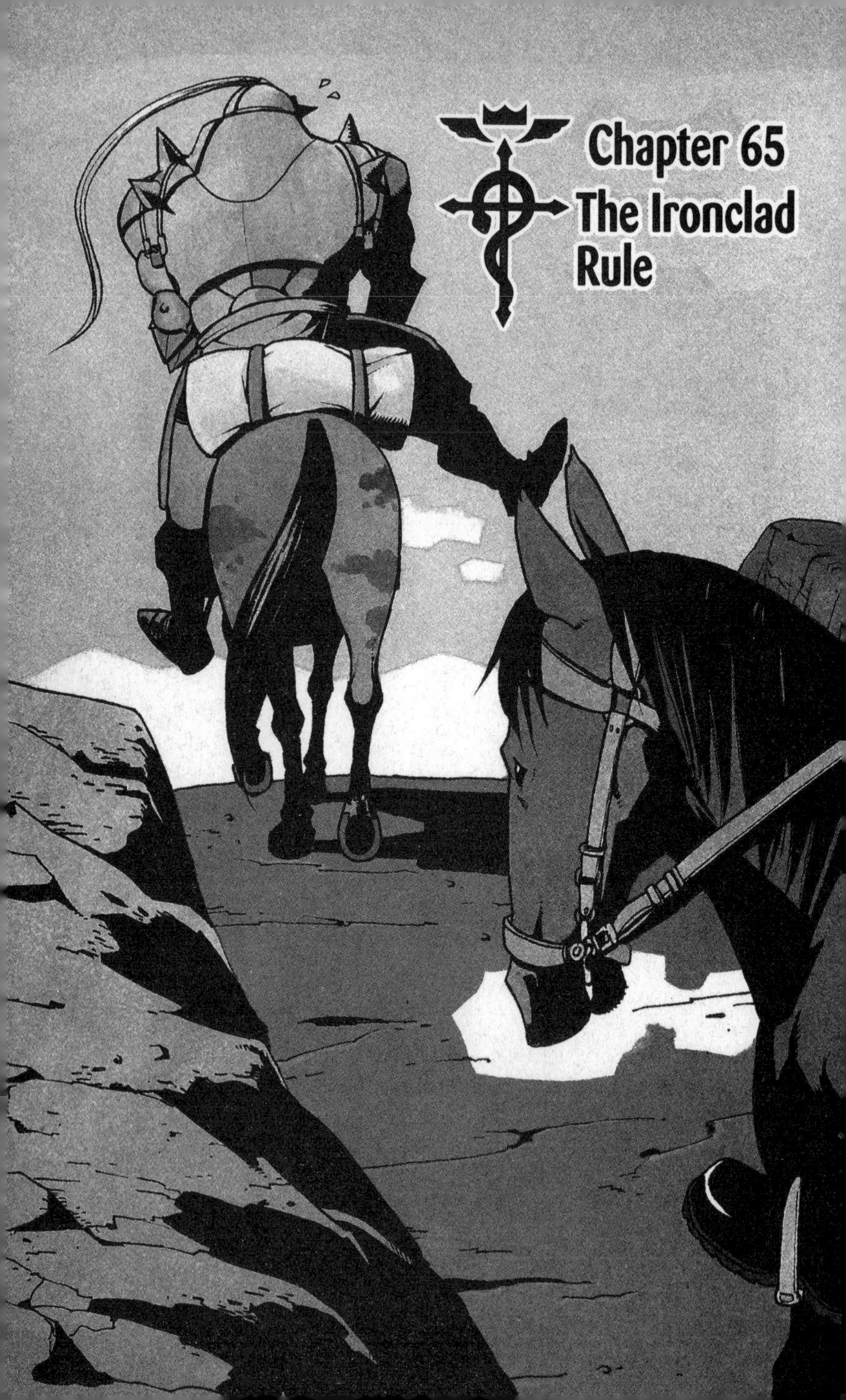
Chapter 65
The Ironclad Rule

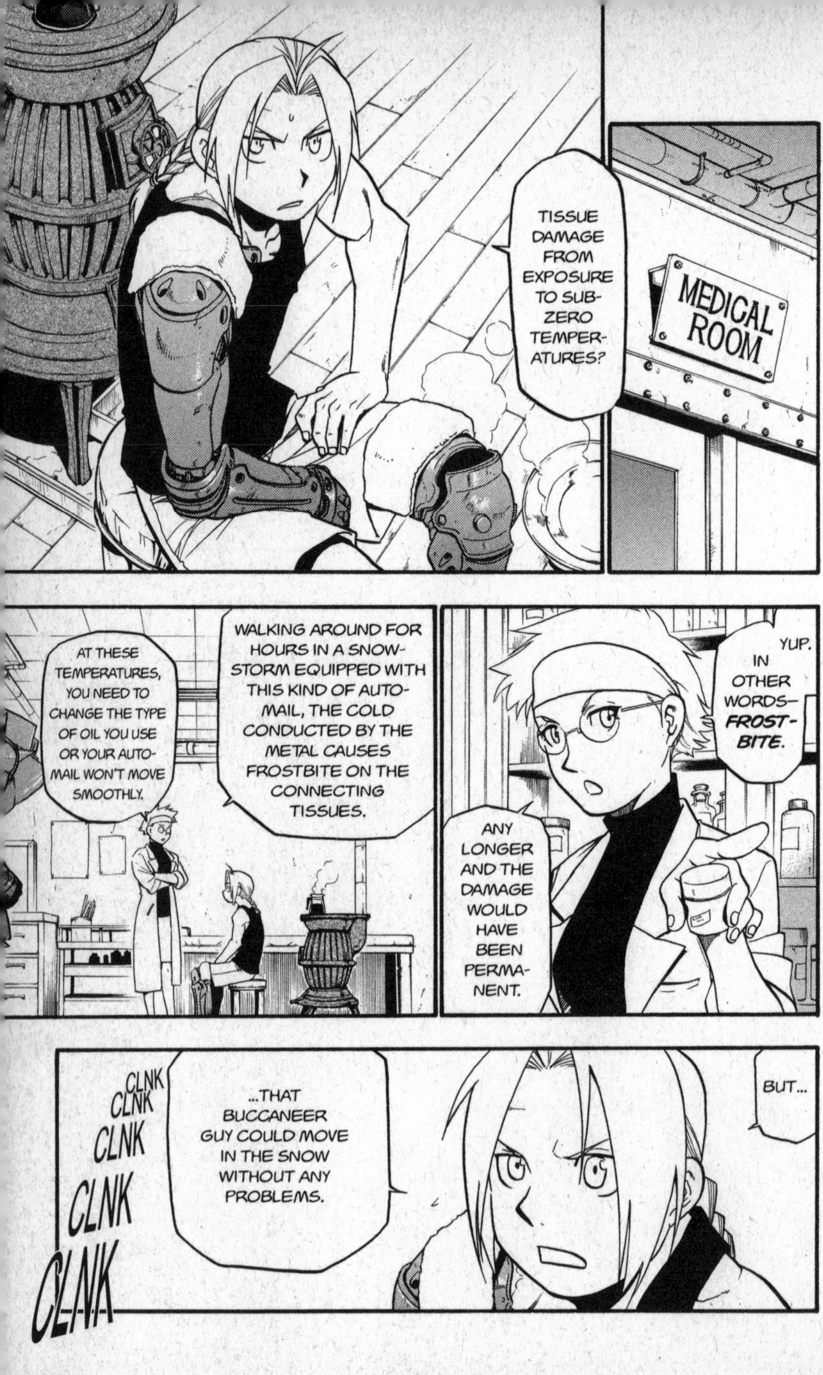
MEDICAL ROOM
TISSUE DAMAGE FROM EXPOSURE TO SUB-ZERO TEMPERATURES?
YUP. IN OTHER WORDS—*FROSTBITE*.
ANY LONGER AND THE DAMAGE WOULD HAVE BEEN PERMANENT.
WALKING AROUND FOR HOURS IN A SNOWSTORM EQUIPPED WITH THIS KIND OF AUTOMAIL, THE COLD CONDUCTED BY THE METAL CAUSES FROSTBITE ON THE CONNECTING TISSUES.
AT THESE TEMPERATURES, YOU NEED TO CHANGE THE TYPE OF OIL YOU USE OR YOUR AUTOMAIL WON'T MOVE SMOOTHLY.
BUT...
...THAT BUCCANEER GUY COULD MOVE IN THE SNOW WITHOUT ANY PROBLEMS.
CLNK CLNK CLNK CLNK CLNK

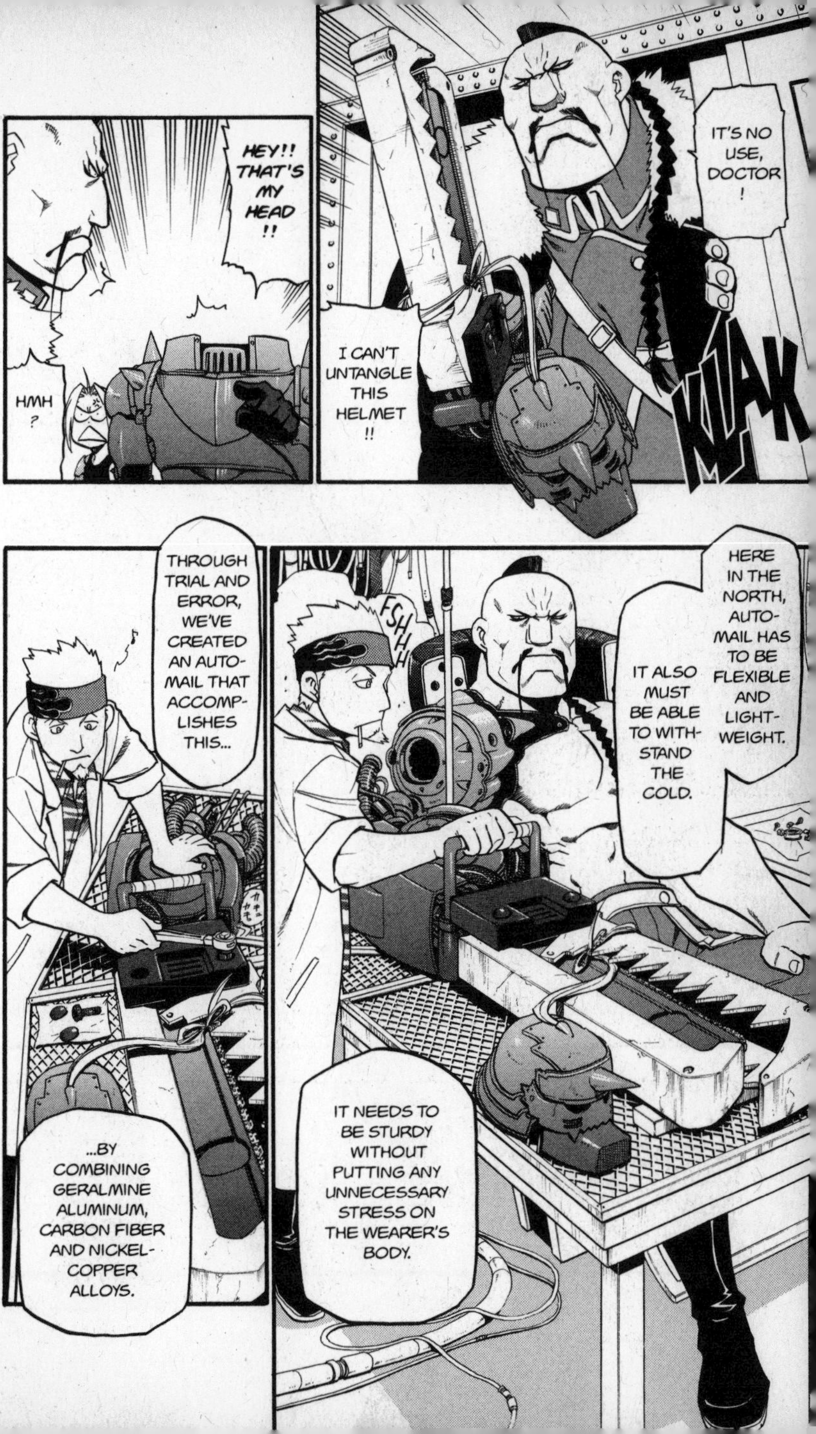
IT'S NO USE, DOCTOR!
I CAN'T UNTANGLE THIS HELMET!!
KLAK
HEY!! THAT'S MY HEAD!!
HMH?
HERE IN THE NORTH, AUTOMAIL HAS TO BE FLEXIBLE AND LIGHTWEIGHT.
IT ALSO MUST BE ABLE TO WITHSTAND THE COLD.
FSHH
IT NEEDS TO BE STURDY WITHOUT PUTTING ANY UNNECESSARY STRESS ON THE WEARER'S BODY.
THROUGH TRIAL AND ERROR, WE'VE CREATED AN AUTOMAIL THAT ACCOMPLISHES THIS...
...BY COMBINING GERALMINE ALUMINUM, CARBON FIBER AND NICKEL-COPPER ALLOYS.

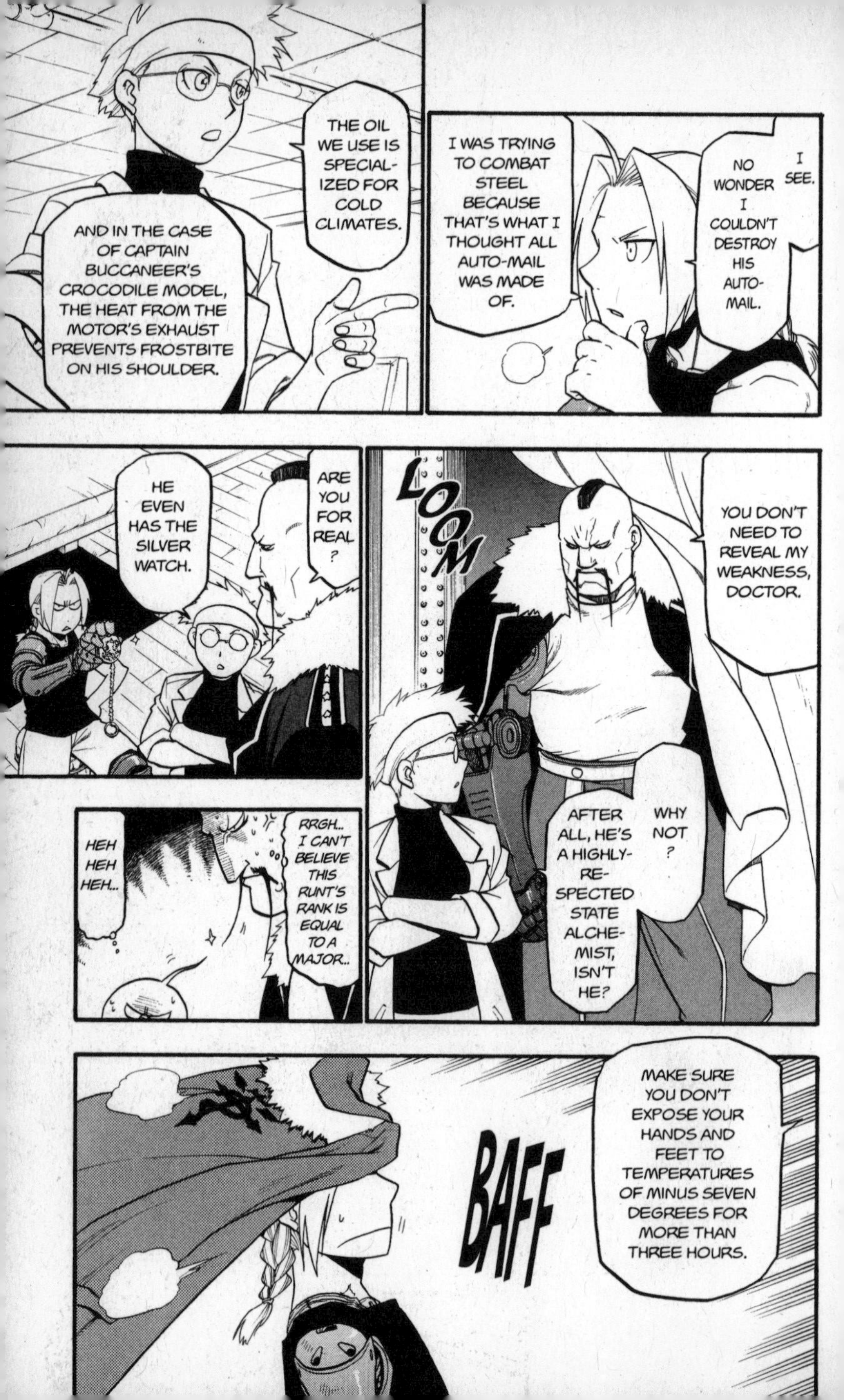
I SEE.
NO WONDER I COULDN'T DESTROY HIS AUTO-MAIL.
I WAS TRYING TO COMBAT STEEL BECAUSE THAT'S WHAT I THOUGHT ALL AUTO-MAIL WAS MADE OF.
THE OIL WE USE IS SPECIAL-IZED FOR COLD CLIMATES.
AND IN THE CASE OF CAPTAIN BUCCANEER'S CROCODILE MODEL, THE HEAT FROM THE MOTOR'S EXHAUST PREVENTS FROSTBITE ON HIS SHOULDER.
LOOM
YOU DON'T NEED TO REVEAL MY WEAKNESS, DOCTOR.
WHY NOT?
AFTER ALL, HE'S A HIGHLY-RE-SPECTED STATE ALCHE-MIST, ISN'T HE?
ARE YOU FOR REAL?
HE EVEN HAS THE SILVER WATCH.
RRGH... I CAN'T BELIEVE THIS RUNT'S RANK IS EQUAL TO A MAJOR...
HEH HEH HEH...
MAKE SURE YOU DON'T EXPOSE YOUR HANDS AND FEET TO TEMPERATURES OF MINUS SEVEN DEGREES FOR MORE THAN THREE HOURS.
BAFF

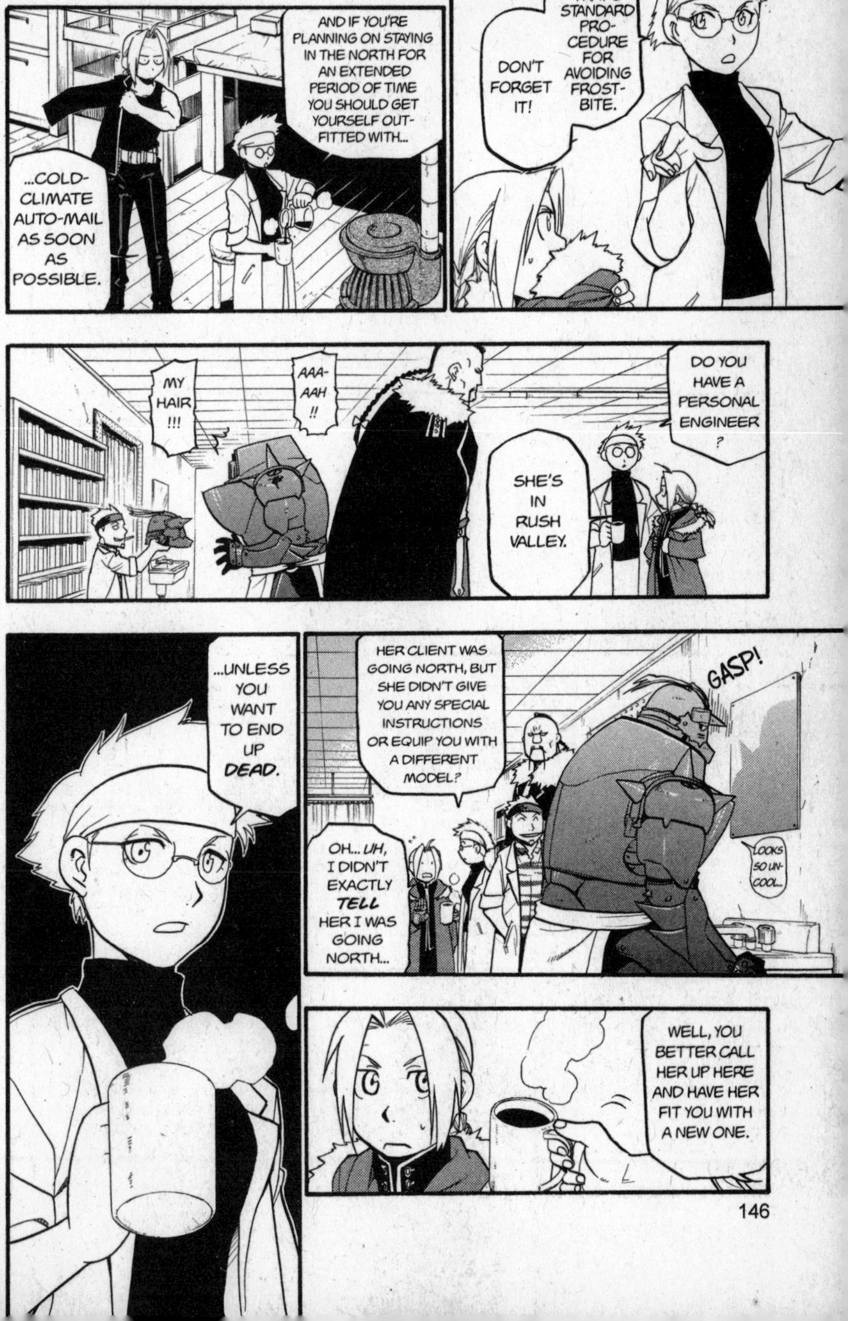
THAT'S STANDARD PROCEDURE FOR AVOIDING FROST-BITE.
DON'T FORGET IT!
AND IF YOU'RE PLANNING ON STAYING IN THE NORTH FOR AN EXTENDED PERIOD OF TIME YOU SHOULD GET YOURSELF OUT-FITTED WITH...
...COLD-CLIMATE AUTO-MAIL AS SOON AS POSSIBLE.
DO YOU HAVE A PERSONAL ENGINEER?
SHE'S IN RUSH VALLEY.
AAA-AAH!!
MY HAIR!!!
GASP!
HER CLIENT WAS GOING NORTH, BUT SHE DIDN'T GIVE YOU ANY SPECIAL INSTRUCTIONS OR EQUIP YOU WITH A DIFFERENT MODEL?
LOOKS SO UN-COOL...
OH... UH, I DIDN'T EXACTLY TELL HER I WAS GOING NORTH...
WELL, YOU BETTER CALL HER UP HERE AND HAVE HER FIT YOU WITH A NEW ONE.
...UNLESS YOU WANT TO END UP DEAD.

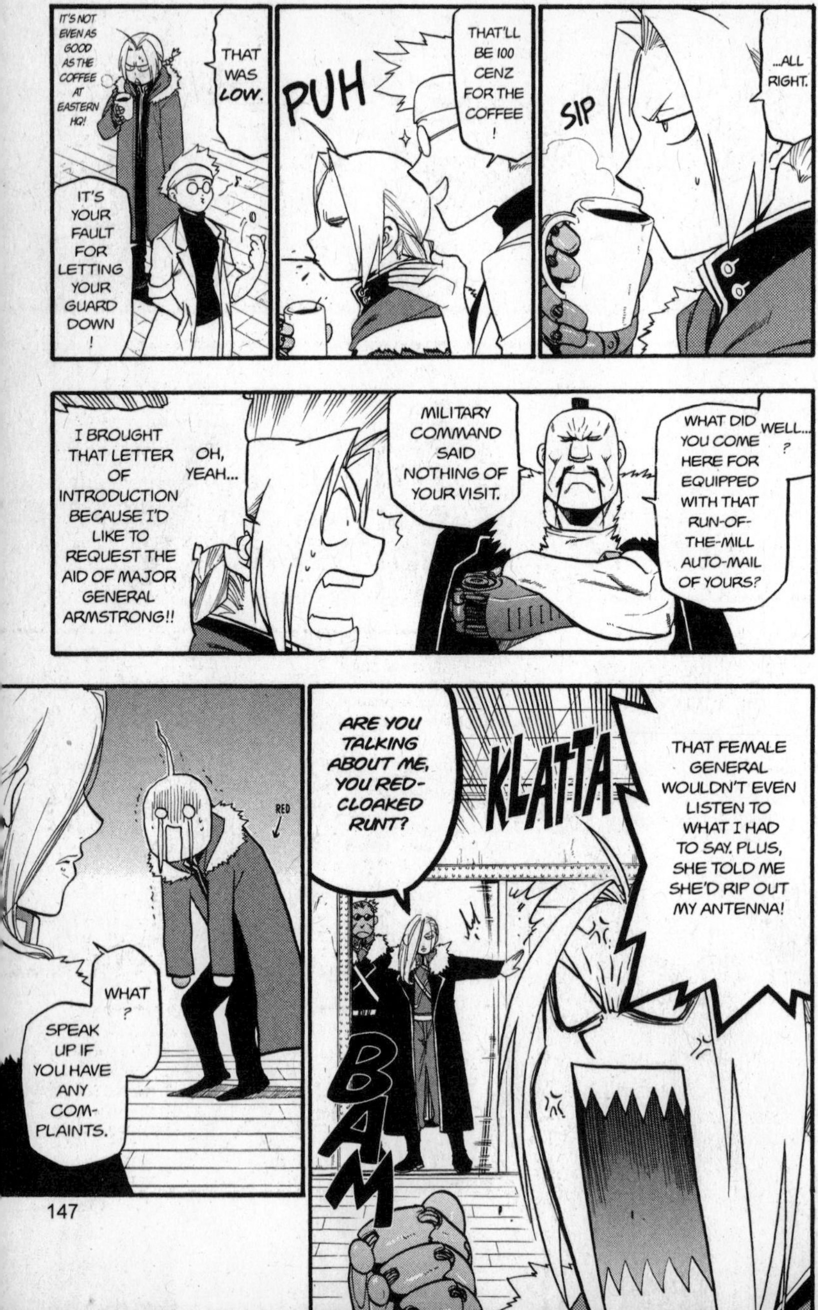
...ALL RIGHT.
SIP
THAT'LL BE 100 CENZ FOR THE COFFEE!
PUH
THAT WAS LOW.
IT'S NOT EVEN AS GOOD AS THE COFFEE AT EASTERN HQ!
IT'S YOUR FAULT FOR LETTING YOUR GUARD DOWN!
WELL...?
WHAT DID YOU COME HERE FOR EQUIPPED WITH THAT RUN-OF-THE-MILL AUTO-MAIL OF YOURS?
MILITARY COMMAND SAID NOTHING OF YOUR VISIT.
OH, YEAH...
I BROUGHT THAT LETTER OF INTRODUCTION BECAUSE I'D LIKE TO REQUEST THE AID OF MAJOR GENERAL ARMSTRONG!!
THAT FEMALE GENERAL WOULDN'T EVEN LISTEN TO WHAT I HAD TO SAY. PLUS, SHE TOLD ME SHE'D RIP OUT MY ANTENNA!
KLATTA
ARE YOU TALKING ABOUT ME, YOU RED-CLOAKED RUNT?
BAM
RED
WHAT?
SPEAK UP IF YOU HAVE ANY COMPLAINTS.

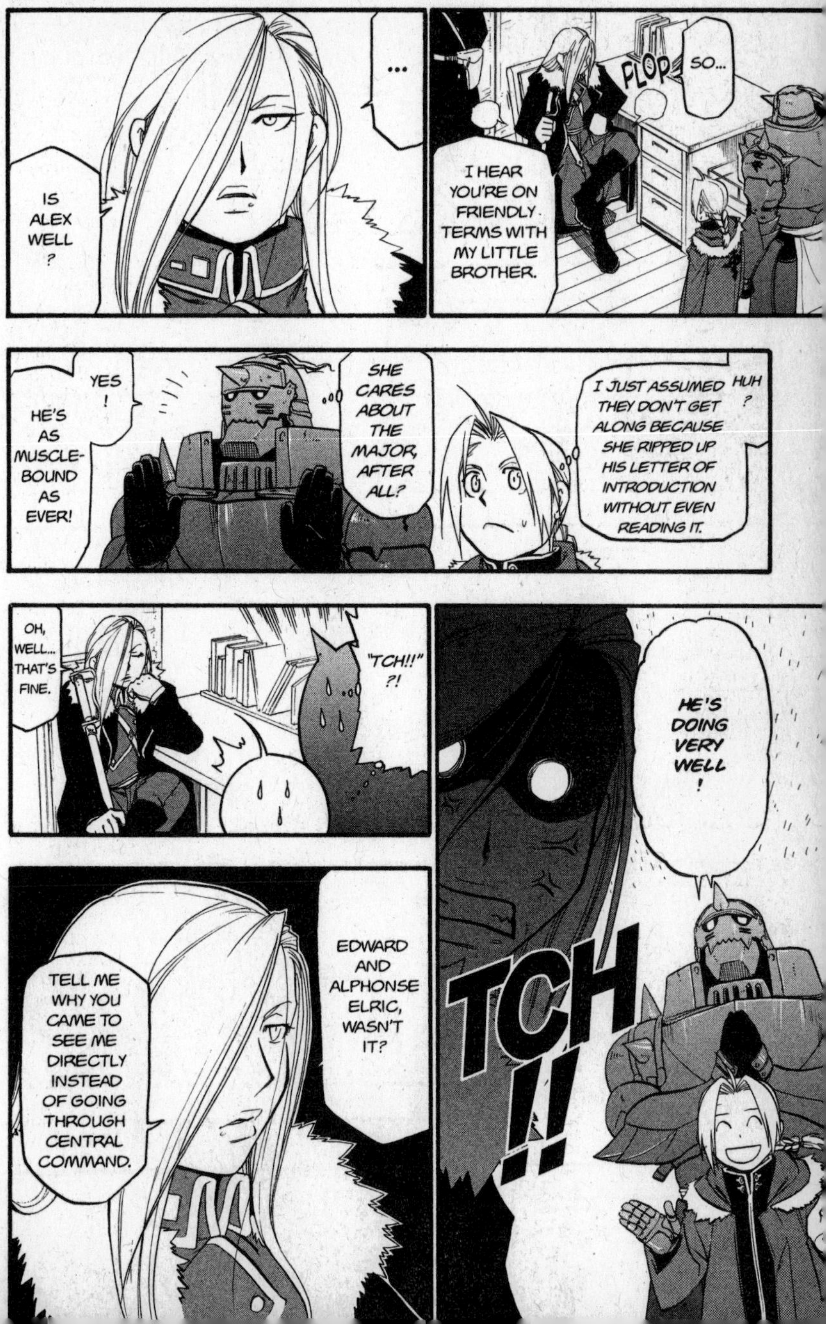
PLOP
SO...
I HEAR YOU'RE ON FRIENDLY TERMS WITH MY LITTLE BROTHER.
...
IS ALEX WELL?
HUH?
I JUST ASSUMED THEY DON'T GET ALONG BECAUSE SHE RIPPED UP HIS LETTER OF INTRODUCTION WITHOUT EVEN READING IT.
SHE CARES ABOUT THE MAJOR, AFTER ALL?
YES!
HE'S AS MUSCLE-BOUND AS EVER!
HE'S DOING VERY WELL!
TCH!!
"TCH!!"?!
OH, WELL... THAT'S FINE.
EDWARD AND ALPHONSE ELRIC, WASN'T IT?
TELL ME WHY YOU CAME TO SEE ME DIRECTLY INSTEAD OF GOING THROUGH CENTRAL COMMAND.

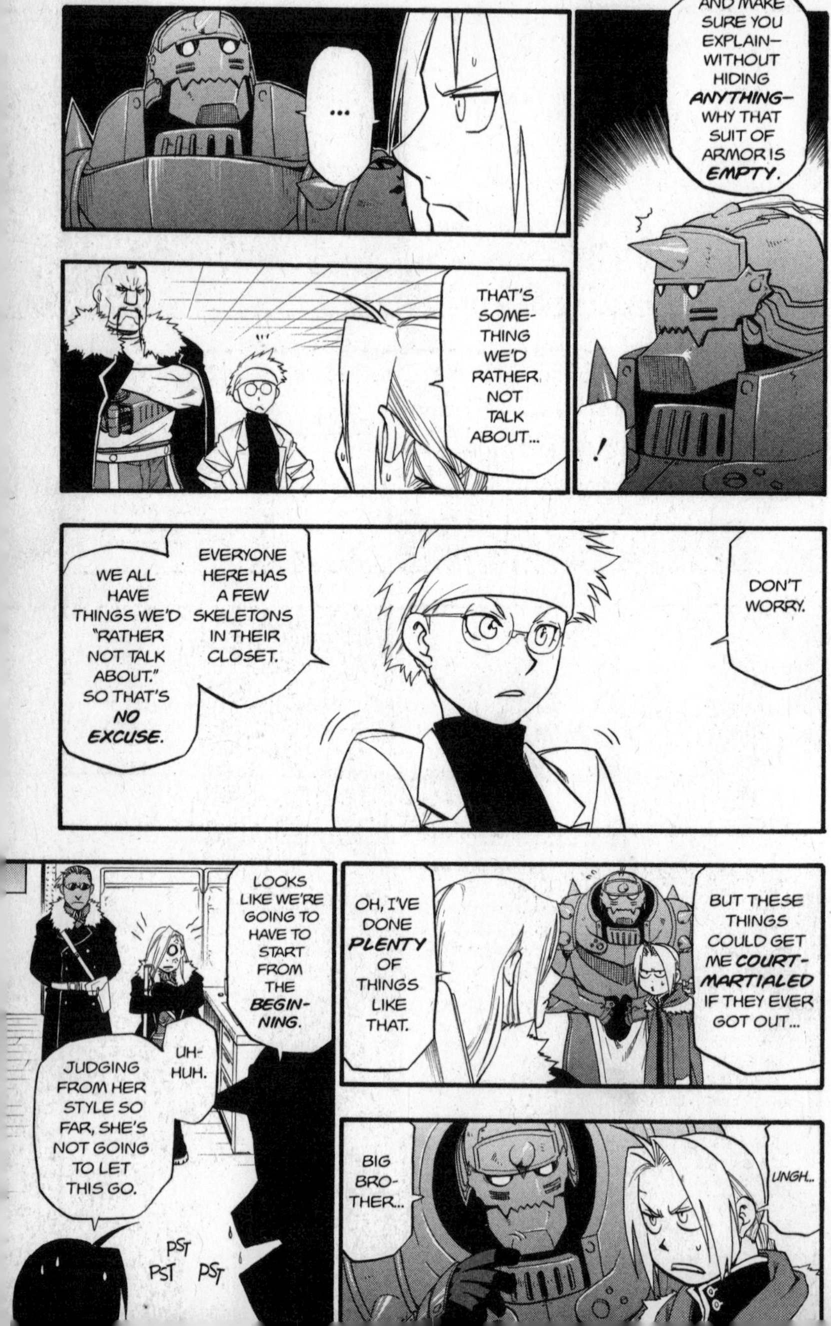
AND MAKE SURE YOU EXPLAIN— WITHOUT HIDING ANYTHING— WHY THAT SUIT OF ARMOR IS EMPTY.
!
...
THAT'S SOMETHING WE'D RATHER NOT TALK ABOUT...
DON'T WORRY.
EVERYONE HERE HAS A FEW SKELETONS IN THEIR CLOSET.
WE ALL HAVE THINGS WE'D "RATHER NOT TALK ABOUT." SO THAT'S NO EXCUSE.
BUT THESE THINGS COULD GET ME COURT-MARTIALED IF THEY EVER GOT OUT...
OH, I'VE DONE PLENTY OF THINGS LIKE THAT.
UNGH...
BIG BROTHER...
LOOKS LIKE WE'RE GOING TO HAVE TO START FROM THE BEGINNING.
UH-HUH.
JUDGING FROM HER STYLE SO FAR, SHE'S NOT GOING TO LET THIS GO.
PST PST PST

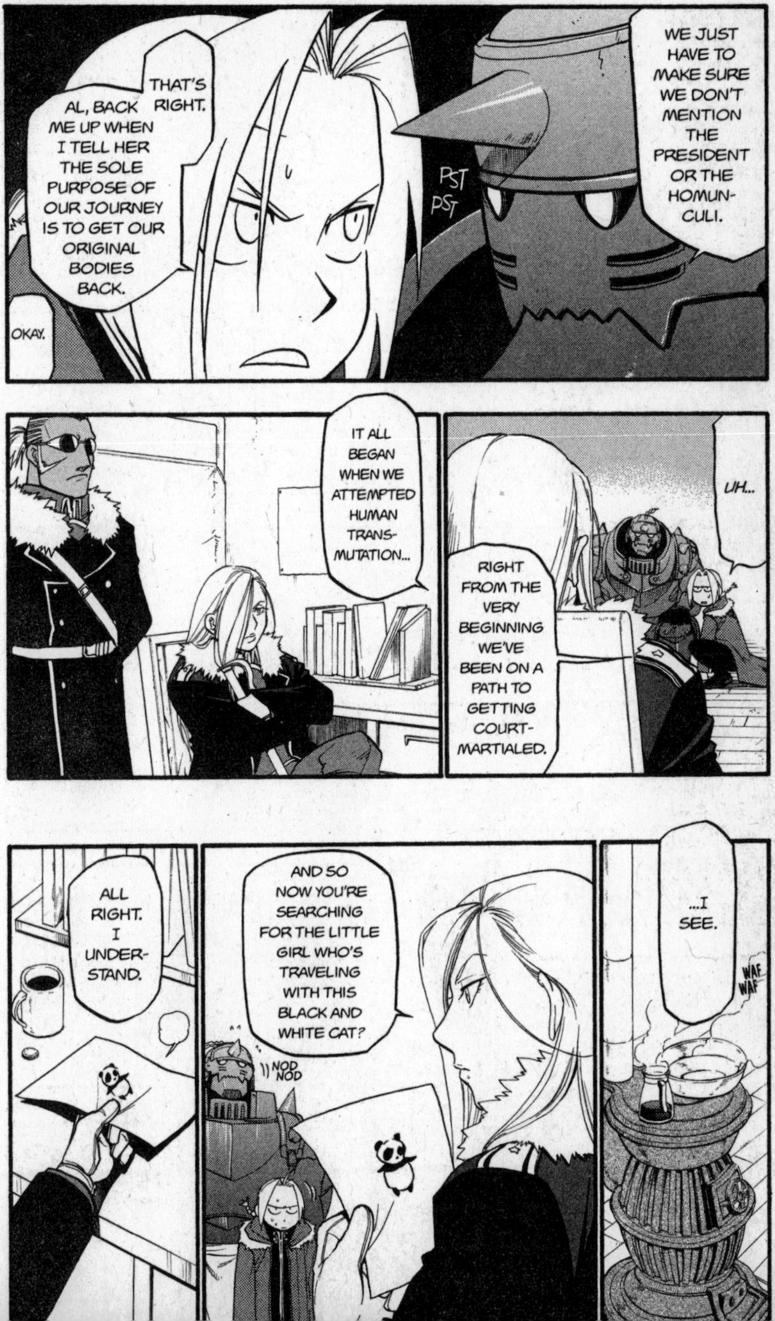
AL, BACK ME UP WHEN I TELL HER THE SOLE PURPOSE OF OUR JOURNEY IS TO GET OUR ORIGINAL BODIES BACK.
OKAY.
PST PST
WE JUST HAVE TO MAKE SURE WE DON'T MENTION THE PRESIDENT OR THE HOMUN-CULI.
THAT'S RIGHT.
IT ALL BEGAN WHEN WE ATTEMPTED HUMAN TRANS-MUTATION...
UH...
RIGHT FROM THE VERY BEGINNING WE'VE BEEN ON A PATH TO GETTING COURT-MARTIALED.
ALL RIGHT. I UNDER-STAND.
NOD NOD
AND SO NOW YOU'RE SEARCHING FOR THE LITTLE GIRL WHO'S TRAVELING WITH THIS BLACK AND WHITE CAT?
...I SEE.
WAF WAF

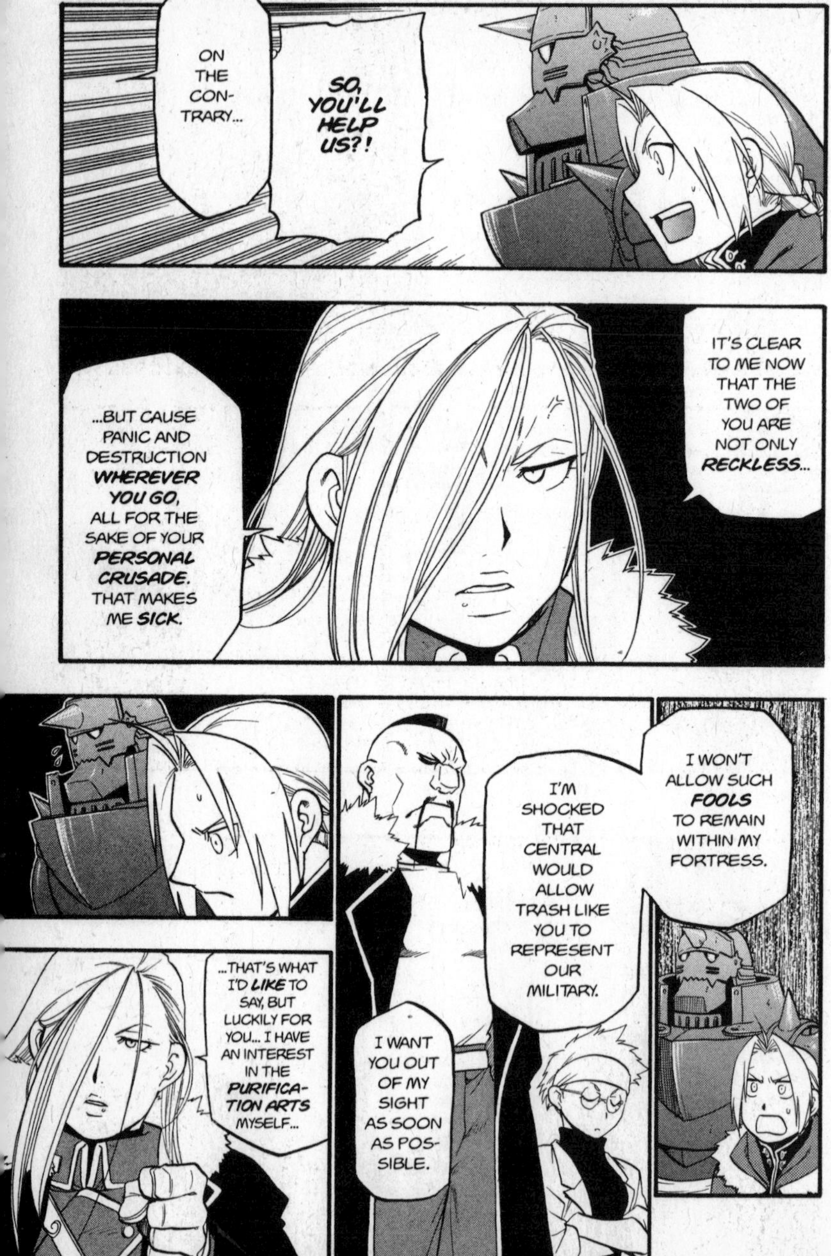
SO, YOU'LL HELP US?!
ON THE CON- TRARY...
IT'S CLEAR TO ME NOW THAT THE TWO OF YOU ARE NOT ONLY RECKLESS...
...BUT CAUSE PANIC AND DESTRUCTION WHEREVER YOU GO, ALL FOR THE SAKE OF YOUR PERSONAL CRUSADE. THAT MAKES ME SICK.
I WON'T ALLOW SUCH FOOLS TO REMAIN WITHIN MY FORTRESS.
I'M SHOCKED THAT CENTRAL WOULD ALLOW TRASH LIKE YOU TO REPRESENT OUR MILITARY.
I WANT YOU OUT OF MY SIGHT AS SOON AS POS- SIBLE.
...THAT'S WHAT I'D LIKE TO SAY, BUT LUCKILY FOR YOU... I HAVE AN INTEREST IN THE PURIFICA- TION ARTS MYSELF...

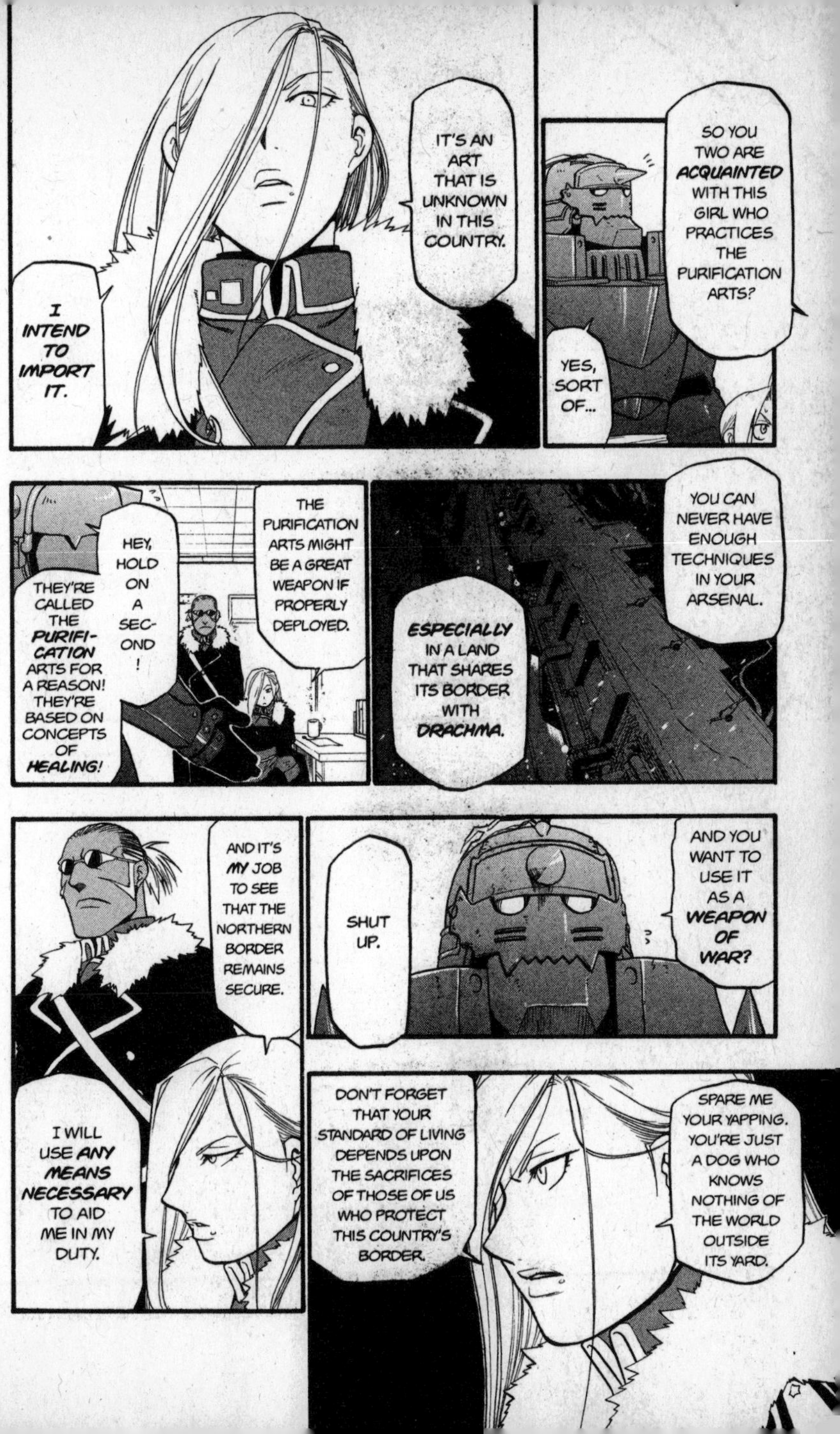
SO YOU TWO ARE ACQUAINTED WITH THIS GIRL WHO PRACTICES THE PURIFICATION ARTS?
YES, SORT OF...
IT'S AN ART THAT IS UNKNOWN IN THIS COUNTRY.
I INTEND TO IMPORT IT.
YOU CAN NEVER HAVE ENOUGH TECHNIQUES IN YOUR ARSENAL.
ESPECIALLY IN A LAND THAT SHARES ITS BORDER WITH DRACHMA.
THE PURIFICATION ARTS MIGHT BE A GREAT WEAPON IF PROPERLY DEPLOYED.
HEY, HOLD ON A SEC-OND!
THEY'RE CALLED THE PURIFI-CATION ARTS FOR A REASON! THEY'RE BASED ON CONCEPTS OF HEALING!
AND YOU WANT TO USE IT AS A WEAPON OF WAR?
SHUT UP.
SPARE ME YOUR YAPPING. YOU'RE JUST A DOG WHO KNOWS NOTHING OF THE WORLD OUTSIDE ITS YARD.
DON'T FORGET THAT YOUR STANDARD OF LIVING DEPENDS UPON THE SACRIFICES OF THOSE OF US WHO PROTECT THIS COUNTRY'S BORDER.
AND IT'S MY JOB TO SEE THAT THE NORTHERN BORDER REMAINS SECURE.
I WILL USE ANY MEANS NECESSARY TO AID ME IN MY DUTY.

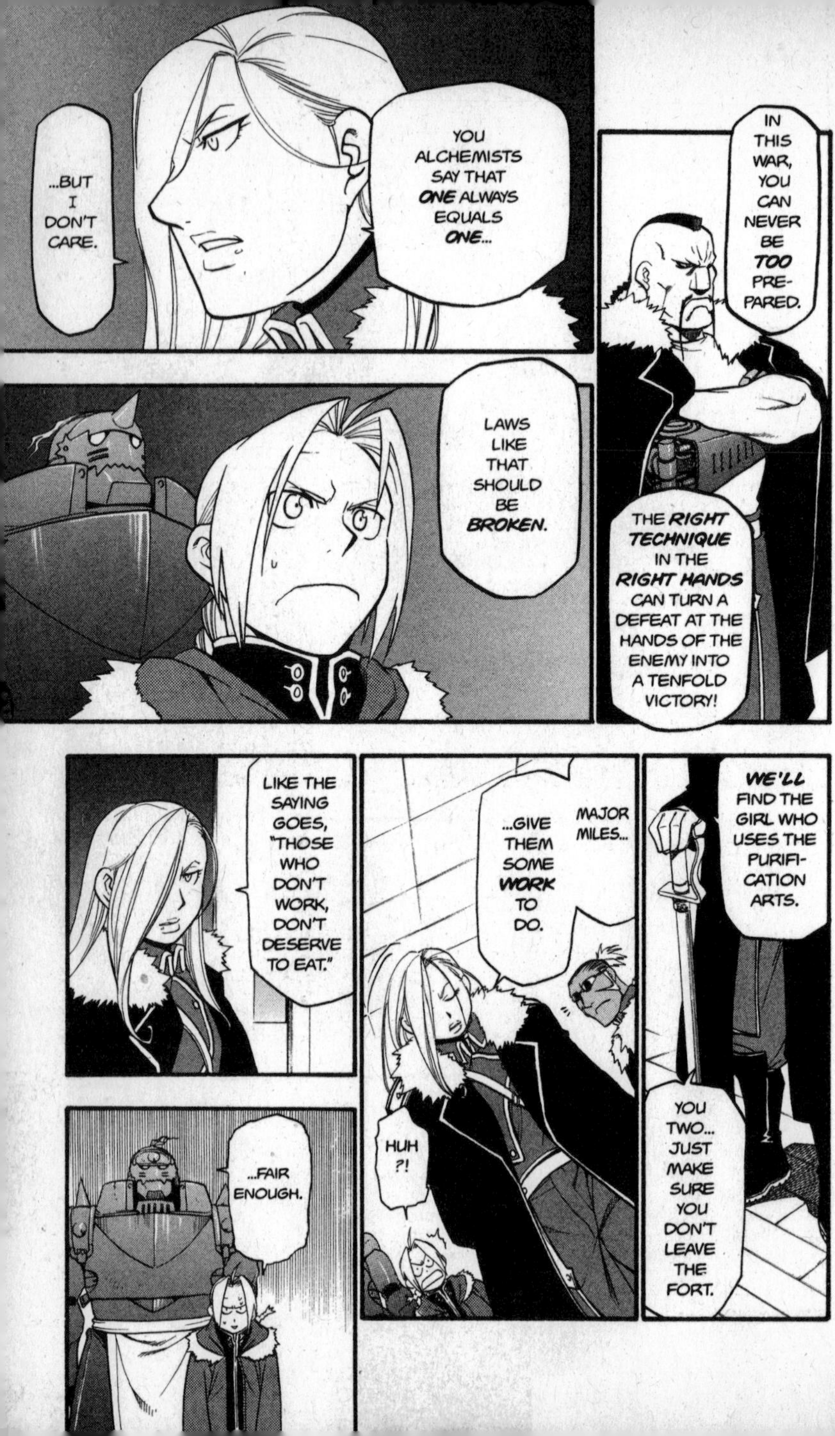
IN THIS WAR, YOU CAN NEVER BE TOO PREPARED.
THE RIGHT TECHNIQUE IN THE RIGHT HANDS CAN TURN A DEFEAT AT THE HANDS OF THE ENEMY INTO A TENFOLD VICTORY!
YOU ALCHEMISTS SAY THAT ONE ALWAYS EQUALS ONE...
...BUT I DON'T CARE.
LAWS LIKE THAT SHOULD BE BROKEN.
WE'LL FIND THE GIRL WHO USES THE PURIFICATION ARTS.
YOU TWO... JUST MAKE SURE YOU DON'T LEAVE THE FORT.
MAJOR MILES...
...GIVE THEM SOME WORK TO DO.
HUH ?!
LIKE THE SAYING GOES, "THOSE WHO DON'T WORK, DON'T DESERVE TO EAT."
...FAIR ENOUGH.

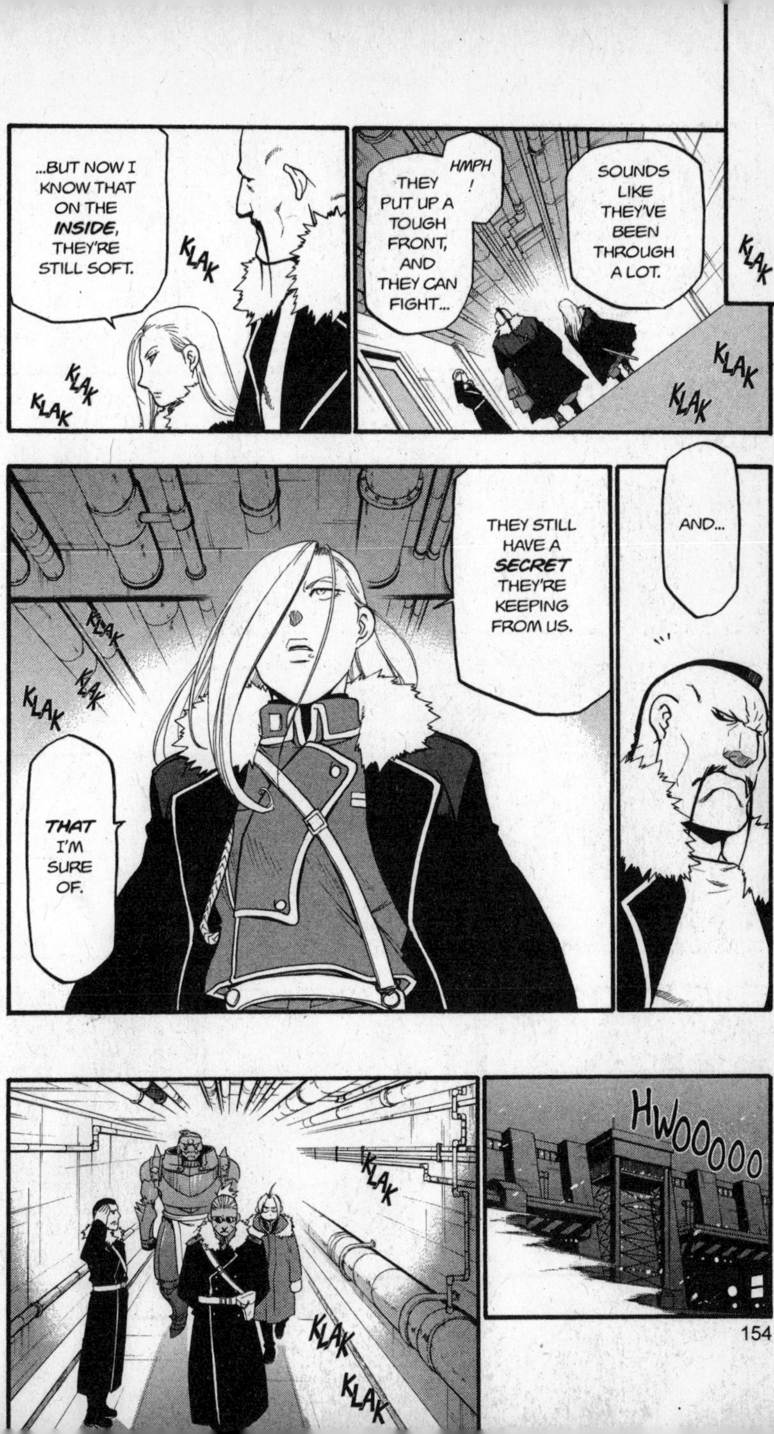
KLAK
SOUNDS LIKE THEY'VE BEEN THROUGH A LOT.
HMPH!
THEY PUT UP A TOUGH FRONT, AND THEY CAN FIGHT...
KLAK
KLAK
...BUT NOW I KNOW THAT ON THE ***INSIDE***, THEY'RE STILL SOFT.
KLAK
KLAK
KLAK
AND...
THEY STILL HAVE A ***SECRET*** THEY'RE KEEPING FROM US.
KLAK
KLAK
KLAK
THAT I'M SURE OF.
HWOOOOO
KLAK
KLAK
KLAK

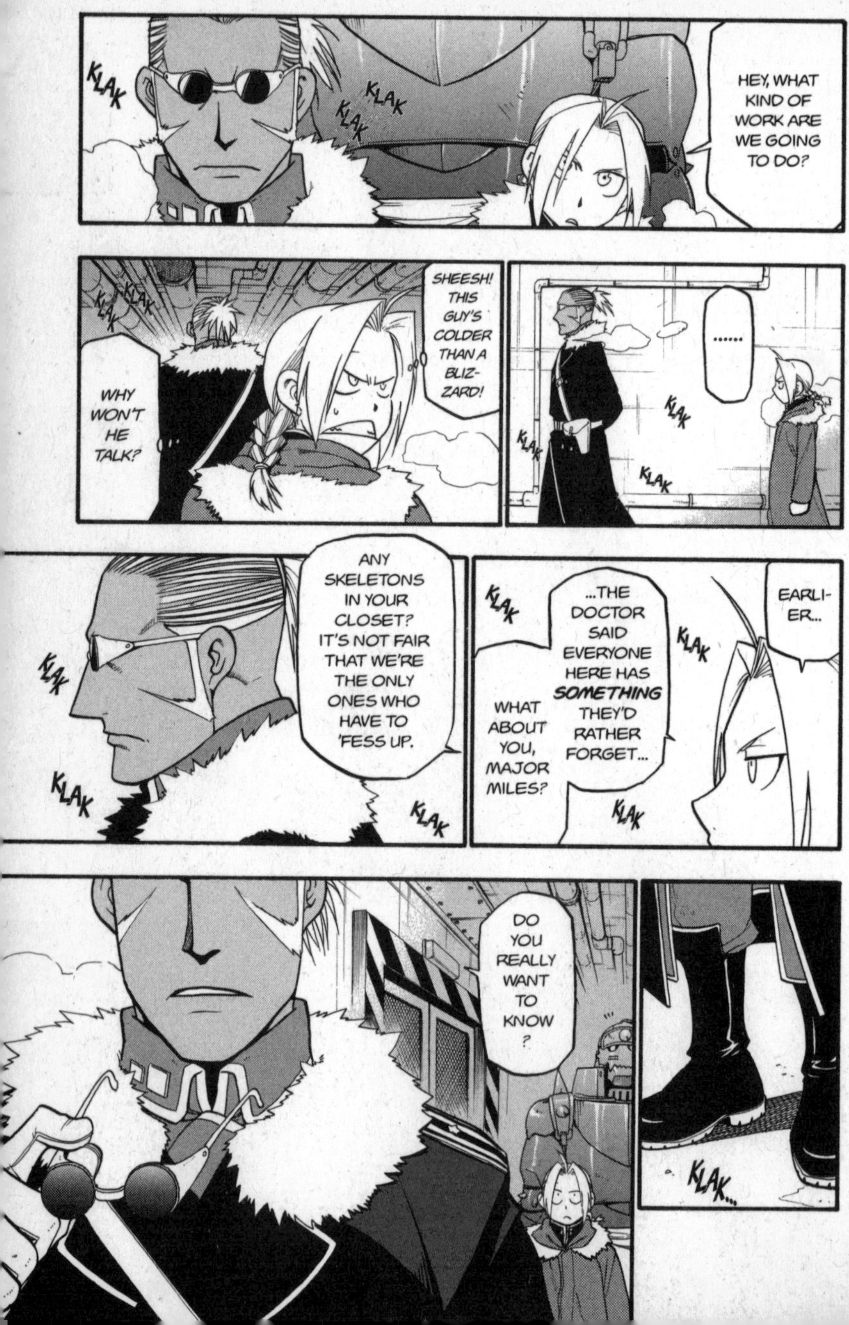
HEY, WHAT KIND OF WORK ARE WE GOING TO DO?
KLAK
KLAK
KLAK
......
KLAK
KLAK
KLAK
SHEESH! THIS GUY'S COLDER THAN A BLIZ-ZARD!
KLAK
KLAK
WHY WON'T HE TALK?
EARLI-ER...
...THE DOCTOR SAID EVERYONE HERE HAS SOMETHING THEY'D RATHER FORGET...
KLAK
WHAT ABOUT YOU, MAJOR MILES?
KLAK
KLAK
ANY SKELETONS IN YOUR CLOSET? IT'S NOT FAIR THAT WE'RE THE ONLY ONES WHO HAVE TO 'FESS UP.
KLAK
KLAK
KLAK
KLAK...
DO YOU REALLY WANT TO KNOW?

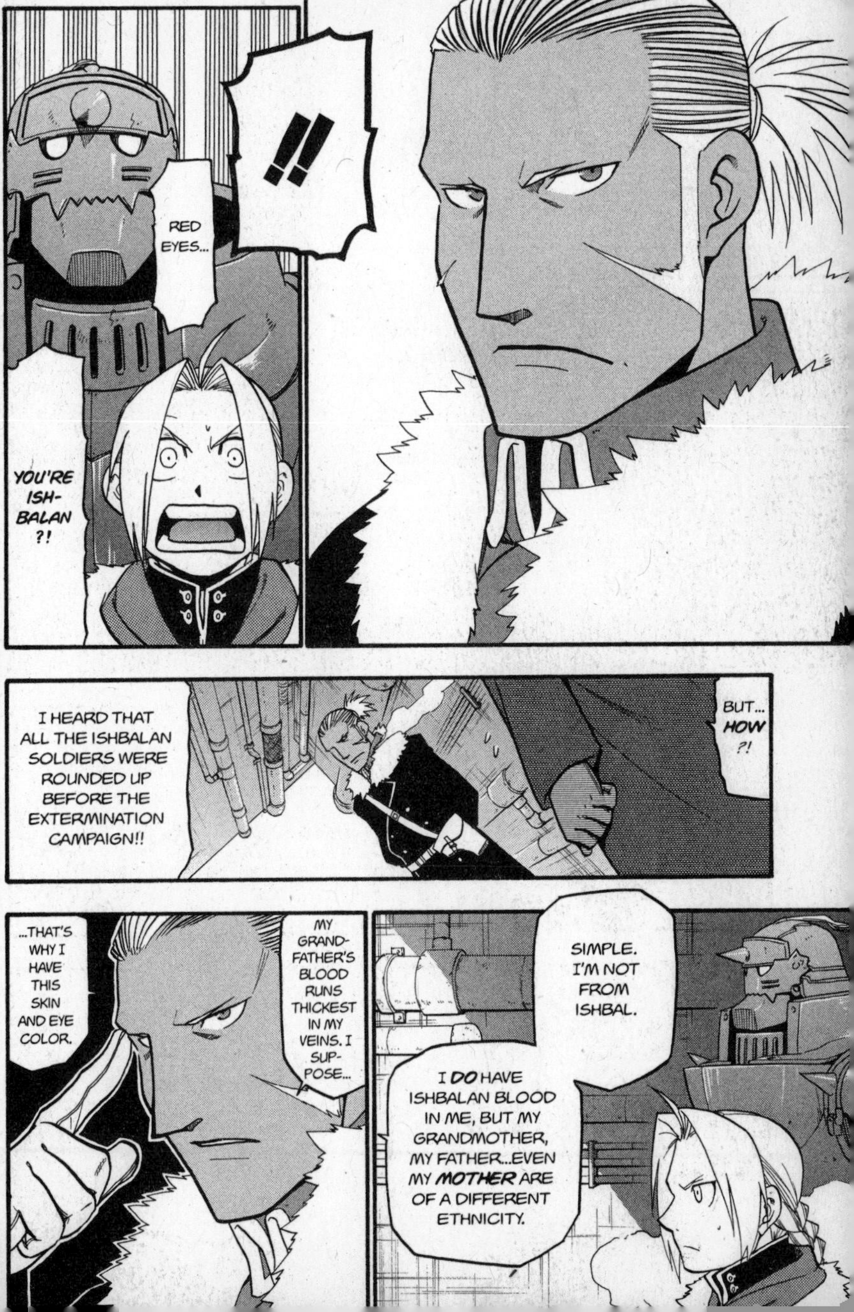
!!
RED EYES...
YOU'RE ISHBALAN ?!
BUT... HOW ?!
I HEARD THAT ALL THE ISHBALAN SOLDIERS WERE ROUNDED UP BEFORE THE EXTERMINATION CAMPAIGN!!
SIMPLE. I'M NOT FROM ISHBAL.
I DO HAVE ISHBALAN BLOOD IN ME, BUT MY GRANDMOTHER, MY FATHER...EVEN MY MOTHER ARE OF A DIFFERENT ETHNICITY.
MY GRANDFATHER'S BLOOD RUNS THICKEST IN MY VEINS. I SUPPOSE...
...THAT'S WHY I HAVE THIS SKIN AND EYE COLOR.

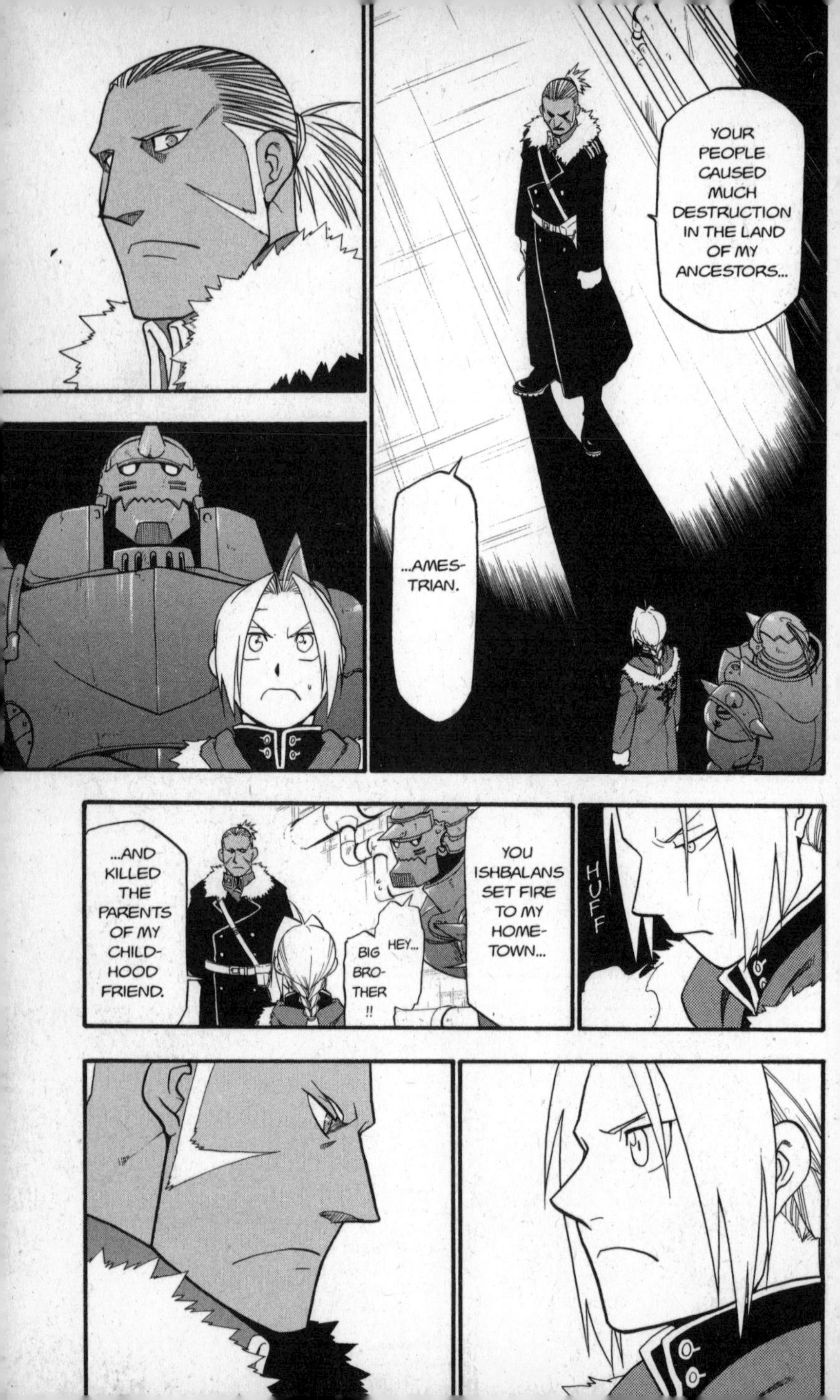
YOUR PEOPLE CAUSED MUCH DESTRUCTION IN THE LAND OF MY ANCESTORS...
...AMES-TRIAN.
HUFF
YOU ISHBALANS SET FIRE TO MY HOME-TOWN...
HEY... BIG BRO-THER !!
...AND KILLED THE PARENTS OF MY CHILD-HOOD FRIEND.

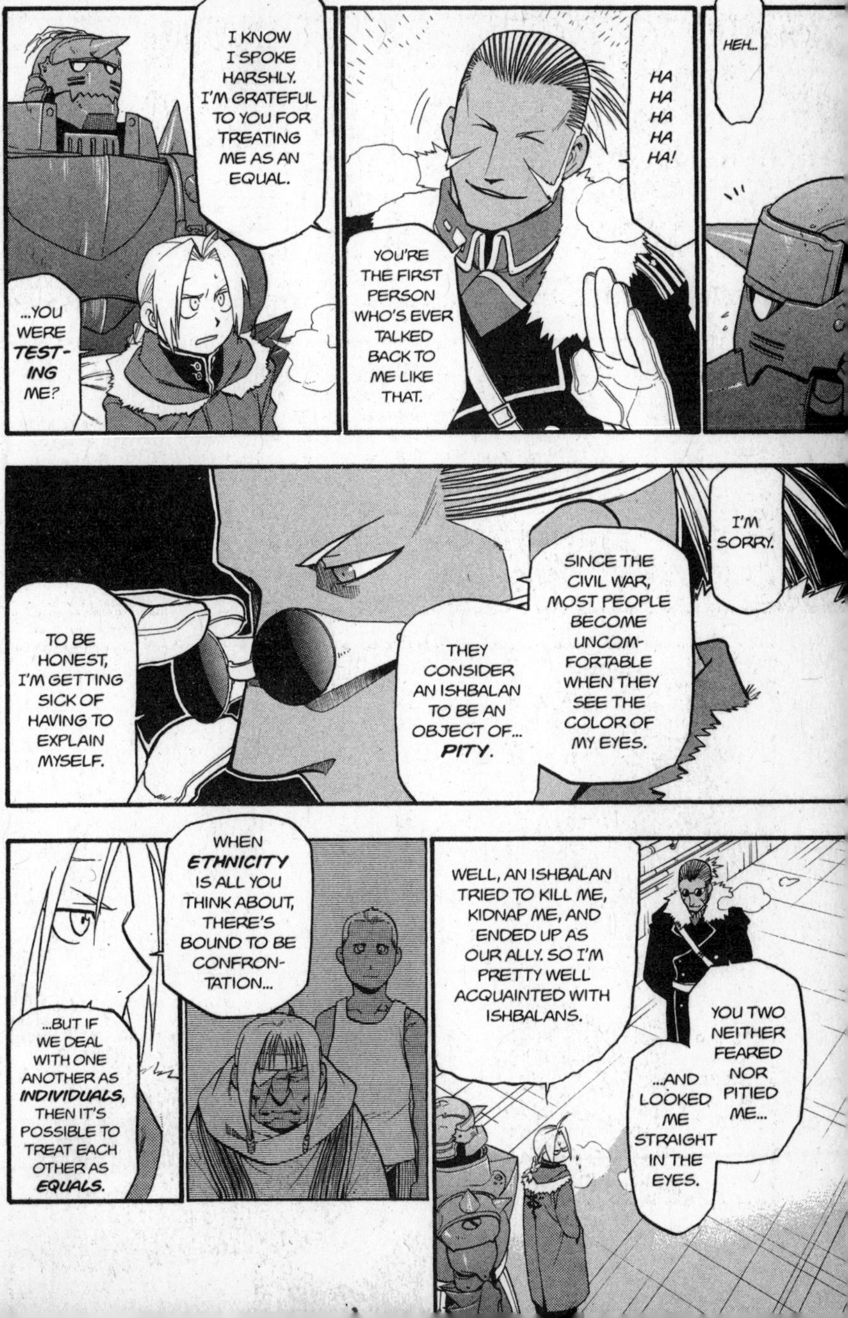
HEH...
HA HA HA HA HA!
YOU'RE THE FIRST PERSON WHO'S EVER TALKED BACK TO ME LIKE THAT.
I KNOW I SPOKE HARSHLY. I'M GRATEFUL TO YOU FOR TREATING ME AS AN EQUAL.
...YOU WERE TEST-ING ME?
I'M SORRY.
SINCE THE CIVIL WAR, MOST PEOPLE BECOME UNCOM-FORTABLE WHEN THEY SEE THE COLOR OF MY EYES.
THEY CONSIDER AN ISHBALAN TO BE AN OBJECT OF... PITY.
TO BE HONEST, I'M GETTING SICK OF HAVING TO EXPLAIN MYSELF.
YOU TWO NEITHER FEARED NOR PITIED ME...
...AND LOOKED ME STRAIGHT IN THE EYES.
WELL, AN ISHBALAN TRIED TO KILL ME, KIDNAP ME, AND ENDED UP AS OUR ALLY. SO I'M PRETTY WELL ACQUAINTED WITH ISHBALANS.
WHEN ETHNICITY IS ALL YOU THINK ABOUT, THERE'S BOUND TO BE CONFRON-TATION...
...BUT IF WE DEAL WITH ONE ANOTHER AS INDIVIDUALS, THEN IT'S POSSIBLE TO TREAT EACH OTHER AS EQUALS.

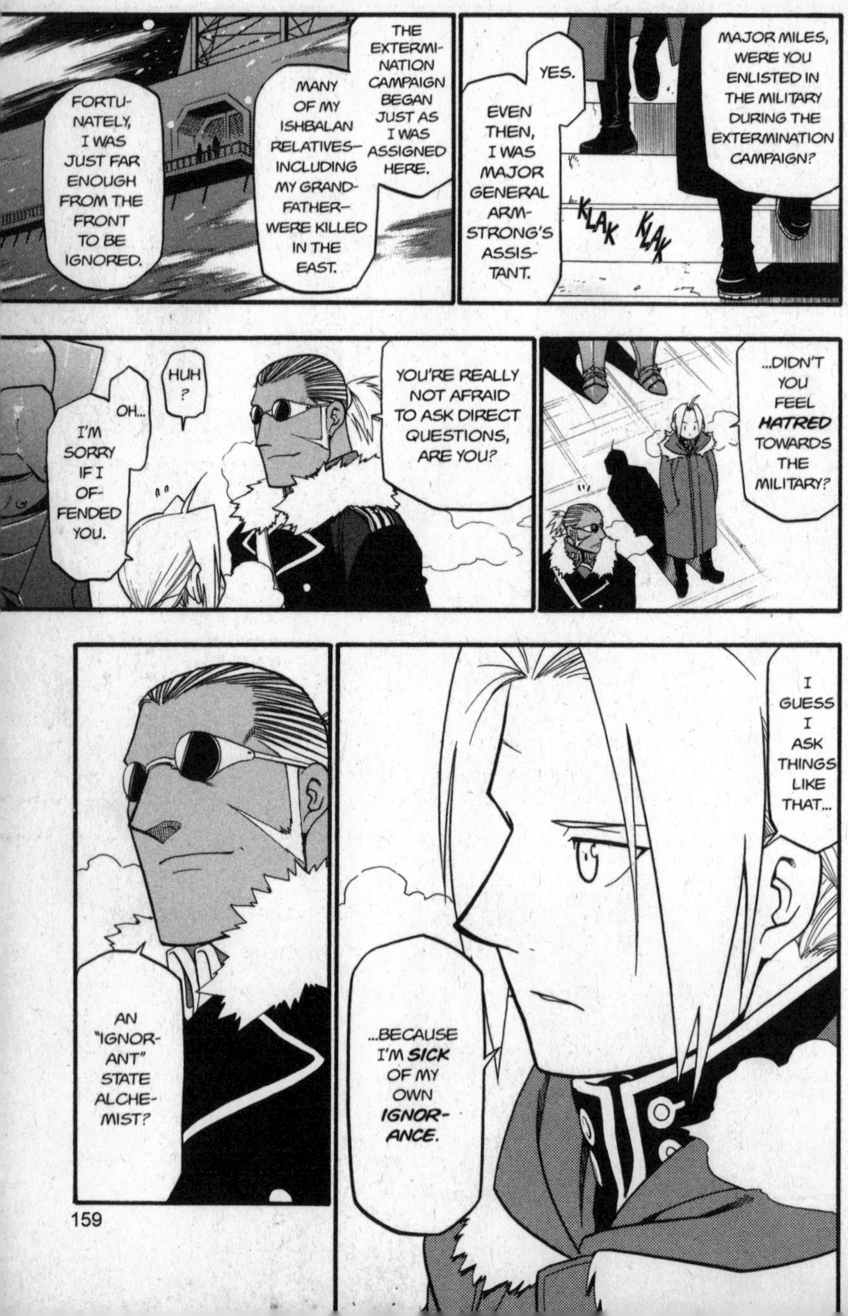
MAJOR MILES, WERE YOU ENLISTED IN THE MILITARY DURING THE EXTERMINATION CAMPAIGN?
KLAK KLAK
YES.
EVEN THEN, I WAS MAJOR GENERAL ARMSTRONG'S ASSISTANT.
THE EXTERMINATION CAMPAIGN BEGAN JUST AS I WAS ASSIGNED HERE.
MANY OF MY ISHBALAN RELATIVES—INCLUDING MY GRANDFATHER—WERE KILLED IN THE EAST.
FORTUNATELY, I WAS JUST FAR ENOUGH FROM THE FRONT TO BE IGNORED.
...DIDN'T YOU FEEL **HATRED** TOWARDS THE MILITARY?
YOU'RE REALLY NOT AFRAID TO ASK DIRECT QUESTIONS, ARE YOU?
HUH?
OH... I'M SORRY IF I OFFENDED YOU.
I GUESS I ASK THINGS LIKE THAT...
...BECAUSE I'M **SICK** OF MY OWN **IGNORANCE**.
AN "IGNORANT" STATE ALCHEMIST?

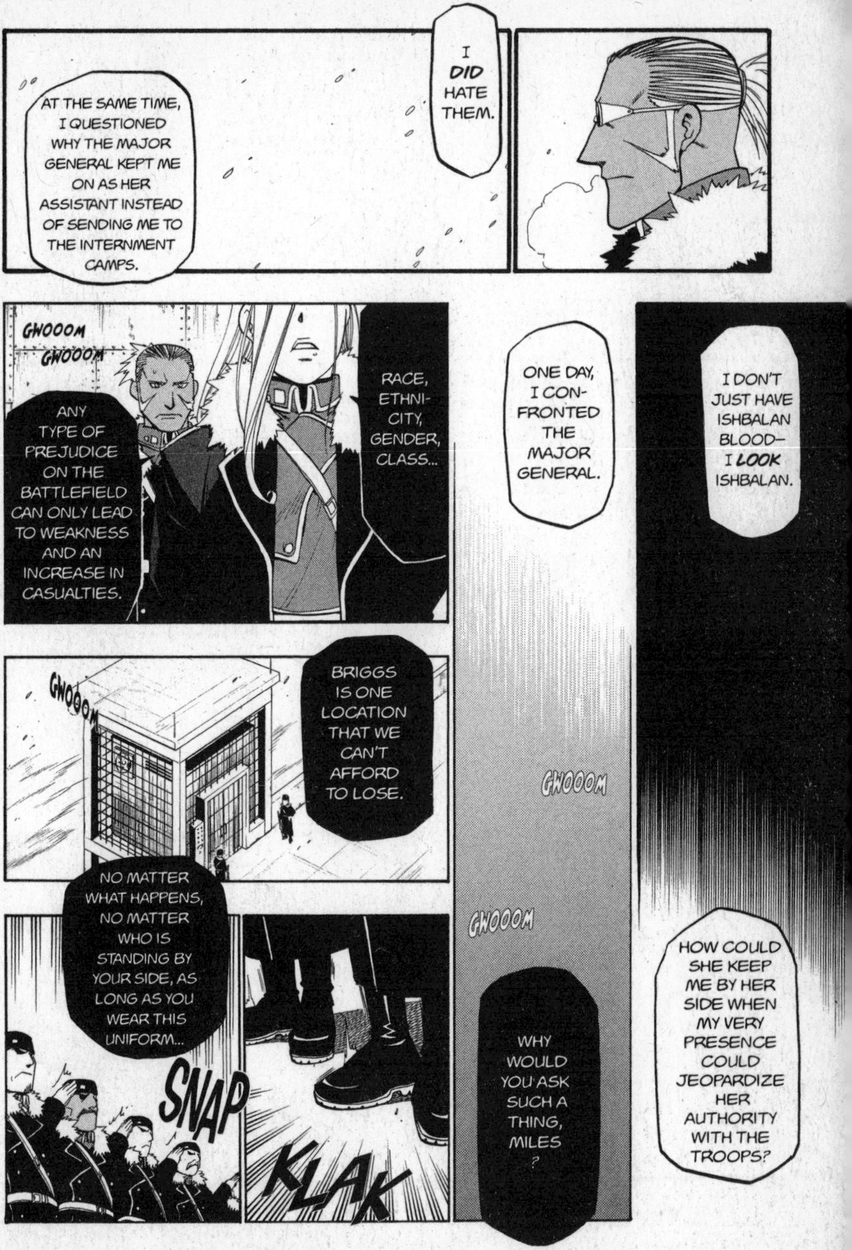
I DID HATE THEM.
AT THE SAME TIME, I QUESTIONED WHY THE MAJOR GENERAL KEPT ME ON AS HER ASSISTANT INSTEAD OF SENDING ME TO THE INTERNMENT CAMPS.
I DON'T JUST HAVE ISHBALAN BLOOD— I LOOK ISHBALAN.
HOW COULD SHE KEEP ME BY HER SIDE WHEN MY VERY PRESENCE COULD JEOPARDIZE HER AUTHORITY WITH THE TROOPS?
ONE DAY, I CON-FRONTED THE MAJOR GENERAL.
GWOOOM
GWOOOM
WHY WOULD YOU ASK SUCH A THING, MILES?
RACE, ETHNI-CITY, GENDER, CLASS...
GWOOOM
GWOOOM
ANY TYPE OF PREJUDICE ON THE BATTLEFIELD CAN ONLY LEAD TO WEAKNESS AND AN INCREASE IN CASUALTIES.
BRIGGS IS ONE LOCATION THAT WE CAN'T AFFORD TO LOSE.
GWOOOM
NO MATTER WHAT HAPPENS, NO MATTER WHO IS STANDING BY YOUR SIDE, AS LONG AS YOU WEAR THIS UNIFORM...
KLAK
SNAP

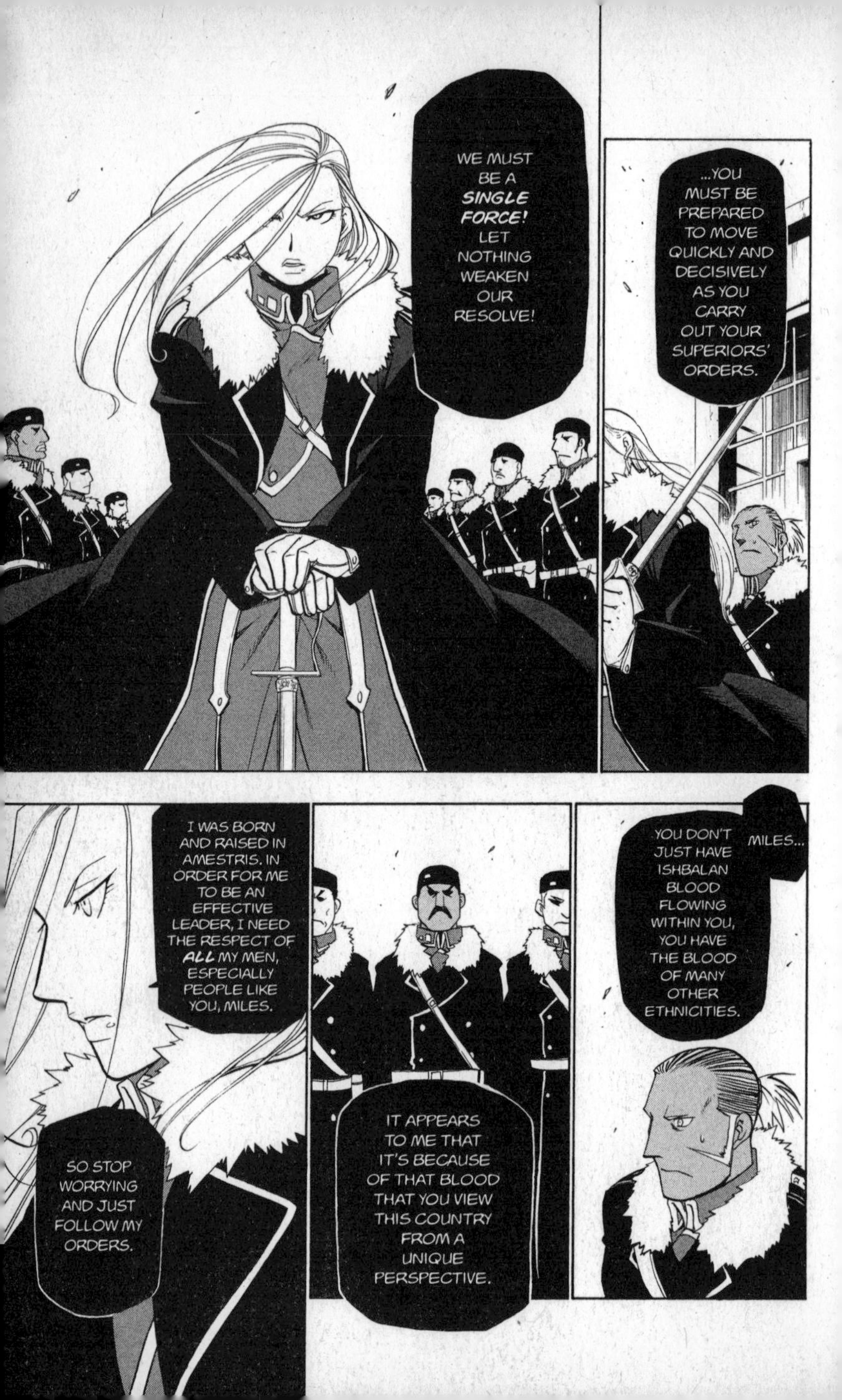
...YOU MUST BE PREPARED TO MOVE QUICKLY AND DECISIVELY AS YOU CARRY OUT YOUR SUPERIORS' ORDERS.
WE MUST BE A *SINGLE FORCE!* LET NOTHING WEAKEN OUR RESOLVE!
MILES...
YOU DON'T JUST HAVE ISHBALAN BLOOD FLOWING WITHIN YOU, YOU HAVE THE BLOOD OF MANY OTHER ETHNICITIES.
IT APPEARS TO ME THAT IT'S BECAUSE OF THAT BLOOD THAT YOU VIEW THIS COUNTRY FROM A UNIQUE PERSPECTIVE.
I WAS BORN AND RAISED IN AMESTRIS. IN ORDER FOR ME TO BE AN EFFECTIVE LEADER, I NEED THE RESPECT OF *ALL* MY MEN, ESPECIALLY PEOPLE LIKE YOU, MILES.
SO STOP WORRYING AND JUST FOLLOW MY ORDERS.

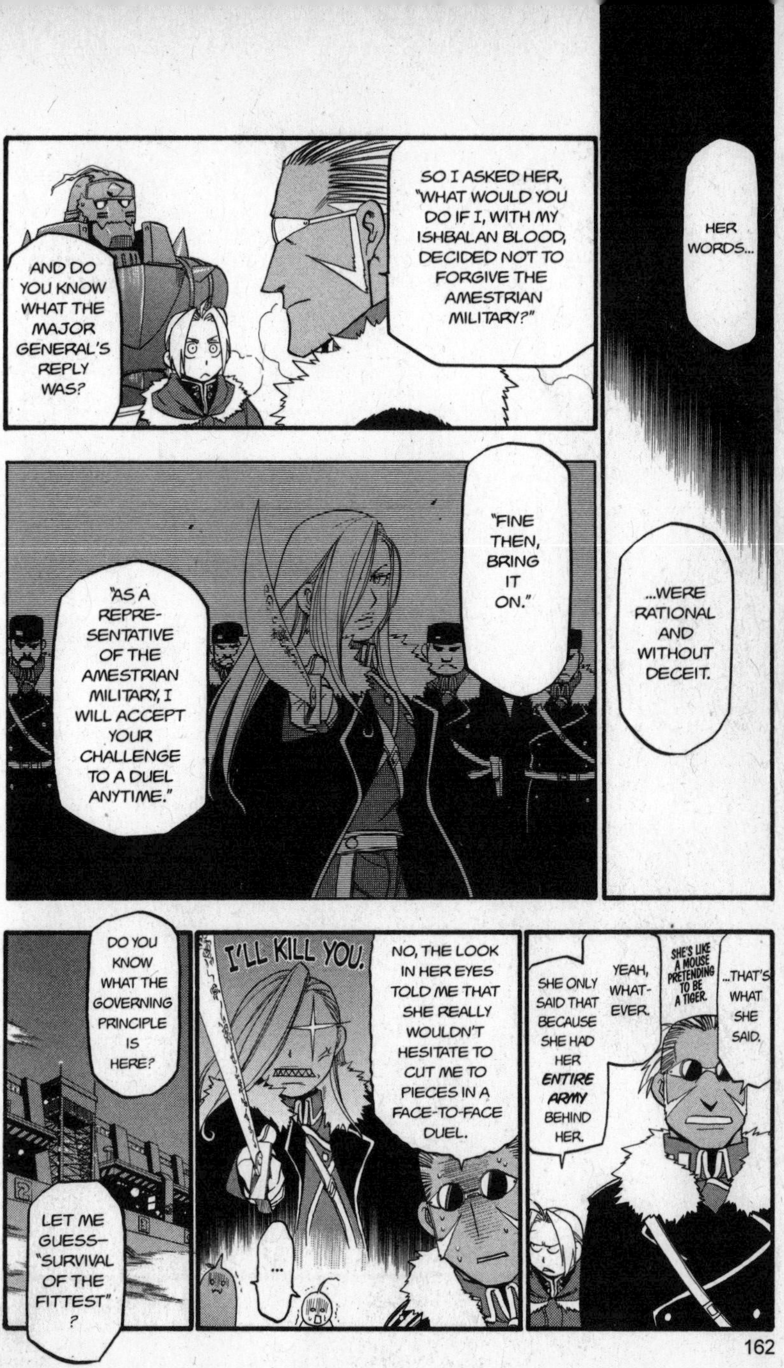
HER WORDS...
...WERE RATIONAL AND WITHOUT DECEIT.
SO I ASKED HER, "WHAT WOULD YOU DO IF I, WITH MY ISHBALAN BLOOD, DECIDED NOT TO FORGIVE THE AMESTRIAN MILITARY?"
AND DO YOU KNOW WHAT THE MAJOR GENERAL'S REPLY WAS?
"FINE THEN, BRING IT ON."
"AS A REPRESENTATIVE OF THE AMESTRIAN MILITARY, I WILL ACCEPT YOUR CHALLENGE TO A DUEL ANYTIME."
...THAT'S WHAT SHE SAID.
SHE'S LIKE A MOUSE PRETENDING TO BE A TIGER.
YEAH, WHAT-EVER.
SHE ONLY SAID THAT BECAUSE SHE HAD HER *ENTIRE ARMY* BEHIND HER.
NO, THE LOOK IN HER EYES TOLD ME THAT SHE REALLY WOULDN'T HESITATE TO CUT ME TO PIECES IN A FACE-TO-FACE DUEL.
I'LL KILL YOU.
...
DO YOU KNOW WHAT THE GOVERNING PRINCIPLE IS HERE?
LET ME GUESS— "SURVIVAL OF THE FITTEST"?

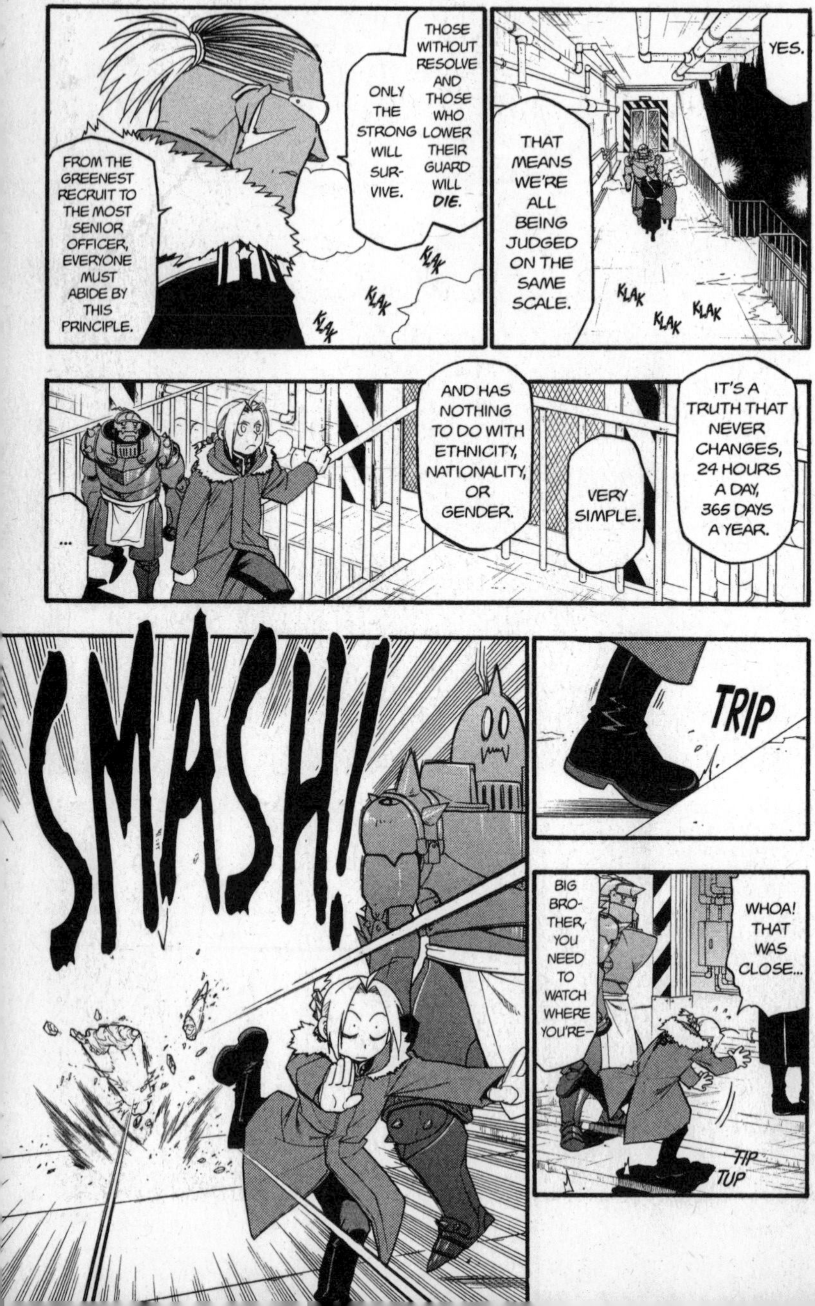
YES.
THAT MEANS WE'RE ALL BEING JUDGED ON THE SAME SCALE.
KLAK
KLAK
KLAK
THOSE WITHOUT RESOLVE AND THOSE WHO LOWER THEIR GUARD WILL DIE.
ONLY THE STRONG WILL SUR-VIVE.
FROM THE GREENEST RECRUIT TO THE MOST SENIOR OFFICER, EVERYONE MUST ABIDE BY THIS PRINCIPLE.
KLAK
KLAK
KLAK
IT'S A TRUTH THAT NEVER CHANGES, 24 HOURS A DAY, 365 DAYS A YEAR.
VERY SIMPLE.
AND HAS NOTHING TO DO WITH ETHNICITY, NATIONALITY, OR GENDER.
...
TRIP
WHOA! THAT WAS CLOSE...
BIG BRO-THER, YOU NEED TO WATCH WHERE YOU'RE-
TIP
TUP
SMASH!

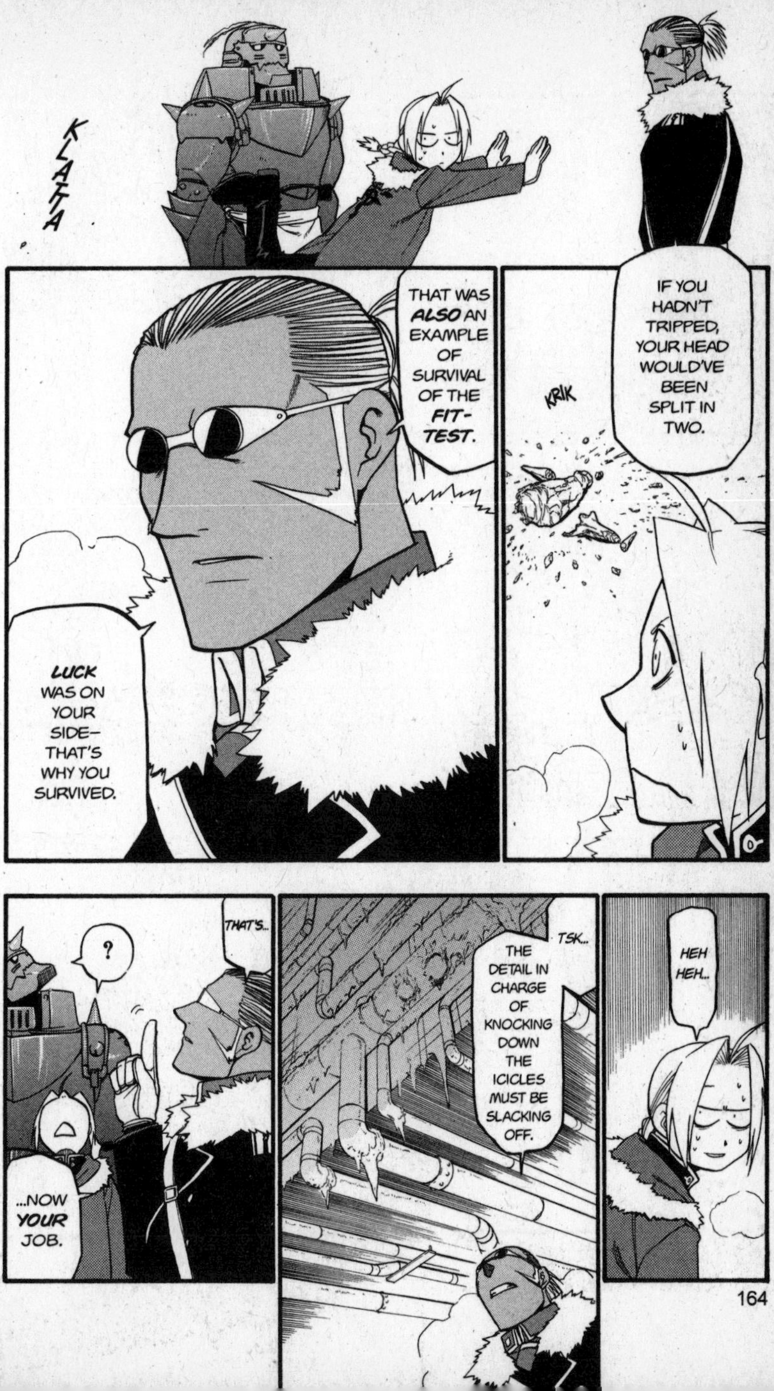
KLATTA
IF YOU HADN'T TRIPPED, YOUR HEAD WOULD'VE BEEN SPLIT IN TWO.
KRIK
THAT WAS ALSO AN EXAMPLE OF SURVIVAL OF THE FIT-TEST.
LUCK WAS ON YOUR SIDE— THAT'S WHY YOU SURVIVED.
HEH HEH...
TSK...
THE DETAIL IN CHARGE OF KNOCKING DOWN THE ICICLES MUST BE SLACKING OFF.
THAT'S...
?
...NOW YOUR JOB.

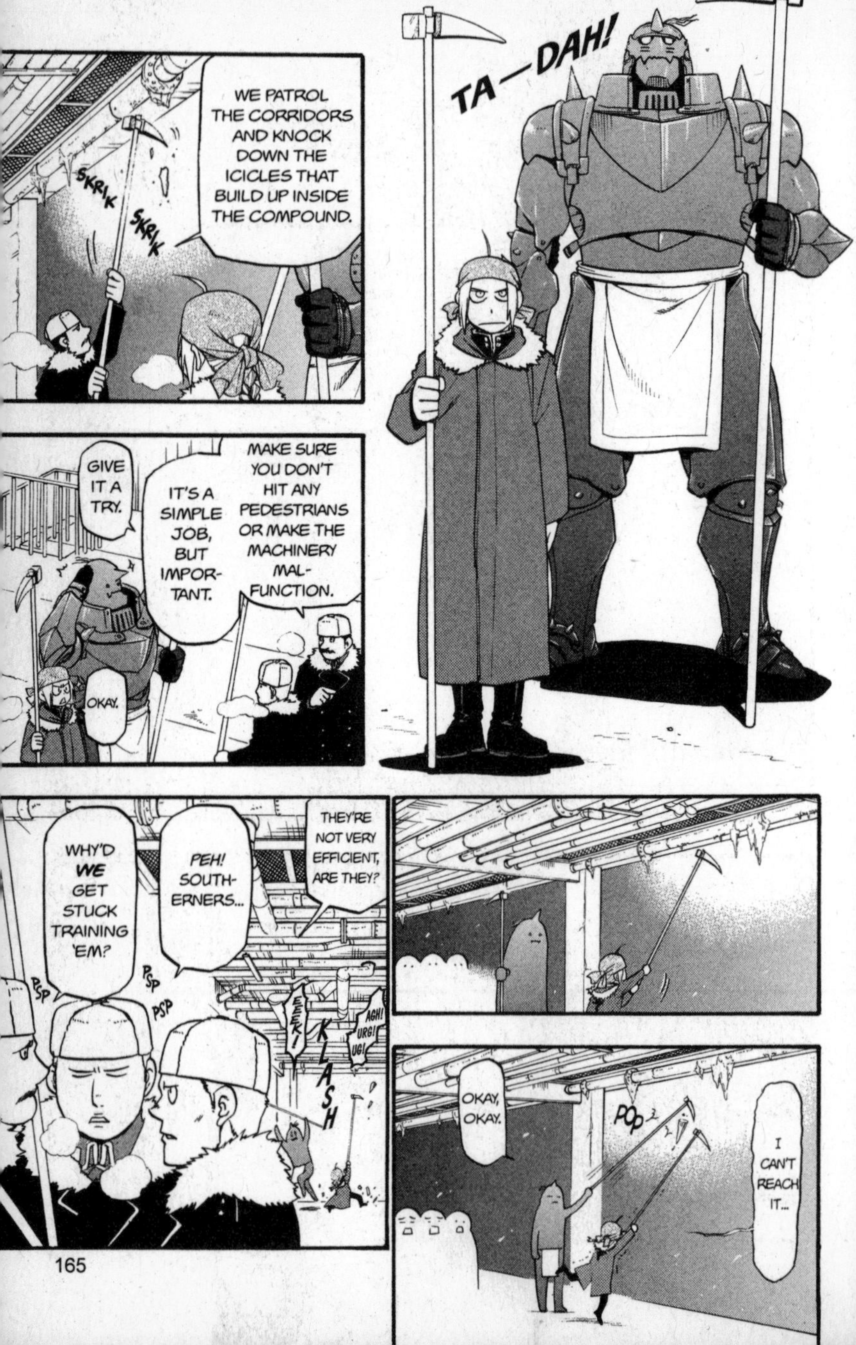
TA—DAH!
WE PATROL THE CORRIDORS AND KNOCK DOWN THE ICICLES THAT BUILD UP INSIDE THE COMPOUND.
SKRIK SKRIK
MAKE SURE YOU DON'T HIT ANY PEDESTRIANS OR MAKE THE MACHINERY MAL-FUNCTION.
IT'S A SIMPLE JOB, BUT IMPOR-TANT.
GIVE IT A TRY.
OKAY.
I CAN'T REACH IT...
POP
OKAY, OKAY.
THEY'RE NOT VERY EFFICIENT, ARE THEY?
PEH! SOUTH-ERNERS...
WHY'D WE GET STUCK TRAINING 'EM?
PSP PSP PSP PSP
AGH! URG! UG!
KLASH
EEEK!

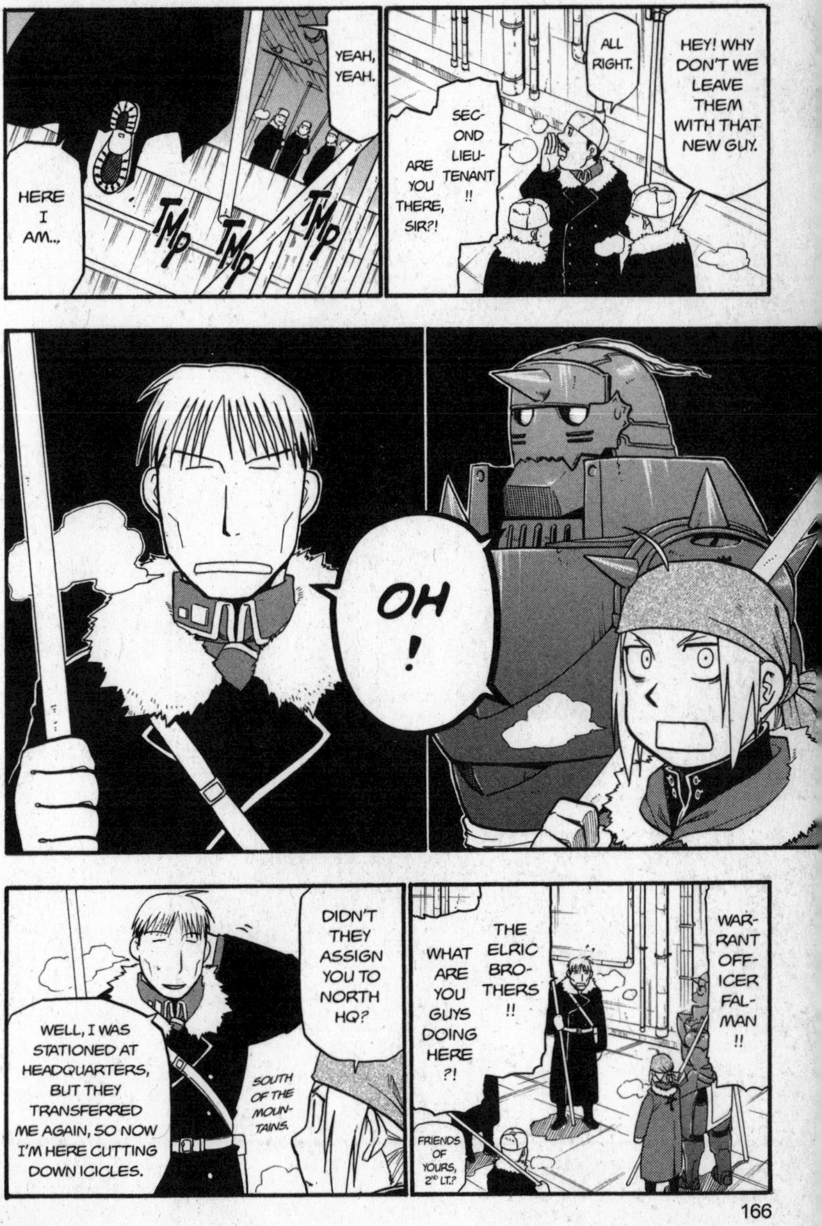
HEY! WHY DON'T WE LEAVE THEM WITH THAT NEW GUY.
ALL RIGHT.
SECOND LIEUTENANT!!
ARE YOU THERE, SIR?!
YEAH, YEAH.
TMP TMP TMP
HERE I AM...
OH!
WARRANT OFFICER FALMAN!!
THE ELRIC BROTHERS!!
WHAT ARE YOU GUYS DOING HERE?!
FRIENDS OF YOURS, 2ND LT.?
DIDN'T THEY ASSIGN YOU TO NORTH HQ?
SOUTH OF THE MOUNTAINS.
WELL, I WAS STATIONED AT HEADQUARTERS, BUT THEY TRANSFERRED ME AGAIN, SO NOW I'M HERE CUTTING DOWN ICICLES.

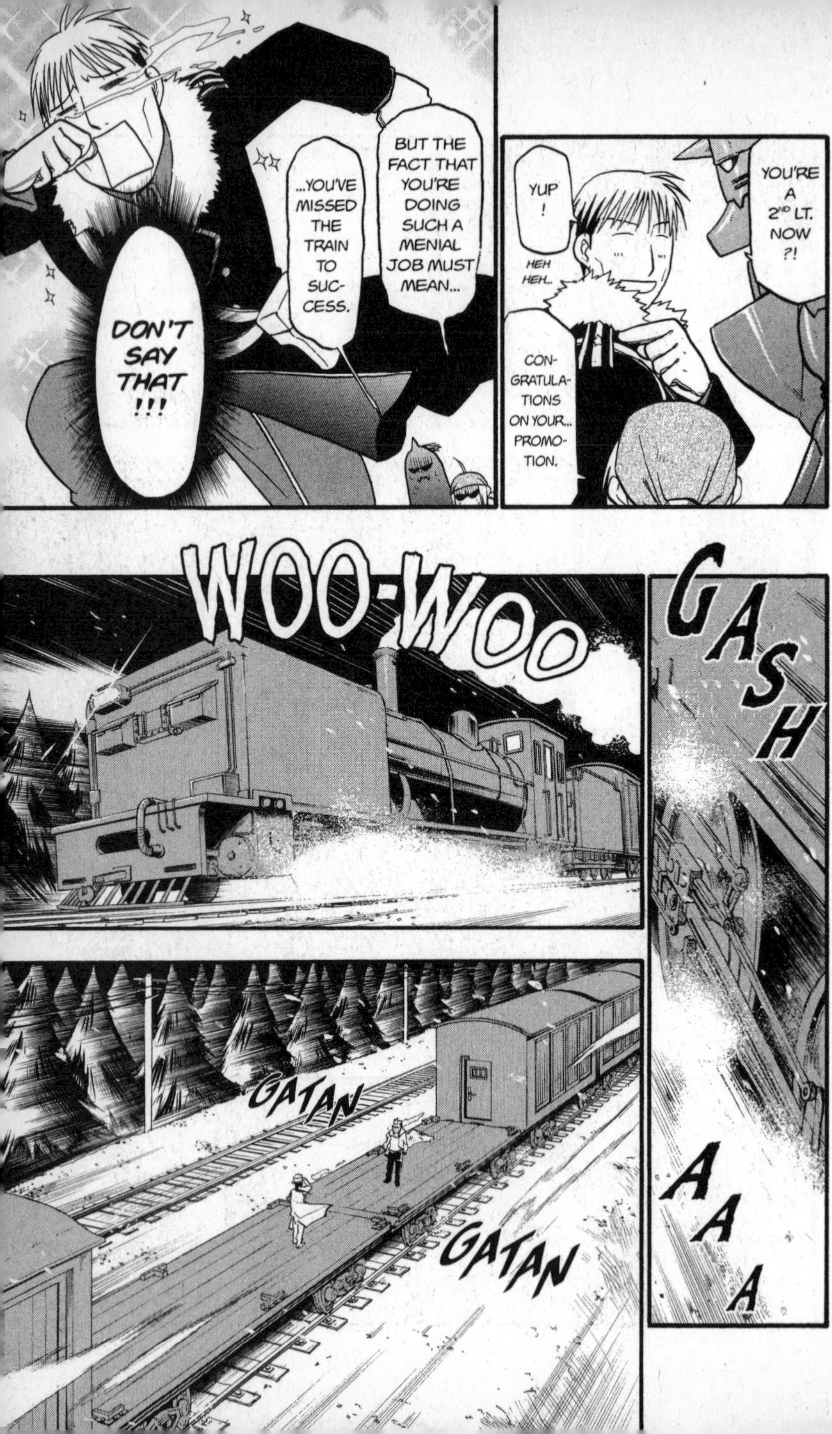
YOU'RE A 2ND LT. NOW?!
YUP!
HEH HEH..
CONGRATULATIONS ON YOUR.. PROMOTION.
BUT THE FACT THAT YOU'RE DOING SUCH A MENIAL JOB MUST MEAN...
...YOU'VE MISSED THE TRAIN TO SUCCESS.
DON'T SAY THAT!!!
GASH
AAAA
WOO-WOO
GATAN
GATAN

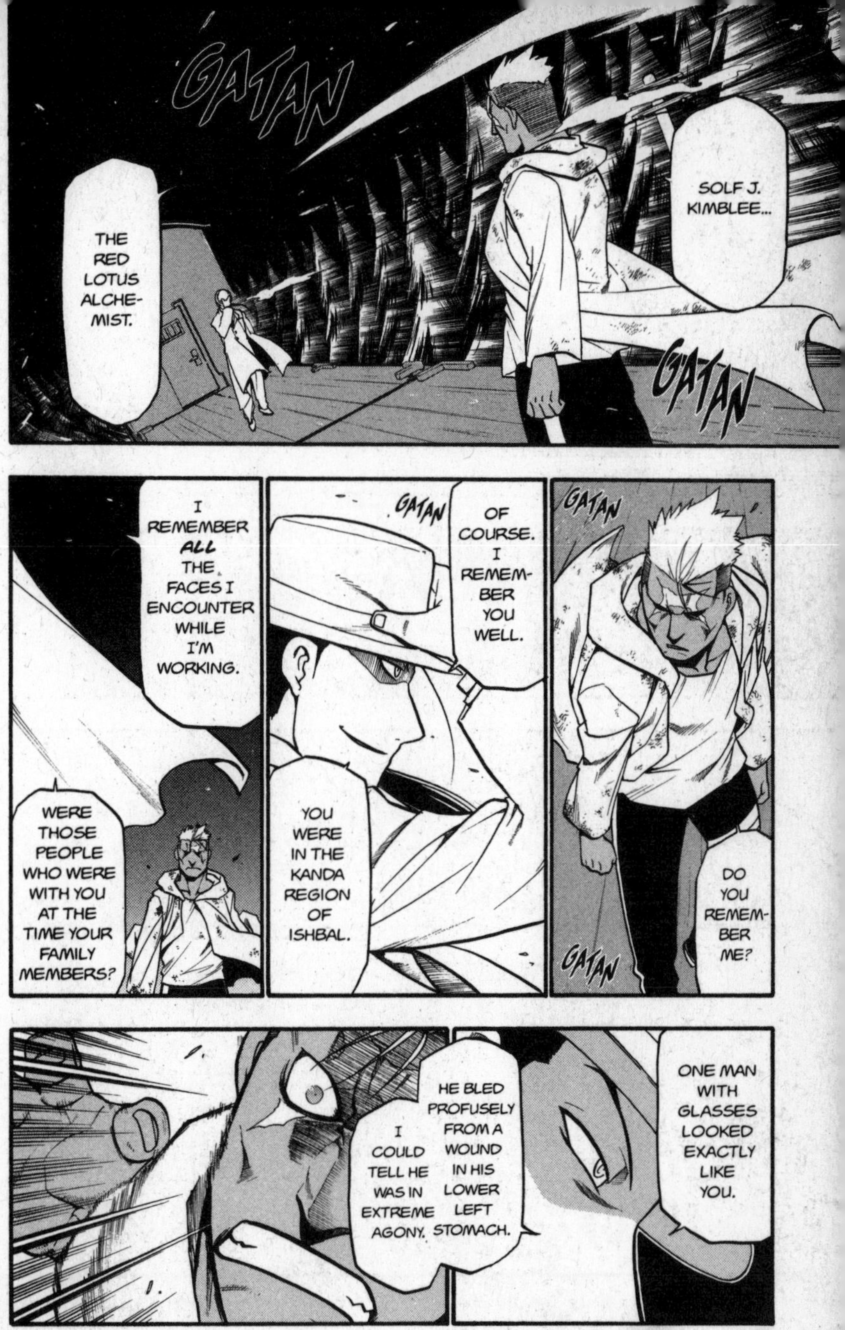
GATAN
SOLF J. KIMBLEE...
THE RED LOTUS ALCHEMIST.
GATAN
GATAN
DO YOU REMEMBER ME?
GATAN
GATAN
OF COURSE. I REMEMBER YOU WELL.
YOU WERE IN THE KANDA REGION OF ISHBAL.
I REMEMBER **ALL** THE FACES I ENCOUNTER WHILE I'M WORKING.
WERE THOSE PEOPLE WHO WERE WITH YOU AT THE TIME YOUR FAMILY MEMBERS?
ONE MAN WITH GLASSES LOOKED EXACTLY LIKE YOU.
HE BLED PROFUSELY FROM A WOUND IN HIS LOWER LEFT STOMACH.
I COULD TELL HE WAS IN EXTREME AGONY.

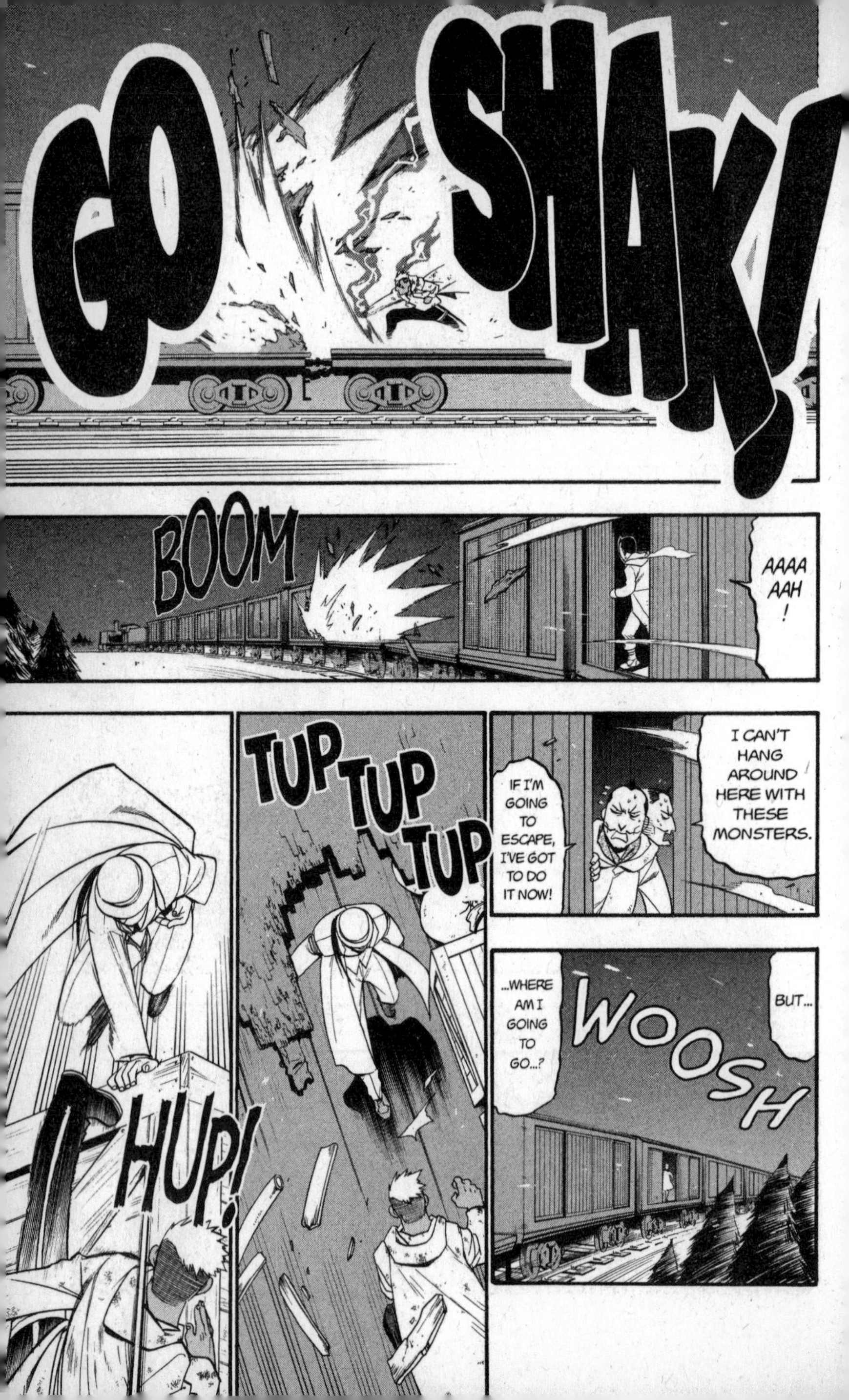
GO SHAK!
AAAA AAH !
BOOM
I CAN'T HANG AROUND HERE WITH THESE MONSTERS.
IF I'M GOING TO ESCAPE, I'VE GOT TO DO IT NOW!
BUT...
...WHERE AM I GOING TO GO...?
WOOSH
TUP TUP TUP
THUP!

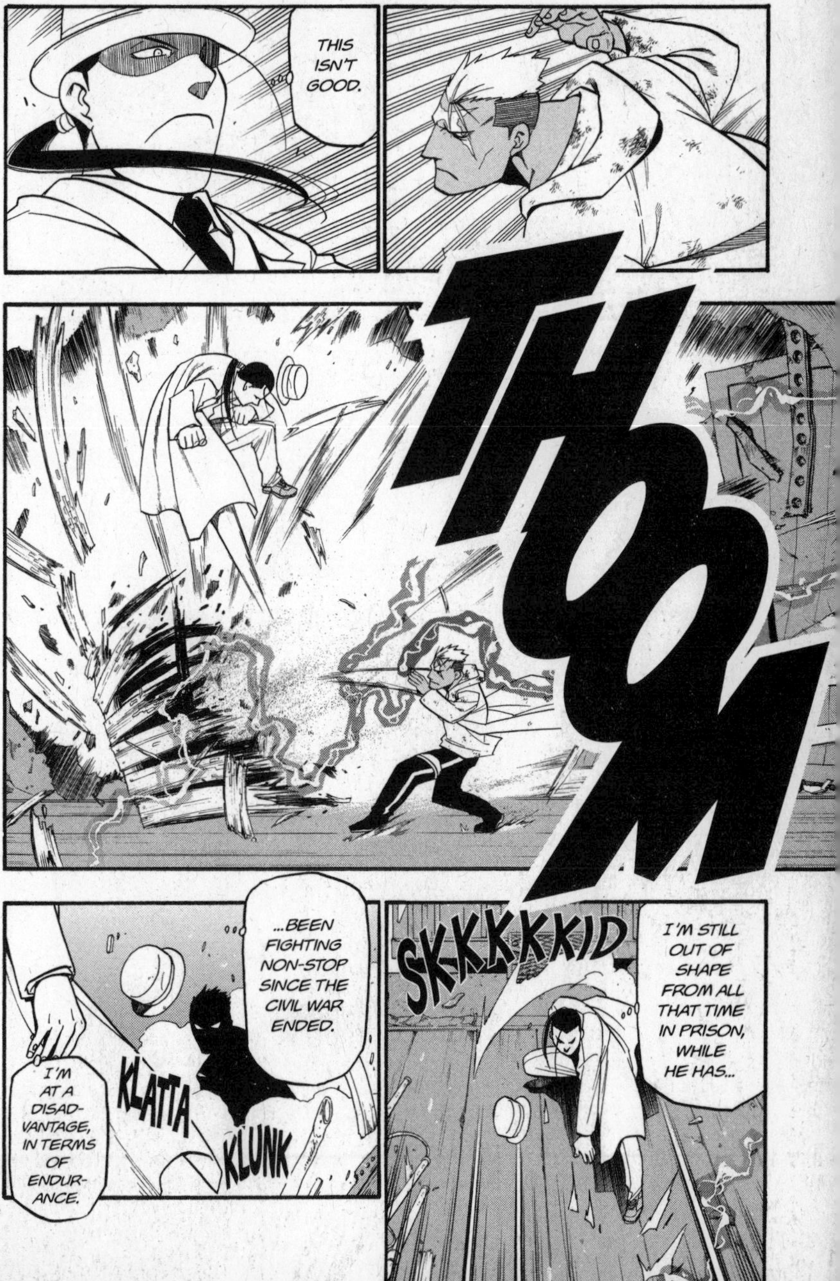
THIS ISN'T GOOD.
THOOM
SKKKKKID
I'M STILL OUT OF SHAPE FROM ALL THAT TIME IN PRISON, WHILE HE HAS...
...BEEN FIGHTING NON-STOP SINCE THE CIVIL WAR ENDED.
KLATTA
KLUNK
I'M AT A DISAD-VANTAGE, IN TERMS OF ENDUR-ANCE.

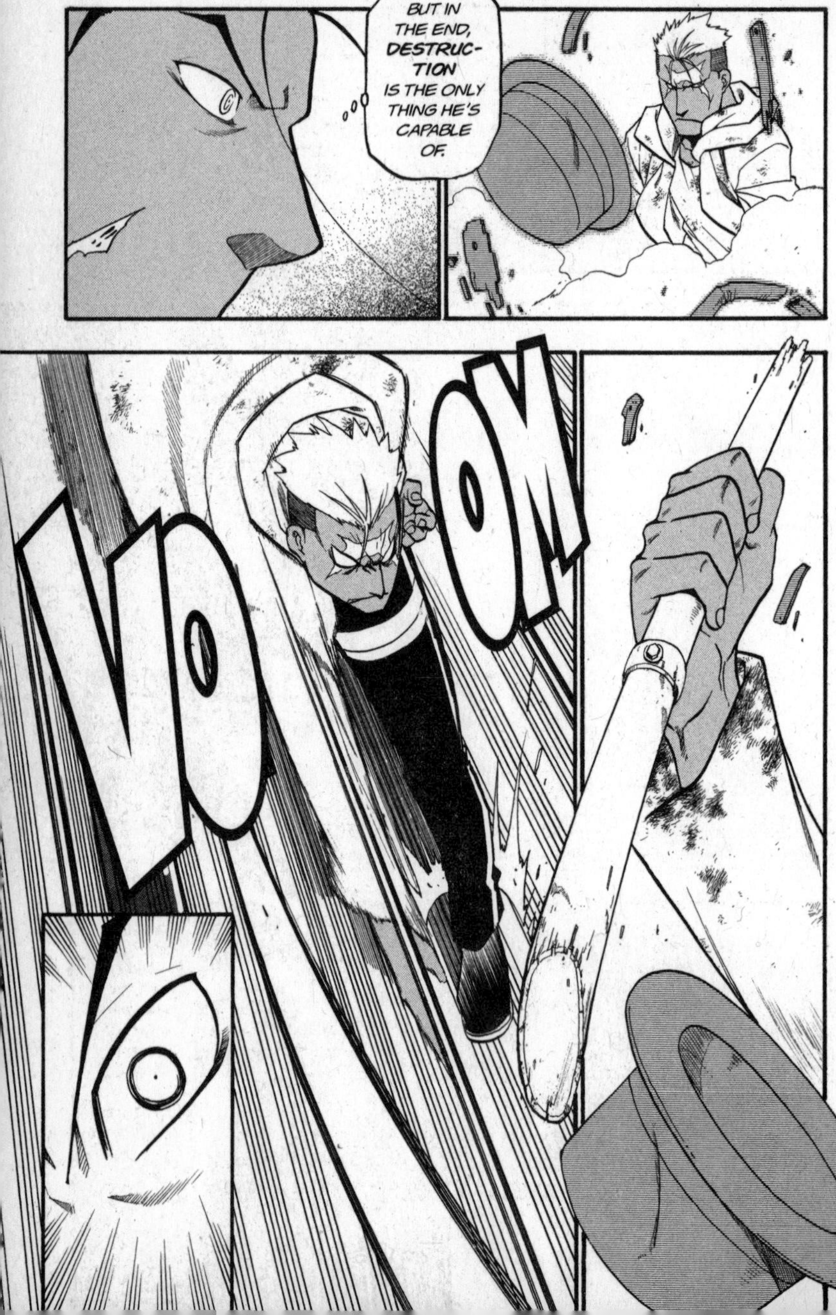
BUT IN THE END, **DESTRUCTION** IS THE ONLY THING HE'S CAPABLE OF.
VOOOM

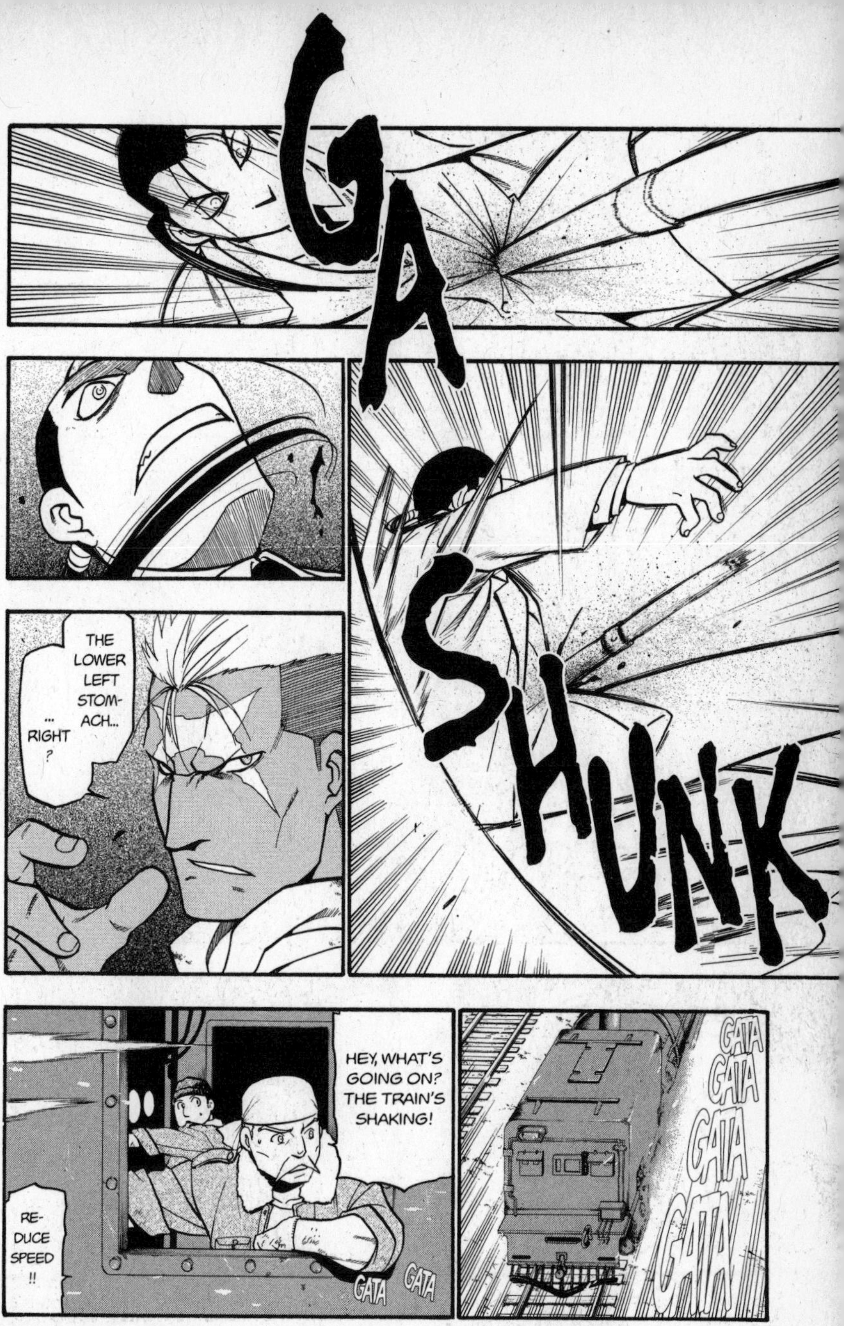
GA
SHUNK
THE LOWER LEFT STOMACH...
... RIGHT?
GATA GATA GATA GATA
HEY, WHAT'S GOING ON? THE TRAIN'S SHAKING!
RE-DUCE SPEED !!
GATA GATA

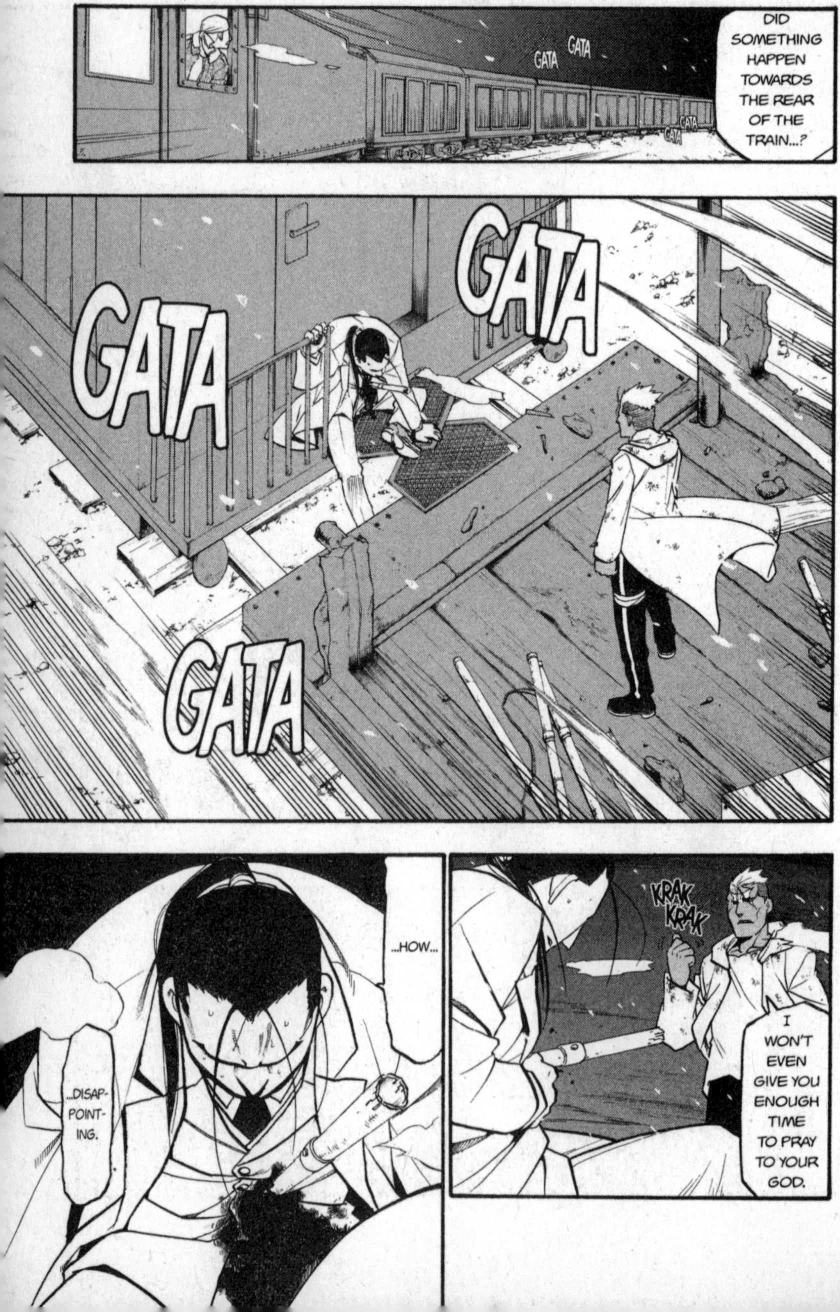
DID SOMETHING HAPPEN TOWARDS THE REAR OF THE TRAIN...?
GATA GATA
GATA GATA
GATA
GATA
GATA
KRAK KRAK
I WON'T EVEN GIVE YOU ENOUGH TIME TO PRAY TO YOUR GOD.
...HOW...
...DISAP-POINT-ING.

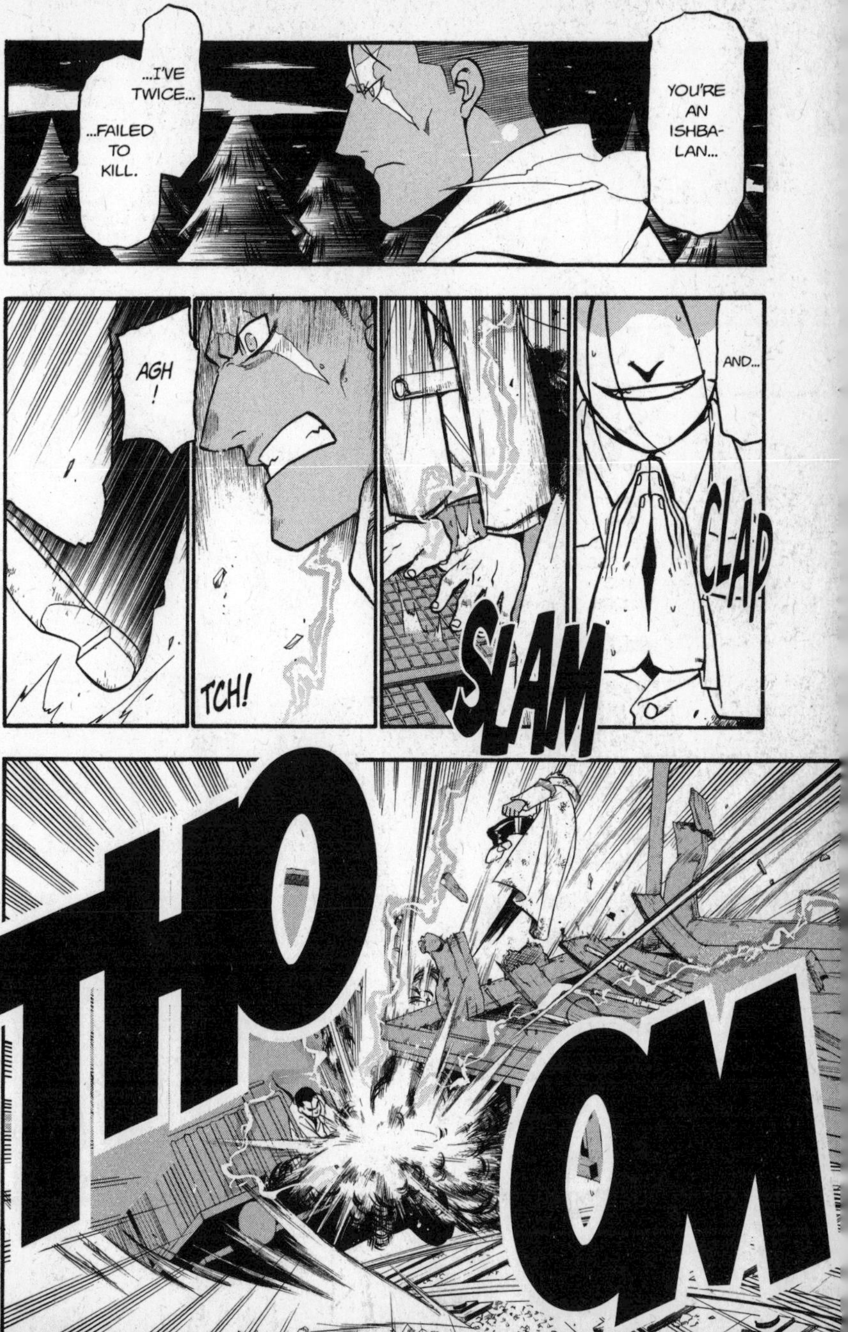
YOU'RE AN ISHBA-LAN...
...I'VE TWICE...
...FAILED TO KILL.
AND...
CLAP
SLAM
TCH!
AGH!
THOOM

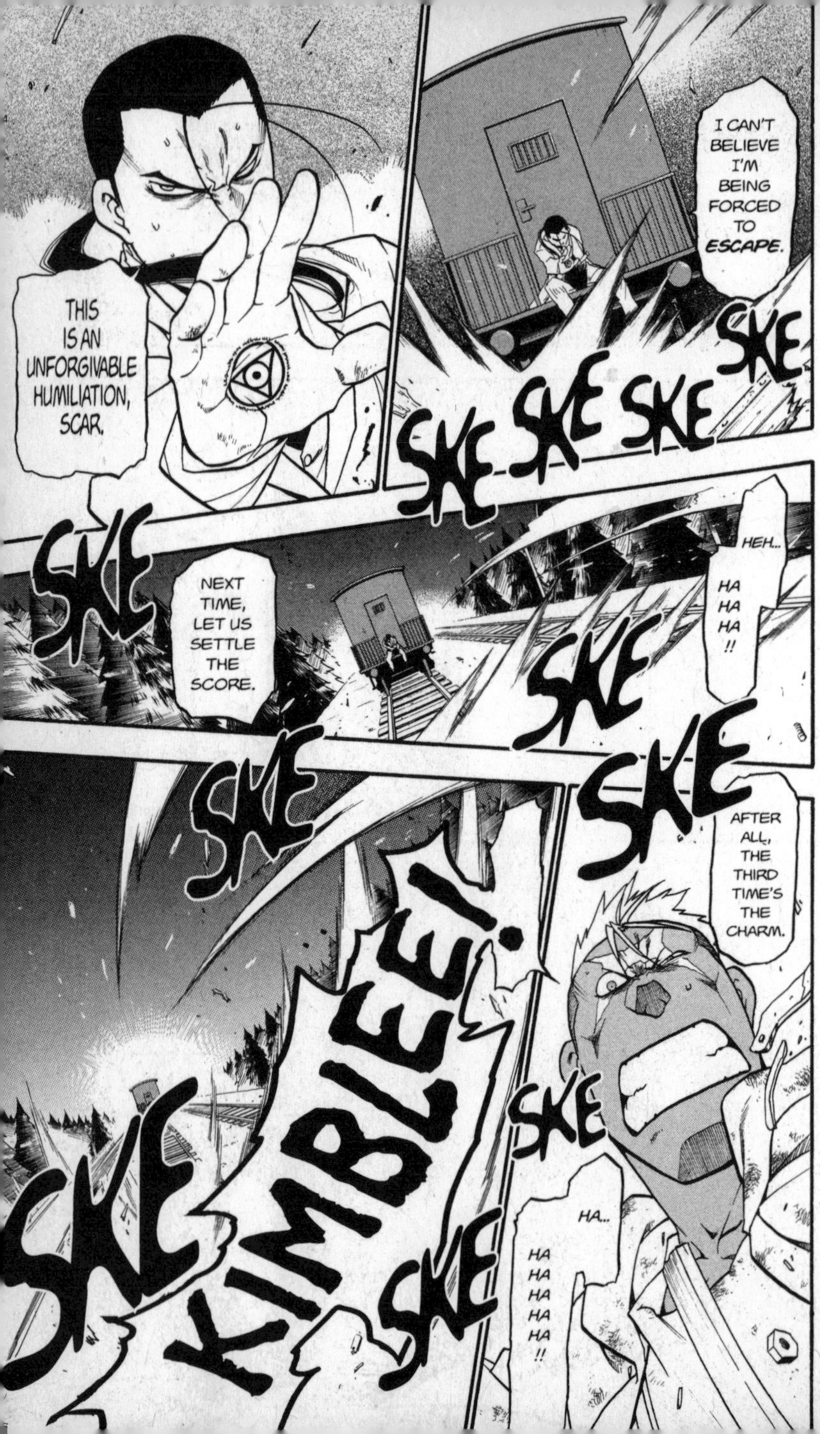
I CAN'T BELIEVE I'M BEING FORCED TO *ESCAPE.*
SKE SKE SKE SKE
THIS IS AN UNFORGIVABLE HUMILIATION, SCAR.
HEH... HA HA HA!!
SKE
NEXT TIME, LET US SETTLE THE SCORE.
SKE
SKE
AFTER ALL, THE THIRD TIME'S THE CHARM.
SKE
HA... HA HA HA HA HA!!
SKE
KIMBLEE!
SKE
SKE

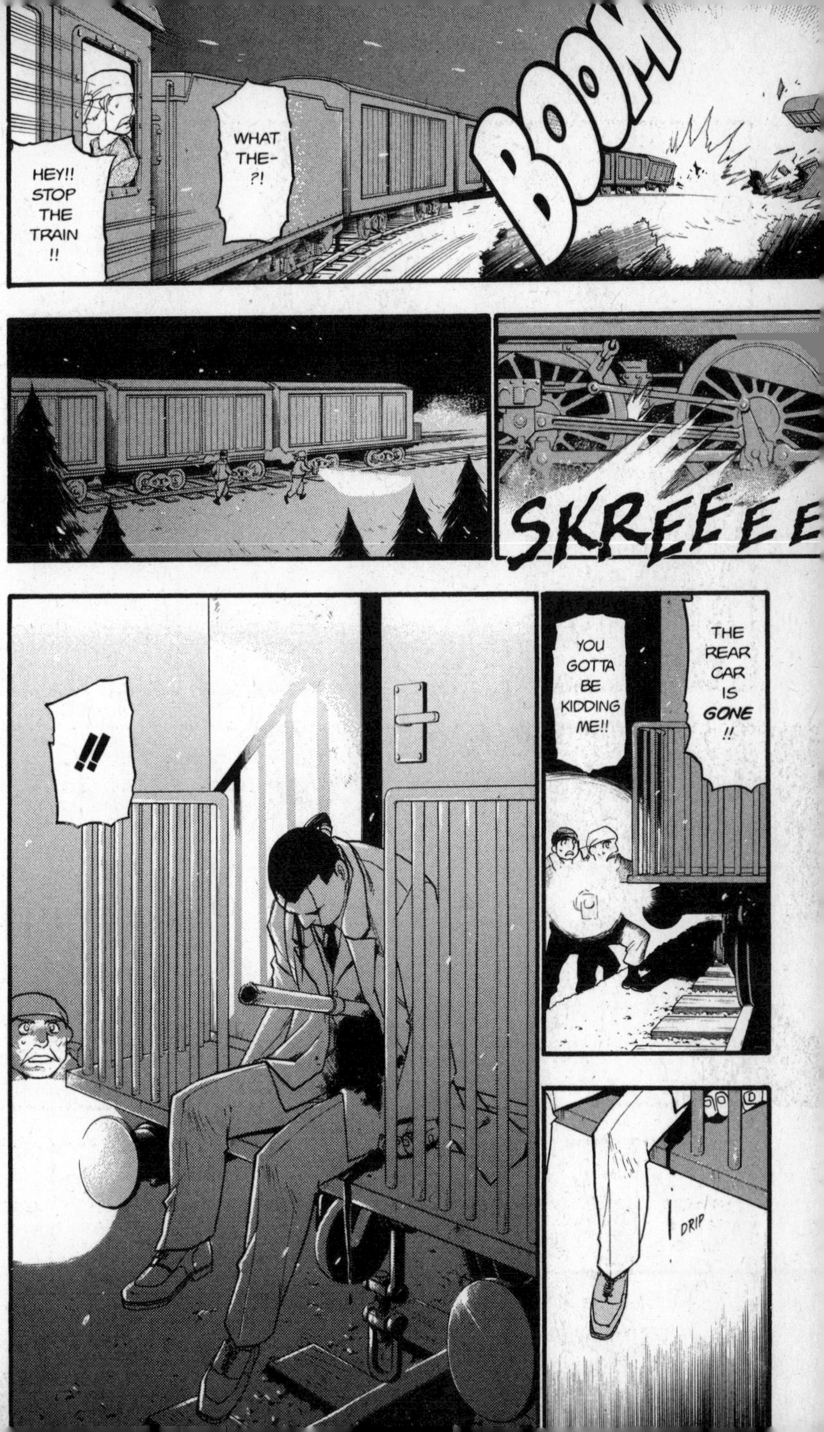
BOOM
WHAT THE-?!
HEY!! STOP THE TRAIN!!
SKREEEEE
THE REAR CAR IS GONE!!
YOU GOTTA BE KIDDING ME!!
DRIP
!!

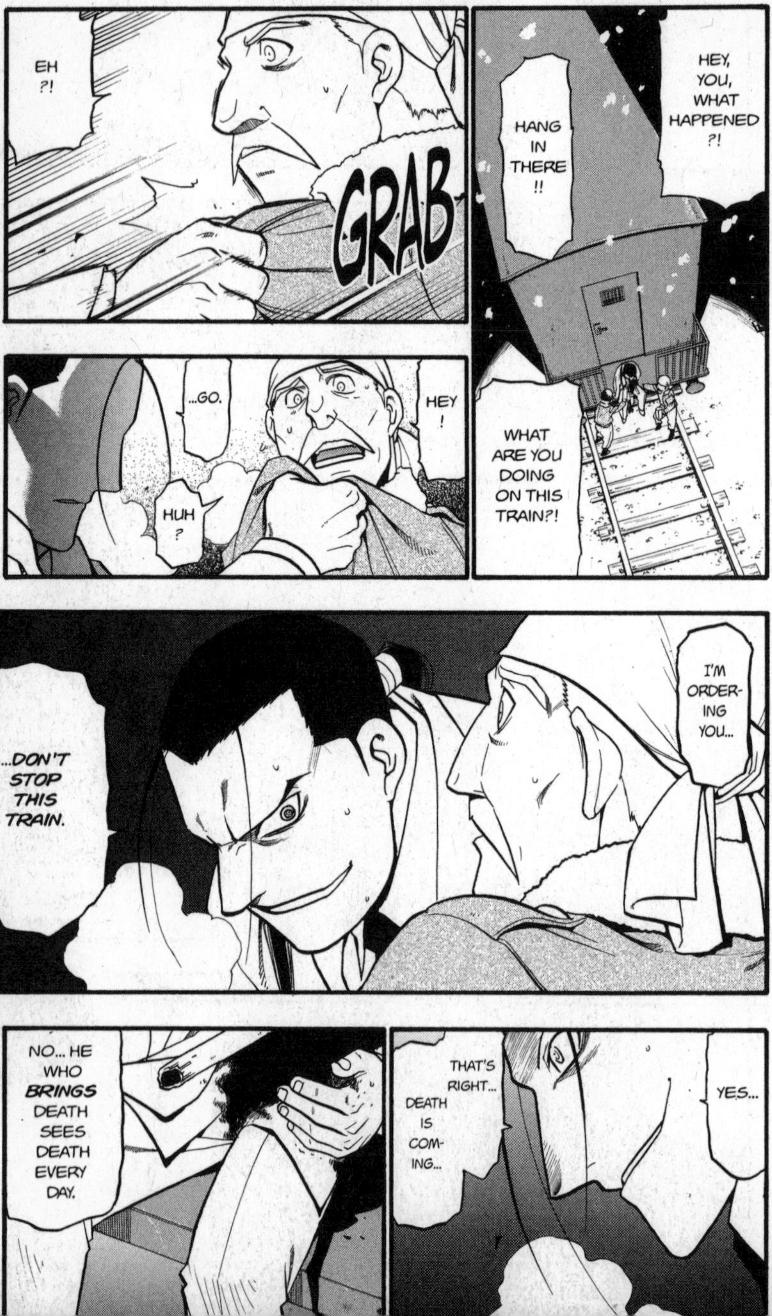
HEY, YOU, WHAT HAPPENED ?!
HANG IN THERE !!
WHAT ARE YOU DOING ON THIS TRAIN?!
EH ?!
GRAB
HEY !
...GO.
HUH ?
I'M ORDER-ING YOU...
...DON'T STOP THIS TRAIN.
YES...
THAT'S RIGHT...
DEATH IS COM-ING...
NO... HE WHO BRINGS DEATH SEES DEATH EVERY DAY.

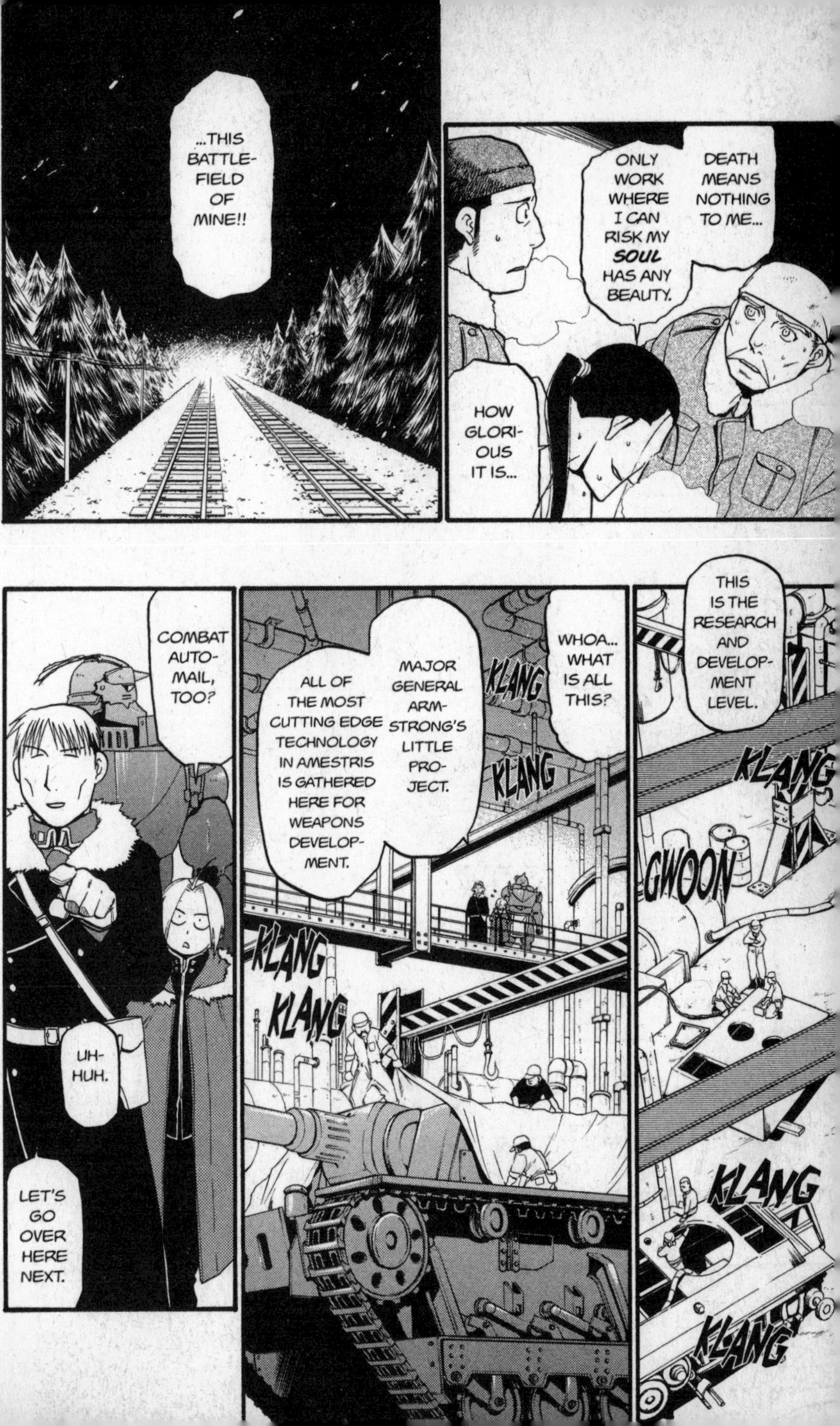
DEATH MEANS NOTHING TO ME...
ONLY WORK WHERE I CAN RISK MY **SOUL** HAS ANY BEAUTY.
HOW GLORIOUS IT IS...
...THIS BATTLEFIELD OF MINE!!
THIS IS THE RESEARCH AND DEVELOPMENT LEVEL.
KLANG
GWOON
KLANG
KLANG
WHOA... WHAT IS ALL THIS?
KLANG
KLANG
MAJOR GENERAL ARMSTRONG'S LITTLE PROJECT.
ALL OF THE MOST CUTTING EDGE TECHNOLOGY IN AMESTRIS IS GATHERED HERE FOR WEAPONS DEVELOPMENT.
KLANG
KLANG
COMBAT AUTOMAIL, TOO?
UH-HUH.
LET'S GO OVER HERE NEXT.

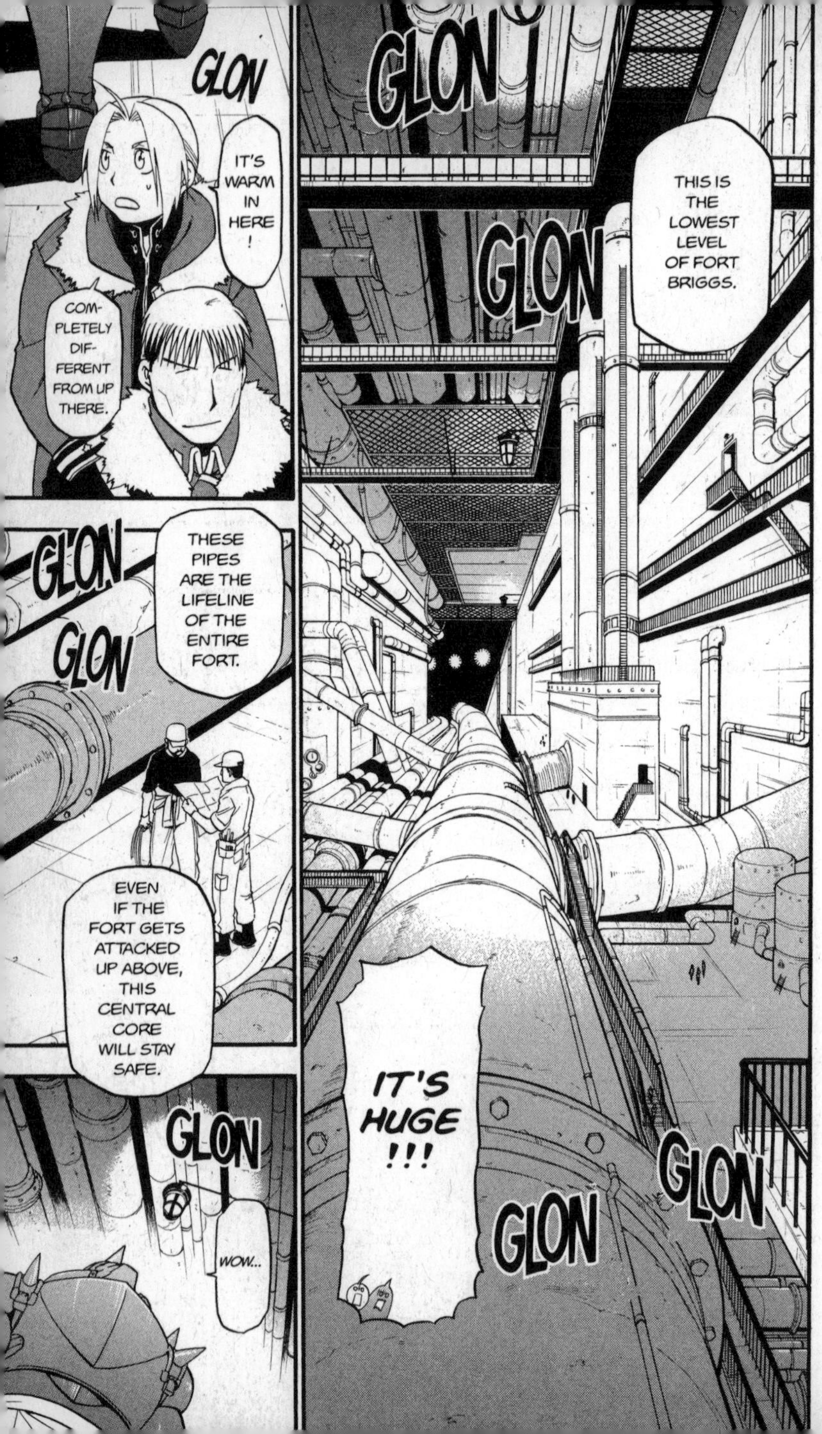
GLON
GLON
THIS IS THE LOWEST LEVEL OF FORT BRIGGS.
IT'S HUGE!!!
GLON
GLON
GLON
IT'S WARM IN HERE!
COMPLETELY DIFFERENT FROM UP THERE.
GLON
GLON
THESE PIPES ARE THE LIFELINE OF THE ENTIRE FORT.
EVEN IF THE FORT GETS ATTACKED UP ABOVE, THIS CENTRAL CORE WILL STAY SAFE.
GLON
WOW...

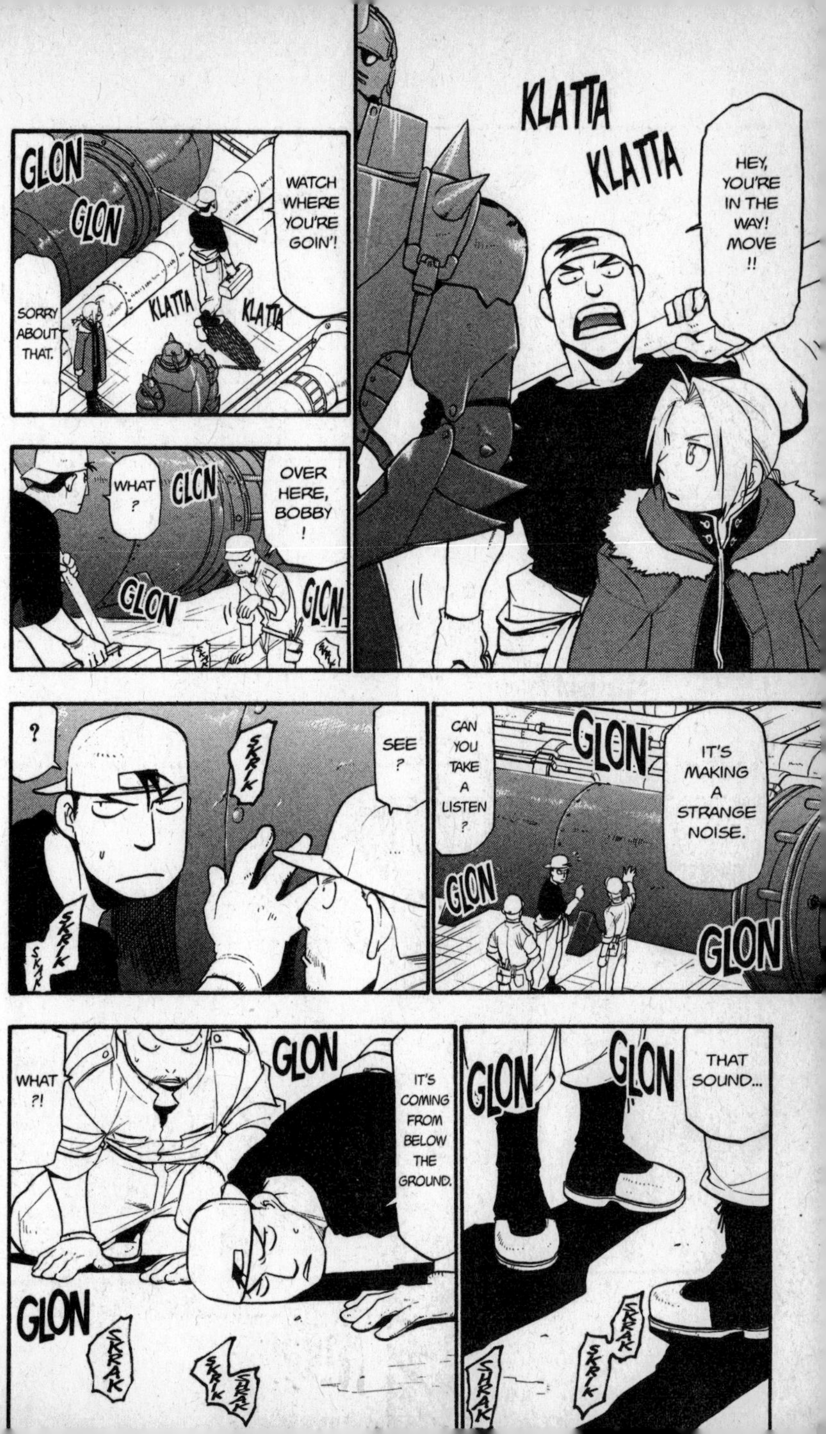
KLATTA
KLATTA
HEY, YOU'RE IN THE WAY! MOVE !!
GLON
GLON
WATCH WHERE YOU'RE GOIN'!
KLATTA
KLATTA
SORRY ABOUT THAT.
OVER HERE, BOBBY !
GLCN
WHAT ?
GLON
GLCN
SKRIK
SKRAK
GLON
IT'S MAKING A STRANGE NOISE.
CAN YOU TAKE A LISTEN ?
GLON
GLON
SEE ?
...
SKRIK
?
SKRIK
SKRAK
THAT SOUND...
GLON
GLON
SKRAK
SKRIK
SHRAK
IT'S COMING FROM BELOW THE GROUND.
GLON
WHAT ?!
GLON
SKRAK
SKRIK
SKRAK

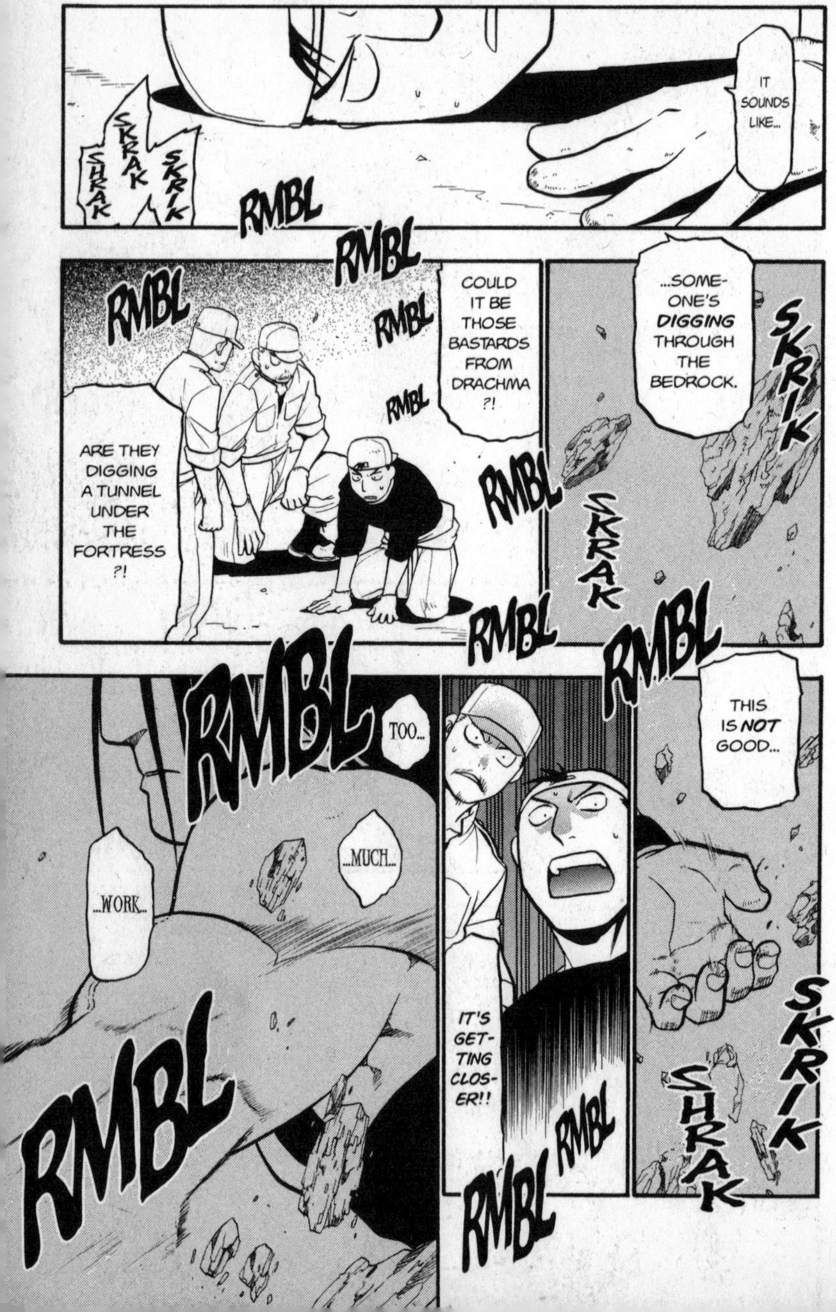
IT SOUNDS LIKE...
SKRIK
SKRAK
SHRAK
RMBL
RMBL
...SOME-ONE'S *DIGGING* THROUGH THE BEDROCK.
SKRIK
SKRAK
COULD IT BE THOSE BASTARDS FROM DRACHMA?!
RMBL
RMBL
RMBL
ARE THEY DIGGING A TUNNEL UNDER THE FORTRESS?!
RMBL
RMBL
RMBL
THIS IS *NOT* GOOD...
SKRIK
SHRAK
IT'S GET-TING CLOS-ER!!
RMBL
RMBL
RMBL
TOO...
...MUCH...
...WORK...
RMBL

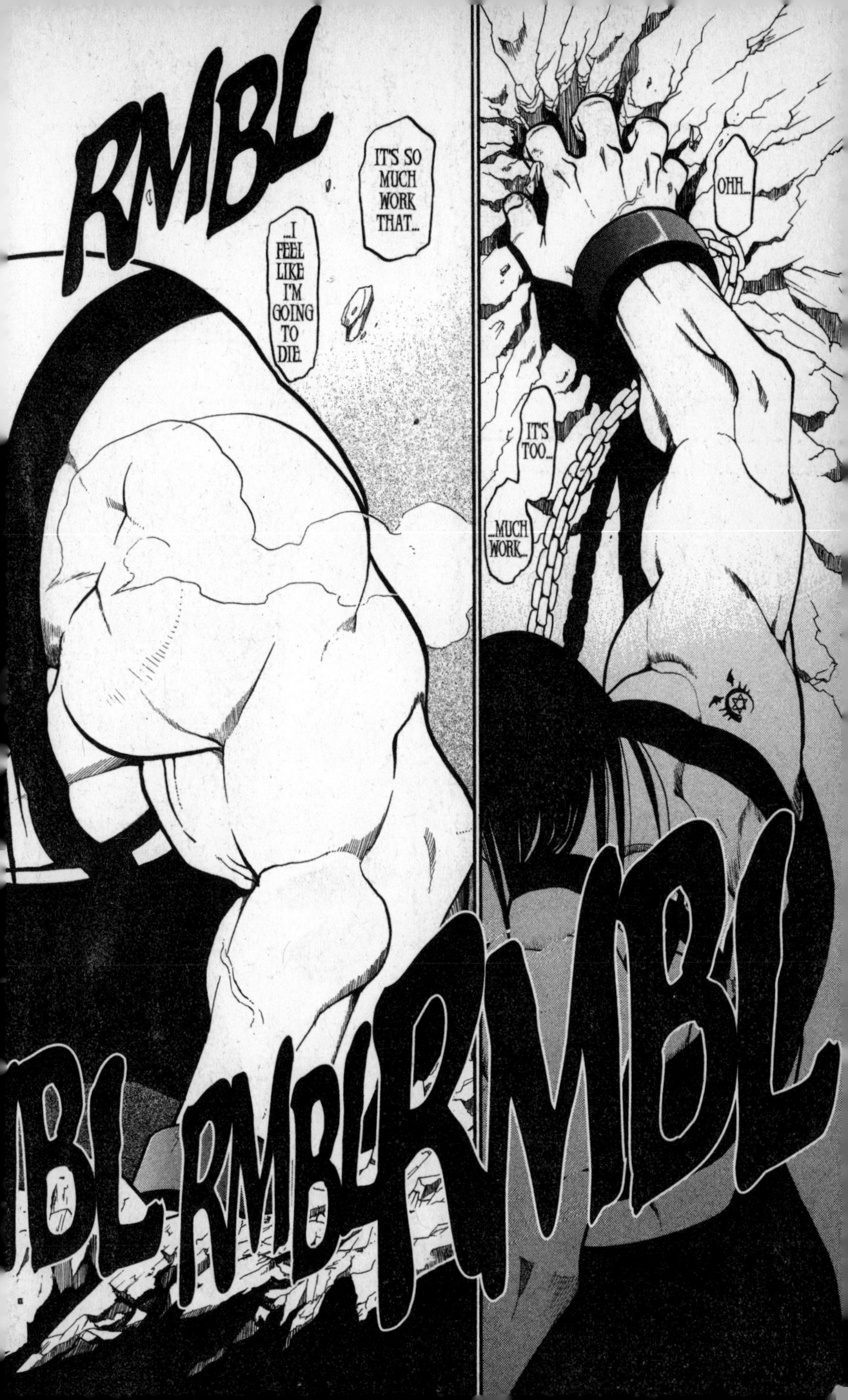
OHH...
IT'S TOO...
...MUCH WORK...
RMBL
RMBL
IT'S SO MUCH WORK THAT...
...I FEEL LIKE I'M GOING TO DIE.
BLRMBL

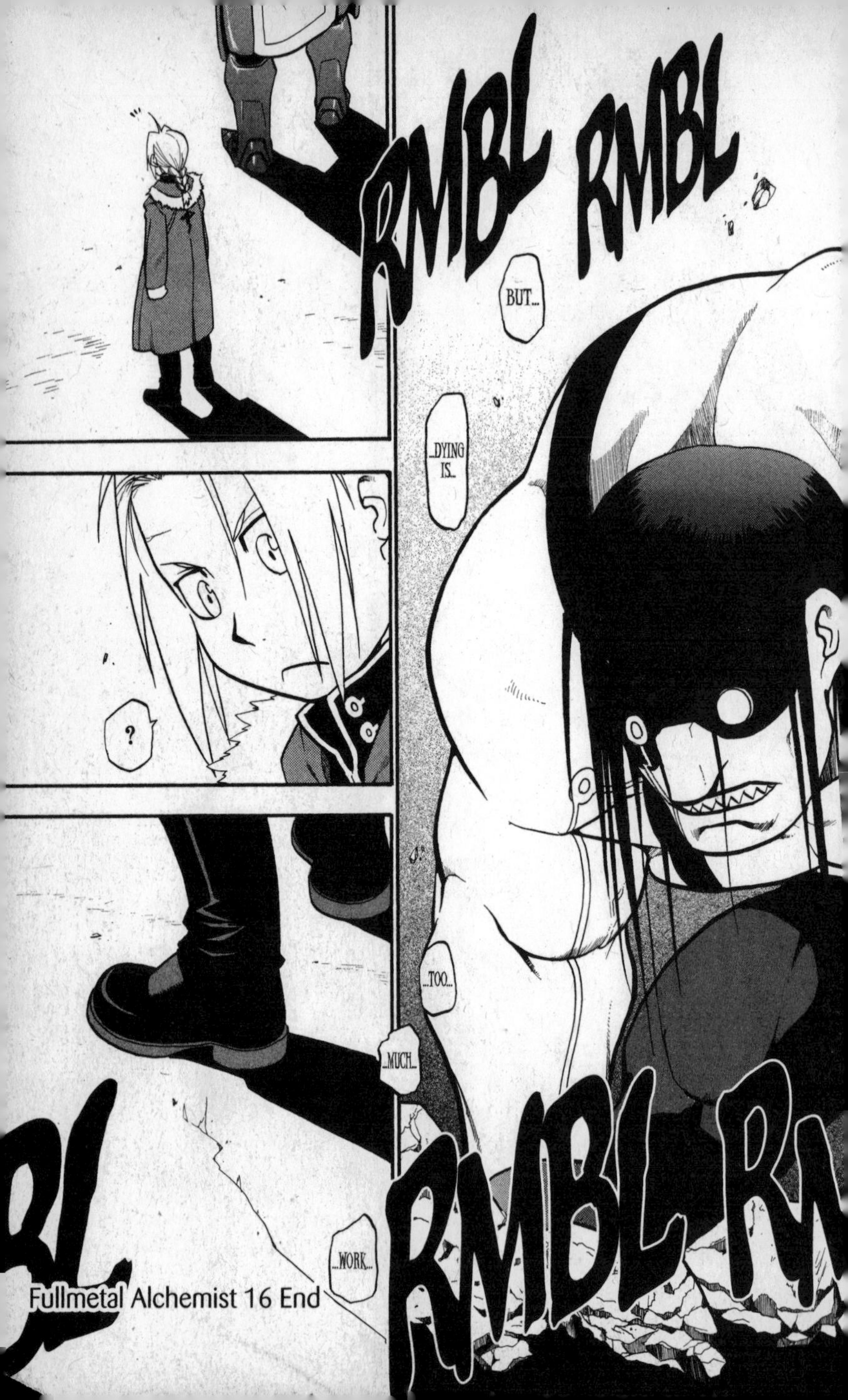
RMBL RMBL
BUT...
...DYING IS...
...TOO...
...MUCH...
...WORK...
RMBL RM
?
BL
Fullmetal Alchemist 16 End

FULLMETAL
ALCHEMIST

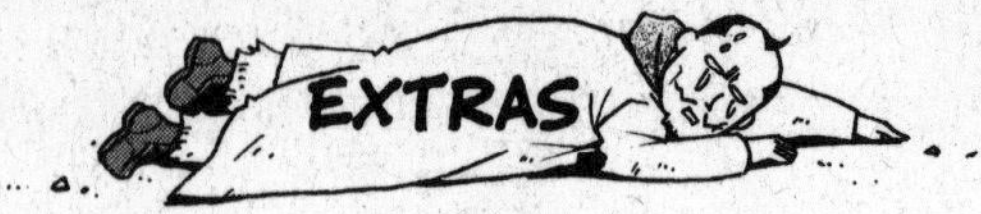
EXTRAS

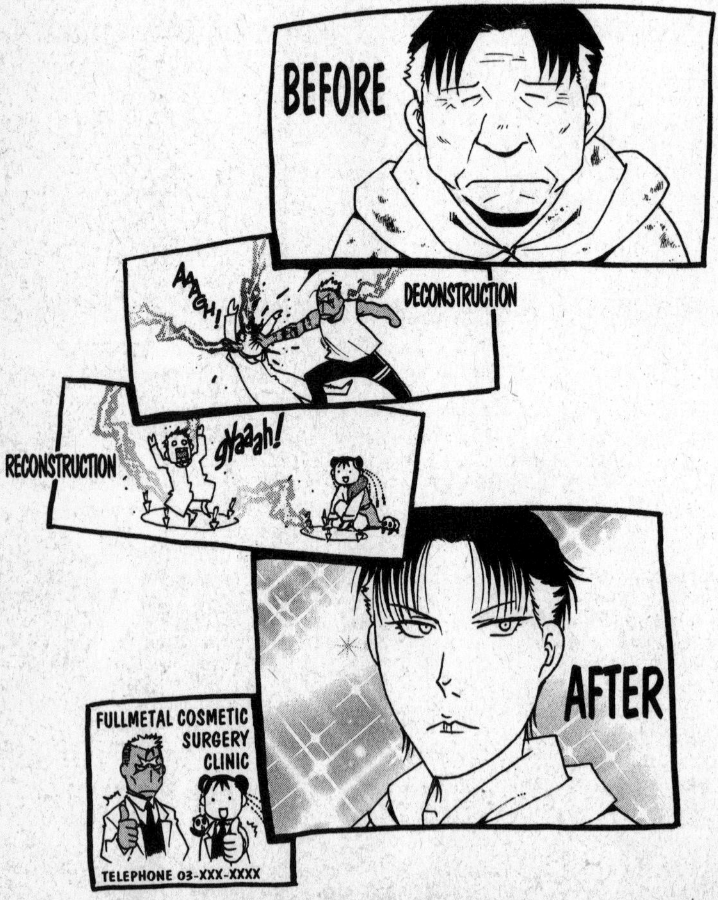
BEFORE
DECONSTRUCTION
AAAGH!
gYaaah!
RECONSTRUCTION
AFTER
FULLMETAL COSMETIC SURGERY CLINIC
TELEPHONE 03-XXX-XXXX

EDWARD AND THE MAGIC LAMP 2

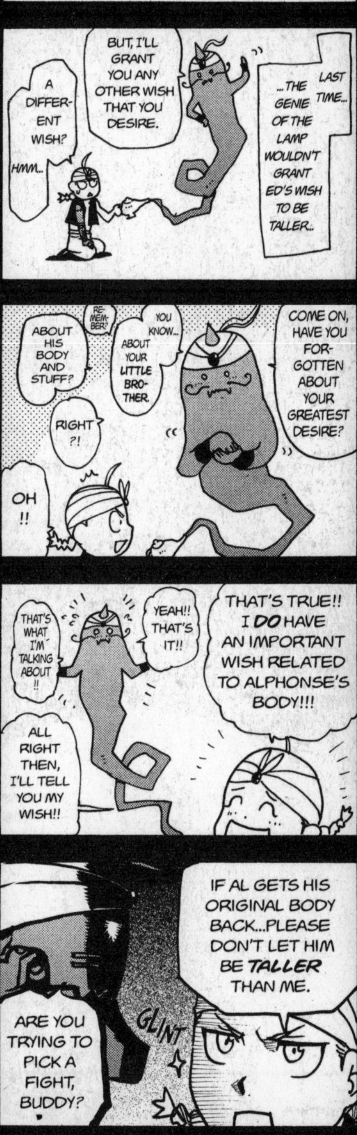
LAST TIME... ...THE GENIE OF THE LAMP WOULDN'T GRANT ED'S WISH TO BE TALLER..
BUT, I'LL GRANT YOU ANY OTHER WISH THAT YOU DESIRE.
A DIFFERENT WISH?
HMM..
COME ON, HAVE YOU FORGOTTEN ABOUT YOUR GREATEST DESIRE?
YOU KNOW... ABOUT YOUR LITTLE BROTHER.
REMEMBER?
ABOUT HIS BODY AND STUFF?
RIGHT?!
OH!!
THAT'S TRUE!! I DO HAVE AN IMPORTANT WISH RELATED TO ALPHONSE'S BODY!!!
YEAH!! THAT'S IT!!
THAT'S WHAT I'M TALKING ABOUT!!
ALL RIGHT THEN, I'LL TELL YOU MY WISH!!
IF AL GETS HIS ORIGINAL BODY BACK...PLEASE DON'T LET HIM BE TALLER THAN ME.
GLINT
ARE YOU TRYING TO PICK A FIGHT, BUDDY?

SECRETS ARE REVEALED

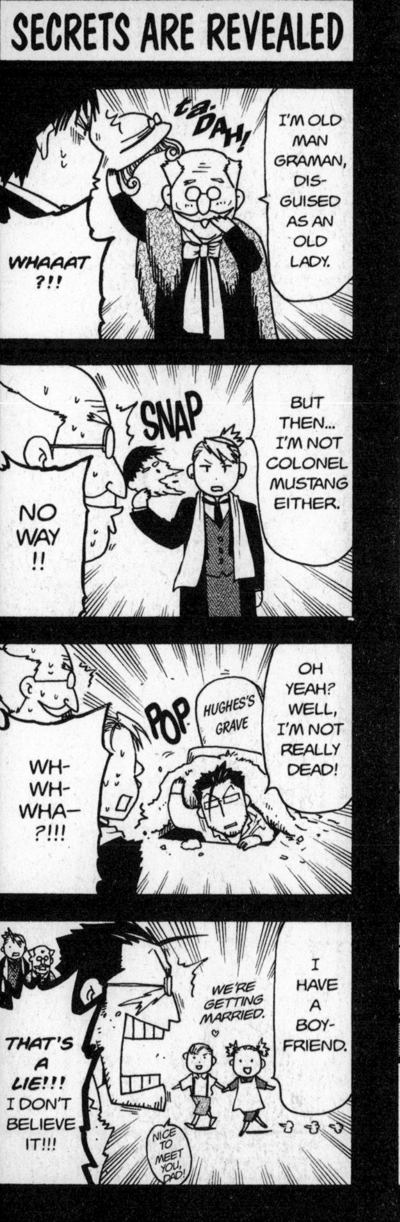
I'M OLD MAN GRAMAN, DISGUISED AS AN OLD LADY.
ta-DAH!
WHAAAT?!!
BUT THEN... I'M NOT COLONEL MUSTANG EITHER.
SNAP
NO WAY!!
OH YEAH? WELL, I'M NOT REALLY DEAD!
HUGHES'S GRAVE
POP
WH-WH-WHA-?!!!
I HAVE A BOYFRIEND.
WE'RE GETTING MARRIED.
NICE TO MEET YOU, DAD!
THAT'S A LIE!!! I DON'T BELIEVE IT!!!

MATERIALS ON-LOCATION

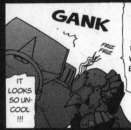

THE TASSEL ON MY HEAD GOT FRIZZY IN MY BATTLE WITH CAPTAIN BUCCANEER!!
GANK
FRIZ FRIZ
IT LOOKS SO UN-COOL !!!
BIG BRO-THER, LOOK...
FRIZ FRIZ
HUH? UH-HUH.
SO? GO FIND SOME STUFF TO FIX IT WITH.
YAAANN
GOOD NIGHT.
SNORE
...
......
I THINK THE HAIR ON THE TOP OF MY HEAD MIGHT BE THINNING...
REALLY ?
TRA-LA-LA...
BLONDE HAIR

FULLMETAL ALCHEMIST 16

SPECIAL THANKS to:

KEISUI TAKAEDA
SANKICHI HINODEYA
JUN TOHKO
AIYABALL
NONO
YOICHI KAMITONO
MASASHI MIZUTANI
SAKAMAKI
MR. COUPON
NORIKO TSUBOTA
MASANARI YUZUKA sensei
MANAGER MR. YOICHI SHIMOMURA

AND YOU!!

AL, WHAT DO YOU PLAN TO DO WHEN YOU GET YOUR ORIGINAL BODY BACK?
ANY DREAMS FOR THE FUTURE ?
I WANT TO CREATE MY OWN KINGDOM OF CUTE GIRLS.
DREAM BIG!!
YOUNG MAN!

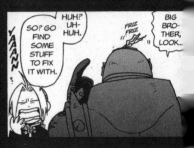

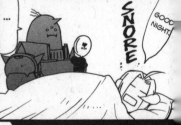

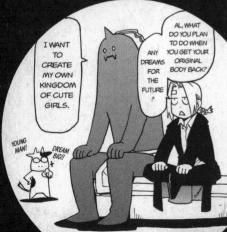

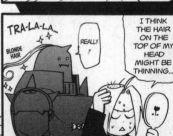

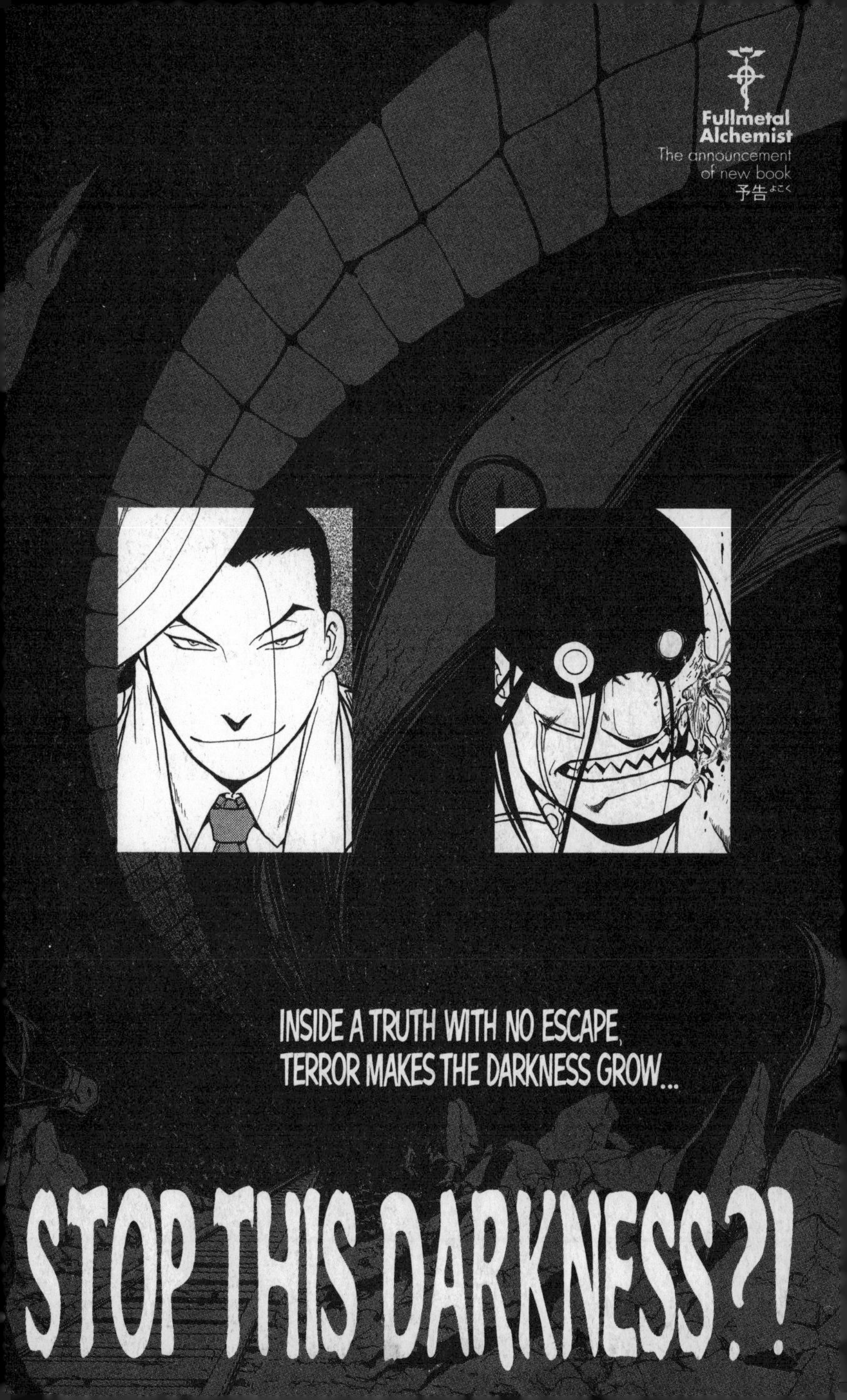
Fullmetal Alchemist
The announcement of new book
予告よこく
INSIDE A TRUTH WITH NO ESCAPE, TERROR MAKES THE DARKNESS GROW...
STOP THIS DARKNESS?!

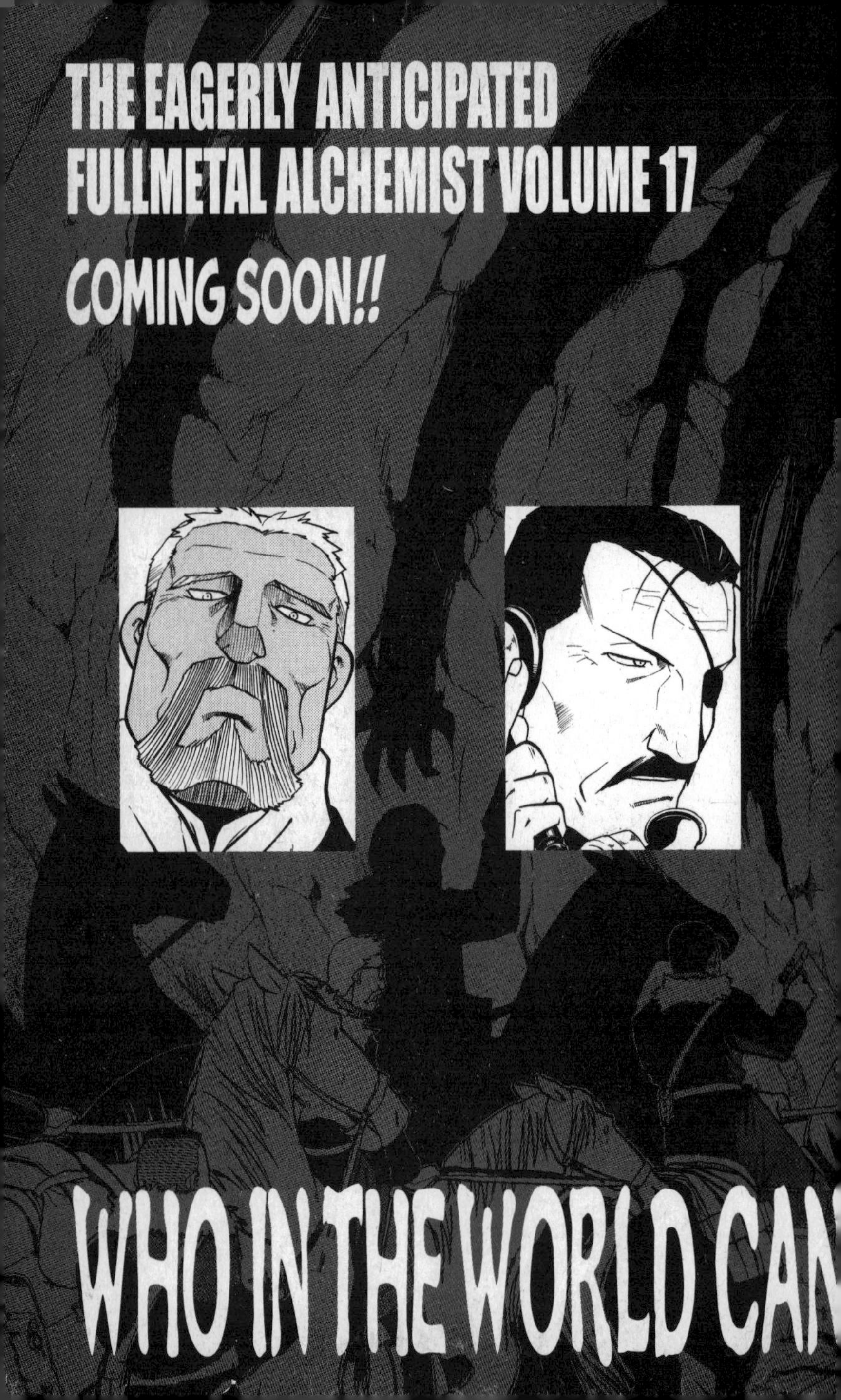
THE EAGERLY ANTICIPATED
FULLMETAL ALCHEMIST VOLUME 17
COMING SOON!!
WHO IN THE WORLD CAN

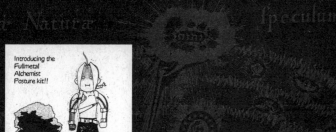

Introducing the Fullmetal Alchemist Posture kit!!
Strap on this handy device and you'll be striking Ed's pose in no time!!

FOR GOOD KIDS.
VERY USEFUL SCIENCE
IN VOLUME 16 WE'RE SUPPOSED TO HEAD NORTH, BUT...
WHICH WAY IS NORTH ?
I THINK YOU BOYS NEED...
TA-DA!
...AN ELECTRO-MAGNET!
PLEASE TEACH US, MS. RIZA! (LESSON #2)
LET'S MAKE AN ELECTROMAGNET!!
FIRST, WE WIND THIS COPPER WIRE AROUND A SOFT IRON CORE.
LOOP
LOOP
LOOP
NEXT...
SHAA
MEGA BATTERY
...WE ADD ELECTRICITY!
BZZT
BATTERY
ARRRGH!!
BZ
AAAP!
AS YOU CAN SEE...
...THE ELECTRICAL CURRENT MAGNETIZES THE SOFT IRON CORE, TRANSFORMING IT INTO A MAGNET.
SO NORTH IS...THAT WAY?!
THANKS, BIG BROTHER!
DUE NORTH
TRY IT, IF YOU GET LOST!
THE SECRET IS TO USE A SOFT IRON CORE!
TIP
ACTUALLY, THE STEEL IN ED'S AUTO-MAIL CONTAINS MORE THAN 1% CARBON, SO IT'S HARDLY SOFT IRON!
SOFT IRON: IRON WHICH CONTAINS LESS THAN 0.02% CARBON.
A WARNING FROM THE EDITORIAL DEPARTMENT: PLEASE DON'T TRY THIS AT HOME!

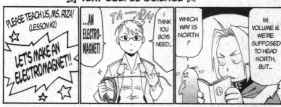

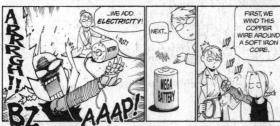

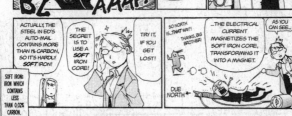

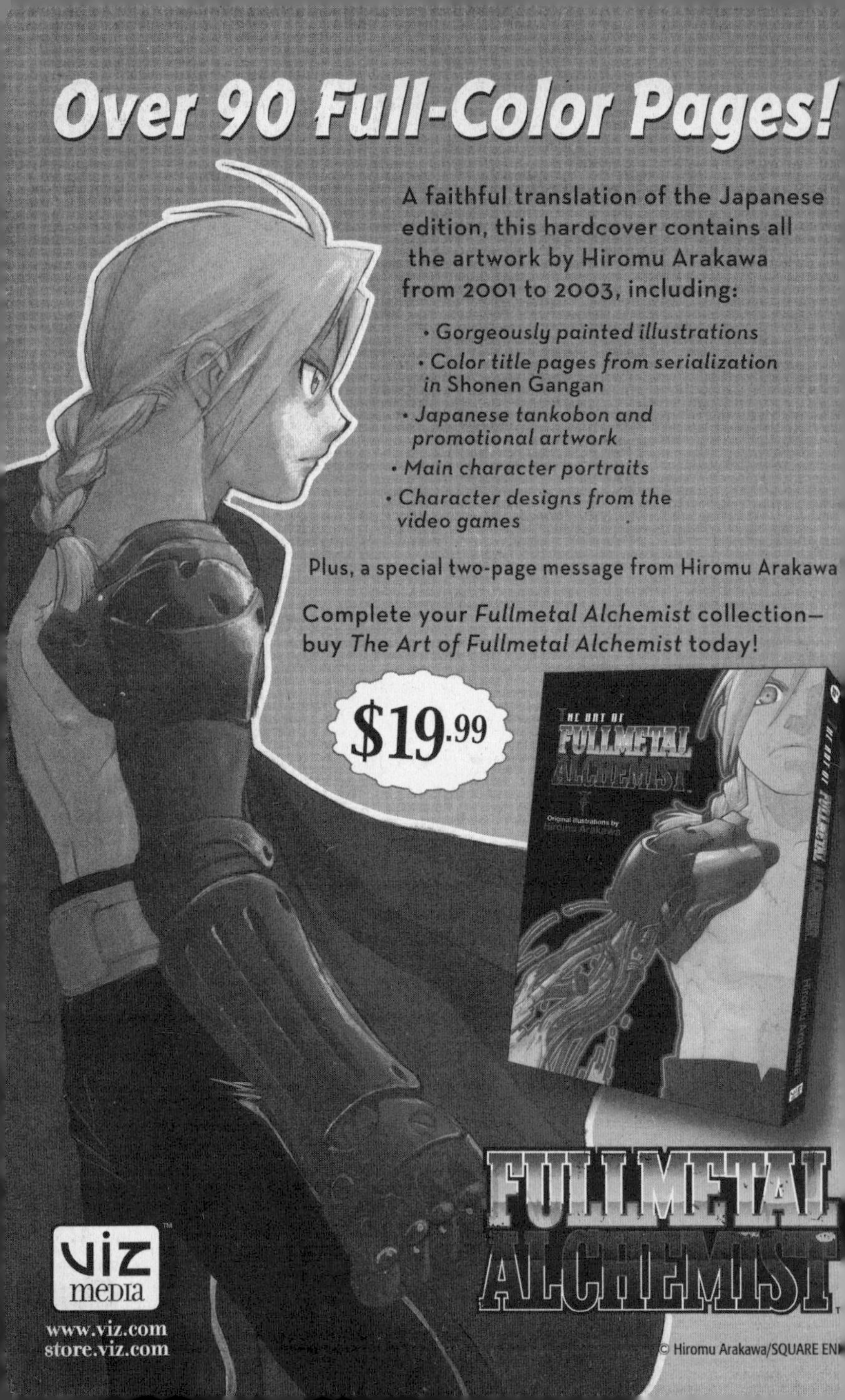
Over 90 Full-Color Pages!
A faithful translation of the Japanese edition, this hardcover contains all the artwork by Hiromu Arakawa from 2001 to 2003, including:
• Gorgeously painted illustrations
• Color title pages from serialization in Shonen Gangan
• Japanese tankobon and promotional artwork
• Main character portraits
• Character designs from the video games
Plus, a special two-page message from Hiromu Arakawa
Complete your Fullmetal Alchemist collection—buy The Art of Fullmetal Alchemist today!
$19.99
THE ART OF FULLMETAL ALCHEMIST
Original illustrations by Hiromu Arakawa
FULLMETAL ALCHEMIST
viz media
www.viz.com
store.viz.com
© Hiromu Arakawa/SQUARE ENI

LOVE MAN[GA]?

LET US KNOW WHAT YOU THINK!

OUR MANGA SURVEY IS NOW
AVAILABLE ONLINE. PLEASE VISIT:
VIZ.COM/MANGASURVEY

HELP US MAKE THE MANGA
YOU LOVE BETTER!